T0281843

MEN OF NO REPUTATION

Ozarks Studies

EDITED BY
BROOKS BLEVINS

OTHER TITLES IN THIS SERIES

*Newspaperwoman of the Ozarks: The Life and
Times of Lucile Morris Upton*

Twenty Acres: A Seventies Childhood in the Woods

Hipbillies: Deep Revolution in the Arkansas Ozarks

The Literature of the Ozarks: An Anthology

Down on Mahans Creek: A History of an Ozarks Neighborhood

MEN OF NO REPUTATION

Robert Boatright,
the Buckfoot Gang,
#and the Fleecing of
Middle America

KIMBERLY HARPER

The University of Arkansas Press
Fayetteville
2024

Copyright © 2024 by The University of Arkansas Press. All rights reserved.
No part of this book should be used or reproduced in any manner without prior
permission in writing from The University of Arkansas Press or as expressly
permitted by law.

978-1-68226-245-0 (cloth)
978-1-61075-809-3 (electronic)

28 27 26 25 24   5 4 3 2 1

Manufactured in the United States of America

Designed by Daniel Bertalotto

⊚ The paper used in this publication meets the minimum requirements of
the American National Standard for Permanence of Paper for Printed Library
Materials Z39.48–1984.

Cataloging-in-Publication Data on file at the Library of Congress.

For Ross and Henry

The past is a foreign country; they do things differently there.

—L. P. HARTLEY

Anybody can tell lies: there is no merit in a *mere* lie, it must possess *art*, it must exhibit a splendid & plausible & convincing *probability*; that is to say, it must be powerfully calculated to *deceive*.

—MARK TWAIN

C<u>O</u>NTENTS

ACKNOWLEDGMENTS

Turn every page. Never assume anything. Turn every goddam page.

—ALAN HATHWAY, quoted in Robert Caro's "The Secrets of Lyndon Johnson's Archives"

After spending thousands of dollars on copy fees, I may be Robert Boatright and John Mabray's final mark. While researching my first book *White Man's Heaven*, I stumbled across Boatright's story and spent over a decade chasing his paper trail across the country. I was aided by a number of archivists, but I am most indebted to Sarah LeRoy of the National Archives. Patrick G. Williams told me what I needed to hear while Jarod Roll generously shared drafts of his study of the Tri-State Lead and Zinc Mining District. I benefited from the assistance of Jeff Woodmansee at the University of Arkansas at Little Rock Bowen School of Law; Steve Weldon, retired director of the Jasper County Records Center in Carthage, Missouri; Shelly Croteau, John Korasick, Christina Miller, Michael Everman, and the staff of the Missouri State Archives; Dennis Northcott of the Missouri Historical Society; and Coreen Gray of the Pottawattamie County, Iowa, Court Clerk's Office.

I want to extend my gratitude to the staff of the National Archives for their help, especially Eric Bittner in Denver, Martin Tuohy in Chicago, Shane Bell in Atlanta, Barbara Rust and Rodney Krajca in Fort Worth, and Lori Cox-Paul and the staff in Kansas City. Mary Smith kindly shared the Omaha newspaper notes of her late husband, Dr. Raymond Smith. The volunteers at the Garland County Historical Society in Hot Springs, Arkansas, were especially helpful. The individuals who have preserved court records and newspapers across the country deserve gratitude for their crucial, yet often underappreciated work. In 1898 members of the Missouri Press Association founded the State Historical Society of Missouri; it is thanks to their vision that I was able to tell this story.

My mother Kay Harper has always encouraged my endeavors even though history was her least favorite subject. Words cannot express how grateful I am for her support over the years. Together we have traveled many a mile on the backroads of the Ozarks. She and my in-laws,

Charles and Jonnie Brown, generously paid for last-minute copy fees—
thank you. I am especially grateful to Brooks Blevins for accepting this
work as part of the Ozarks Studies series. His guidance was invaluable
as I refined the manuscript. Many thanks to Mike Bieker, David Scott
Cunningham, Janet Foxman, Jenny Vos, David Cajías Calvet, Melissa
King, Daniel Bertalotto, Charlie Shields, and Sam Ridge of the University
of Arkansas Press. Everyone needs a copyeditor; fortunately, James
Fraleigh was mine. Jim Coombs graciously accommodated my request
for his carefully crafted maps. A friend can make all the difference; thank
you, Dean. Most importantly, I want to thank my husband, Ross, who is
without equal. He is a wonderful husband, father, friend, and partner. We
are two mules pulling together. This book is dedicated to Ross and our
son Henry—the best of both of us.

MEN <u>of</u> NO REPUTATION

INTRODUCTION

Anyone with money is worth playing for. Just bring him in,
and I'll take something from him.

—ROBERT BOATRIGHT

It is doubtful whether there has ever been a greater scoundrel
than Robert Boatright.

—JUDGE SMITH M^CPHERSON, *Clay v. Waters*, 161 FED. 815

No one knew why the mausoleum was broken into in the waning days of winter in 1994. A simple limestone affair in an undistinguished plot in Webb City Cemetery, it was a far cry from the ostentatious tombs in nearby affluent Mount Hope Cemetery. Situated between the faded southwest Missouri mining towns of Joplin and Webb City, it could have been a grave in any small-town cemetery. An observer might have noticed that three epitaphs decorated its otherwise unremarkable exterior. Unless, of course, one knew that within its walls lay the remains of one of the most successful confidence men in American history. Or did they? On closer inspection, the epitaph for Robert P. W. Boatright, the scoundrel in question, read, "not dead, but gone before." Had Boatright pulled off the greatest con of his career almost one hundred years earlier in 1904?

This is the story of how a gang of midwestern and southern confidence men in the Ozarks swindled millions of dollars from their fellow man, a story that has been forgotten over time, but one that reveals the seedier side of late nineteenth- and early twentieth-century rural America. By their nature, confidence men wish to avoid detection and leave little, if any, evidence behind. Robert "Buckfoot" Boatright and the activities of his gang in the turn-of-the-century Missouri Ozarks set off a series of court cases that reveal much about the inner workings of one of history's most gifted but little-known con men and his confederates.

Scholar David W. Maurer asserted Robert Boatright was "the dean of modern confidence men," but he remains an obscure figure in the annals of crime. While he did not invent the foot race swindle, he used it to improve and perfect the big store concept purportedly invented by mid-western gambler Benjamin Marks. Instead of simple fixed games of three-card monte, Boatright and an extensive network of associates across the country developed an elaborate form of criminal theater they deceptively called the Webb City Athletic Club. Posing as wealthy businessmen, they cultivated victims by guaranteeing a sure bet on fixed athletic contests. As Roger H. Williams, one of the gang's members, observed, a success-ful con needed one thing: a man with "enough Grand Larceny in him to make a good first class horse thief." The greedy victim unwittingly arrived at the gang's headquarters in Webb City, Missouri, or another predeter-mined location to wager significant sums of money on fraudulent foot races and prizefights. Unbeknownst to the victim, however, the only cer-tain outcome was that their man would lose just as he was on the verge of victory. The sprinter's foot would buck upon hitting a dirt clod or even a rock, causing them to stumble, fall, and lose the race. This led the press to style Boatright and his confederates the "Buckfoot Gang."

Seemingly aided by a local Democratic Party boss, they operated with impunity in Jasper County, Missouri, for almost a decade. When their activities attracted too much attention, they retreated to Hot Springs, Arkansas, and Colorado Springs, Colorado—resort towns full of gullible tourists and gambling. Relying on fear of embarrassment to ensure their victims' silence, the gang found themselves in trouble when a victim filed a lawsuit that exposed their criminal activities. The Republican *Joplin News-Herald* and the Democratic *Jasper County News* devoted coverage to each lawsuit that was filed. Taking aim at corruption, they drew addi-tional scrutiny to the gang.

Far from being disinterested bystanders, the newspapers were guided by personal and partisan bias. Jasper County Democratic chieftain Gilbert Barbee, owner of one of the Ozarks' most influential newspapers, the *Joplin Globe*, feuded with political rival William H. Phelps whose ally, Cornelius Roach, published the Carthage *Jasper County Democrat*. The two men engaged in a proxy war against each other in the golden age of print journalism. The Republican publishers of the *Carthage Evening Press* and the *Joplin News-Herald* were more than willing to launch attacks on their Democratic foes. All four publications took sides over Barbee's alleged patronage of Boatright's Buckfoot Gang as did smaller local newspapers. Despite their fallibility newspapers provide the broadest insight into Boatright and Mabray's cons. Court records, too, provide invaluable understanding of the gang's schemes.

When members of the Boatright and Mabray gangs took the stand, they, too, fashioned their own truth. Although they rarely testified under oath, two did at length: Edward E. Ellis and Roger H. Williams. Both men demonstrated a clear-eyed caginess that indicated they were telling the truth—but only to a certain degree. Several Jasper County attorneys both represented and helped prosecute the gang at various times, though even they were not above suspicion. The gang's zealous legal opponent Hiram W. Currey allegedly attempted to blackmail the gang in exchange for money. Currey's chief adversary, Boatright attorney George R. Clay, went so far as to testify under oath that Currey offered to conspire with Clay to defraud Robert Boatright's mother and a bankruptcy trustee.

Maurer, who corresponded with dozens of career confidence men about who among them had been the most successful, believed Boatright stepped "from legitimate life into the big con and made a success of it." But he was never legitimate; his first con began when he was a boy in St. Louis. As an adult he and his confederates snared bankers, farmers, a future governor of Kansas, lawmen, merchants, and a Yale graduate in their intricate web of deception. His legacy lived on as the remnants of his gang, led by another confidence man, John C. Mabray, continued to prey upon the country's moneyed fools until the federal government ended their mischief in 1909.[1] And yet, the game continued.

Individually, and sometimes as part of a larger criminal enterprise, many of the original members of the Buckfoot Gang continued to swindle victims before newer cons emerged that were far more lucrative than the old schemes of the past. Cons are never new, Boatright could tell you, because the goal remained the same: separate the sucker from his money.

The literature of swindling is vast, but only a handful of works make fleeting references to Robert Boatright and John Mabray. There are no known contemporary accounts of the Buckfoot Gang outside of court records and newspapers, but an Arkansas deputy did chronicle Mabray's exploits. Surviving accounts of Boatright, Mabray, and their fellow confidence men resemble colorful folklore where one must attempt to determine what is true and what belongs to the greater mythology of the past. As Jill Lepore observed, "The work of the historian is not the work of the critic or of the moralist; it is the work of the sleuth and the storyteller, the philosopher and the scientist, the keeper of tales, the sayer of sooth, the teller of truth."[2] And so this book relies upon the work of a keeper of tales, David Maurer, a linguist who spent decades corresponding with the aristocrats of crime who shared their rich, opinionated stories. Maurer's *The Big Con: The Story of the Confidence Man* is perhaps the most famous and influential work. Prior to the book's 1940 publication, Maurer conducted research for *The Big Con* when some of Robert Boatright's contemporaries were still alive. The stories he relates about Boatright have a ring of truth to them—especially when compared against court records and newspaper accounts. Maurer often obscured the names and activities of his correspondents. Because Maurer's papers were destroyed after his death, it is impossible to know their identities. Mabray merited little mention in Maurer's work—perhaps because many of his cronies held grudges.[3]

In 1924 Texas rancher J. Frank Norfleet recounted being swindled by Denver's Blonger Gang in his memoir, *Norfleet*.[4] Amy Reading examined his experience in *The Mark Inside: A Perfect Swindle, a Cunning Revenge, and a Small History of the Big Con*. She convincingly argues confidence men have been part of the fabric of American identity since the country's founding. Reading explores the evolution of the American confidence game and the criminals who engaged in what she—echoing David Maurer—called, "a perfectly constructed piece of theater."[5] Robert Boatright, however, is not mentioned, while John Mabray merits only a few pages.

Although neither man is referenced in Chic Conwell's *The Professional Thief by a Professional Thief*, it is an invaluable source for understanding confidence men from 1900–1925. Conwell (a pseudonym) wrote the manuscript, which was then edited by sociologist Edwin H. Sutherland. Conwell's account closely mirrors those of David Maurer's correspondents.[6] A con man who critiqued Conwell's manuscript contended confidence men needed an attractive personality, intelligence, ego, and an aptitude for acting. The most successful confidence men, like Boatright and Mabray, learned the game from expert practitioners.[7] They often worked in groups known as mobs; mobs existed when several confidence men worked together to pull off complex schemes like Boatright and Mabray. The use of the word *mob* may confuse readers; Conwell was not referring to what might be referred to as the mafia. As such, I have elected not to use the terms *mob* or *con mob* except when necessary; I have instead chosen to use the word *gang* as that is how Boatright and Mabray's contemporaries referred to them.[8]

While Conwell focuses on early twentieth-century confidence men, historian David Johnson traces the development of the intercity criminal networks that gave rise to Boatright and Mabray.[9] The origins of intercity criminal activity in the nineteenth and early twentieth centuries began with criminals devising new ideas that sometimes required elaborate organizations. Cities provided an ideal environment in which to test their schemes and collaborate with other criminals. From the 1840s to the 1880s, one of the most important groups to do so were confidence men.[10] Taking advantage of a favorable environment initially created by gamblers, confidence men seized upon the circular swindle and—after the Civil War—green goods and bucket shop scams. They developed managerial skills to supervise employees and negotiate relationships with local authorities as they plied their trade in prosperous downtowns.[11] These bright-light districts varied little; confidence men could rely on their predictability and familiarity as they traveled from one city to another.[12]

This led to what was likely the "beginning of a cohesive underworld based on extensive, stable institutions for the first time." The expansion of the country's rail system during Reconstruction encouraged urbanization

In the 1890s Robert Boatright's Buckfoot Gang—headquartered in Webb City, Missouri—also pulled off confidence schemes in Hot Springs, Arkansas; Galena, Kansas; Colorado Springs, Colorado; and Salt Lake City, Utah. After Boatright's demise, several of his confederates fell in with John C. Mabray. Mabray and his cronies operated in major cities across the United States but became closely identified with Council Bluffs, Iowa. *Map by Jim Coombs.*

and new opportunities for criminals. From the 1880s until World War I, confidence men like Boatright and Mabray flourished. Throughout this era, they refined their intercity operations with little outside interference.[13] The big con was among the most notable scams to emerge during this period; Boatright and Mabray proved to be masters. For the swindle to be successful, the victim had to have faith in both the confidence man and the scheme in order to willingly part with large sums of money. Trust was easy to establish for confidence men who traveled by train and stayed in luxury hotels. They could glean details about their victim over dinner, playing cards, or sharing a passenger car. Once rapport was established, they relied on associates at rail centers to arrange protection and take care of the remaining details. By the 1890s the framework and foundation for big cons were well established throughout the United States.[14]

Johnson asserts this was when con men operated as loosely structured syndicates. Big cons needed intercity connections to succeed. Skilled professionals could participate in a single scheme or an entire season. Both Boatright and Mabray oversaw criminal enterprises that operated in this manner.[15] Confidence men who joined a syndicate received a fixed percentage. Individual syndicates were not permanent; if the principal organizers withdrew, it dissolved. Former members might form a new syndicate. The period from the nineteenth century to the early twentieth century was a time of innovation and experimentation for confidence men; they continued to refine their craft through trial and error with little interference. As Progressives challenged the boss system, their calls for honest, efficient, professional government reshaped the relationship between politicians and crime. Joplin's Gilbert Barbee and Omaha's Tom Dennison saw reform efforts challenge their rule. Police departments, too, professionalized and became more adept at combating crime. After the 1920s, migration to the suburbs disrupted criminal activities, bright-light districts faded in popularity, and confidence men were forced to adapt. By this time the con had evolved beyond Boatright and Mabray's outdated schemes.[16]

As for Boatright's vandalized mausoleum, the *Joplin Globe* reported two men were arrested for breaking into it. Police found the scattered bones of the Boatright family, but the thieves did not provide a motive. Officers surmised they were searching for jewelry.[17] Were the men simply opportunists? Or had they heard stories of Boatright and his big store? Whatever their motives, Robert Boatright would have taken pleasure in the fact that he had tricked two more suckers from beyond the grave almost one hundred years after his death.

In short, everyone in this story is a liar.

1

"BLOOD FOR BLOOD"

An attempt at murder in a Criminal Court is not unknown in the annals of crime;
but, for deliberate intent and swift, terrible and daring execution, that of
R. P. W. Boatwright upon the life of Charles Woodson yesterday in the Criminal
Court, has never been surpassed.

—*St. Louis Democrat*, MARCH 16, 1875

Reverend Edward Woodson survived the horrors of slavery. Born in servitude in Virginia, he found freedom on the western frontier. While enslaved in Missouri, he hired himself out and used the money he earned to purchase freedom for himself, his wife, and his children. Woodson became a Baptist preacher in St. Louis and helped other enslaved people secure their emancipation. In the years following the Civil War, he worked as a janitor at the St. Louis County Courthouse, a position of prestige for an African American. It must have come as a shock to Woodson on the afternoon of March 15, 1875, that he was a spectator in a courtroom in the city's Four Courts Building where his twelve-year-old son, Charles F. Woodson, was on trial for second-degree murder. A man of faith, Woodson must have hoped his son would be spared once the jury learned the details of the case.[1]

Charley, as the child was known, was small for his age; his head barely rose above the back of his chair. He sat next to his defense counsel, former Missouri lieutenant governor Charles P. Johnson and his brother John D. Johnson, two of the state's most distinguished criminal attorneys.[2] As the trial began, prosecutor Seymour Voullaire recounted the details of Charley's alleged crime. The previous year on Washington Avenue, just east of Fourteenth Street, a group of St. Louis capitalists had been in the process of converting a pair of private residences into a hotel. During the renovation, the rubble attracted the attention of neighborhood children.

The debris became contested territory that led to animosity between the Seventeenth Street Boys, "a band of turbulent spirits" and their rivals, the "Sixteenth Street young'uns."[3]

On September 21, 1874, Charley Woodson and his brother stood near the corner of Sixteenth and Morgan Streets exchanging taunts with a group of boys across the street. Tensions mounted and soon the two sides were throwing rocks at each other.[4] Oscar J. Boatright, a seventeen-year-old white youth, was struck in the head and collapsed.[5] He was carried to the family home where, after lingering for weeks, he died of lockjaw. With his death, the family had only one surviving, grief-stricken child, Robert P. W. Boatright. Edward Woodson brought Charley to the Boatright home and had Oscar's father, Robert M. Boatright, flog him. Fearful Boatright was not satisfied, Woodson brought Charley to him a second time, but the bereaved father told Woodson he had whipped him enough and wanted the law to take its course.[6]

After police officers convinced the elder Boatright to press charges, Charley was put on trial for second-degree murder. Now the two fathers watched the proceedings; one had already lost a child, the other feared he was about to lose his own. When prosecutor Voullaire sought to introduce Woodson's admission to the crime, the defense objected, pointing out their client's confession had been obtained under duress. Robert M. Boatright, the Johnsons argued, extracted the confession from Woodson at gunpoint. Boatright was called to the witness stand and the jury retired from the courtroom while Judge William Cuthbert Jones questioned him. The Johnsons, Voullaire, and Edward Woodson stood listening at the bottom of the judge's bench.[7]

Before his son Oscar died, Boatright had asked who threw the rock that struck him, but Oscar refused to name the guilty party until shortly before his death. Only then did Oscar tell his father Charley Woodson threw the rock. The day after Oscar's death, Boatright confronted Charley with a loaded pistol and ordered him to tell the truth or he "would BLOW HIS DAMN HEAD OFF." When Judge Jones asked Boatright if he would have shot Woodson if he had not been forthcoming, Boatright responded he would have. As Jones considered whether to admit the confession, a young white man slipped into the courtroom.

While both sides gathered at the judge's bench, little Charley sat alone at the defense table. Few noticed as the young man walked purposefully past empty courtroom seats, entered an area reserved for court officials, and stopped behind the diminutive defendant. He pulled a large knife from inside his coat and lunged at Charley from behind, yelling, "You killed my brother, and I will kill you!" Everyone in the courtroom was "horror-struck—even paralyzed—not a motion was made to save the little fellow."[8]

Judge Jones saw the flash of the assailant's knife as it plunged downward. Before the attacker could stab Woodson a second time, Jones leapt from the bench and together with Voullaire apprehended Robert P. W. Boatright, Oscar's brother. As the courtroom erupted in chaos, court clerk Andrew Clabby grabbed the knife from Boatright, who offered no resistance. Charley Woodson stretched out his hands toward Charles P. Johnson and cried out, "Oh God!" before he ran forward and collapsed into his lawyer's arms. Johnson gently laid the boy on the floor as court officers quickly cleared the courtroom. A deputy marshal escorted young Boatright downstairs to a holding cell.[9]

The noise in the courtroom attracted the attention of physicians J. J. O'Brien and Anselm Robinson. Robinson brought a mattress for the boy to lie on while O'Brien examined him. The doctors found Woodson's intestines protruding from a vicious, seven-inch-long wound. It was thought, however, that the wound would not prove fatal unless it became infected. Woodson was carefully removed from the courtroom and taken home by ambulance. Upon examination, the nearly twelve-inch knife was found to have a freshly sharpened blade. Several notches and the initials O. J. B. were carved into the handle.[10]

St. Louis chief of police Laurence Harrigan visited Boatright in his cell. The youth told Harrigan he "was much affected by his brother's death, and just half an hour before [Oscar] died he promised that he would KILL THAT N[——]." If Woodson did not die, Boatright vowed to kill him some other time.[11] A reporter found Boatright sharing a cell with four other boys and wrote that he "assumed a bravado air. His coolness, however, was not real, for at one moment he laughs with well simulated glee when he refused to answer any questions, and then he immediately scowled and frowned as though angry." The reporter noted, "his face is full of cunning."[12] If Boatright was fearful of the consequences of his murderous action, he showed little sign of it. Whether he faced a charge of attempted or first-degree murder depended on the fate of his victim.

Despite his initially optimistic diagnosis, Charley Woodson died the next day.[13] A coroner's inquest convened over his tiny body. After two hours of eyewitness testimony, the jury found Woodson died from peritonitis caused by the knife wound.[14] Boatright was subsequently charged with first-degree murder.[15] The trials that ensued may have been the first major con that Boatright pulled off in his storied career as one of the Midwest's greatest confidence men.

Born in 1859, Robert P. W. Boatright spent his early years in Franklin County, Missouri. In 1861, his father, Robert M. Boatright, left to join the secessionist Missouri State Guard and spent the rest of the Civil War in the Trans-Mississippi theater as a member of the Fifth Missouri Infantry Regiment. After the war's end Boatright returned home to his young family: wife Priscilla and sons Oscar and Robert P. W. His third son, born after he left for the war, died before his return.[16]

Postwar life in Franklin County paled in comparison to the opportunity found in St. Louis, fifty miles to the east. Established south of the confluence of the Missouri and Mississippi rivers by the French in 1764, the muddy trading post grew into a cosmopolitan community with the fortunes of the fur trade. In 1803 St. Louis became part of the United States through the Louisiana Purchase. In time it became the heart of midwestern river traffic and western trade.[17] Throughout its early history St. Louis struggled with outbreaks of disease. Following a destructive fire in 1849, a devastating cholera epidemic swept through the city killing thousands. Although the causes behind cholera and typhoid outbreaks were poorly understood at the time, after 1849 the need for sewers was apparent. The city installed a new underground sewer system to combat waterborne diseases as the city's population increased.[18]

The Civil War brought new challenges. The city remained loyal to the Union but paid an economic price when Confederates blockaded the Mississippi.[19] Once the shackles of war lifted in 1865, St. Louis sought to become "the future great city of the world."[20] A visitor could recognize the economic power of the city merely by glancing skyward. Due to the city's reliance on soft coal, heavy columns of smoke poured forth from factories, residences, and steamboats.[21] Refusing to submit to the misfortunes of the past, St. Louis emerged as a midwestern metropolis that attracted thousands of postwar arrivals, including the Boatrights.

By 1867 Robert M. Boatright had moved his family to St. Louis, where he worked as a carpenter. Four years later he was a deputy constable, and two years after that he became a deputy sheriff. In 1874 Boatright made an enterprising but short-lived leap into publishing, partnering with Charles Gonter to produce the *St. Louis Advertiser*. The paper did not survive more than a year, perhaps a casualty of a weakened economy following the Panic of 1873. When his son first went on trial for murder, he was employed as a private detective.[22]

Although St. Louis presented greater economic opportunity for Boatright and his family, they lived in a city plagued by common societal ills. The family moved often, living in less-than-desirable neighborhoods.

When they first arrived in St. Louis, the Boatrights resided on the edge of Kerry Patch, an impoverished, working-class Irish area. Shanties built by squatters crowded up against one another like a mad architect's dream. The humble dwellings were characterized by broken doors and rags stuffed into empty windowpanes. In time the Boatrights moved to a less squalid area.[23] In 1874 they lived at 1615 Christy Avenue. Some of their neighbors owned homes, but many others lived in poverty. Boys from the neighborhood, one observer asserted, became thieves and eventually ended up in the Missouri State Penitentiary.[24]

It was amid the rabble of St. Louis that Robert P. W. Boatright came of age. In 1870, despite city leaders' efforts to improve public health, he contracted typhoid. He was, according to some, never the same. When Boatright was fourteen, he was sentenced to the city's House of Refuge for incorrigibility. Established in 1856, the House of Refuge was a reform school for juvenile offenders. Not all of its inmates, however, were delinquents. Orphaned and abandoned children were also housed within the institution's imposing twenty-foot-tall walls. The young inmates came from a variety of backgrounds, but poverty and neglect were common threads that bound them together.[25] Although the House of Refuge was for some a welcome alternative to living on the streets, life there presented its own set of challenges.

Overcrowding was a constant problem. Boys and girls slept in bunk beds in separate dormitories. Each child was permitted to keep only a small box of clothing and personal items.[26] As one historian noted, the institution acted as "a school, a workhouse, and a prison." Some inmates were hired out; those who were not worked seven-hour days learning a trade in one of the facility's workshops. Once they finished working, inmates attended at least three hours of school each day.[27]

If education failed to transform inmates into respectable citizens, corporal punishment was permitted. In 1872, the year Boatright entered the House of Refuge, a St. Louis grand jury indicted Superintendent F. S. W. Gleason for willful oppression and abuse of authority after finding Gleason and staff members mistreated their young charges. Outside observers skeptically declared, "At best, institutional life is bad. The children of public institutions and asylums cannot, as a general rule, become very excellent citizens. The effect of association and discipline in orphanages and reform schools is generally of a character which does not recommend such institutions as the foster-mothers of the future citizens of our land." Despite its barred windows and high walls, Boatright escaped from the House of Refuge on May 8, 1873, and did not return. During his absence from home, his eight-month-old sister Lillie had died of small-pox.[28] Boatright's time at the House of Refuge did little to temper his incorrigibility; less than two years later, he murdered Charley Woodson.

Boatright's trial did not begin until the following year. Because he killed Woodson in the St. Louis Criminal Court, his case was moved to the St. Louis Circuit Court.[29] On February 21, 1876, Boatright's case was called before Judge James J. Lindley. Prosecutor James C. Normile asked for a continuance given that Edward Woodson—Charley Woodson's father and a key witness—was dead, and he needed to secure additional witnesses.[30] Lindley ordered the case to proceed. As the trial began on March 7, a pale and expressionless Robert P. W. Boatright sat next to his parents. With an air of indifference, he spat tobacco between his legs as Normile made his opening statement to the jury.[31] A similar, highly publicized situation only a few years prior had catapulted Normile into public office.

In 1869, twenty-five-year-old James Normile arrived in St. Louis with little legal experience. He had studied law at Georgetown and Columbia Colleges but had not graduated and kept this fact hidden. Normile's meteoric rise in St. Louis legal circles was the result of being selected to defend Joseph H. Fore from murder charges. Fore, a handsome alcoholic wastrel who beat his wife, killed his unarmed, invalid brother-in-law Munson Beach in 1872 after Beach gave shelter to Fore's wife.[32]

From the outset, Normile faced what many believed was an insurmountable battle. Fore's irredeemable character stood in stark contrast to Beach's virtuous reputation as a middle-class bookkeeper and temperance worker. Perhaps most daunting of all was Normile's opponent, the formidable prosecutor Charles P. Johnson. With no other viable options available, Normile relied on the increasingly popular insanity defense. After fierce oratorical combat between the novice and the veteran, the jury found Fore not guilty.[33]

Buoyed by his success, Normile was elected to a four-year term as a St. Louis circuit attorney. In one of his first cases, he prosecuted his former client after Fore attacked his wife with a hatchet. Fore's attorney again employed the insanity defense, but Normile convinced the jury that Fore was sane. In subsequent trials in which the insanity defense was used, Normile was able to secure not only convictions but even death sentences. During the prosecution of William Morgan for the murder of his wife, Normile mocked such defenses as "the flimsy fabric of insanity reared round the accused."[34]

The veneer of mental illness was all that stood between Robert P. W. Boatright and death. Normile declared he would prove Boatright threatened Charley Woodson days before he callously murdered him. As he held up the murder weapon a collective shiver rippled through the audience. Neither Boatright nor his parents reacted. Judge William Jones and Charles Johnson, Woodson's attorney, were the first to testify. Woodson's sister, Susan Reed, was next. She testified that three weeks prior to the murder, she was sweeping snow from the front steps of her parents' residence while Charley skated on the icy street. Robert P. W. Boatright walked up and declared, "You God damn you n[— —], you God damn son of a bitch, you are skating now, but before you skate much longer I'll send you to hell."[35] Boatright's attorneys repeatedly objected throughout Reed's testimony, but she remained unshaken.

While the first day of the trial produced little new information, the second day revealed details about Boatright's mental state. Newspaper reporters jockeyed with the public for seats in the packed courtroom. Despite Boatright having a deathly pallor from confinement, a reporter noted his strong, active appearance. Boatright was dressed in a dark suit; his "strangely bright" eyes glittered feverishly. He remained still and expressionless, prompting one journalist to wonder if Boatright was aware of his surroundings.[36]

Frank Turner, one of Boatright's two attorneys, opened for the defense.[37] Turner announced his client chose to plead not guilty by reason of insanity. The defense, he told the jury, would prove Boatright was insane because he had a family history of epilepsy, lost his intelligence when stricken by typhoid, became mentally unstable after the death of his brother, and twice attempted to commit suicide. Defense witness A. L. Bagwell, who worked for Boatright's grandfather in Franklin County, testified that Boatright's deceased aunt Ann sometimes had three epileptic fits in a day.[38] He was followed by witnesses whose testimony portrayed a disturbed young man.

Former St. Louis neighbors testified about their interactions with the defendant. Joseph Miller thought Boatright a "quiet, intelligent, clean, orderly, obedient boy until his illness." Henry Tice, whose sons were Boatright's playmates, said he "was very bright, intelligent, neat and orderly." After the Boatright family moved, Tice had only seen the young man twice and noticed he appeared mindless. Tice's wife Matilda remarked that Boatright had been well-mannered, affectionate, friendly, and fond of his schoolbooks. After his illness, Mrs. Tice noticed his behavior changed. When she spoke to him in the street, he stared at her as if frightened. Byron Truesdale recalled Boatright talked unintelligibly while ill with typhoid. On cross-examination Truesdale commented, "I noticed that he was more stupid than he used to be."[39] E. O. Pickering observed that after Boatright's illness he played with toddlers, laughed idiotically, and acted peculiar. He admitted, "I always considered him an imbecile; I never knew the boy to do a sensible act in his life."[40]

Bennett B. Brown knew young Boatright from the fall of 1872 until he left St. Louis in 1874. Based on his own observations, Brown believed Boatright was insane. He had seen Boatright frequently gesturing wildly and talking incoherently to himself. Brown found Boatright's behavior so disturbing he told his wife that she and their children were not to associate with him.[41] Bookkeeper William Hicks, who lived with the Boatrights during the summer of 1874, recalled that Boatright stood in the street "for a long time as though he was looking for some person and when asked what he wanted or who he was looking for, could not tell or give an intelligent answer." When given new clothes, Boatright would cut them to pieces and act like a child. Like Brown, Hicks believed Boatright was of unsound mind.[42]

Three of Boatright's former employers took the stand. Stonecutter Alex S. Hughes employed Boatright prior to Charley Woodson's murder. The young man could do a good job, he testified, but sometimes faltered. The morning before the murder Boatright told Hughes he could not get Woodson out of his head. Boatright also occasionally complained of pain in the left side of his head and "at those times he was more stupid than usual."[43] William Sinclair employed Boatright for six to seven months before the murder and claimed he was unlike other boys his age, seemed dull, and did not engage in conversation. When Boatright finished cutting a stone, "he would destroy it with an ax, and when asked about it would answer only with a strange look, which I could not understand, and would not say anything about it." Because of his behavior Sinclair dismissed him twice but took him back after the elder Boatright begged him to keep the boy occupied. Sinclair remarked he never thought Boatright was insane, just strange.[44] Cabinetmaker C. L. Ream hired Boatright after the boy's father pleaded with him to hire his son, but the moody Boatright lasted only six weeks.[45]

Before the second day of the trial ended, Robert M. Boatright—the defendant's father—testified. He recounted his family's history of epilepsy; both a brother and a sister suffered from the disorder. Boatright then explained that after Robert P. W. contracted typhoid in January 1870, he and his wife found the boy they knew had disappeared. The son who once made them proud no longer seemed "to have any mind or be able to control himself."[46] Young Boatright disappeared from the family home for days at a time, only to return without explanation. He seemed unable to remember things; he showed little interest in books and destroyed his clothes. Only Oscar could control the boy, though Robert P. W. was not afraid to hit him. He also struck a woman without provocation while playing ball with his brother and father.[47] The jury was left to consider the words of the elder Boatright overnight as court adjourned for the day.

The trial received considerable coverage in St. Louis newspapers, and by the third day nearly every seat in the courtroom was taken, many by African Americans. Robert M. Boatright explained that of his eight children, the defendant was the only one still alive; three had died of convulsions. After Robert P. W.'s bout with typhoid left him incorrigible, the elder Boatright had petitioned Judge John Colvin of the St. Louis Court of Criminal Correction to admit him to the House of Refuge in March 1872. Strangely, Boatright did not consult a physician about his son's behavior. Prosecutor Normile asked Boatright why he did not have his son committed to the St. Louis County Insane Asylum, but Turner objected, arguing it was an unfair question. Boatright was excused from the witness stand without answering.[48]

As Boatright stepped down, the eerie sound of dirge music unexpectedly filled the courtroom while the funeral procession for Mabel Hall, a ballet dancer murdered by a spurned suitor, passed by the courthouse. Several people left their seats to watch the spectacle as mourners made their way to the cemetery. After order was restored, Boatright's mother Priscilla was called to the witness stand. Like her husband, she too claimed her son's behavior changed after contracting typhoid; he had twice attempted to hang himself.[49]

After the jury reconvened from a brief recess, the trial's first medical expert, Dr. Louis Bauer, was called. Bauer, a German immigrant, had practiced medicine for over three decades. Educated at European and American universities, he had been an expert witness in thirty to forty similar cases. Defense attorney Turner presented Bauer with a hypothetical case identical to that of Boatright. He then asked, "What was the condition of the prisoner at the time of the alleged homicide?" Bauer replied, "If those facts were proven, that such a person was insane at the time of the commission of the act." The exchange between Normile and Bauer has not survived, though Bauer remarked Boatright "looked very stupid and idiotic."[50]

Dr. William B. Hazard, resident physician at the St. Louis County Insane Asylum, next took the stand. He, too, agreed the individual in the hypothetical case "was undoubtedly insane at the time of alleged homicide." Hazard, who previously served an assistant physician at New York's Kings County Hospital, believed an epileptic seizure could change the moral character of a man, but that an epileptic should not be held responsible for their conduct. On cross-examination, Hazard told

Normile that "physicians were the only thoroughly qualified persons to judge of insanity." Normile testily responded his "profession would have something to say about it."[51]

The next day, after the prosecution finished questioning rebuttal witnesses, defense attorney Frank Turner began his closing statement by emphasizing his client's alleged insanity. Turner's co-counsel, Joseph R. Harris, conceded, "We do not deny the killing, but we do say that at the time the act was done, the person that did it was not sane, was not a reasonable being, was not within the purview of the law." Harris declared, "If this fact was not established to [your] satisfaction [you] ought to convict; if it was [then you] should acquit." Harris recounted the testimony of witnesses who knew Boatright as an intelligent, active, obedient, and loving boy struck down by illness. After an arduous recovery, Boatright's parents realized the child they knew was gone; in his place was a boy who "was to be a care, perhaps for a lifetime." The shock of his brother's death brought back the disease that had preyed upon his mind. The law, Harris passionately insisted, was meant to protect even the insane. The court then adjourned.[52]

Just after ten o'clock the next morning, prosecutor James Normile approached the jury to present his closing remarks. In a spirited speech, Normile asserted that the physicians who testified Boatright was insane relied on a "pretended science, as uncertain and false as the science of their predecessors who caused seventeen [year] old women to be hung in England." It was "insane" for Dr. Bauer and Dr. Hazard "to say that only physicians understand the human mind."[53] Normile singled out Boatright's parents as unreliable. "They were unworthy [of] the respect of humanity if they would not tell a lie to save their son from ignominy, disgrace and death," he charged, noting his charity toward their "unreliable testimony." These accusations stung Boatright's mother; she shook with indignant rage as she listened.[54] Normile reminded jurors that perpetrators whose criminal acts were accompanied by forethought, reflection, and willfulness were to be held responsible. Normile stood at the prosecution's table. "A stick might have injured, or a pistol might not have gone off," Normile reasoned, "but in close quarters a knife is the most terrible weapon." He held up Boatright's knife. Pausing for a moment to let the sight sink in, Normile then asked the jury to find Boatright guilty. If they did, he vowed, he would use his influence with the governor to have the death sentence commuted to life imprisonment. If, however, competent medical experts pronounced Boatright insane, he would ask the governor to pardon the defendant and commit him to an insane asylum.[55] After Normile finished, Judge Lindley issued jury instructions.

On March 13, 1876, after two days of deliberations, the jury announced they could not return a verdict.[56] Boatright's attorneys requested bail, but Lindley denied the request. When Harris pushed the matter, Lindley snapped he would not release an individual prone to homicidal mania and remanded Boatright to the custody of the jailer.[57]

In May 1876, the St. Louis grand jury returned a new indictment against Boatright, and the next month his attorneys failed to appear in court to answer it.[58] One of his visitors during this time was his cousin B. F. Sloane. On one occasion Sloane brought a basket that contained a prepared meal. He asked jailer Jerry Coakley to deliver it to Boatright and then left. Suspicious, Coakley opened the basket's lid. At first, all he saw were peas and neatly arranged slices of meat. Upon closer inspection, he discovered a rag concealing two knives: one an old case knife and the other modified into a crude saw. After a brief investigation, the jailers believed Boatright tried to obtain the tools for another inmate and not for himself.[59]

Whatever Sloane's intent was, Boatright remained in jail.[60] The second trial began on December 19, 1876, with most of the same witnesses and experts from the first trial. No transcript of the second trial exists and newspapers gave it less attention than the first, but from their brief accounts it seems little, if any, new information emerged.[61] Altogether, it took the defense and prosecution ten and a half hours to deliver their closing statements. As the jury deliberated, St. Louis's homeless gathered in the courtroom to enjoy a respite from the chill winter air. Boatright, motionless, sat flanked by his mother and a female relative.[62] Finally, on December 27, 1876, the foreman reported there was no hope of consensus. Judge Lindley, who wanted to avoid a third trial, reluctantly thanked the jury. Once again—and after costing thousands of dollars—the trial ended with the jury split ten to two for acquittal.[63]

Boatright returned to the streets of St. Louis. During his imprisonment, his parents had had another child, Elijah Gates Boatright, but Boatright spent only a short amount of time with him as the infant died of convulsions on April 1, 1877. Boatright was not listed in the 1877 city directory, but in 1878 he was listed working as a laborer and living with his parents. He does not appear in the 1879 and 1880 directories, though his father was listed as a private detective. This may have been because on February 24, 1880, Boatright and another man were arrested for first-degree robbery.[64] "Boatright is well known in criminal circles," the *Post-Dispatch* remarked, "and this arrest is not the first time that he has enjoyed life behind the bars."[65] In April 1880 Judge Lindley dismissed the murder charge against him.[66] The following month Boatright was charged with violating the city's revised ordinances prohibiting individuals from associating with "thieves, burglars, pickpockets, pigeon droppers, bawds, prostitutes or lewd women, or gamblers, or any other person, for the purpose or with the intent to [cheat someone]." Boatright, it seemed, had found friends among St. Louis's sinners.

The city was not immune from vice; one resident noted confidence men were extremely active in 1878. Con men, pickpockets, and other criminals successfully plied their trade on the gullible, greedy, and unsuspecting, who fell for scams such as three-card monte, the country merchant game, and even land racket schemes. These were the people Boatright was likely associating with when he was arrested; they may have been old friends from St. Louis's shabby neighborhoods or new acquaintances from jail. Boatright pled guilty and was fined $500. The fine was delayed for twenty-four hours to allow him time to leave the city.[67]

If he left St. Louis, Boatright returned in time to be included in the 1881 city directory as a clerk living with his parents. In 1882 he was absent, but for the next two years Boatright was listed as a blacksmith living at home. In 1885, in his final entry in the St. Louis city directory, he was simply listed as "river," which may indicate he worked on the city's bustling riverfront, but that same year his father curiously described himself as an "explorer." The following year the Boatrights disappeared from the city.[68]

It is unknown when exactly the Boatrights arrived in southwest Missouri, but by 1891 they lived in Jasper County, perhaps drawn by the boom of the Tri-State Lead and Zinc Mining District. The district's lead and zinc fields were rich not only with ore but also with the potential to elevate the common man into the ranks of the wealthy, provided he was unafraid of risk and hard work. It was a time of speculation and scheming, when wealth could also be found concealed in others' greed. Robert P. W. Boatright would find his riches not in the earth, but in the pockets of his fellow man.[69] If he were truly insane, he showed little sign of it as he fleeced the gentry of the Midwest in one of the greatest cons of all time.

2

"NO PLACE FOR 'SISSIES'"

The facts will show you, gentlemen, that this commenced in 1897, that in 1898 a
good many of these races were run or prepared to be run and a large amount of
money was got, and in 1899 and 1900 it began to get common.

—JOHN W. HALLIBURTON, *State of Missouri v. Robert Boatright,*
Ed E. Ellis, and Bert Bromley

The marks came from everywhere. They came from Indian Territory, the Kansas plains, dusty Texas; they came from across the country to a mining town on the edge of the Ozark foothills. Located in Jasper County, where the Missouri Ozarks give way to the vastness of the Great Plains, was the unassuming mining town of Webb City. It had once been open rolling prairie farmed by John C. Webb, but after lead was discovered there Webb found royalties and real estate more profitable. A settlement, first known as Webbville and later Webb City, was established in 1876, one of dozens of mining camps spread out across the Tri-State Mining District. Encompassing almost 1,200 square miles, the district extended from southwest Missouri into southeast Kansas and northeast Oklahoma. Prior to the Civil War individuals engaged in pick-and-shovel prospecting and, after the war, resumed mining with vigor. By 1875, Missouri was the nation's leading zinc producer. The landscape was riddled with deep mine shafts and littered with hulking chat piles. Mines were christened with names such as Goodenough, Hello Dad, Sweet Relief, Yellow Dog, Billy Sunday, Ino, Uno, Damfino, Damfuno, and Hell-on-Earth. One by one, many of the old mining camps disappeared, leaving only a handful of communities to survive. Webb City was among the survivors.[1]

It sat between cross-county rivals Joplin and Carthage. Joplin, the heart of the mining district, was less refined than Carthage, the county

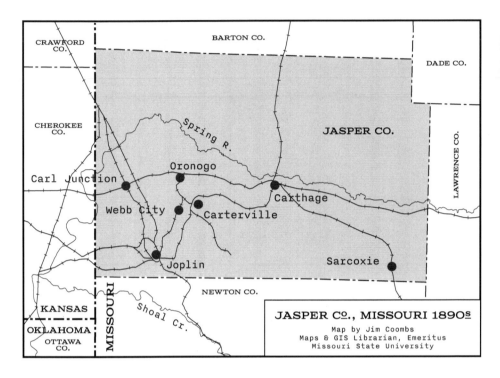

Map of Jasper County, Missouri, 1890s. *Map by Jim Coombs.*

seat where many wealthy denizens preferred to live. Carthage native and prominent Democratic Party leader Emily Newell Blair recalled, "The two towns do not like each other. Joplin thinks Carthage is smug and superior. As strangers are told when they ask about it, 'Oh, Carthage—it's where dead men walk about.' And Carthage thinks that Joplin is crude and self-sufficient." "Joplin citizens referred laughingly to Carthage as the 'holy city,'" the *Carthage Evening Press* remarked, "because this town never had any ambition to be known as a frontier of civilization. Joplin intimated that one could not reside in Carthage long without sprouting wings and getting a halo."[2] Webb City, however, was neither holy nor civilized.

Years after the lead and zinc mines fell silent, Webb City was remembered as "no place for 'sissies.'" Miners from Webb City and neighboring Carterville met at Ben's Branch, a stream dividing the two towns, to fight with "pick handles and fists." In 1877 when a Carterville resident was arrested in Webb City, his friends shot up the town.[3] Although lead sparked the town's creation, it was zinc—also called blackjack—that led to its being called the "Town That Jack Built." Webb City's fortunes rose and fell with the markets, but as it successfully transitioned from mining camp to town, much of its growth was financed by the Exchange Bank of Webb City. Located on Allen Street, the bank was founded in 1889 by the Stewart family and fellow shareholders of the Center Creek Mining Company. One resident recalled the thoroughfare's saloons, bawdy houses, and barber shops led "church people, the [Woman's Christian Temperance Union] members, and some other do-gooder groups" to believe "the devil had his habitat up and down the length of the east side of Allen Street." But, he continued,

> Some, there were, who said the east side was the wrong side of the street. Others disagreed. One thing is sure; the length and breadth of this famous street provided entertainment for the most cosmopolitan, both rich and poor. The west side provided the genteel items for everyday living. Intermingled with these were the luxury stores demanded by the newly rich. However, on the west side of the street things were recorded which were not always of an orthodox nature. The well capitalized bank [Exchange Bank] across the street, on the west side of Allen Street, loaned huge sums of money to the mine operators, to the grand stores which flanked each side of the beautiful entrance, and to the individual miners who could establish credit.[4]

James Stewart served as the bank's cashier and his cousin Joseph Stewart as president; together they kept a firm grip on the financial institution. During the Panic of 1893 the Exchange Bank suspended operations after having loaned heavily to new mining companies but did not suffer any losses.[5] By the 1890s Webb City boasted an opera house, the Newland Hotel, a Baptist college, and four newspapers. The city's population, 5,043 in 1890, nearly doubled to 9,201 by 1900. As historian Brooks Blevins noted, "Between 1890 and 1910, Jasper County experienced a population explosion, growing from fifty thousand people to almost ninety thousand."[6]

Christian missionary H. A. Northcutt predicted, "It is only a matter of short time when Joplin, Webb City, Carterville, Oronogo, and Carthage will be one city." Northcutt continued, "Christianity is at a low ebb while saloons and gambling houses are prosperous. A new saloon was opened while I was in Webb City, the furniture of which is said to have cost ten thousand dollars. They advertised free drinks for the opening day. It was heart-sickening to see the hundreds of young men going into this place. One of these saloon keepers said some Saturdays from noon till midnight

Allen Street, Webb City, Missouri, 1900. The Newland Hotel is at left.
Courtesy Carthage Public Library.

he would take in across the counter three thousand dollars."[7] Webb City, rough and unassuming, suited Robert Boatright's purposes.

Boatright was just one of many gamblers to take up residence in Jasper County. By the end of the decade, it must have seemed to a missionary like Northcutt that the gates of hell had opened in this part of the Ozarks. A Carthage paper reported, "There is a lively time on in Webb City and the saloons are feeling the effect of the efforts of certain people to regulate them. Webb City is a 'wide open' town and in the language of the dead game sport 'everything goes' in that place but according to some 'everything' has gone almost too far."[8] Webb City, however, was on the periphery of a much larger gambling hell.

By the end of the nineteenth century Joplin had become the "metropolis for a territory three hundred miles in circumference." In 1899 Sedalia

Fourth and Main Streets in Joplin. This photo, taken after 1902 but before 1906, shows the commercial heart of the Tri-State Mining District. The House of Lords is visible at left. *Author's Collection.*

journalist Charles M. Barde marveled, "Joplin is certainly a world within itself. Immense buildings are going up everywhere, and houses, too. Hundreds of people are living in tents, so scarce are houses." Ragtime pianist Percy Wenrich recalled the north end of Joplin's "Main Street was as wide open as a barn door." Periodically, though, the spirit of reform overtook the city.[9]

"Gambling in Joplin must stop," declared Jasper County prosecuting attorney Hiram Shannon in 1899.[10] He then issued sixty warrants for gamblers. Joplin constable Austin Harvey told the *Joplin News-Herald*, "Heretofore we have been handicapped because of a misunderstanding in certain official circles, but the prosecuting attorney has settled that matter and this thing will be fought to a finish."[11] Gaming house proprietors expressed skepticism at the prosecutor's intent. They scoffed the crusade would be short-lived and their joints would "probably stay closed up until this term of circuit court is about over."[12] The *Joplin Globe* expressed disgust that wide-open gambling houses offered every game in existence and questioned if Shannon was sincere or if he was giving criminal defense attorney T. Bond Haughawout an "opportunity to make another 'shake down.' "[13]

Fifty gamblers were fined and public gaming houses ordered closed. A Joplin resident told the *Globe*, "The public gambling houses have been supported by the miners and since they have been closed this time men who never took their wages home before went home last Saturday night with bundles of clothing and provisions for the family and with money in their pockets."[14] Sports were angry after gambling joints remained closed in some, but not all, Jasper County cities. "There is no justice in closing up the gambling houses in Joplin and allow them to run wide open in Webb City," an indignant gambler spat. "It is an unjust discrimination. Mr. Shannon's jurisdiction over Webb City is the same as that over Joplin. If the gamblers are to be run out of the one place they must be driven out of the other. The prosecuting attorney ought to be consistent."[15] Shannon insisted, "If I get the support in this matter that seems assured me, you will see no more gambling in Joplin. I have every reason to believe that the promises that have been made me will be kept."[16] Those promises rang hollow as gambling flourished in Jasper County. In this ideal environment Boatright easily transitioned from gambling to operating gambling houses to organizing fake athletic contests. To do it, he relied upon a confederacy of confidence men whose own colorful stories began long before the Buckfoot Gang.

Decades after Bud Gillett was buried in in the Flint Hills, old-timers in Greenwood County, Kansas, still spoke of him with a mix of pride and bitterness. The Gillett family lived on Dry Creek five miles northeast of Quincy. Local lore had it that Bud and his brother Frank often went to town, with Frank on horseback riding at a lope and Bud running alongside holding on to Frank's saddle strings. Six feet tall with a powerful physique and a slim waist, Bud Gillett was a natural. When he practiced on a hundred-yard track alongside the rail line in Quincy, a gaggle of boys waited halfway down the stretch. When Bud began running, they shot off like bottle rockets but never beat him. Local sports called him "the fastest sprinter in the world." Quincy native Glenn S. Slough remembered, "I never saw Bud Gillett run a race but, as a child, I did see him practice sprints. While the untrained eye of a child is not reliable, it seemed to me that Bud was the fastest sprinter to date."[17]

Life in nineteenth-century rural America was full of amusements quaint by modern standards. One of the most common, though now forgotten, was foot racing. Together with horseracing, it could be held almost year-round and was popular during community events such as the Fourth of July.[18] But this seemingly innocent pastime was easily corrupted. Large amounts of money were often wagered, which presented savvy individuals the perfect opportunity. Some foot racers traveled the country with promoters; others worked alone. The simplest way to make money was to arrange the outcome of the race in advance, with one of the runners agreeing to throw the contest. Gillett, however, won race after race without a whiff of suspicion. By 1894 he was known throughout the Verdigris River valley as the man to beat in the hundred-yard dash.

It may have been that his family struggled to earn a living in an area characterized by rugged, rocky soil. It could have been that he believed criminal behavior was acceptable; his brother Frank had several scrapes with the law. Or, it could have been an easy way to make a living for someone to whom running came so naturally. Dozens of newspaper articles bear testament to Bud's speed and athleticism during the early 1890s and show how he became the pride of tiny Quincy. Somewhere along the way, though, Bud chose to start running fixed races.

The beginning of the end came during the summer of 1894. On July 20 Bud was matched with Jesse Rossel Jr. from nearby Eureka. The race drew a large crowd of several hundred spectators and "every man had a wad of money that he wanted to bet on the Quincy champion." Bud's brother Frank walked up and down the racetrack with fistfuls of five-dollar bills challenging spectators to bet an unlimited amount as Quincy "had the fastest runners, the surest shooting guns and the fattest hunting dogs." No one took his offer. The race, scheduled to begin at four in the afternoon, got off to a late start after the runners came up to the start line forty or fifty times without committing. At six o'clock, with the crowd restless and ready to go home for the evening, the race official finally fired his starting pistol. Gillett had a two-foot advantage off the line as he sprinted down the track. An exhausted Rossel tried but failed to close the gap. Gillett ran easily enough, though some observers wondered if it was his best effort.[19]

On September 9, Gillett raced Carl Bush in Quincy. The *Eureka Democratic Messenger* noted several Eureka citizens, hoping to recoup their losses on the Gillett–Rossel race, recruited Bush. The Eureka boys went to Quincy in high spirits but shortly before the race they discovered their ringer had been compromised. Betting on Bush stopped. After a series of false starts, Gillett waved at the crowd and yelled, "Get back there, we are coming this time." The two men took off; Bush quickly got a lead on Gillett, but at fifty yards he was eight feet behind. Suddenly Bush began running faster, so fast that "some of the unsophisticated thought for a moment they were yet to win their bets" but Bush "knew his business and carefully checked his advance in time to avoid winning."

Gillett won by eighteen inches. Eureka's losses were estimated at $300 to $700. Doubts about Gillett surfaced. Some expressed their belief that the race was fair; others were confident a swindle had taken place. Despite such misgivings, Gillett's victory solidified Quincy's faith in the home-town champion.[20]

Two months later, Gillett was matched with Ralph Martin of Columbus, Kansas. News of the race spread like wildfire and the Santa Fe Railroad added extra cars to bring spectators to watch the contest. "Sainted people" bet everything they could on Gillett—cash, pocket watches, and IOUs for cattle, saddles, and horses.[21] No eyewitness or news account of the race is known to exist, but at least two papers noted the outcome. The *Eureka Herald* marveled, "There isn't a timepiece, except a 'grandfather's clock' and that stopped long before the war and while Buchanan was president, left in the east-end of the township."[22] Martin and his backer took home an estimated $7,000 ($242,872 in 2022), or, as one paper put it, "the price of several good farms. . . . Another popular idol has fallen," the *Yates Center News* lamented. "We are sorry for Gillett," it declared, "But his defeat is a good thing for his community if it will only put a stop to the further development of the sporting spirit in that neighborhood. They have run wild down there and not only the men but the women and children bet loyal and to the limit on Gillett."[23] The *Toronto Republican* agreed, "The defeat of Gillett has done more to cure the foot-race disease than all other remedies applied."[24]

Gillett's loss did not endear him to the townsfolk who once cheered him. A year after his ignominious loss, Gillett was spotted in town. A Eureka paper groused he was a professional "not averse to being beaten by an amateur provided the betting has been properly arranged." Gillett now lived in Webb City, Missouri, and had not lost a race since Quincy. The paper observed, "From an athletic and rather unsophisticated appearing young farmer, he has blossomed into an all-round sport of the first water. His clothes, carriage, and conversation all bear testimony to the evolution." Gillett could run 100 hundred yards in "9⅖ seconds—when he wants to—and hopes to equal the world's record—9¾ seconds—during the coming year."[25]

And yet, even though it was widely publicized Bud Gillett was a fraud, locals could not resist the allure of a sure thing. In the summer of 1897, he again toed the starting line with Ralph Martin. A crowd of over a thou-sand men, women, and children waited for two hours in sweltering heat to watch, but the race turned out to be less than eventful. Gillett failed to start and scratched.[26] Days later, when Gillett passed through Eureka, the *Democratic Messenger* noted dryly, "He was going to Texas to win or throw a race."[27] Gillett was not the only one.

Athletes like Gillett were essential to Boatright's con. Yet Boatright also needed men gifted with patience, persuasion, and nerve. They had to be actors, psychologists, and salesmen who inspired trust. Each man was instinctively a risk-taker. One of the best was a slender westerner skilled at cards. Lucius E. Hindman—the Honey Grove Kid—came from a small town of the same name in the Red River valley of northeast Texas.[28] In the winter of 1898 he drifted into the railroad town of Sedalia, Missouri. Boosters called it "the Queen City of the Prairies," but Sedalia had a less than savory reputation. Originally a cattle town on the Shawnee Trail, its infamous red-light district had led the *St. Louis Post-Dispatch* to call it the "Sodom and Gomorrah of Missouri." Decades later vice and crime still flourished there. Thus it was no surprise Hindman was recruited by local sports to skin the Woodward brothers, who had been beating everyone at the game of "coon can."[29] Hindman could pick up his cards and "foretell the result of the game without ever missing it, just as if he had scanned every card in his opponent's hand." The brothers quickly realized they were being hustled. One local remarked if the Kid had kept his mouth shut, he could have won. Instead, his skilled play signaled he was "a world-beater at 'coon can.' "[30] Although he did not skin the Woodward brothers, Hindman remained in Sedalia.

On February 1, 1899, Hindman and another man engaged Oscar Strand, a Missouri Pacific engineer, in a game of chance. Strand had no idea he was playing with professionals. By the time he caught on to the scheme, Strand had lost ninety-five dollars. Indignant, he demanded his money back. Hindman promised to square the matter at the Hotel Huckins, but upon arrival he failed to do so. Strand grabbed Hindman by the coat and demanded, "If this is a confidence game I want to know it." He again asked for his money back. The diminutive Texan drew a revolver and barked, "God damn you, I ought to kill you anyhow." When a hotel clerk tried to intervene, Hindman waved his revolver and threatened, "God damn it, don't anybody touch me or I'll kill them." He then shot Strand two inches below the heart, mortally wounding the engineer. In the ensuing chaos, Hindman escaped into the night.[31]

Hindman, the *Sedalia Evening Sentinel* proclaimed, was "a frequenter of one of the hell holes of gambling with which the city is surfeited." Another paper confirmed the Texan made his living from the track and gambling rooms. He was "only 21 years old, is of good address, always neatly attired and is a good mixer in the truest sense of the term." The Kid may have relied on his revolver because ot his slight build; he was only five feet, five inches and 127 pounds. Sedalia acquaintances claimed this was the first time he had ever been in trouble.[32] Although he had a head start, officers were waiting for Hindman when he got off the Missouri Pacific No. 6 train in St. Louis. Hindman claimed he was a farmer named Harry Russell, but after an hour in police custody he confessed to shooting Strand.[33] Upon his return to Sedalia, Hindman better resembled "a well-fed, well-dressed clerk in a city broker's office than a professional gambler and murderer."[34]

Unsurprisingly, Hindman was a smooth talker and well informed. Only three years earlier he had been a clerk in his hometown of Honey Grove, Texas, when he began playing poker. Once he discovered he was good at cards, Hindman became a professional gambler. While in custody, he told a reporter he had only been arrested once and that was for having too much money in Omaha. He falsely claimed Confederate general Thomas C. Hindman was his grandfather, no doubt an attempt to impress the gullible. A woman vowed to put up every dollar in the world for him, but Hindman could not make $10,000 bond.[35] The Kid wrote the boys at home to "refrain from 'the butterfly life'" and express regret he had not remained employed at the town's livery stable.[36] Eventually he posted $7,500 bond and left Sedalia.[37] On April 4, 1899, Hindman was indicted for the murder of Oscar Strand. In the fall the well-dressed gambler was spotted in Joplin, where he split his time between the southwest Missouri mining town and Indian Territory.[38] A year after his indictment, Hindman went on trial in Sedalia. The proceedings lasted a week, but after twelve hours the jury found him not guilty. His confident performance on the witness stand and the state's failure to cross-examine him helped secure his freedom. Hindman moved on from Sedalia and, although left unsaid, to new victims.[39]

Lest one lose themselves in the romanticism of the con and its practitioners, Leon Lozier was one of the more disreputable individuals in the Buckfoot Gang, though one of the most impressive in terms of tricking bettors while clearly looking past his prime as a sprinter. With Lozier it can be said that prejudice did not blind Boatright to finding the best men for the job. As a child he immigrated with his family to America from Obersitzko in Prussia (modern-day Obrzycko, Poland), where the Loziers were part of the town's Jewish community.[40] When he first began to compete as a sprinter is uncertain, but by the early 1880s Lozier's athletic prowess made him a common fixture in Midwest sporting news. He traveled across the region challenging local runners to compete against him for $50 to $500 ($1,555 to $15,557) a side.[41] "Short and heavy set, with muscles hard as steel," he ran with a "short, quick step," and was gifted with "great activity and endurance."[42] His professional and personal behavior, however, left much to be desired.

Lozier skipped out on his bills. He was arrested in Scranton, Iowa, for allegedly raping the city marshal's seven-year-old daughter in 1884.[43]

Leon Lozier. *National Archives and Records Administration.*

Hired to help the Sioux Falls, South Dakota, fire hose team win the 1885 Dakota State Firemen's Tournament, he stumbled and fell as the team approached the finish line. An angry mob of Sioux Falls citizens attacked Lozier. In a sensational account published a decade later, one participant claimed someone tried to secure a rope around the sprinter's neck. As a desperate brawl erupted between Sioux Falls and Sioux City spectators, Sioux City marshal James Shaley and Sioux City fire chief Harvey Hawman grabbed Lozier and fought their way into an empty exhibition building. They shoved the bleeding sprinter in a room and locked the door. Outside the mob attacked the building with axes and breached a wall. With assistance, Lozier barely escaped.[44] One spectator claimed the story was exaggerated, but decades later in 1930 a fellow race participant recalled, "Lozier was certainly lucky to get away without more serious injury than he received."[45] Despite the publicity generated by Lozier's near lynching and his growing notoriety across the Midwest as a fraud, he continued to swindle victims.[46]

Lozier occasionally took part in more seemingly legitimate athletic events. In 1888 he competed in a professional sprinting championship in St. Louis.[47] More often than not, though, he ran in local races. As with Bud Gillett, a regional mythology enveloped Lozier. In 1937 Omaha sports editor Frederick Ware and local sports enthusiast Pat Connell reminisced about Nebraska foot racing. According to Connell, in 1893 Frank "Kid" Sullivan dominated the small sprinters, W. H. Copple ruled the big ones. But, he recalled, there was another sprinter, faster than anyone he ever saw except for Sullivan. No one knew with certainty how fast Leon Lozier was, but he supposedly inspired the gamblers' adage, "I won't bet on anything that can talk." "He would lose races that appeared on the soundest evidence to be cinches," Connell recollected. "He would win when pitted against champions and near-champions. It wasn't surprising that his enemies among people who bet on foot racers increased rapidly. He got a bad name, which may not have been entirely deserved."[48]

In 1892 Lozier participated in the Milwaukee Caledonian Games under a fake name. More than one hundred people protested that the outcome of the two-hundred-yard professional race was fixed.[49] The next year he was arrested after a fraudulent race in Whiting, Iowa, but the charges were dismissed. Lozier was later arrested on a charge of conspiracy, but by the fall of that year he lost a race to William H. Copple.[50] Notorious in sporting circles, he became more widely infamous when he was accused of sexually assaulting a five-year-old girl at his residence in Council Bluffs, Iowa. Officers in neighboring Omaha apprehended him on a Missouri Pacific train. From his cell Lozier hollered to a reporter he was innocent, but not everyone agreed. Later that night a man in a Council Bluffs saloon yelled, "Let's lynch him!" A smoldering fire of public opinion erupted into a firestorm of riotous outrage.

Within minutes, yells rent the air as angry men spilled out into the streets and converged on the jail. Two thousand men and boys bellowed, "Bring him out!" Pottawattamie County sheriff John T. Hazen and four deputies as well as Council Bluffs police chief John Scanlan and three officers confronted the mob. Standing on the jail steps, Hazen ordered the unruly crowd to disperse. A rope surfaced. Hazen barked, "We have armed men in this building and will defend it with our lives." Lacking a leader, the mob milled around without direction. Lewis Berger, an African American, made a short inflammatory speech declaring if Lozier was a Black man, the crowd would have lynched him. Berger demanded, "Give me the rope, I will lead the crowd." Officers removed him from the scene.[51]

Sheriff Hazen sent a message to Governor Frank Jackson requesting the services of the Iowa National Guard. Captain William E. Aitchison and twenty-seven armed infantrymen were ready within thirty minutes. At 11:00 p.m. Aitchison and his men marched over a half-mile of icy pavement to the jail, passed the howling mob, and took up positions inside the building. By 2:00 a.m. the crowd had dispersed. Not wanting to tempt fate, Sheriff Hazen transported Lozier to the Iowa State Penitentiary.[52] The Pottawattamie County grand jury recommended Lozier's case be dismissed. The decision sparked public outcry, but jurors determined the allegations were the result of a family feud.[53]

The home life of the itinerant sign painter and sprinter did not improve; the following spring Lozier left his wife and children in desperate straits. The children had battled scarlet fever for two weeks and one was near death. Upon learning of the family's difficulties, Chief Scanlan raised money to buy groceries for the Loziers.[54] In 1898 Lozier and two associates were sued for $5,000 in Macon County, Illinois, by victim Bernard Stein of Chicago. Stein alleged the men tricked him into betting $2,000 in cash, diamonds, and his watch on a fixed foot race, but they were found not guilty.[55] It would be far from Lozier's last trouble with the law.

Lozier and Gillett may have been the most prominent sprinters in Boatright's stable of athletes, but the Buckfoot Gang also included at least one prizefighter. Edward "Eddie" K. Morris, whose real name was Eddie K. Steele, was the only African American member of the Webb City Athletic Club. Born in Tennessee, he left home at age twelve. Able to read and write his name, the heavily built fighter stood just under five feet, six inches tall.[56] It is unknown when and where Morris learned to box, but in a 1911 interview Morris remarked he "began and served his apprenticeship in fake prizefighting under Boatright, the head of the Webb City, Mo., organization" and "had been in the game twelve years." Morris emphasized he "never faked a fight where the public was concerned, only where the ones present were the victims and members of our organization."[57] Just how others in the gang felt about Morris is unknown, but at least one member demonstrated an avowed dislike of Blacks.

Bert "Curley" Bromley—sprinter, pugilist, bartender, and baseball umpire—was one of the most pugnacious members of the gang. Stocky and bowlegged, his nickname was the result of a peculiar square formation on the back of his head topped by a curly knot of hair. In 1896 the *Galena Post* reported, "Bert Bromley, better known as 'Curley,' a tin horn gambler of limited standing, is again in trouble. On one of his jamborees at Webb City a few nights ago, he cut a negro so badly it is thought death will be the result."[58] Later that year Bromley and Joseph Fetters Jr. forced their way into Laura Martin's room at the California House in Webb City. Once inside they pistol-whipped Martin before Fetters assaulted her; they also attacked a fellow boarder who tried to intervene.[59] This drew the attention of other occupants, but Bromley and Fetters held them off at gunpoint and escaped, only to be arrested a few minutes later. Threats of lynching circulated throughout town, and an excited mob briefly formed outside the jail. The *Joplin News* sniffed, "The entire outfit is of the sporty element and such scenes are not an unusual happening in Webb."[60] Two years later Bromley pled guilty to assault and battery in neighboring Galena, Kansas, for shooting at William Bartlett because he wanted to "see a n[——] run."[61] That fall Bromley was charged with grand larceny after he stole a pistol and twenty-four dollars of the madam's money from the White Elephant brothel in Galena.[62] Not all the gang's members were as rough around the edges as Bromley.

Edward Elias Ellis grew up in nearby Granby, Missouri. After rich lead deposits were discovered in the 1850s, thousands participated in the "Granby Stampede" to try their hand at mining. By 1859 eight thousand people lived in the township. Outside investment poured in from St. Louis capitalists.[63] Fought over for the duration of the Civil War, Granby became a ghost town. Three months after the end of the war, a visitor found the town overgrown with brush. Within a year production resumed, and Granby attracted a new wave of miners "infected with gambling instinct."[64] Among those who sought their luck in postwar Granby was Edward's father, James R. "Dick" Ellis, a Mississippian who brought his young family to the Ozarks.[65]

Ed Ellis left Granby and drifted through the region's mining camps until he landed in Webb City. There, "handsome, of a naturally refined, gentlemanly disposition," he caught the attention of Robert Boatright. Ellis could "have been a different man with his natural talents cultivated and training in an elevating and Christian manner . . . for with all his evil training there was nothing sneaking about him." Boatright, recognizing Ellis's shrewd mind and talent for handling money, recruited the youth to be his chief lieutenant. The young Ozarker became a skilled confidence man who plied his trade on ocean liners. He loved to brag about how he talked his way into a millionaire's lawn party in Colorado Springs, Colorado, mingled with the wealthy guests, and then cleaned them out playing auction bridge.[66]

Ellis's urbane manner was matched by George W. Ryan, who grew up further east on the Springfield Plateau where the Ozark hills yield to the prairie. Ryan came from a reputable family. His mother, Laura Sherman

Ed Ellis. *National Archives and Records Administration.*

Ryan, claimed descent from a signer of the Declaration of Independence. His father, William S. Ryan, was a Union veteran. After the war, the elder Ryan married and purchased a farm in Lawrence County, Missouri. He was elected sheriff twice before his career in law enforcement came to an inglorious end in 1883 after five inmates escaped from jail. Still, Ryan's fellow citizens trusted him to collect taxes, and he served one term as county collector. By the time George was sixteen, his father was operating a drug store. In 1889 the elder Ryan died after an angry customer struck him with a brick.[67] When Ryan left home and what he did following his father's death is unknown, but by 1897 he had moved to Hot Springs, Arkansas. In 1902 he and former Garland County, Arkansas, deputy sheriff Ed Spear operated a fight store together there, though it is unclear if they were operating separately from or together with Boatright.[68]

Another of the more colorful members of the gang hailed from the Bluegrass State. Kentuckian Roger H. Williams was born in 1862 in Carrollton, located between Louisville and Cincinnati, Ohio. He led a roving life from early boyhood before marrying in 1886.[69] When the cry went up that gold had been discovered in the Klondike region, he joined the mad scramble to the Yukon. Whether he sought his fortune as a prospector or as a gambler is unknown, but he became snowbound and almost starved to death. His obituary would state he was a painter, but Williams promoted athletic contests and occasionally engaged in the mining business. The Honey Grove Kid put it more bluntly: Williams was a professional gambler.[70] Although Williams was not an alcoholic, his sister wryly remarked, "He was not averse to try his fortunes with the cards." After his wife's death, he made sure his only child, Leland A. Williams, attended school.[71] Others came from less settled backgrounds.

George R. Thompson was the son of a Crimean War veteran who emigrated with his wife from Britain to the United States in 1861. After serving in the Union Army during the Civil War, Thompson's father operated hotels in Kansas.[72] In 1900 Thompson lived in Cherryvale, Kansas, next to Garrette Orville "G. O." Stansbury. Stansbury was one of the oldest members of the gang. Born in 1851 and orphaned young, by 1883 he was identified in Kansas and Missouri newspapers as a gambler who operated gaming devices.[73] Stansbury, like Gillett and Lozier, also participated in fraudulent foot races. In 1887, using the alias Thomas Brown, he ran a fixed race against William Crider in Tuscola, Illinois. He operated a billiards parlor in the Axtell Hotel in Cherryvale, seventy-five miles west of Webb City, Missouri.[74]

At least one member already had a juvenile record when he joined the gang. The son of a railroad baggage master, Harry Wasser grew up in Girard, Kansas. In 1893 he worked in his grandfather's hardware store in Webb City. Suspected of stealing from the firm, Wasser's alleged transgressions were overlooked until he and an accomplice stole several firearms and $350. Convicted of burglary and larceny, Wasser received a two-year term at the Missouri State Training School for Boys in Boonville. His juvenile delinquency did not deter his marriage prospects; in 1900 Wasser, his wife, and young son lived down the street from Robert Boatright in Webb City. Like Boatright, Wasser listed his occupation as gambler.[75]

At least one member of the gang was an educated professional. Dr. Robert Edward Lee Goddard, the son of a Georgia physician who moved to Texas after the end of the Civil War, was an 1894 graduate of the Kentucky School of Medicine in Louisville. In 1900 he and his family lived in Dallas; Goddard specialized in treating alcoholics, which gave him access to vulnerable individuals.[76]

Harry "Bud" Wasser, third from left, at the Missouri State Training School for Boys in Boonville. *State Historical Society of Missouri (P0138).*

Boatright needed men with financial resources when things got hot; the most important was Charles "Charley" A. Parker. A longtime Webb City resident and proprietor of the 16 to 1 Saloon at 117 North Allen Street, Parker gave bond when called upon by Boatright.[77] Parker had extensive mining interests, large land holdings, a meat market, and was said to be worth at least $100,000. An ardent Democrat, Parker reportedly served as a delegate to every local convention. Parker was not to be messed with; in his saloon, money was stacked on the bar without a guard. His name frequently appears in court records, most often for gambling and selling liquor on a Sunday.[78] Boatright conducted much of the gang's business at Parker's saloon. Victims were taken there to bet, and after every race his co-conspirators held high carnival at the bar.[79]

The names of other Buckfoot Gang members fleetingly appear in newspaper articles and in court cases. Presumably they staged athletic contests, roped victims, and acted as shills. John "Cash" Grimm, William Crider, John "Jack" Kivlin, Oro Fields, Ed C. Moore, Dick Beatte, Ben Ansel, and Jesse Ansel were all sprinters. Except for Oklahoman Beatte, the Ansels who lived in Kansas and Oklahoma, and Crider who was from Illinois, many of the men were from Iowa. Chicago welterweight Walter R. Nolan was also likely affiliated with the gang. Many more individuals were only referred to by their surnames and, in some cases, their aliases. As court records demonstrate, gang members often used each other's surnames instead of their own when interacting with victims.[80] It was a motley union of scoundrels and liars, but together these otherwise unremarkable men were part of one of the most successful turn-of-the-century confidence gangs in the United States.

3

"MEN OF NO REPUTATION"

—ROBERT MOONEYHAM, *State of Missouri v. Robert Boatright, Ed E. Ellis, and Bert Bromley*

It was a story that even a sheriff shared with relish. One summer as the locusts sang, Robert Boatright's Webb City Athletic Club challenged the Carthage baseball team for $600 a side. The Carthaginians readily accepted the offer. By the time they took the field against Webb City, both sides had put up $1,600. During the first inning, two Webb City players were injured. At a loss for replacements and with money at stake, the Webb City players went to a nearby mine. Two grimy men emerged from the mineshaft, put on uniforms, and took the field. "Such ball playing as they did was never seen there before," it was said. One of the substitutes only allowed two hits. Boatright had imported "professionals from an Eastern league team," one of whom had reportedly pitched for Philadelphia that season. Unsurprisingly Webb City won the game.[1] Despite occasional deviations from their usual method of separating suckers from their money, the Buckfoot Gang made the bulk of their money off individual cons and public sporting events.

In the heart of the Tri-State Mining District, Boatright and his fellow "men of no reputation" convincingly posed as wealthy mine operators. Served by the Kansas City, Fort Scott, and Memphis, St. Louis–San Francisco, and Missouri Pacific railroads, Webb City was accessible from the Midwest and Southwest, as well as from neighboring Joplin and Carthage via the region's extensive interurban trolley system. Protected by local law enforcement and politicians, Boatright operated with impunity. When local protection was not enough, he hired attorneys George E. Booth and George R. Clay to defend him in court. Most important of all, Boatright had the cooperation of the Exchange Bank of Webb City and, later, the Joplin Savings Bank, providing him the legitimacy needed to pull off his schemes.[2]

Webb City Mining District, 1902. *State Historical Society of Missouri (P0018).*

Although it can be divined from court records that Boatright engaged in illegal gambling during the 1890s in Jasper County, it is uncertain when the gang itself was organized.[3] Records indicate some members were gambling in Webb City around the same time.[4] Newspaper accounts indicate others were running fixed races in the 1890s, but it is unknown if they were working alone, with another fixer, or with Boatright's front, the Webb City Athletic Club. Where and when Boatright met the other members is unclear. It is even uncertain when and how Boatright learned the scheme he perfected—he may have even been a victim. While the gang's origins are unknown, a few intriguing details have survived.[5]

Various dates for the gang's formation appear in court records. One lawyer believed the Webb City Athletic Club "commenced in 1897, that in 1898 a good many of these races were run or prepared to be run and a large amount of money was got, and in 1899 and 1900 it began to get common." In another account, the club was founded in 1891.[6] In 1895 an organization by that name was granted sanctions by the St. Louis Cycling Racing Board. This was the first known appearance of the Webb City Athletic Club in print.[7] Banker James Stewart testified the Webb City Athletic Association was founded in the 1890s during the height of the bicycle craze.[8] This is supported by an apocryphal story about Boatright staging a bicycle race. He brought a rider from out east, but on the day of the race the cyclist injured his foot. Boatright, who had bet heavily on the Easterner, found a substitute in a cigar store clerk. To bettors' surprise, the clerk was an even better rider than the injured cyclist; Boatright had planted him in the store in advance.[9] No record for the association or the club's incorporation exists. Boatright likely appropriated its name for his purposes; at least one victim alleged Boatright used the club's stationery with Stewart's name on it.[10] Boatright's specialty, however, was fixed foot races and prizefights.

While there were confidence men who wrote memoirs, unsurprisingly not one member of the Buckfoot Gang left behind an account of their life. Court records and newspaper accounts, however, provide both a general framework and intimate details of their cons. The gang's scheme relied solely on an individual's greed. Individuals known as ropers went out on the road to look for a mark; that is, a victim. Sometimes they snared wealthy visitors in resort towns like Hot Springs, Arkansas, and Colorado Springs, Colorado. Mostly, however, they found their quarry in small towns located on rail lines across the country. They used various methods to identify marks. Sometimes they secured employment in a town and became a fixture in the community; other times they relied on previously established relationships. In some cases, their own victims helped them rope friends. Once they had an individual in mind, the ropers inquired around town to determine if the sucker was worth skinning.

Satisfied the mark had money and access to letters of credit, the ropers approached the individual and spun an enticing yarn about the Webb City Athletic Club, a group of millionaire mine operators who enjoyed betting on athletic contests. Sometimes a roper claimed to be an athlete shortchanged by club members. In other situations, the roper claimed to be a sprinter who wanted to bet against himself without fellow club members knowing it. All the roper needed, he assured the mark, was the assistance of an unknown man of means who was willing to bet the roper's money on his behalf. The mark would not have to bet any of his own money, the roper earnestly asserted, so there was no risk. In exchange for this service, the roper would provide the mark a share of the winnings, often 25 percent.

The story was tailored to each individual victim, but the intended outcome was the same: to convince him to come to Webb City flush with letters of credit, bank drafts, or cash. Once there he was introduced to club members who demanded to know that the stranger in their midst was, like them, a man of means. The mark was then asked to establish his financial standing by drawing on his letters of credit at the Exchange Bank of Webb City. Bank cashier James Stewart nodded when asked if the club president, Robert Boatright, was trustworthy. Cash in hand, the mark was privately assured by the ropers his money would be returned to him. The race, unbeknownst to the mark, was fixed. Then it was time to place bets, the foot race or boxing match would be held, and the victim parted from his money. When he returned to the bank, Stewart would gravely inform him the letters of credit had already been sent for collection. If he were lucky, the mark might receive money for a return ticket home.

David Maurer, who corresponded with Boatright's peers in the criminal underworld, comes closest aside from court records in documenting how their schemes worked. While court records explain how a victim fell for the con in their own words, Maurer's work offers a window into how Robert Boatright's con worked from the viewpoint of its practitioners.

Boatright and his confederates were participants in what Maurer described as a "carefully set up and skillfully managed theater where the victim acts out an unwitting role in the most exciting of all underworld dramas." This theater, known as the big con, was a "big-time confidence game in which a mark is put on the send for his money, as contrasted to a short con where the touch is limited to the amount the mark has with him." The send, a technique that emerged during this era, made it possible to increase the amount a victim wagered because it required him to go home and return with more money, rather than just betting whatever sum he might have on his person. Victims were brought to the big store (in this instance an athletic club), which served as the stage for the coming drama.[11] The big store only functioned while the mark was being swindled. Otherwise, it was empty. As Maurer noted, it had little formal organization but was "held together by loose but effective bonds."[12]

Together Boatright and his associates were, in criminal argot, a "con mob." A con mob, when referring to a big con operation such as Boatright's Webb City Athletic Club, meant the personnel of the big store: the inside-man, manager, ropers, and shills.[13] Each man had a role or, depending on the situation, more than one. Some had specialized talents. For example, George W. Ryan, Irven E. Johnson, and Lucius "Honey Grove Kid" Hindman excelled as ropers (also known as steerers or outsidemen),

men tasked with snaring a mark and bringing him to the store to be fleeced. A roper was "armed only with a smooth tongue, a deep disillusion regarding the motives of mankind, and some notes on human psychology which are not to be found in the textbooks." Ed Ellis and Roger H. Williams often alternated as manager of the big store. Shills were often locals hired to encourage the mark to bet. Boatright's shills—locals like Daniel Maloney, James R. "Dick" Ellis, and his father Robert M. Boatright—acted the part of wealthy miners.[14]

An insideman in an outfit like Boatright's stayed near the big store to receive the mark. They possessed "a superb knowledge of psychology to keep the mark under perfect control during the days or weeks while he is being fleeced."[15] Maurer praised Boatright as "one of the best insidemen who ever trimmed a sucker." Boatright's peers believed he was "one of the best . . . a 'natural.'"[16] The insideman, who owned and financed the big store, directed the manager, who oversaw it.[17] To make a profit the insideman needed several ropers on the road, in some cases dozens, while he remained at the big store to handle the marks as they arrived. The insideman used an appointment book to schedule multiple marks.[18] Boatright recorded the gang's business in two books; one for swindles and the other for keeping track of the gang's correspondence. When they communicated by mail, members did not use their real names; instead, they closed the message with an assigned number. When Boatright received a letter, he checked the number against a list of names to see who it was from—the numbers went as high as 114.[19] Not only did Boatright excel at choosing ropers, handling victims, recruiting shills, and paying off the authorities, he also elevated the big store concept to a new standard.

Boatright, according to Maurer's criminal confidants, "made several innovations" to the fight store concept and "raised it to a high peak of perfection." He devised the idea of giving the victim part of the money for the play. This move made him eager to obtain more money. Boatright used shills to bet money he furnished so the greedy mark would raise his own bet. He also placed money in a safe in front of the mark, who assumed the money was secure when it was actually stored in a double-sided safe. Money could be secretly removed by a confederate and handed to a shill to bet.[20] Boatright needed more than trusted associates and a bank willing to accommodate him; he also needed political influence. Fortunately, it was available at a price he could afford.

Cities like Chicago and New York were initially popular places for confidence men to ply their trade but soon gained a reputation as sanctuaries for scoundrels. It evolved, then, that it was better for big cons to operate in smaller cities, preferably with the protection of local politicians and law enforcement. Under those conditions, confidence men felt free to "'rip and tear'—that is, to grift without restraint as long as they avoided" swindling locals.[21] Boatright wisely cultivated a reputation in Webb City "as a sort of philanthropist and public benefactor . . . If money is needed for any public enterprise, Mr. Boatright's name goes down for $100— and some greenhorn from Texas pay the freight."[22] Most importantly, Boatright and his gang needed victims unafraid to profit at the expense of others. As Maurer observed, "A confidence man prospers only because of the fundamental dishonesty of his victim."[23] Luckily, the country was full of suckers.

Individuals who read the local papers at this time would have noticed an increase in articles covering area sporting events. To the casual reader, the items would not have likely raised any suspicion, but Webb City residents would have recognized Boatright's machinations. An 1898 contest featuring Bud Gillett in Webb City was "the biggest foot race ever run in the southwest." Gillett won $2,200 ($79,346) and an estimated $9,600 ($333,081) changed hands. This may have been the first fixed race the gang pulled off when they swindled Kansas City cattle buyer H. Purcell. Purcell brought suit in the December 1898 term of court, but it was disposed of the following year. The next year Gillett, "the noted foot racer of Webb City," arranged a race between fellow Buckfoot member Ben Ansel and John Keagy.[24] In 1899 fights arranged by the Webb City Athletic Club in Galena, Joplin, and Webb City began to appear in the news. More often than not, however, they held races.[25]

On April 6, 1900, a large crowd of spectators watched Duke Bishop beat Bert Fisher; $3,000 changed hands on the eighty-yard race.[26] The next month the Buckfoot Gang skinned Charles D. McIlroy of the McIlroy Banking Company of Fayetteville, Arkansas, for $2,000.[27] Later that summer, a hundred-yard race was held in Webb City between Jerry Cockrill and Duke Bishop.[28] In early October Cockrill and his brother Stewart roped Kansas farmers Monroe Griffith and John S. Owen on a fixed race. When Griffith realized he had been duped, he noticed the other spectators were conspicuously armed. He and Owen quietly returned home.[29]

Winter's arrival did not deter sporting enthusiasts. In December a large sum of money changed hands when Bud Gillett beat Tom Sawyer by three feet in Webb City;[30] another race took place a few weeks later.[31] When the weather grew too cold, the gang transitioned to prizefights. On January 6, 1901, the Galena Athletic Club announced three twenty-round boxing contests featuring Eddie Morris.[32] Morris was accustomed to taking blows in the ring; now the gang received a counterpunch from one of its victims.

The first case to appear in the press was filed by Guy Berger against Boatright. Berger claimed he made a $500 wager with Ed Ellis that Bud Gillett could beat sprinter H. W. Carruthers. Berger claimed he was forced into involuntary bankruptcy as result of the fixed race. The jury sided with Berger.[33] His success may have emboldened the next complainant. William Reger of Sullivan County, Missouri, sued Ed Ellis, Robert Boatright, and other members of the Webb City Athletic Club. Garrette O. Stansbury, using the alias Bert Hansel, had arrived in Harris, Missouri, and befriended many locals, one of whom was Reger's son, Bruce. Upon learning Bruce managed his father's farm and had access to his bank account, Stansbury convinced Bruce to travel to Webb City to bet $2,000 on a race. In his suit the elder Reger asserted James Stewart of the Exchange Bank was president of the Webb City Athletic Club and Robert Boatright was manager.[34] William Reger received a $2,000 judgment.[35] In the meantime, the gang skinned Henry Cohn of Collinsville, Illinois, for $4,350.[36] The gang was starting to attract the press's attention, but they showed no signs of slowing down— there were too many marks to fleece.

In Cleburne, Texas, portly Stephen E. Moss was riding high. He had sold his stake in the National Bank of Cleburne and had interests in two other banks. The owner of a large ranch in Bosque County, Texas, Moss was exploring his options in the burgeoning oil industry when Lucius "Honey Grove Kid" Hindman roped him in March 1901.[37] With a $1,000 draft from Hindman in hand, Moss traveled to Webb City.[38] Within minutes of the Texan checking into his room at the Newland Hotel, Hindman came to greet him. He was followed by Robert Boatright, who affirmed the club was chartered in Missouri and the race would be a square contest. He confided the Exchange Bank was the only bank "friendly to our business" and that Moss would have to show the bank he was financially sound before betting. "You needn't be afraid to trust me," Boatright told the Texan, "you are a banker and you just ask the bank who I am."[39]

Boatright walked Moss across the street to the Exchange Bank, where he introduced him to James Stewart and left. When Moss asked about Boatright's reputation, Stewart responded he was one of Webb City's best men. Acting on Boatright's orders, Moss had Stewart telegram banks in Cleburne, asking if they would honor separate drafts of $5,000. Finished, Moss went to the 16 to 1 Saloon, where Boatright introduced him to Ed Ellis, Roger H. Williams, Bert Bromley, C. F. Landers, and William Crider, explaining they were millionaire miners. They sidled up to the bar, where Boatright asked the bartender to give Moss some nerve tonic. The Texan estimated he had a dozen drinks before everyone signed a printed contract governing the race. Moss put up $3,000 in forfeit money. A

Robert Boatright, with his hands in his pockets, stands behind the sprinters in the center of the photograph. *Sioux City Journal.*

wild scene ensued as men pushed and shoved to place their bets.[40] The nerve tonic hit Moss hard. He was "pretty well jagged up" when he and Boatright timed Moss's ringer with a stopwatch on the gang's track. As the sprinter cleared the finish line, Boatright hugged Moss and cackled, "That man is the fastest man in the world." The race, he said, would be held in the morning when Moss should be feeling better. Relieved, Moss—a man who did not often drink—"felt mighty bad."[41]

The next morning Boatright told Moss his bank telegrams were satisfactory. Together they downed eight to ten drinks as a crowd filled the saloon. As betting began again Boatright panicked. He told Moss to withdraw some money and hide it in a pocket. Moss retrieved $2,500 from the Exchange Bank. The clamoring throng swarmed him on his return to the saloon and the betting and drinking resumed. Moss and the others downed more nerve tonic as the runners were measured. The crowd decided Moss's man was pretty good, but theirs was better. The saloon door burst open as more bettors arrived. Moss eyed the raucous crowd and told Boatright, "Those fellows are pretty sporty." "Yes," the con man agreed, "a pretty sporty crowd."[42]

When the theatrics finished, a heavily intoxicated Moss thought he had wagered at least $13,000. It was late afternoon when they finally traveled to the track north of town. After the crowd bickered over judges,

Boatright and Moss were selected. An unnamed third man served as referee; he would be the final arbiter should Moss and Boatright disagree on the outcome. Moss thought they were sure to win.[43] After the sprinters changed their clothes in a small cottage, spectators carried them to the track. At the sound of a pistol, the two men ran toward Moss and Boatright, who both stood holding the string for the finish line. Moss watched in disbelief as his sprinter lost. Boatright gasped he should keep quiet or risk getting killed. Moss suddenly noticed the spectators were armed with guns of every description.[44]

Moss and the gang returned to the 16 to 1 Saloon. They crowded around him, and one said with a smirk, "Now, what have you got today?" Moss replied he had nothing; he had been skinned. Back in Dallas Moss stayed in his hotel room for four days. He felt close to death; he had never felt so bad before in his life. In all, Moss estimated he lost $18,500 ($667,230).[45]

When the gang was not staging races for the likes of Moss, they promoted local fights often officiated by a questionable referee. On the evening of June 19, 1901, Eddie Morris squared off against Bob Long in front of 2,600 spectators at Webb's Hall in Webb City. Long was backed by his manager William H. "Billy" Gibson, "Cherokee" Tom Cox, and Garrette Stansbury. Gibson, like Morris and Stansbury, was a member of the Buckfoot Gang. In the fifth round Morris hit Long in the clinch; referee Ed F. Burke declared Long the winner. The *Galena Republican* opined, "Ed. Burke has lost his prestige as a referee among the sports of this section on account of his rotten work at the Morris-Long scrap. The Carterville Rocket says: 'We think that Ed. Burke of Springfield, is no more fitted, scientifically nor morally, to referee than an Arkansas mountain mule.' "[46]

Such swindles did not go unnoticed. In response to allegations of crime and corruption in Jasper County, Judge Hugh Dabbs convened a special grand jury in July 1901. Although the records appear to have been lost, surviving newspaper accounts provide some insight into the proceedings. In what was perhaps one of the longest charges given to the grand jury, Dabbs instructed jurors to investigate crimes including gambling, operating bawdy houses, and selling liquor on Sunday. He singled out Webb City's foot races and told jurors it had "become an organized business" in the county.[47] Dabbs pointedly stated it was a disgraceful, illegal practice. The grand jury should investigate the charges and, if they found them to be true, indict the guilty parties. Dabbs also directed jurors to investigate rumors that public officials had been bribed. He concluded, "This is a matter of greatest importance to the citizens of your county. Every man has a right to demand that the law be enforced in his community. Every man has a right to demand that all who violate the laws shall be punished."[48]

The day after Dabbs's instructions to the grand jury, Robert Boatright appeared in circuit court and was asked to testify as to his net worth. He responded he did not have any property or bank notes. When asked if he had cash, Boatright replied, "Yes, sir, I have $33,000 in bills, which I always carry, and I have it now, here in my pocket. Besides that, I have some silver too." The *Joplin News-Herald* did not doubt his statement. The *Jasper County Democrat* remarked there was "no provision in the statutes of Missouri that a judgment or any other debt can be collected by taking money from one's person, and Boatright with his $33,000 was exempt from collection of a cent of the judgment." The only way for a victim to get money out of Boatright, it believed, was to force bankruptcy proceedings.[49]

If Boatright got nervous as additional victims continued to surface, he showed little sign. An anonymous Kansan commented on the grand jury's investigation to the *Joplin Globe*. He recalled an incident that convinced him the Webb City crowd were "pretty smooth people." Some fellow Kansans lost large sums of money on a fixed foot race. Their attorney traveled to Missouri ready to fight but found it impossible to quarrel with the apologetic race managers. In fact, the managers were so disappointed with the outcome that they had discussed the possibility of a second race. If his clients would let their bets stand, they would prove they were fair by scheduling another race. The Kansans agreed and their attorney placed his own side bet on the second race. All three returned home empty handed. Neither the lawyer nor his clients had been willing to discuss the matter, but the story had still somehow surfaced.[50] It may have been planted in the *Globe* to discredit any future marks as the gang's notoriety increased.

While the battle between law and vice in Jasper County played out in the grand jury room, another fight erupted in the local newspapers. A schism between the county's two most powerful Democrats erupted into public view. Gilbert "Gib" Barbee of Joplin and Williams H. Phelps of Carthage, though little remembered today, were influential figures in Missouri's turn-of-the-century Democratic Party. The fight may have originated over politics, but the struggle evolved into a conflict that presented one Democrat with an opportunity to smear the other with accusations of "Buckfootism." The gang was brought into the forefront as the two political bosses vied for control of the local party.

A native of New York, attorney William H. Phelps entered politics in 1868 when he became chair of the Jasper County Democratic Committee.

He served as a delegate-at-large to the Democratic National Convention in 1872 and two years later was elected to the Missouri House of Representatives. In 1875 he was shot by fellow attorney James F. Hardin in court. A year later Hardin was shot and killed. Phelps and his brother Charles were arrested, but both men were acquitted of Hardin's murder. He became a railroad lobbyist—first for the St. Louis–San Francisco Railroad and later the Missouri Pacific—and amassed significant power. "Straight as an arrow and with heavy gray moustache and imperial, he moves about more like a gentleman of the old school than anything else," a contemporary remarked of Phelps. "He is reserved almost to the point of taciturnity, and while ever courteous, hates effusiveness and dislikes 'glad-handing.' Yet with his friends he is a charming companion, and a man of deep feelings and warm affections." Phelps built his political clout with "the power of the pass." It was said no legislator or anyone of political influence in Missouri had to pay railroad fare on the Missouri Pacific thanks to Phelps. He used this leverage to ask legislative favors on behalf of his client, the railroad, "which usually got what it wanted." Phelps supported William Joel Stone's gubernatorial bid, but the two men quarreled over railroad legislation. After Stone left public office, he became an outspoken critic of Phelps, charging his former supporter was a shameless lobbyist. Phelps memorably responded, "I am a lobbyist. I admit it. But so is Stone. We both suck eggs, but he hides the shells." Despite a handsome limestone mansion in Carthage and another on a large stock farm outside the city, Phelps did not live a completely charmed life; he suffered a series of personal tragedies.[51] His chief rival in Jasper County was also a fierce political operator.

A native Ozarker, Gilbert "Gib" Barbee was self-made, having walked barefoot from neighboring Newton County to seek his fortune in Jasper County. He sunk a shaft on Parr Hill and worked alone when the common practice was to work in a two-man team. Barbee "held his drill with one hand and he pounded the steel with the free arm. And he drew two days' pay for every day he worked. The early life made a magnificent man out of him." Through hard work and determination, he became one of the most influential men in the Ozarks. Whereas his rival Phelps favored a refined Van Dyke beard, Barbee sported a prominent mustache. The *Sarcoxie Record* described him as "one outstanding, colorful, forceful personality, rather short and bulky of complexion, wearing a slouched hat." Although he accumulated wealth and political power like Phelps, Barbee operated behind the scenes and yet was "the most widely known man in southwest Missouri." While he owned substantial real estate holdings, none were as significant as his three-story brick building near the corner of Fourth and

Main streets. It was from there that he exercised his power.[52] It housed the city's most famous establishment, the House of Lords, where Barbee frequently held court. It, along with Barbee and Boatright, were drawn into the public eye with accusations of corruption and lawlessness.

Located at 319 Main Street, the House of Lords was hailed as the Delmonico's of the West. The first proprietor, William "Billy" Patton, could not settle on a name until a visiting Englishman suggested naming it after the upper house of Parliament. On the ground floor visitors could find a cigar stand, restaurant, and bar. The clientele included many of Joplin's prominent citizens who socialized with "eastern capitalists who were in the district to conclude mining deals and other business ventures." Men conducted business over whiskey and cigars in secluded booths at the rear of the bar; society women and demimondaines dined at the restaurant but "remained well within their respective spheres."[53]

Behind the bar hung a large painting of a nude woman. Ragtime composer Percy Wenrich recounted, "I heard colored fellows play all the time, and there were piano players you never heard of and no one ever will—a piano and all its keys was just a toy to them." The House of Lords boasted it never closed its doors and its reputation spread far and wide. Around the world travelers from Joplin would be asked, " 'And how is the House of Lords?' If the person to whom the question was addressed happened to be a missionary, he would lift his eyes to the sky and reply: 'Ah, my friend, Satan is in the ascendancy yet.' " A sport's response was, "Still there and going strong." The establishment changed management over the years, but Barbee's *Joplin Globe* always asserted neither the building's owner nor the restaurant and bar proprietors had anything to do with the illicit businesses conducted above on the building's upper stories.[54]

The activities that took place on the second and third floors led to accusations of corruption and lawlessness. The second floor housed gambling rooms; and the third floor, a notorious brothel.[55] The first proprietor of the gambling den was Bill Hunter, who allegedly had several notches on his gun. Daniel E. Saighman, a "well-educated, polished man," followed Hunter. Orphaned at an early age, Saighman became a gambler before making a fortune in Kansas City real estate. After suffering significant losses, however, he returned to gambling and moved to Joplin in 1897.[56]

The House of Lords was not a blood-bucket establishment; though fights took place, there were few fatalities over the years. One of these rare incidents happened just days before Judge Dabbs convened the grand jury, when Wilkins Taylor, son of Joplin capitalist John H. Taylor, shot and fatally wounded Will Moore over an argument that began in the

Fourth and Main, Joplin. The House of Lords is at far left; its name is painted between the building's second and third floors. *Author's Collection.*

House of Lords.[57] Barbee was not oblivious to the activities taking place in his building. There was a walkway built over an alley that connected the House of Lords to the *Joplin Globe* building on Virginia Avenue so Barbee could go back and forth between his apartment at the *Globe* and the upper rooms "where the boys were."[58]

Although Joplin's reputation for wickedness was exaggerated over the years, Barbee and the House of Lords fueled the folklore. Oklahoman Will Rogers recalled his parents admonishing, "Now whatever you do, don't you ever go to that bad place, Joplin!"[59] Thomas Hart Benton's family was certain "the town offered too many opportunities for a seventeen-year-old boy to go to hell." Years later the artist vividly remembered downtown Joplin: "The saloon doors—and there were plenty of them—swung constantly . . . Everything was there—drugstores, slot machines, real-estate slickers, soliciting preachers, and off the main street, a row of houses devoted to insinuatingly decorated girls."[60] With Barbee's name firmly identified with debauchery and Joplin's reputation as a wide-open town unquestioned, Buckfootism became the bane of those seeking to clean up the town. It would be difficult, however, because

Gilbert Barbee's crown jewel happened to be one of the most influential papers in the Ozarks.

In 1899 Barbee purchased a majority interest in the *Joplin Globe* and hired a coterie of talented journalists. Among them were business manager Dan Dugan, editor Bart B. Howard, and reporter Ben H. Reese. Later, after leaving the *Globe*, Howard and Reese joined the *St. Louis Post-Dispatch*. There Howard won a Pulitzer Prize for editorial writing

Joplin Globe, 1902. Author's Collection.

and Reese became managing editor of the vaunted broadsheet. Barbee used their talent and the newspaper like a cudgel, simultaneously attempting to control local politics and viciously attacking his political and personal rivals, most often William Phelps. The *Globe's* editorial page featured "Barbee-inspired thunderbolts [that] were directed by Bart Howard at those not in accord with the Barbee program."[61]

Those thunderbolts flew after the election of 1900 when, despite a solid Democratic victory in Jasper County as well as the Fifteenth Congressional District, Barbee attacked Phelps in the *Globe*. This divided the party at the county level, but according to longtime political observers, Barbee triumphed. The breach between the two led Phelps and his supporters to whet their knives. Cornelius Roach, editor and publisher of the Carthage *Jasper County Democrat*, was a Phelps man. Republicans Edward S. Hosmer of the *Joplin News-Herald* and William J. Sewall of the *Carthage Evening Press* joined Roach in opposing Barbee. Together these men and their newspapers battled Barbee and the *Globe* over the coming years. The opening salvos were fired as Dabbs's grand jury conducted its investigation.[62]

As the jurors met, the *Jasper County Democrat* fumed at the *Globe's* insinuation that if gambling in Joplin were eliminated it would be as dull as the *Democrat's* city of Carthage. The paper huffed, "If a grand jury that threatens to stop gambling will make a 'graveyard' of Joplin, then the lead and zinc metropolis better be a graveyard at once. If such an affair as the 'club rooms' over the House of Lords is essential to a city's prosperity, then the Missouri statutes better be dispensed with, and courts and juries overthrown for riot, revolution, robbery and murder." Jurors should "see 'the sights' during their sojourn to Barbeeville" and take in the poker table, crap table, and roulette wheel.[63]

Over the course of twelve days, jurors questioned almost two hundred witnesses and issued fifty-two indictments. Not all the names of those indicted were published and little was disclosed about the jury's findings. Barbee's *Globe* crowed when the jury exonerated county officials.[64] Within days the *News-Herald* proclaimed gambling had stopped. "Club Rooms Upstairs" signs were removed from saloon windows and the doors locked.[65] Daniel Saighman and other House of Lords denizens packed up their gaming equipment and left for El Reno, Oklahoma Territory.[66] Boatright's crony Charley Parker, proprietor of Webb City's 16 to 1 Saloon, was found guilty of selling liquor on Sunday.[67] Questions about the jury's findings were left mostly unanswered.

The *News-Herald* groused, "There's a violent eagerness to know just what the jury has done." If the investigation was disclosed, "we shall then be able to determine whether the whole thing was a grandstand play or a serious effort on the part of a Democratic administration to correct the flagrant abuses which have existed under the Mooneyham regime," referring to prosecutor Robert A. Mooneyham. After railing against debauchery permitted by local officials, the paper continued, "The 'so and so fixed men' spoken of by this judge, as officials who had betrayed their trust are not vague, indefinite, nameless creations of rumor, but Democratic officeholders whose cognomens can be learned without being obliged to keep your ear on the ground." The *News-Herald* predicted a coat of whitewash would be the only result.[68]

It could not have helped when the editor of the *Carterville Rocket* received a copy of an affidavit to be filed with the court prior to the grand jury concluding its investigation that accused Boatright and his associates of pulling off an illegal prizefight. Witnesses purportedly included Mooneyham, his father Thomas, and Constable Len Rich. Mooneyham denied any knowledge of the case.[69] Although the grand jury records seemingly no longer exist, it seems Boatright escaped scrutiny. Mooneyham, the Democratic successor to Republican prosecutor Hiram Shannon, was no more successful than Shannon at curbing crime.

Other battles played out in the pages of the local press. Angered by an article tying him to gambling published a month earlier in the *Jasper County Democrat*, Gilbert Barbee used the *Globe* to counterattack his political rivals. Roach, Barbee thundered, was the *Democrat*'s owner, but William Phelps owned Cornelius Roach. Barbee acknowledged he owned the building in which the House of Lords was located, but what took place there was beyond his control as he had leased it for five years. He published an affidavit from gambler and boxing referee Ed F. Burke stating Barbee was not affiliated with Burke or his slot machines in the House of Lords. Barbee charged that John W. McAntire, the attorney who had drawn up the lease, had gossiped about him. McAntire, he snapped, knew he did not have control over the House of Lords. Barbee sourly noted if gambling was wrong—and he conceded it was—then it was wrong in any other house.[70]

Turning his attention to his old political enemy William Phelps, Barbee growled, "Everybody who knows him and his piratical methods knows that his policy all through life has been to ruin anyone who he cannot rule, not stopping at the assassination of private character or anything else." The *Democrat*, he spat, was trying to destroy "my influence or supposed influence in a political way. There is a little crowd of political desperadoes in Carthage of justice of the peace caliber and supreme court aspirations who have sworn to have my political scalp, and that is the milk in the coconut. They care nothing about slot machines, gamblers and gambling."[71]

Phelps and his ally Roach would not let Barbee's attack go unanswered. Buckfoot was about to become a household name in Jasper County. Yet for now—in the midst of it all—the Buckfoot Gang flourished.

4

"AND A FUNERAL WILL BE
THE END OF THESE RACES"

—CARTHAGE *Jasper County Democrat*, SEPTEMBER 9, 1901

T he game continued. In the summer of 1901 Boatright's Webb City Athletic Club received word from George Siler, sporting editor of the *Chicago Tribune*, that he would officiate the upcoming Eddie Morris–Bob Long fight. Touted as the best contest held in the Southwest, the match was jeopardized when Morris was arrested in nearby Galena, Kansas, for assault with intent to kill. He was at the home of Elnora Franklin when David Price came to collect a bill. If Price did not know Morris was a prizefighter, he soon found out. When Morris told Price that Franklin was not home, Price tried to get in the house and struck Morris. Morris knocked Price down and kicked him, then knocked out a man who had accompanied Price.[1]

As the gang promoted the match, the Jasper County grand jury's indictments trickled out, charging multiple individuals with running gambling rooms. Two justices of the peace were indicted for collecting illegal fees and committing fraud in office. Daniel Saighman, who ran the House of Lords club rooms, was also indicted.[2] That same day, the Webb City Athletic Club notified Dan Dugan, the *Joplin Globe*'s business manager and stakeholder for the event, that the Morris–Long fight was postponed as referee Siler had taken ill. Dugan had long been associated with the gang's boxing contests. In 1899 he backed Frank Purcell in a bout promoted by the Webb City Athletic Club, one that Ed F. Burke refereed— the same Ed Burke who signed an affidavit published in the *Globe* that stated Gilbert Barbee was not associated with slot machines in Joplin.[3]

On the evening of August 6, 1901, hundreds of boxing enthusiasts gathered to watch Eddie Morris fight Bob Long in Webb City. George Siler, whose ill health had delayed the original match, officiated. A preliminary bout featuring Buckfoot "colt" Bert Bromley entertained the crowd before Morris and Long entered the ring to applause. One of Morris's cornermen was James "Bow Tie" Bronson; Long's cornermen were Buckfoot associates William H. "Billy" Gibson and Garrette Stansbury. The fifteen-round fight lasted four; Long won after landing a wicked right to Morris's abdomen. Siler's decision was unpopular; many spectators claimed Long fouled Morris. Some even growled Morris had sold out his Joplin backers.[4] Yet public allegations of impropriety did not impede the gang's enthusiasm for swindling suckers: two weeks later Merwin Bangs, a Yale graduate and Kansas resident, lost $5,000 on a race.[5]

The prizefights, foot races, and gambling were more than some locals could tolerate. Joplin resident William M. Carter was so disgusted by the city's alarming "hordes of lazy, worthless, dangerous renegades—male and female—white and black" that he publicly denounced city authorities for failing to adequately fund the police to protect homes and families from "this vile and degraded class—base and conscienceless, refugees from towns all around us" and urged his fellow citizens to act.[6] The day after Carter's plea, as if to support his claim that Joplin and, by extension, Jasper County were going to hell in a handbasket, the *Joplin News-Herald* published a brief exposé of the Buckfoot Gang's latest con.

Iowa farmer Everett L. Phelps was roped by an old acquaintance, William "Billy" Gibson, the former manager of famed midwestern wrestler "Farmer" Martin Burns. After Phelps balked, Boatright sneered that "every county officer and all police authorities at Webb City did his bidding; that no candidate for a county office or a municipal office in Webb City could win without the support of the Webb City Athletic Club." Phelps returned home unscathed.[7] The *Jasper County Democrat* weighed in on Buckfoot and his comrades: "Their game is getting thread-bare, getting notorious, injuring the reputation of the county—a county that cannot afford to harbor a species of confidence operators, whose methods match the green goods, gold brick, gentry."[8]

The two newspapers were not alone in calling out the Buckfoot Gang and their gambler brethren. The editor of the *Carterville Rocket*, one Mr. Kuhn—who had waged war on the gamblers and had the gaming houses there closed twice—spent four hours exhorting the town's three preachers to join his antigambling crusade when he realized he had been "pulling weeds in the wrong patch." Only one of the clergymen volunteered to support a mass meeting of Carterville citizens to discuss how to close the gambling houses.[9] Two days later gamblers assaulted Kuhn, but he escaped serious injury.[10] There were signs, though, his assailants and their ilk might soon be on the run.

Buried in the September 5, 1901, *Joplin Globe* was news that Leon Lozier and James "Jack" Cherry had been arrested. The two men had arrived the previous week to run a race; Lozier won. Local backers won $5,000 on the contest. A second race between Cherry and Lozier, held on the afternoon of September 4, had just concluded when a deputy sheriff emerged from the crowd and arrested the sprinters. Stories circulated knives and guns had been flashed during the arrest, but the *Globe* dismissed the allegations as hyperbole.[11]

One of Cherry's backers was Sheriff Henry Phillips of Cuming County, Nebraska.[12] Phillips, Cherry, and Lozier had met in West Point, Nebraska, when the racers arrived during the town's Old Settlers Picnic. Their slick talk attracted the attention of the local sporting fraternity. Phillips agreed to serve as Cherry's financial backer with Lozier acting as business manager. After the arrangement was made, Cherry and Lozier obtained money under false pretenses from Phillips's friend Fred Sonnenschein. Although the sheriff learned of their actions, he accompanied them to Webb City. Phillips bet $5,000—every cent he had—as well as money borrowed from friends. At the track Cherry stumbled and fell in the last ten yards. Realizing he had been buncoed, Phillips wired Nebraska authorities, who then telegrammed Jasper County sheriff Albert Rich asking him to arrest Lozier and Cherry.[13]

The *Globe*, perhaps attempting to get ahead of the story and engage in damage control, lambasted Phillips for having Cherry and Lozier arrested. Phillips, it charged, had tried to arrange another race in Kansas City.[14] He moved to have the sprinters requisitioned, but they fled before the papers could be served, leaving bondsman Charley Parker liable for $1,000. Shortly after Phillips returned home the gang's attorney arrived and gave him $2,200. It was little consolation; the sheriff was still out $3,000.[15] Lozier and Cherry's absence meant there would be "two less of Buckfoot's coterie of seventy runners."[16]

Despite the unwanted publicity, the gang held another race in Webb City. This time the victims were Texans Henry S. Wright, a middle-aged farmer and deputy sheriff, and his friend, Robert M. Duncan. Wright bet $6,000 and his pocket watch; Duncan bet only his watch. As Frank Landers and William Crider stepped to the line, Wright noticed Landers's posture looked odd. He growled at Boatright the race was fixed. Despite reassurance from Boatright, Wright's instincts were right. With nothing left to do but go home empty-handed, he and Duncan returned to their hotel for the night.[17]

The next morning Duncan found Boatright outside the Exchange Bank. Duncan gushed about the strength of Boatright's con; it was so good he wanted in on it. He told Boatright about a wealthy doctor in Texas he thought could be taken for $20,000 to $50,000. Boatright nonchalantly responded he could send a good man or two to rope the doctor. In exchange he would give Duncan a percentage and reimburse Wright for some of his losses. Duncan warned Boatright that Wright would "dog him." Boatright snorted, "I would like to know what he could do. We have got the people with us; we have got the officers with us; and we have got the bank with us, and I would like to know what in the hell is left for them."[18]

Later, while waiting at the depot, Duncan and Wright encountered Boatright and Hindman. Wright snapped at Boatright, "If you have got the honor of a son-of-a-bitch, you will give me my money." Hindman scolded Boatright to return Wright's money. Boatright left and returned with the men's watches. "If you want to rob me, I want you to clean me," Wright hissed. Boatright handed the watches to Duncan. Wright roared, "Don't you take it." Duncan ignored him.[19] The two men returned to Texas worse for wear.[20]

Cornelius Roach, editor of the Carthage *Jasper County Democrat* and political foe of Gilbert Barbee, kept the gang in the news. After the *Webb City Sentinel* questioned the *Democrat*'s ability to end the foot races, Roach barked that the question was whether officers would enforce the law. The *Sentinel* mused, "Now it remains to be seen who has the most influence with the county officials, the Democrat or the 'Buckfoot' crowd. We venture to say that the foot races will be pulled off as usual until some fellow with lots of nerve and a big gun will kill somebody when he finds his money gone. This is where the thing is leading and a funeral will be the end of these races."[21] Most victims, however, avoided bloodshed.[22] Yet an even bigger story emerged as one of the gang's most prominent victims was about to make headlines.

The story broke when the front page of the Republican *Fort Scott Daily Monitor* of Kansas blared a banner masthead that mockingly declared, "The Idea of a Man Who Has Been through a Session of the Kansas Legislature Being Taken In and Robbed by a Missourian. He Ought to Resign." The *Monitor*'s Democratic rival, the *Fort Scott Daily Tribune*, shrieked, "JONATHAN M. DAVIS BET $5,000 AND LOST IT."[23]

The son of a Kansas farmer, Davis left his studies at the University of Nebraska after his father's death and returned home to his family's 1,700-acre Little Osage Farm outside Bronson. Davis stumped for William Jennings Bryan before he was appointed postmaster of Eve, Kansas, in 1899. The following year he was elected to the Kansas House of Representatives. Things were going well for Davis until he met Bud Gillett.[24] Earlier in the year Gillett had married Bronson native Maude

Hiner and moved to his bride's hometown, where he befriended the young politician. Soon thereafter Gillett and Garrette O. Stansbury arrived at Davis's farm and confided they needed someone to bet $4,500 on a foot race; for his trouble Davis would receive $1,000. Like many others before him, Davis travelled to Webb City where he met Boatright and signed a contract. Although he did not get drunk, what he did imbibe had a strange effect on him. Gillett sprained his ankle and lost the race. As the crowd of spectators left, a groggy Davis found himself out $5,000.[25]

He returned home to a dire situation, one that may have originally prompted him to take a chance on Gillett and Stansbury's scheme. A severe summer drought had ravaged Davis's farm and left him with 250 head of mortgaged cattle in need of sustenance. Financially strapped, he was forced to turn them over to agents of the Bank of Fort Scott, who sold them for far less than their value during a market downturn. After his mother repaid a separate debt to the Bank of Bronson, Davis signed over his equity in the family farm to her to avoid creditors. Eager to recoup his losses, he hired Fort Scott attorney Jacob Sheppard to pursue Boatright.[26]

Bank officials launched an investigation into Davis's financial irregularities. He had hoped to keep details of the affair secret, but Davis came clean when one of the banks threatened to prosecute him for obtaining money under false pretenses. Bank attorney Willard W. Padgett spoke to prosecutor Mooneyham who confirmed Boatright had pulled off fixed races for years without any interference. If true, Mooneyham's failure to prosecute the gang is inexplicable; Padgett did not elaborate on what, if any, explanation Mooneyham may have given for his inaction.[27] Bourbon County prosecutor Charles B. Griffith filed complaints against Robert Boatright, Ed Ellis, Garrette Stansbury, and Bud Gillett. Judge William Margrave issued arrest warrants for the four men for obtaining $5,000 under false pretenses. If Missouri officials would not act, then Kansas authorities would.[28]

Bourbon County sheriff William Brooks caught Bud Gillett by surprise when he arrested the sprinter in his father-in-law's barn in Bronson.[29] Retired banker and former Fort Scott postmaster Charles H. Osbun mysteriously provided Gillett's bond on behalf of the Bank of Carthage.[30] Brooks apprehended Garrette Stansbury in bed at his Cherryvale, Kansas, residence. Stansbury told Brooks he did not want to go to Fort Scott without Boatright and Ellis and convinced the sheriff to take him to Webb City to talk to them. Upon their arrival Sheriff Brooks and Stansbury went to the 16 to 1 Saloon where they met Robert Boatright and an attorney. Brooks sized up Buckfoot as a man who "has every appearance of being a leader in the profession he follows." When he asked

Boatright to return to Kansas with him, Boatright declined, but bragged he could post $100,000 bond. As Brooks and Boatright spoke, the sheriff granted Stansbury permission to use the washroom. Brooks soon realized Stansbury had escaped. Before he left, Brooks learned that Boatright, the "king bee of Webb City" controlled the town's elections and "had hundreds at his call." Back in Fort Scott, he discovered Bud Gillett had arranged to be locked up in the jury room at the county courthouse under armed guard instead of at the county jail. He promptly ordered Gillett behind bars.[31]

Boatright's attorney George Booth arrived in Fort Scott to confer with Bud Gillett's local counsel. When asked if he thought Boatright, Ellis, Gillett, and Stansbury would be tried in Kansas, Booth laughed. He showed no signs of concern, either, when a warrant was issued for James Stewart, cashier of the Exchange Bank of Webb City. Stewart's complicity, the *Daily Monitor* asserted, was obvious. When Stewart received confirmation from the Bank of Bronson that Davis was good for $5,000, he immediately sent Davis's draft to the bank for collection instead of sending it to a Kansas City bank, which was its usual method of conducting business. Davis's attorneys believed this deviation from normal operating procedures indicated Stewart knew the transaction was fraudulent and wanted to obtain the money before the scheme was discovered and payment was stopped. To add insult to injury, Stewart charged Davis seven dollars to cash his $5,000 draft.[32]

On the eve of Bud Gillett's preliminary hearing, court officials were mortified to learn the records regarding Gillett's case, including bond papers, had been stolen from the county attorney's office. The court clerk later found them—minus one envelope of records—stuck behind a mailbox inside the courthouse. Had the papers not been located, the *Fort Scott Daily Tribune* groaned, Gillett could have walked free without any bond to hold him.[33] Jonathan Davis's testimony lasted for hours. When he recounted meeting Robert Boatright, a smile crossed Gillett and Booth's faces. Seated next to them at the defense table was former Kansas attorney general Louis C. Boyle. Davis's attorney Jacob Sheppard introduced evidence implicating Exchange Bank cashier James Stewart.[34] Gillett was bound over for trial, but the gang was not hesitant to push back against their persecutors.

Sheriff Brooks received a telegram saying Garrette Stansbury was in the custody of Webb City authorities and left to bring him back to Fort Scott. What followed is demonstrative of the gang's influence. Within minutes of Brooks's arrival in Webb City, Jasper County sheriff Albert Rich served him with a warrant charging him with the attempted kidnapping of Stansbury. After he was arraigned, Brooks gave bond and hired an attorney. If convicted, Brooks faced two to ten years in prison. Perhaps out of guilt, Rich took Brooks to dinner. Stansbury, meanwhile, was released after the court held that the alleged crime was committed in Missouri and therefore Kansas did not have jurisdiction. As Stansbury prepared to leave, an officer presented him with a fugitive warrant Sheriff Brooks swore out earlier as a precaution. Boatright and Charley Parker paid Stansbury's $500 bond.[35]

A Fort Scott paper complained Boatright and his gang were "so shielded by the authorities and prominent people of Webb City who profit from their revenue that it is almost impossible to reach them at all. One newspaper man down there says they have nearly every officer and the courts and all in their influence, and that they pay the newspapers so much per month not to mention their dealings nor their troubles."[36] Reports circulated Davis's case might be settled out of court, but he vowed to recover in a civil action.[37] His attorney Jacob Sheppard swore, "It is a fight to the death. Those men will either be wearing stripes or they will get out with only the expense of employing a lawyer to defend them. We have no idea of settlement."[38] Sheriff Brooks vowed, "You can rest assured that the officers of Bourbon county, Kansas, are in this case to fight to a finish, and that finish is a penitentiary sentence for some of if not all of the so-called Buckfoot gang."[39] Unfazed, the gang continued to fleece suckers.

Boatright's Webb City Athletic Club held a highly publicized fight between Billy Stift and Bob Long; one of the two preliminary bouts featured Eddie Morris. The main event was so well received—the audience applauded referee Ed Burke's decision in favor of Stift—that the *Joplin News-Herald* declared, "The Webb City Athletic club last night regained the prestige lost in former exhibitions by entertaining this large crowd of sports with the Stift-Long glove contest."[40] The gang may have realized their lopsided fights had drawn too much scrutiny. While the fight received the attention of the local press, curiously only one Jasper County newspaper reported Robert Boatright was in federal court at Springfield "fighting an attempt to throw him into bankruptcy."[41]

Boatright's vulnerability to legal claims first surfaced when victim Guy Berger sued him claiming involuntary bankruptcy. Earlier in the year Berger had won a $500 judgment against Boatright. Four days after US district judge John Finis Philips heard the new case in Springfield on October 5, 1901, Berger withdrew the suit and paid his debts. No explanation was given for Berger's sudden decision, but he may have settled with Boatright outside of court.[42]

Some victims paid a much higher price than the loss of their pride and pocketbook. One of the gang's youngest victims, Frank C. Youmans, lost $5,000 on a fixed race. Angry, he traveled to Springfield, Illinois, for the purpose of getting revenge. Although the details are vague, Youmans met Johnny Connors—a boxer and saloonkeeper he alleged was part of the gang—as well as two Buckfoot confederates. He then went to Detroit, Michigan, where he wired his father to meet him because he "had a job fixed up." While there Youmans was arrested for embezzlement, having obtained money to bet on the race under false pretenses from the Traders' Bank of Kansas City. Tragically George W. Youmans, the young man's father, died in a train wreck on his way to meet his son. Frank Youmans returned to Kansas City in the custody of a detective on the same train that carried his father's body in a baggage car. The charges against Youmans were dropped when no one from the bank appeared in court. While many men lost money to the Buckfoot Gang, with some even declaring bankruptcy, Youmans was the only known victim who lost a family member due to his involvement with the gang.[43]

As Youmans mourned his loss, Harry Wasser and Ben Ansel were searching for a new mark in Oklahoma Territory. They found thirty-five-year-old farmer and real estate dealer Robert E. Hobbs in El Reno, a railroad town twenty-five miles outside Oklahoma City. Sticking to his well-worn script, Wasser boasted to Hobbs about his athletic prowess and showed him newspaper clippings about his success on the track. He confided that although he had won many races on behalf of the Webb City Athletic Club, the club's members had chosen not to share their winnings with him. Wasser claimed that Robert Boatright, the club's president, and James P. Stewart, the club's banker, disagreed; they thought he should receive part of the money he had made on the club's behalf. Disgruntled, Wasser wanted Hobbs to travel to Webb City, where Wasser would race Ansel and Hobbs would secretly bet Wasser's money on Ansel. Wasser would then throw the race and make a large sum of money. In exchange, he would pay for Hobbs's train ticket and give him 25 percent of the proceeds. Of course, Hobbs was welcome to bet his own money on the race.[44] Despite initially declining Wasser's proposition, Hobbs found it too tempting. Three days later he left for Webb City on the three o'clock train, armed with letters of credit. After betting $5,000, Hobbs was unknowingly treated to a first-rate theatrical performance.[45]

Daniel Maloney, a large imposing man, began arguing with Boatright over the amount of money in the purse. Emitting a string of curses, he ordered Boatright to count the money. Boatright drew a long breath and suddenly looked pitiful, as if he would rather be somewhere else. Maloney protested and the two men began arguing again. Feeling ill, Hobbs left the room. Ansel followed him.[46] Ansel whispered that Maloney and the others would kill Boatright because the purse was short. Hobbs needed to withdraw another $3,000 to make up the difference. They could then hold the race and Hobbs would get his money back. His mind spinning, Hobbs said he wanted out. "My God," Ansel exclaimed, "we are ruined if you lay down—we are ruined." Hobbs drew the rest of his money from the Exchange Bank. The fix was in.[47]

At ten o'clock that morning Hobbs, the sprinters, and the club members made the short trek to the club's racetrack. Once there Ellis and the others tried but failed to instigate a new round of betting. Wasser and Ansel went to the line and took off running. When the dust settled, Ansel had lost. Wasser, who was supposed to have thrown the race, was the victor. Stunned, Hobbs demanded his money back. Boatright sobbed he did not have the money and that he, too, was ruined. He told Hobbs the only way to get his money back was to rope other people and bring them to Webb City. As Hobbs watched in disbelief, Boatright took off running across the prairie shouting he was ruined. Hobbs returned to El Reno a wiser man.[48]

It would have been little consolation to Hobbs, but he was outwitted by a man the *Lamar Democrat* called an "accomplished gambler and a man of iron nerve." Boatright was a clever "Napoleon of 'Con' " with a "fine appearance," "engaging manners," and a "splendid physique." To ensure they did not get shot by an angry victim, Boatright and his associates cleverly denied being armed and then asked to use their victim's revolver as a starter pistol. The anxious bettor would hand his gun to one of the gang, who then deftly extracted all the cartridges except the one he was going to fire and then return the empty weapon.[49]

As stories of Buckfoot's cunning surfaced, Cornelius Roach of the *Jasper County Democrat* pointed out Missouri law prohibited gaming houses and that it was unlawful for property owners to permit gambling on their premises. He called attention to the fact Democratic state committeeman Gilbert Barbee, owner of the House of Lords, was violating the law. The *Joplin News-Herald* grumbled, "The Local Democracy's spasm of virtue spent itself before the grand jury farce had scarcely gotten out of the present tense . . . and now, secure in the privilege for which they pay the gamblers, fake foot-racers, proprietors of bucket shops, and all the rest of the be-damned et cetera merrily ply their trades in Jasper County."[50] Mooneyham's failure to act was troubling. But the prosecutor was not the paper's only target; the *News-Herald* also swiped at the *Webb City Register* by insinuating it purposefully ignored the gang's activities.

The *Register* clapped back: "The Joplin News-Herald says 'that either through a terrorized or subsidized press the fake footracers continue to operate at Webb City.' Our predecessor became so wealthy by subsidization that he retired from business and we are only awaiting the chance." The *News-Herald* retorted, "We said that the gang of footracers operating in Webb City had become so powerful that either a terrorized or subsidized press dare not make a critical comment upon them. The press of Webb City is not responsible for the presence of the Boatright outfit, though its silent toleration is blamable." Instead, it blamed Mooneyham for not prosecuting the gang, noting, "The game goes on with never a growl of disapproval from Bobby."[51] The *News-Herald*'s rebuke may have been prompted by the news Barbee and former Missouri governor William Joel Stone had purchased interests in the *Carterville Record*, the *Sarcoxie Farm Record*, and the *Webb City Register* with the intent of controlling the Jasper County Democratic Party.[52]

The *Democrat*'s support of Mooneyham faltered when he went on vacation. Roach lambasted the prosecutor's failure to keep his campaign promises to "bolt and bar the doors of the gambling hells of Joplin." Mooneyham, Roach sarcastically claimed, "is further convinced that other Democratic officials, including the judges of the circuit court and the sheriff with his deputies should share with him the responsibility of 'weakening the party' by enforcing the law against gamblers, thieves, thugs, foot racers, robbers and murderers."[53]

In response, the *Joplin News-Herald* caustically commended the *Democrat* for finally acknowledging Mooneyham's inaction. It pointedly noted his failure to prosecute Gilbert Barbee, who, it claimed, avoided being indicted by the grand jury by leasing his building in which the House of Lords operated. The *Democrat* and *News-Herald*'s hysterics about crime and gambling in Jasper County were validated a few days later when gambler Frank Fay was shot in the House of Lords.[54] Mooneyham ordered Joplin gambling houses shuttered, but the edict did not dissuade the Buckfoot Gang.[55] The gang continued to promote fights, though they were not always careful to conceal their fraudulent methods.

Eddie Morris wrote to Lou Houseman, sporting editor of the *Chicago Inter Ocean* and manager of welterweight Walter Nolan, that "The Club is anxious to have Nolan & I fight and if you will bring Nolan here to fight me.... There are a lot of rich mine owners out here that will lose as much as $20,000 as I have licked everybody that came here to fight me they even want to bet $10,000 that I can beat Joe Wolcott now you can imagine how green they are."[56] If they fought on the square, they would only make four hundred dollars to split between them; if they fought a fixed bout, they could earn three to four thousand. Houseman published Morris's letter and his own sarcastic response that read in part, "About the time you say the club wants to bring off the contest at Joplin I shall be busy holding up the west-bound overland limited trains on the Nevada desert."[57] Sports across the country who read Houseman's column were now aware Morris and the Webb City Athletic Club were frauds.

A fight between "Cherokee" Tom Cox and Billy Everts at Webb's Hall was postponed after prosecutor Mooneyham issued warrants to arrest fight participants.[58] Rich and his deputies kept close watch, but no fight transpired. Mooneyham may have become more proactive as a result of Cornelius Roach repeatedly roasting him in the *Jasper County Democrat*. Building on his earlier editorial that scolded Mooneyham, the paper published a story about Joplin's crime rate, noting police officers "have bitten the dust during the 'reign of the criminal.'"[59]

Mooneyham admitted he had a laissez-faire attitude when it came to enforcing the law. He told the *Globe*, "I believe in local self-government and I feel and have always felt that as far as could be made consistent with duty, every town and city should be allowed to govern its own affairs." Mooneyham advised Webb City residents could file a complaint with a justice of the peace and he would prosecute the offenders. He exasperatedly grumbled he did not understand what more people expected him to do.[60]

Mooneyham had attended a fight held in Webb's Hall, the *Webb City Sentinel* asserted, and now he had the audacity to announce prizefighting was illegal. The *Sentinel* asked if "the statute of limitations has not run against the prizefight he witnessed, and if he is the great reformer that he would have people believe he is, why not arrest those who took part in the fight he witnessed?" If he had forgotten the names of the fight's participants, the paper pointed out, they were easily obtainable. Mooneyham, the *Sentinel* sniffed, believed he must first give "the city a chance to enforce the law before he is supposed to take a hand. Such rot. A layman who never read anything except Poor Richard's almanac knows better."[61] As the *Sentinel* judged Mooneyham and found him wanting in the court of public opinion, the train from St. Louis pulled into Webb City with a new victim.

Produce buyer A. N. Randall was in the region purchasing apples when he met Roger H. Williams. Like countless marks before him, Randall lost money on a race. Almost all the money he lost belonged to his employers. Terrified, Randall swore out a warrant for Williams's arrest. "The foot racers," the *Webb City Sentinel* reported, "are resting easy under the assumption that they have committed no crime; as Randall is as guilty as they and cannot be heard to complain."[62] One source claimed Boatright returned $4,500 to Randall. If the remainder was not returned, Randall vowed to sue.[63] His employers, Charles J. Becker and George P. Lang, founded their wholesale grocery business in the fall of 1896; together they had fifty years of experience in the produce trade.[64] Instead of worrying about the fall crop, Becker and Lang were faced with the actions of a rogue employee and a substantial loss of capital.[65]

The Carthage *Jasper County News*—long silent on the gang's activities—acidly observed, "There are thirty-three men composing the Buckfoot gang, all well known in Webb City. Businessmen and police nudge each other when a stranger comes to town and is seen with any of these thirty-three men, and say: 'Another sucker for Buckfoot.' Not a hand is raised in warning him of the robbery about to be perpetrated, not a voice to whisper caution in his ear." Victims were faulted for losing money: " 'Wanted to rob others and got robbed!' That excuse might have saved paradise for Satan if he had only thought of it. . . . No viler crew ever scuttled a ship nor cut a throat," the paper proclaimed, "It is now time for action, Jasper county has been disgraced long enough by this gang of highway robbers and villains of deepest dye." It further declared, "There are men in high positions who have been bribed and the evidence can be produced against them. Woe to them when public wrath is turned upon them. The end is now, near, let them return their ill-gotten gains whence it came, and do their duty, else let the consequences rest upon their own heads."[66]

In the wake of Randall's story, the *Carthage Evening Press* joined the anti-Buckfoot fray and predicted Webb City would become known "as one of the most notorious and sporty gambling resorts in the west." The races "are run almost every day it seems, on the open prairie out north of Webb City, where crowds assemble to see the sport. How the unwary stranger can escape without a hint or a warning wink when all the town people are onto the swindle is certainly a mystery." The *Press* believed newspaper exposés were futile after a victim spent time "in Carthage previous to the race, and the papers here have been full of Buckfoot exposition." As for Randall's threat to sue the gang, the paper shrugged, "But what can he do?"[67] Despite the public outcry, the marks still came.

To the north, in Iowa, John R. Black was threshing on his farm when he spotted a wagon in the distance. As it drew near, he recognized an old acquaintance, William Kyle, who was accompanied by a stranger. After exchanging pleasantries, Kyle introduced Black to Frank Hamilton. Kyle explained he had met Hamilton on the morning train and that he wanted to sell 175 head of cattle in Jasper County, Missouri. When Hamilton asked if he knew of any prospective buyers in the area, Kyle had thought of Black.[68] Black agreed to go look at the cattle. He obtained a $10,000 letter of credit from the Bank of Griswold and traveled with Hamilton to

Joplin. Stepping off the train, he was surprised to find his friend William Kyle had made the same journey. As Kyle looked on, Hamilton introduced Black to Robert Boatright at the train depot.[69]

When Hamilton said he could not show Black the cattle right away because the owner was out of town, Boatright rattled off his racing spiel. Black fell for it.[70] At Boatright's suggestion, Black went to the Exchange Bank of Webb City. He assured cashier James Stewart he had credit in Iowa as well as with the Strahorn-Hutton-Evans Commission Company of Chicago. At Stewart's suggestion he wired the firm, which specialized in cattle loans, to see if it would honor his draft for $5,000. The next day Stewart informed Black that Strahorn would honor his draft. Black deposited $2,600 Boatright had given him to bet on the race; this clever ploy was intended to encourage the victim to bet their own funds. After the money was deposited, Hamilton, Kyle, and Black headed to the 16 to 1 Saloon.[71]

Inside, bettors excitedly called out wager after wager until club member Daniel Maloney interrupted and a quarrel ensued.[72] Angry with Boatright, the club members left. In a strained voice he told Black, "They are going to force me to count that money; I ain't got but half of it." Giant drops of perspiration appeared on Boatright's face as he began to "sweat like a booger." Boatright looked plaintively at Black. "You are the only man who can save me," he pleaded. Black shook his head no. Boatright stammered he would lose his job and be unable to support his elderly parents. "Can't you help me?" he begged. Boatright suggested Black draw on his telegram from Strahorn. "No, I couldn't think of that," Black retorted. Boatright left to scrape up money by himself.[73]

When Boatright returned, he was still $7,000 short. He persuaded Black to draw $2,000 on the Bank of Griswold in Iowa and $5,000 on his Strahorn account. Black promised to return the money to banker Stewart in twenty minutes after Boatright used it to make his final count of the purse.[74] When Black handed over the money, relief washed across Boatright's face as he chirped, "You saved my life." He slipped the money into a satchel and warned Black, "Don't say a word to the boys." Together they went downstairs to the street where a carriage awaited them.

At the track Black felt uneasy and told Boatright there was no need to run the race. As the two men argued, Black's man tripped two-thirds of the way down the track and hit his head. Boatright informed Black he did not have Black's money; he had left the satchel with the cash behind but would return the money to him later. Black scowled; he knew he had been conned. The cattleman returned to the Exchange Bank and informed Stewart he could not return the $7,000. The bank cashier said little in response. As it was already late in the evening, Black caught a trolley to Joplin. When he arrived, the streets were crowded as miners, flush with payday cash, enjoyed a raucous evening. It was a sleepless night.[75]

The next morning Black contacted Strahorn and his bank. The bank replied that it would protest the draft from the Exchange Bank, and Strahorn sent the firm's confidential man, R. E. Lee, to investigate the Exchange Bank. Lee arrived in Webb City on the first train out of Chicago and confirmed Black's story. When he left town, the *Joplin News-Herald*'s front page trumpeted, "FINISH OF THE BUCKFOOT GANG. The End of the Notorious Swindling Regime That Has Disgraced Webb City and the County Administration is in Sight. LATEST VICTIM WILL PROSECUTE."[76]

Black hired attorneys who found the gang had woven a damning financial web. Stewart, once Black had left the bank, had sent the cattleman's drafts for payment. Hamilton Wilcox, president of the Bank of Griswold, believing Black had purchased cattle, honored the $2,000 draft and mailed payment to the Exchange Bank. Shortly thereafter Wilcox received Black's telegram asking to stop payment. The banker telegraphed Webb City postmaster William H. Haughawout to stop delivery of the letter.[77] After a flurry of telegrams from Haughawout, Wilcox received a final message stating the letter had been delivered to the Exchange Bank. He frantically wired the Chicago exchange and asked payment be stopped on the draft. His request was honored.[78]

Wilcox angrily assumed postmaster Haughawout was working with Boatright. One of Black's attorneys, Loren L. DeLano, traveled to Webb City to investigate. Haughawout claimed when he sent the first telegram, he was unaware of the procedures regarding stopping delivery of a letter. When he looked it up, he discovered he would violate postal regulations if he did so, which led him to send a second telegram. After the letter arrived, James Stewart walked into the post office and demanded it. Haughawout, without a request from the Griswold postmaster to hold the letter, was required to give it to Stewart. Haughawout told Stewart he heard Black was protesting payment of the drafts, but Stewart assured the postmaster that even if the drafts were not paid, the Exchange Bank would not lose any money.[79]

Armed with this information, DeLano went to the Exchange Bank to talk to Stewart. The cashier was not available; he was out of town to answer a suit brought against him in federal court charging him with violating postal laws. His cousin Joseph Stewart, the bank's president, was available. When DeLano told Stewart why he was there, the banker curtly responded, "All foot racers looked alike to me" and that Black "was just as bad as the man that beat him . . . A Buckfoot from Iowa was as bad as a Buckfoot in Webb City." He then asked DeLano to leave. Keeping his composure, DeLano recounted his conversation with Haughawout and asked Stewart why his cousin said the bank would not lose any money. Stewart retorted his cousin would not have said that, but if so, he must have meant that the bank would take $7,000 from Boatright's account. Surprised, DeLano asked Stewart why the bank would do that. Stewart replied, "The bank had an understanding with Boatright." Shocked Stewart would make such a bold admission of guilt, DeLano returned to Iowa armed with evidence.[80]

Closer to home, the gang's success—having won an estimated $200,000 in the past eighteen months—meant their legal troubles intensified. Boatright and his associates were indicted in federal court for using the mails to defraud Jonathan Davis.[81] When Jasper County deputy sheriff Jeff Plummer went to serve papers, he could only find Boatright; the rest of the gang were at a race. Buckfoot rounded them up so Plummer could serve everyone. Plummer and Boatright laughed about how Boatright had been so poor upon his arrival in Jasper County that he could not afford tobacco. Plummer, who worked in the same mine as Boatright, gave him a plug of tobacco. Boatright repaid him the following Saturday.[82] While the bunco king may have been on the square in the past, that was no longer the case—the gang was beginning to feel the pressure of a justice system beyond their influence.

When Boatright, Ed Ellis, and Bud Gillett appeared before US commissioner David M. Roper in Carthage to answer the indictment from the federal grand jury in Fort Scott, Boatright jauntily tossed his hat on Roper's desk. As Roper read the indictment, Boatright twirled his mustache and shifted in his chair. Charley Parker and Alfred G. Carter, Ellis's brother-in-law, promptly paid their bonds. At James Stewart's appearance later that day, his lawyer lamented, "Jim is in a bad fix for doing banking with those men."[83] When Jonathan Davis was swindled, Stewart did not cash Davis's check. Instead, he sent it by mail to the bank on which it was drawn. When Stewart did this, he made himself liable for fraudulent use of the mails.[84] The following day Davis's attorney received a letter from attorney Loren DeLano recounting John Black's experience. Buckfoot's victims were beginning to seek each other out; only time would tell if they would band together as their numbers continued to grow.[85]

As Christmas of 1901 approached Boatright and his associates prepared to enjoy the season's festivities, likely assuming the new year would be just as lucrative as the last. It would be anything but.

5

"HE HAD TO HAVE ENOUGH GRAND LARCENY IN HIM TO MAKE A GOOD FIRST CLASS HORSE THIEF"

—ROGER H. WILLIAMS, *In re R. H. Williams*

The Watkins brothers never should have trusted the dapper man with glittering gold teeth. The day before New Year's Eve 1902 in southwest Oklahoma, where the Red River slowly unfurls across the Great Plains, T. J. Watkins, a restaurateur in the gold rush town of Wildman, and his sibling James, a stockman from Sterling, found themselves in Webb City at the behest of their friend Jesse Ansel. Ansel, whom they had known for nine years, asked them to bet money on his behalf over Christmas dinner with Ansel's nattily attired friend Harry Clark. The Watkins brothers proved amiable and, upon their arrival, were taken to the Webb City Athletic Club's clubrooms. In the chaotic betting that ensued, T. J. Watkins put up a $750 bank draft while his brother James reluctantly handed one over for $600. A squabble ensued among the bettors, and the Watkinses were ushered to the Banks Hotel in Galena, Kansas, by Ben Ansel, variously identified as both Jesse's brother and cousin, who registered as "Lamont." This irregularity did not raise the Oklahomans' suspicion.

The following day the Watkins brothers returned to the clubrooms, where they wisely avoided drinks but accepted dinner. After they finished everyone headed to the track. When it came time for the race, no starter pistol could be found. James Watkins hesitantly offered his .38 Smith & Wesson, which Boatright examined before giving it to Bob Long, who the *Joplin News-Herald* noted was, "a gentleman of color, who belongs to Buckfoot and poses in the fistic arena as a prize fighter." Long emptied all but one of the chambers and then fired it. Ten yards from the

73

finish line, the Watkins' sprinter fell and was knocked unconscious. The Oklahomans demanded their money back, but Boatright refused. They hurriedly attempted to stop payment on their drafts before leaving for Joplin. Penniless, they swore out a warrant against Ben Ansel, Robert Boatright, Harry Clark, and Jesse Ansel. Jesse was arrested and jailed on a charge of conspiracy to defraud but insisted he had lost $550 on the race.[1]

Downtown Joplin came to a standstill the next morning as a resplendent coach-and-six navigated the city's streets. "There was a blare of trumpets, a clatter of the hoofs of fiery Arabian steeds, and a rumble of carriage wheels" as six handsome horses arrayed in a glittering silver-mounted harness pulled a "rig fit for the Queen of Sheba." The gleaming carriage rolled to a stop in front of Justice James M. McAdams's court. Onlookers watched as Robert Boatright, a "large and portly man of agreeable manners," and three of his colts stepped down and walked into court. Streetcar service between Webb City and Joplin, it seemed, was far too pedestrian. A Buckfoot representative allegedly already had met with the Watkins brothers and paid them off; the *Globe* cackled they would likely not appear for the trial. When Boatright learned one of the Oklahomans complained his bond was too low, he gamely told Justice McAdams to make it any size and he would pay it. After satisfying their bonds and seeing Jesse Ansel released from custody, the men repaired to the House of Lords for an elaborate midday meal before returning to Webb City.[2] Other victims took their chances in court and won.

Charles O. Hodges of Dallas, Texas, filed suit against the gang for $4,620. A jury awarded him $4,804 after Robert Boatright and others failed to appear.[3] This news was compounded by a story that Buckfoot confederate George Thompson and victim William J. Laughlin were under arrest in Kansas City. Jackson County prosecuting attorney Herbert S. Hadley had charged them, together with Robert Boatright and Ed Ellis, with trying to sell forged instruments in January 1902.[4] Hadley, just beginning his meteoric rise in Missouri politics, was a progressive Republican reformer who spearheaded cases against jury tampering and gambling—not a political hack who could be purchased.[5]

Laughlin, a clerk from Denver, Colorado, had taken three checks totaling $5,000 to bet on a race. When Robert Boatright saw Laughlin's drafts were on a Denver bank, he told Laughlin "nothing but Kansas City paper could be used." Laughlin obtained drafts at a printing office, altered them to say "National Bank of Kansas City," and signed the cashier's name. When he returned, Boatright snatched the drafts from Laughlin's hand; Laughlin said the frenzied crowd of bettors made it impossible to retrieve them. After the race did not take place, Laughlin told Boatright the drafts were no good, but Boatright gave the drafts to Thompson to cash, prompting their arrest.[6] The *Jasper County Democrat* crowed, "From all indications the Buckfoot gang have been roped into a neat little confidence game themselves."[7]

George Thompson was released on $3,000 bond provided by his brother-in-law George E. Cole. Boatright and Ed Ellis provided their own bail money with former Kansas attorney general Louis Boyle cosigning their bonds. A reporter found Boatright "very dark with black moustache and hair. He dresses rather roughly and looks like a well-to-do miner or cattleman. He has a keen eye and looks one squarely in the eye when he talks to him." Ellis had "a sandy complexion" with reddish hair and moustache. The "smooth faced and stout" Thompson looked like "a well-fed clerk with sporting tendencies."[8]

When the time came, William Laughlin did not want to testify. In a letter to the judge he noted the gang had never been convicted and was scared they would harm him. Hadley was not dissuaded. "We will take steps to make Laughlin testify," he vowed. "There is a way of doing it and we will get him."[9] In court Boatright and Thompson, dressed "stylishly, but flashily," watched Hadley spar with Boyle.[10] Hadley told the judge the defendants had fleeced victims out of $300,000. Their victims had been beaten, drugged, and had their lives threatened. "When Laughlin was here at the preliminary hearing he was so terrorized by these men that he almost had nervous prostration," Hadley explained. "It appeared that it was their purpose to kill Laughlin. These persons for some reason can't be tried in their own county." He insisted, "We have a prosecution here and testimony that if the case is continued to give us an opportunity to get Laughlin here, I am confident we can send them to the penitentiary."[11] As Hadley spoke, Boatright shook his head and "looked so fierce" a deputy marshal stepped toward him. The judge continued the case, but the final disposition is unknown. Hadley's assertion he could send Boatright and Thompson to the penitentiary seems to have gone untested—perhaps Laughlin could not be compelled to appear.[12]

While Boatright grappled with legal entanglements, Garrette Stansbury was arrested in Denver and extradited to Kansas.[13] Almost a week later, attorney Harry Armstrong of Xenia, Ohio, arrived in Jasper County to represent Maggie Day.[14] Day's husband, George, had taken $3,000 from her bank account at the Citizens' National Bank and lost it on a Buckfoot race in early February 1902. Under Ohio law, George was prohibited from withdrawing money from his wife's account without her written consent. Once Maggie learned what her husband had done, she notified her bank. Officials there stopped payment on the drafts that

George gave Boatright. The Jasper County Circuit Court issued a temporary injunction to stop the Joplin Savings Bank from delivering the drafts to Roger H. Williams, who had left them for collection. The gang had turned to the Joplin Savings Bank after the Exchange Bank of Webb City had been garnished in the William Reger and Guy Berger cases in November 1901; after that date the Exchange Bank did not handle any of the gang's transactions. Boatright, the *Evening Press* explained, could go to the courts "with his illicit cause if he has the effrontery" but it looked like he "might be beaten at his own game."[15]

Boatright must have been pleased, then, when the *Joplin Globe* gave a "pink carnation of approval" to prosecutor Mooneyham, who was expected to run for reelection. The paper's rival, the *News-Herald*, was outraged. Not a week went by that the Buckfoot Gang did not fleece someone, the paper insisted, and "it is not extravagant to say that in the whole country there is perhaps no other place where organized outlawry flourishes so openly as right here in Jasper county under" Mooneyham's administration. "Someday there'll be a climax of blood in the Buckfoot story," the paper warned, "and it will probably be written on the race track at Webb City." It then asked, "When murder has been added to the long list of robberies by the Buckfoot gang, will Mr. Mooneyham feel that a sufficient cause for action has appeared?" The paper concluded, "Murder on the race track at Webb City would not mean the end of the Buckfoot swindle, if what has transpired in our own city under Mooneyham's administration is a criterion. Joplin has had its gambling hells, it has had bloodshed in one of those gambling hells. Joplin has its gambling hells today. Through all this Jasper county has had, and still has, Mooneyham."[16]

The *News-Herald's* outcry may have led to the circulation of a petition calling for a special grand jury to investigate several flagrant criminal offenses in Jasper County—most prominently corruption and the activities of the Buckfoot Gang. The petition—which, the *Carthage Evening Press* noted, created "a profound sensation in political and other circles in the county"—denounced the gang, prizefights, gambling, and a bucket shop openly advertising in the local papers. It was given to Gilbert Barbee's political rival William H. Phelps, who was temporarily serving as a special judge. Phelps demurred, not wishing to act on it. Instead, he would give it to Judge Joseph Perkins upon his return.[17]

Boatright suffered a minor setback in March 1902 when a jury awarded St. Louis produce merchants Lang and Becker $2,344.85 in their damage case against the bunco king.[18] A few days later the gang conned Drayton W. Powell and Albert B. Blocker Jr. of Marshall, Texas.[19] Powell ran a cotton yard; Blocker worked in the county tax collector's

Joplin News-Herald, 1902. *Author's Collection.*

office. Powell could only muster $750; Blocker $300. When the duo complained they had been fleeced, the gang laughed and said if they had known they were going to get such a small sum they would not have roped them. Powell and Blocker refused $300 to sign an agreement not to prosecute the gang. When they returned to the Joplin Savings Bank, Blocker told bank president George W. Layne he had been robbed and that Layne was a party to the robbery. Layne laughed, "You boys have been caught."[20] Such stories were attractive fodder for Barbee's enemies.

The *News-Herald's* penchant for publishing stories about Boatright's victims led to a counterattack by its chief rival. Jasper County Democratic chieftain Gilbert Barbee's *Joplin Globe* lashed out at the *News-Herald* and its owner, Edward S. Hosmer. In a series of stories and sworn affidavits from Daniel Saighman and Robert Boatright, the *Globe* alleged Hosmer met multiple times with Saighman. Hosmer, it asserted, repeatedly offered to turn a blind eye to gambling in Joplin in exchange for $100 a month. He also allegedly asked Saighman to relay an offer to Robert Boatright: for $200 a month ($6,936) he would stop publishing stories about Boatright. Buckfoot declined but countered he would pay Hosmer $100 a month to stop attacking him and "roast" his opponents. Hosmer declined. A few weeks later, the *Globe* maintained, he reconsidered and said would take $100 a month. Boatright declined. He explained the *News-Herald* could not possibly inflict any more damage. Or, as Saighman explained it, Boatright said "the News-Herald's graft was so much worse than his own that he would have nothing to do with it."[21]

The *Globe* huffed, "It is a fair sample of the tactics pursued by the sheet that is now attempting to win a republican victory in Joplin. Republican victory for this paper and the gang that supports it would mean only a chance for them to loot the treasury of the city." Hosmer, the paper alleged, met with *Globe* business manager Dan Dugan to discuss a scheme to enrich the owners of both papers through a bidding war for the city's official printing contract. After Dugan rebuffed him, Hosmer then supposedly made his failed bid to secure hush money from Boatright.[22] The *Globe* concluded that Joplin residents "will refuse to endorse the methods of this stranger who comes into the city and allies, or attempts to ally, himself with the forces of vice and who sees in public affairs only a chance to make some money for himself and his paper. They will refuse to endorse the bitter attacks that this wily and slippery alien has made on reputable citizens of Joplin who have lived here most of their lives and have given their time, their energy, and their money to the upbuilding of the city's interests."[23]

Hosmer and the *News-Herald* refuted Barbee's accusations, which were made on the eve of an election. An editorial argued Saighman's affidavit proved Hosmer refused to take hush money and that, if his representations to Hosmer were true, then it demonstrated criminal collusion existed between public officials and criminals. Saighman, Hosmer said, told him Boatright and Joplin gamblers were paying $150 a month to parties on behalf of another Joplin newspaper and that even larger sums were being paid to Joplin and county officials. He did not disclose their names, but voiced his hope he could present the facts to a court of law.[24]

Barbee, Hosmer contended, "rents his property to immense advantage for gambling purposes and among the gamblers he has able lieutenants who render him great service in return for violating the law which his dictum permits. The gamblers are a potent factor in the politics of the undercurrent." They contributed liberally to the "corruption fund" and disbursed the funds to maximum effect. "There isn't a saleable vote in the city of Joplin that the gamblers organization hasn't its eye on. They know how to buy votes and they do it." Bossism and gambling in Joplin had to end. Prosecutor Robert Mooneyham could find "information warranting prosecution by reading the first page of the Globe," notably its admission that Saighman openly operated a gambling house in Barbee's House of Lords building. The *News-Herald*, however, conceded Barbee had lived three decades in Joplin and never been caught.[25]

Going on the attack, the *News-Herald* ran two prominent stories: "Barbee's Gang Self-Convicted" and "Buckfoot Will Be Prosecuted." The stories contended Barbee headed a political ring, whose members included Daniel Saighman and Robert Boatright, that controlled city government for the benefit of criminals who "held [a] high carnival of crime without molestation." After disclosing Barbee's machinations in local politics, the paper concluded, "Another and more conclusive evidence of the gamblers' conspiracy is the fact that when the News-Herald pushed the Globe into a corner with the manifold proofs of the guilt of its crowd, and it was attempting to distract attention by calling 'stop thief,' it instinctively turned to its partners in politics for assistance, and Saighman and Buckfoot appeared as its affidavit makers."[26]

The paper's optimism was also buoyed by the news that Jonathan Davis's attorney Jacob Sheppard had convinced Mooneyham to prosecute Boatright. Mooneyham, who repeatedly claimed he could not do so because of victims' reluctance to appear in court, was forced to act after multiple victims arrived in Webb City. Frank Youmans, Robert Hobbs, Monroe Griffith, John Black, and William Barker, a lightning rod salesman from Council Bluffs, Iowa, had agreed to combine their efforts in pursuing legal action against Boatright and his gang.[27] Across the state line in Kansas, Boatright, Ed Ellis, and Bud Gillett were under bond; Boatright's was set at $2,000 and Ellis and Gillett's at $3,000. "This is a heavy bond," the *Jasper County Democrat* remarked, "and it is said that if the men ever get up in front of Judge Hook they will be given the limit of the law in the case." If the men were convicted of using the mail to defraud, they faced fines of no less than $500 and a prison sentence of eighteen months.[28] The threat of imprisonment did little to deter them.

Late one spring evening in 1902, Eddie Morris visited John Carlson's saloon in Spring Valley, Illinois, accompanied by local butcher Samuel Horner. Carlson, a Swedish immigrant, had made money on Morris's previous fights in Illinois. Horner informed Carlson that Morris was going to "get the best of" Bob Long in Webb City and asked if he would come with them. Carlson was game.[29] Once they arrived in Webb City after midnight on April 22, the trio climbed into a cab at the Missouri Pacific depot. Carlson and Horner sat inside with two fellow travelers while Morris sat with the driver. Gliding through the back streets, the cab rolled to a stop in front of the Webb City Athletic Club. Horner and Carlson were shown the clubhouse and its gymnasium equipped with a punching bag, trapezes, swinging rings, and a walking ladder.[30] The next morning Carlson and Horner met Ed Ellis and other members. At Roger Williams's suggestion, Carlson deposited his money at the Joplin Savings Bank.[31]

The evening of the fight, Carlson and Horner arrived at the club's gymnasium, where Bob Long and Eddie Morris stripped down and entered the ring. In the first round, Morris landed a blow that left Long groggy. The men who had bet on Long congratulated Carlson for backing Morris. During the fourth round, the boxers tangled in the ring and Morris fell with Long on top of him. Morris screamed his leg was broken. He and Williams insisted a bewildered Carlson and Horner take the 8:40 train out of town and promised a rematch.[32] Instead, they visited attorney Hiram Currey, who had unknowingly shared a cab with them the morning of their arrival in Webb City. Currey recalled telling his companion the two men were going to get robbed. Carlson returned home and told acquaintances he had been swindled. But, the Swede declared, he had "hired a lawyer, and was going to try his luck."[33]

Eddie Morris was not the only one roping out on the road. Salesman Irven E. Johnson, one of the gang's most prolific ropers, was hard at work. He could play the long game; several of his victims resisted for months before succumbing. It took Johnson over a year to snare John I. Pittman, who lost $2,500 on a foot race. The financial loss was more than Pittman could bear; his paint and wallpaper business failed.[34] At almost the same time he skinned Pittman, Johnson roped lumberman Peter Doucette. After Doucette's sprinter lost, he noticed one of the gang had something in his hand. "I wasn't certain then whether it was a gun or a stick," Doucette said later, "but I thought it was a gun and I thought if I wanted to see my wife and family again, I had better behave myself." He lost $8,300.[35] Real estate broker J. J. Broussard from Beaumont, Texas, lost money and his hat and boots on a side bet with the Honey Grove Kid.[36]

The gang did not hesitate to protect their lucrative business. Bert Bromley and the Honey Grove Kid attacked victim Frank Youmans in the lobby of Webb City's Newland Hotel shortly after he filed charges against the gang in early 1902. Bromley and the Kid claimed they were talking to Youmans when he pulled a gun. Onlookers intervened and all three were arrested. A *Globe* reporter who conveniently happened to be at the scene asked for an interview. Youmans, dazed from being beaten, was reticent. When he finally spoke, he asserted he was not the aggressor. He claimed they attacked him from behind and that he had not drawn his gun; it had likely fallen out of his pocket when he was knocked to the ground. When pressed to explain what prompted the attack, Youmans snapped he had said enough. The *Globe* likely wanted to humiliate one of the gang's victims given that its owner, Gilbert Barbee, was believed to be protecting them from prosecution.[37] Bromley and the Kid were charged with assault and released on bond, Youmans with carrying a concealed weapon. Boatright's attorney George Booth told the *Globe* Youmans and other victims who had joined forces the previous month were attempting to recoup their losses through criminal prosecution. The *Globe* alleged Youmans threatened to prosecute them in federal court if they did not return his money. This, the paper surmised, was what led to the fight. Animosity between the two sides, it speculated, might result in bloodshed.[38]

The attack prompted Hiram Currey, the gang's legal antagonist, to write a scathing letter published in the *Kansas City Journal*. "This is, we think, the only city in the state of Missouri, which enjoys the distinction of harboring an organized gang of outlaws, who publicly defy legal authority," Currey began. "I doubt if ever before in the history of the state, any gang of men have organized themselves together for the purpose of getting other men's money, by methods purely criminal, and carried on their schemes at one place, without interruption, for any considerable time."[39] Despite employing every illegal trick "known to the art," law enforcement officers had not intervened. Locals even sympathized with them. Currey noted, "On the streets one hears it said many times, any day, that 'these fellows who are being robbed have come here to rob our citizens and get robbed themselves, and it is no matter for us to complain of.'"[40]

Echoing the press, Currey alleged the gang's political influence emanated from their allies' ownership of the "wing of the Democratic party which seems to have charge of the county politics." The other branch of the local Democratic party, he charged, was not much better. The opposing party differed little. Currey believed many Republican leaders "are selecting and pushing candidates who will be friendly to the gambling and saloon influences, and unless the real people take charge of affairs," things would likely remain the same.[41] Currey's letter attracted little attention, though he was not wrong about the gang's brazenness and the need for action.

In response, Boatright's attorney George Booth aired an unflattering story that Currey was driven from Dade County for stealing an old harness and indicted for robbing a widow.[42] Infuriated, Currey filed a libel suit. The *Webb City Sentinel* remarked, "This, no doubt, will be one of the hardest fought causes appearing in our courts in recent years, from the array of legal talent on the side of the plaintiff, and from the fact that the Buckfoot gang will likely interest themselves in the matter and help out the defense."[43]

As the battle raged over the soul of Jasper County, the gang conned sixty-nine-year-old W. A. Blagg of Texas; he was followed by a trio of men from Beaumont, Texas, who were taken for $10,000.[44] Attorney Charles M. Chambers of Clarksville, Texas, was breezily roped by the Honey Grove Kid. After betting had taken place in the gang's brick clubhouse, Chambers watched them caucus and realized he was a sucker.[45] Worried about his safety, he left behind a suitcase with clothes, diamond jewelry, three unsigned drafts for $12,000, and a pocketbook with cash. Chambers wrote Boatright and asked him to send his belongings. Boatright replied he had sent the suitcase and clothes via express charged collect because "they could not use either; but the others they would keep and hoped the trip had taught me that 'suckers' ought to stay at home." Chambers mused, "Being of the same opinion, I let the matter drop."[46]

At least two victims scored a small victory in May 1902. Attorney Frank Forlow, who represented St. Louis produce merchants George Lang and Charles Becker, had the personal property in the Buckfoot Gang's club rooms attached on a judgment for his clients against Boatright, Ed Ellis, Bud Gillett, Bert Bromley, and Roger H. Williams. Located in a double brick building on Tom Street just north of Daugherty Street, the contents included furniture, carpets, curtains, a desk, typewriter, liquor, and a large iron safe. Two deputies were stationed outside as the safe was believed to contain victim's money. The land the building sat on was also seized.[47] Boatright confederate George Thompson quickly went before a justice of the peace and filed a claim of ownership.[48] Lang and Becker then gave the sheriff an indemnifying bond with orders to sell the property.[49] Within a week Thompson and Mary Rice, the wife of Buckfoot member Frank H. Rice, brought suits against Sheriff Rich to recover the furnishings and property.[50] The loss of their headquarters, however, proved inconsequential to the gang's pursuit of money.

Under the auspices of the Fraternal Order of Eagles, a fight was held in Joplin, with local politicians among the 1,200 spectators at the city's regal Club Theater. After the last fight ended, Sheriff Rich arrested the participants. When asked why he allowed the fights to take place, Rich blamed a deputy for not alerting him in time to prevent them. An anonymous source disclosed Rich had been pressured to act and "evidently he was up against it, for he would be damned if he did and damned if he didn't."[51]

The *Jasper County Democrat* expressed its dismay at the "carnival of prize fights" and Sheriff Rich's inaction. "Why he did not the Democrat does not know," the paper groused, "and cannot understand, for he and his deputies and the prosecuting attorney were all in Joplin, and could have put an end to all violation of law and commission of crime by simply putting in appearance and announcing no fight would take place. Mr. Rich says he has no statement to make." The *Democrat* did not ask Mooneyham for a statement because—like Boatright—he was an Eagle and "Eagles enjoy prize fighting much more than prosecuting violators of law." Missouri law, it asserted, made such " 'exhibitions' as that of Thursday night a felony punishable with a term in the penitentiary." The paper upbraided local Democrats for allowing "a band of organized gamblers" to dictate policy. "Jasper county sentiment has always favored the enforcement of law. It is a law-abiding country. It has always had its toughs and its sports, but there never was a time, and never will be a time, when the decent, respectable people submitted, or will submit, in either party to political domination by the lawless element."[52]

As spring turned to summer, there was at least one less Buckfoot confederate in Jasper County: Roger Williams was in Colorado City, Colorado. Founded in 1859, it was a rough frontier town populated by miners, prostitutes, and settlers during the Pikes Peak Gold Rush. Two years later it became the capital of Colorado Territory but lost its bid to become the state capital. Colorado City was then eclipsed by neighboring upstart Colorado Springs, which sought to become the "Saratoga of the West" with luxury hotels, sanitariums, and stately homes. When the wife of the founder of Colorado Springs convinced her husband to prohibit saloons within city limits, Colorado City seized upon the opportunity to offer amenities that its rival could not: prostitution, gambling, and prizefighting. It was no surprise it attracted Williams, but the problems brewing back in the Ozarks followed him. Accompanied by his attorney Haywood Scott of Joplin, he traveled to Colorado Springs to give a deposition for Hiram Currey's suit against the Joplin Savings Bank. It is one of only a few times in which a member of the Buckfoot Gang gave direct testimony about its operations.[53]

The thirty-seven-year-old "promoter for athletic contests and backer of athletes" verbally sparred with Deputy District Attorney Thomas J. Black and attorney Robert L. Hubbard over the course of several days. At times Williams was forthright; he admitted the athletic contests were both fake and genuine. A prizefight between Bob Long and Billy Stift, for example, had been legitimate. He had also been involved in fights between "Bob Long and Eddy Morse, Bob Long and Billy Stift, Tommy Dixon, Jack Madden," but did not explicitly state they were fixed. The fake contests, he conceded, were meant "to mislead the sucker in order to separate him from his money." When asked how he got victims to bet on rigged contests, Williams responded he had to find a man with "enough Grand Larceny in him to make a good first class horse thief." The only ones they had been able to find, he noted, were people with a bad reputation in their local communities. Throughout much of the deposition, though, Williams was evasive. When asked if there was an "athletic club or association at Joplin or Webb City" that promoted contests, Williams coyly responded there was, but he was unsure if it still existed. Robert Boatright was manager and he, along with several others he named, were members.[54]

When Black's schedule did not permit him to continue the deposition, Hubbard took over.[55] When Hubbard inquired if he had personal business transactions with the men he named, Williams objected for the first time, on grounds of self-incrimination. The con man acknowledged he received 4 percent of victim John Carlson's money. He claimed he cashed the certificates of deposit at Carlson's request and insisted his business with the Joplin Savings Bank was personal and unrelated to the Buckfoot Gang. He denied bank president George Layne was involved.[56]

Layne was not the only one accused of questionable conduct. Hubbard asked if emissaries were sent out across the country to rope victims. Williams snapped, "I think that word emissary emanated in the brain of our Honorable man the Hi Currey, and he presumes that such is the case and tries to blackmail his way through, that 'he will do this to you or that to you' if you do not give him some of the money." He explained he did not rope victims, but "if any of the rest of them do I do not know it."[57] Williams explained Currey—representing various victims—threatened the gang with blackmail, including negative newspaper articles, if they did not pay him. The gang had paid him multiple times, he claimed, with the understanding he would leave them alone, but Currey always reneged. Williams huffed, "He is so unreliable in any and every way that we have just absolutely refused to recognize him." The gang could prove Currey's duplicitous behavior thanks to a receipt in his own handwriting they had secreted away. Currey, he said, was reportedly on the verge of being indicted for embezzling from his clients. Williams sniffed, "In fact, he has done so many crooked things that I absolutely think he is the orneriest man I ever saw, and I have seen some pretty bad cases around Webb City."[58]

Williams likely monitored events back in Jasper County, including the bacchanalian atmosphere on the streets of Joplin. The *Jasper County Democrat* howled, "JOPLIN'S DISGRACE; Barbee's House of Lords Building an Unsavory Resort Where Gamblers, Women and Whisky Revel and Fight Nightly." At 9:30 p.m. on a weeknight, pedestrians in the vicinity of Fourth and Main in downtown Joplin were treated to the "most disgraceful battle royal that has taken place in this city for some years." It began in the front room on the second floor of Gilbert Barbee's House of Lords building overlooking Main Street when gamblers "Spooly" Geir and David Cooper McBride got into a physical altercation with madam Belle Robinson and a prostitute named Bulah. The room went dark but there was enough light from the street that pedestrians on the sidewalk below could see the fight, which "waxed warm and furious, and between the upper-cuts, swings, punches, hooks, which were landed, small bunches of hair were also seen to float out upon the atmosphere."[59]

"Those who were lucky enough to hold complimentary tickets to the battle and held front seats," the paper cheekily commented, "report the Ferns-Zeigler bout a tame affair compared with the one of last night." After the police restored order, Spooly and Bulah crept downstairs to the sidewalk. He took off at a "2:04 gait south on Main street," but Bulah gave pursuit "and a sprint event that would put to shame any Buckfoot event that has ever taken place was given." Daniel Saighman's gambling rooms in the building were silent due to poor business. What the rooms would be used for in the meantime was unclear, but the paper ventured, "it is not likely they will be used as a place of worship."[60]

In calling for Mooneyham to act, the paper mentioned that the night before there had been a fight in the House of Lords saloon—separate from the restaurant—on the ground floor of the same building. The *Democrat* declared, "Mr. Barbee's building is becoming notorious," scoffing that "the Joplin Globe, owned by Barbee who also owns the House of Lords, contained no account of these fracases. As a newspaper the Globe is careful to conduct such a policy as will not inform any part of the world of the true character of its owner, the 'alleged' leader of the Democratic party of Jasper county. . . . Nothing," the *Democrat* continued, "gives a better insight into the kind of man Barbee is than the doings of the House of Lords, first, second and third floors. This man with the gamblers of his house is the individual who at present assumes to dictate the policy and management of the democracy not only of Jasper county but of Southwest Missouri."[61] The only question was, how much longer could Barbee protect Buckfoot and his gang?

6

"THE STARS OF THE PROFESSION"

—*Colorado Springs Gazette*, DECEMBER 7, 1902

Gilbert Barbee's confidence and combativeness—useful traits in backroom politics—did not lend themselves to protecting confidence men. At a time when the gang did not need publicity, Barbee channeled his ire toward Hiram Currey and his client, Buckfoot victim John Carlson, through the *Joplin Globe* when it publicized the Swede had been charged with fraudulently obtaining hotel board. Currey claimed Carlson could not speak fluent English, but the hotel manager denied having issues communicating with him. Each time Carlson attempted to speak in court, Currey grunted for him to keep his mouth shut. Assistant Prosecutor Stonewall Pritchett attacked Carlson as a man who sought to rob a set of men who engaged in the business of robbing others, but the jury found him not guilty.[1]

Currey's suit against the Joplin Savings Bank in Jasper County Circuit Court soon followed. He filed it in his name after Carlson assigned him his claim; he hoped to compel the bank to return Carlson's $3,000. Currey argued the bank was not authorized to pay the money to the Buckfoot Gang or anyone else.[2] The preliminary hearing ensnared more than just the Joplin Savings Bank. Jasper County assistant prosecutor Charles S. Creller, handling the case in prosecutor Robert Mooneyham's absence, questioned Ed Ellis about the Webb City Athletic Club. Ellis admitted the Buckfoot Gang's athletic contests were fraudulent and that he was a member of the gang without a legitimate livelihood. Asked to explain the illegitimate means he used, Ellis replied, "Making money on these sporting contests, so-called."

Creller pressed him again, "And these [are] cinches [?]"

"Yes, sir," Ellis nodded.

Incredulous, Judge Hugh Dabbs interjected and questioned Ellis as to what transpired between Carlson and the gang. Creller issued a warrant for Ellis's arrest; he was charged with grand larceny and his bond set at $4,000.[3]

When the case came to trial in August 1902, Hiram Currey prevailed against the Joplin Savings Bank; Judge Dabbs remarked, "No fiction writer had ever woven around his victim a more deliberate or better prepared scheme to deceive" than the plot devised by Buckfoot. Based on the evidence presented by both sides, Dabbs concluded Carlson's bank drafts were obtained by larceny and therefore the bank was liable. When the case against Ed Ellis was called, he was nowhere to be found and forfeited his $4,000 bond.[4] Such losses paled in comparison to what the gang may have been making out west; summering in Colorado Springs, the "invulnerable Bob" was said to have raked in $102,000 ($4,161,518). But trouble in the Ozarks was not far from his mind; Boatright had left behind at least one colt to watch local developments.[5] One came when, while on vacation in Wisconsin, Robert Mooneyham announced he would not run for reelection due to his wife's ill health.[6] A few days later, tragedy struck Webb City.

On August 10, 1902, Webb City marshal Leonard Rich was killed when he responded to a disturbance at a resort. Whitecaps soon visited five of the city's madams and warned them to leave before sundown; otherwise, they would tar and feather the women and burn their furniture. Calling the madams "contemptable," the *Sentinel* declared all good citizens were determined "to purify the moral atmosphere of the city. These houses and these people are the direct cause of the death of City Marshal Rich and the slugging of Policeman James. They are a menace to public order and public decency." No mention of the Buckfoot Gang was made despite its contributions to Webb City's sins.[7]

Carthage editor Cornelius Roach disapproved of Webb City's vigilantes. "All this sounds strange," he remarked, "in an enlightened community of the twentieth century. There is no occasion for resorting to primitive methods for dealing with the problems that confront Webb City or Joplin." Jasper County had elected officials and a circuit court to enforce the law, he argued. Vigilantes who went after "defenseless fallen women," Roach lectured, were not "brave or sensible." The county did not "need the bawd, the pugilist, the gambler, the thug, the murderer, nor the political boss who is responsible for all. Eliminate the political boss and the officer who has not the moral courage to do his duty for fear of the boss will have a much-improved nerve to live up to the requirements of his office."[8]

Roach further railed, "The murder of Officer Rich is a terrible, a deplorable occurrence. It is said he has always protested against the so-called 'wide open policy' of turning the town over to the vile and the vicious. He was, however, only a subordinate official. Poor man!"[9] The *Joplin News-Herald* agreed lax law enforcement had emboldened criminals and now "it is a case of sowing to the wind and reaping the whirlwind."[10] Residents in Joplin's North Heights neighborhood petitioned city officials to purge North Main Street of brothels or else they would use "the plan adopted by Webb City people."[11]

Two days after Rich's murder, the Buckfoot Gang skinned businessman Fagan Bourland of Fort Smith, Arkansas, out of $4,000.[12] Yet in the wake of Rich's death, Barbee's paper shamelessly called out Buckfoot's detractors as hypocrites. The *Joplin Globe* trolled the anti-Buckfoot and anti-Barbee press with the headline, "Democracy's Prosecution of the 'Buckfoot Gang' as Compared with Republican Administration's Record." Both the *Carthage Evening Press* and *Joplin News-Herald*, the *Globe* charged, had made false allegations against the county's Democratic administration. It argued Buckfoot and his gang had flourished under Republican prosecutor Hiram Shannon. A *Globe* reporter sent to analyze court records claimed Shannon had brought only one case against Boatright. Under Democrat Robert Mooneyham, however, six cases had been filed, two of which were settled when the gang returned the victims' money.[13] In response, *Carthage Evening Press* editor and publisher William J. Sewall printed a lengthy comparative analysis. Sewall asserted Shannon had secured almost three times as many convictions as Mooneyham. This, he said, explained how the House of Lords gamblers and Buckfoot Gang had flourished in the last two years.[14]

Some victims pressed ahead; Robert Hobbs's case against Boatright, the Exchange Bank, and James Stewart began in earnest on October 7, 1902. He was aided by the testimony of fellow victim John Black and Black's banker Hamilton Wilcox.[15] Hobbs's case led the *News-Herald* to crow, "The State House Gang and the Buckfoot Democracy are on the Run—Keep Them Going!"[16] The paper's optimism was not misplaced; the jury delivered a unanimous verdict in favor of Robert Hobbs for $6,347. Boatright's attorneys moved to appeal.[17] "If Messrs. Boatright Ellis & Co., forming the close corporation known as the Buckfoot gang, do not get a new victim soon the funds of the company are likely to run low," the *Jasper County Democrat* cackled. "What with putting up bonds for their foot racers to escape punishment, and bribing witnesses and others, they are eating in on the profits of the business."[18]

Following the verdict, Robert Boatright, who had briefly returned to Webb City, headed west. He was followed, one by one, by his colts, who arranged with their bondsmen to pay their forfeited bonds. News soon came from Colorado Springs that Frank C. Lory, a self-described Klondike millionaire from Petersburg, Indiana, had been buncoed out of $65,000 ($2,254,155) on a foot race. The *Colorado Springs Gazette* did not dispute the event took place but expressed disbelief Lory had lost such a large sum of money.[19] Further investigation confirmed the gang had been behind a fight held in the mountains north of Colorado City for $3,000 when the city hosted "the biggest and smoothest bunch of confidence men" that ever met west of the Mississippi. No amount was too small or too large for the bunch, and they had made a fortune from tourists until police intervened. "The stars of the profession," the *Gazette* marveled, "were numbered among the gang."[20] Even far from home, Boatright's notoriety affected the local Democratic Party's fortunes.

The defeat suffered by Democratic candidates at the recent special election in Webb City, Webb City citizen "Old Time Democrat" reasoned, was the result of the "deplorable condition of affairs in this county. The people are tired of the rule of harlot. They stand for law and order and the suppression of vice and crime." He quoted a speech William H. Phelps gave that summer at the Jasper County Democratic convention in which he declared, "The men of this county are tired of their wives and daughters, on their way to church, being jostled from sidewalks by the blear-eyed drunken loafers congregated in front of Sunday saloons. They will support tickets made by men who fear God and love home, but will not support tickets made by gamblers, pimps, and pugilists." The writer lamented two weeks earlier he was standing on Joplin's Main Street when a "drunken, brazen, disgusting prostitute stood in front of a window in the third story of the House of Lords as naked as when she came into the world, in plain view of the hundreds of people walking up and down the street, and not an officer with the courage or decency to prevent it." He described what happened next:

> Ladies were obliged to turn their faces or leave the street; and I am told the proprietor of the [Joplin Hotel] cannot assign a lady a front room because of the character of the occupants in the building across the street. Sodom and Gomorrah were never sunk as deep in the depths of infamy and vice as this, and the prayers of the wives and mothers of Joplin will be answered in November. The mills of the gods grind slowly, but they grind exceeding fine.

He ended his missive with a plea: "Every night of the week, and every week of the year the rattle of the faro chip and the spin of the wheel of fortune can be heard, and no officer will suppress it . . . If it is to be tolerated in this county, let it be done under a Republican and not under a Democratic administration."[21] His plea doubtlessly encouraged hopeful Republicans.

Editor Sewall of the *Evening Press* published a scathing rebuke of Barbee's Democratic *Globe*. The Hobbs trial confirmed Buckfoot's headquarters were in a room above Charley A. Parker's 16 to 1 Saloon. Sewall sourly noted the *Globe* should take note Parker had signed all Buckfoot's bonds. Parker's saloon was permitted to run from May 1, 1901, to May 1, 1902, without paying county and state license fees. It also served as the headquarters of two associate justices of the county court. "Why?" he asked before dryly observing, "This 16 to 1 saloon is run on Allen street, within a block of the office of the assisting prosecuting attorney, to whom tax payers pay one hundred dollars a month to do that business. It is also the home of the sheriff." Sewell asked if it was all just a strange coincidence. He concluded, "Every person within ten miles of Webb City seems to have known of the outrageous robberies except the officers, whose duty it was to arrest and prosecute the offenders. This is Barbeeism as applied in Webb City.[22]

Two days later Sewall exasperatedly reported Boatright, who had a warrant in the sheriff's possession, had arrived in Carthage accompanied by Charley Parker. He strode into the courtroom with a lordly bearing and shook hands with Judge Hugh Dabbs and other court officers. Buckfoot, who stood an estimated five feet, eleven inches tall and weighed around 225 pounds, sported his trademark heavy black moustache. Neatly attired, he wore large diamonds and a confident smile. He paid a $6,000 bond arranged by Dabbs and immediately approved by Sheriff Rich.

Judge Dabbs then left with Boatright's attorney, George Booth, to campaign for the upcoming election. Sewall demanded, "If [the gang] are not favorites of the officers, why, after they have trifled with the court so often, their bonds are not fixed at such sums that they would be required to appear, or in failing to fine them, go to jail. They are not entitled to any more consideration by the court than the St. Louis boodlers, whose bonds were fixed at twenty-five thousand dollars."[23] Voters, he contended, should expel their current county officials in the next election.

The negative press may have inspired judicial action. Having forfeited a $1,000 bond, Bert Bromley was arrested and the amount raised to $5,000. Bromley promptly paid it with James Gammon, one of Robert Boatright's neighbors, and Charley Parker as bondsmen. A few days later Ed Ellis—in high spirits after recently touring Colorado, Nebraska, and Illinois—was arrested for the same reason. Judge Joseph Perkins admonished him for forfeiting bond in Division Two court. He assigned Ellis a $6,000 bond to ensure his presence at trial.[24]

In the run-up to the November 1902 election the *Carthage Evening Press* published cartoons attacking Gilbert Barbee, Robert Boatright, and local corruption. In one, "Jasper County's Dumb Show," law enforcement officers were depicted with their backs to Barbee as he collected sacks of money from a gambler, Sunday saloon keeper, bawdy-house operator, and fake foot racer.[25] Another, "A Joplin Chart That Speaks for Itself," provided an intricate layout of Barbee's property at Fourth and Main Streets, including the *Joplin Globe* and the House of Lords. The caption explained Barbee and Daniel Collins owned 85 percent of the *Globe's* stock and almost four hundred feet in the business block. It also informed readers, "Promiscuous rooming over Globe office and City Hall offices. Stairway between Globe office and City Hall leads up to hallway in 2nd story which leads to back end and into blind bridge across alley into Gambling Hell in 2nd story of House of Lords, and 3rd floor of House of Lords occupied by Painted Women and Bird Cages, Pet Dogs, etc. Blind bridge or passage over alley is within 25 feet of Y.M.C.A. rooms."[26]

The *Joplin News-Herald* joined in denouncing Buckfoot and Barbee. The paper thundered, "CONNIVING WITH CRIME. No Democratic official so far has reported the collection of those forfeited Buckfoot bonds, and none of the gang have been sent to jail on account of the bonds being forfeited several weeks ago. Boss rule has brought about a nice state

THE LOAD IS TOO MUCH FOR THE DEMOCRATIC DONKEY.

Barbee's outsized influence on Jasper County's Democratic Party had negative implications for the party and its candidates; here a donkey symbolizing the Democratic Party struggles under the weight of Gilbert Barbee, Robert Boatright, and politicians J. A. Ristine and Henry Adkins. It bears the brand of the 16 to 1 Saloon on its hindquarter. *Carthage Evening Press.*

A JOPLIN CHART THAT SPEAKS FOR ITSELF.

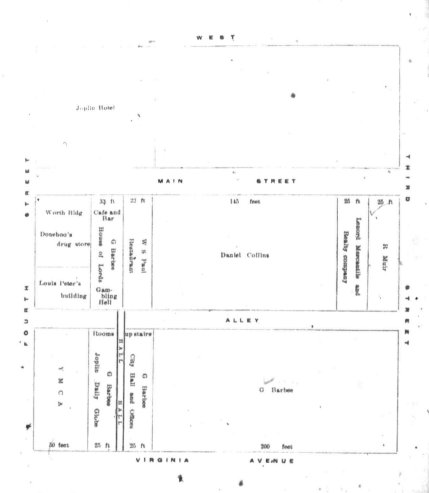

Barbee and Collins own 85 per cent of stock in Globe.   Barbee and Collins own 395 feet out of 600 feet frontage in block.   Globe owners could by this showing stop gambling and other vices in the block.
Promiscuous rooming over Globe office and City Hall offices.   Stairway between Globe office and City Hall leads up to hallway in 2nd story which leads to back end and into blind bridge across alley into Gambling Hell in 2nd story of House of Lords, and 3rd floor of House of Lords occupied by Painted Women and Bird Cages, Pet Dogs, etc.   Blind bridge or passage over alley is within 25 feet of Y. M. C. A. rooms.

Gilbert Barbee's ownership of the House of Lords and the *Joplin Globe*—as well as his association with Robert Boatright—led his political and publishing rivals to attack him. The *Carthage Evening Press* published this rendering of Barbee's *Globe* and House of Lords buildings—taking care to note the walkway connecting the two—to visually link him to crime and corruption in Joplin. *Carthage Evening Press.*

of affairs in Jasper county." The paper observed, "The Globe's wail for Democrats to get out and vote is a call from Boss Barbee for action. The apathy among Democrats is appalling to the boss and the state house ring."[27] A few days later it chided, "THE TWO WON'T WORK. You can't lay claim to good citizenship and at the same time vote for a party whose leaders protect and shield such characters as the Buckfoot gang."[28]

Other critics in the local press redoubled their attacks. William Sewall of the *Carthage Evening Press* again asked why Charley Parker operated his saloon without paying the requisite fees. "Was it for the love of Buckfoot or was there boodle in it," he wondered. He ran more anti-Barbee and anti-Buckfoot cartoons, including one of Barbee walking a Senate candidate on a leash in front of the House of Lords as Boatright and others cheered. Yet another depicted an exhausted Democratic donkey struggling under the weight of Barbee, Boatright, and two Democratic candidates. The *Carterville Republican* asked if citizens would vote the Republican ticket or the Barbee ticket. The election would decide if the county's better element would prevail or if the criminal classes would control the county's affairs. "Buckfootism would be in full bloom today," it stated, "but for the uprising of the people against the swindle, which made it imperative for the officers to act . . . The time has come to bury Barbeeism out of sight, both the carcass and the smell."[29] The *Neosho Miner & Mechanic* reminded readers the Newton County Democratic party and Fifteenth Congressional District were under Barbee's control, "a man whose place of business in Joplin, comprises a saloon on the first floor, gambling house on the second floor, and house of prostitution on the third floor. How can the decent, Christian democrats of Newton county support a ticket dominated by a man of such unsavory reputation?"[30]

The day before the election, the *Globe* guffawed, William H. Phelps, Barbee's Democratic nemesis, put in a day's work begging Democrats to vote the Republican ticket. Phelps, who controlled Republican head-quarters in Carthage, was working to defeat Barbee's Senate candidate, former governor William Joel Stone.[31] The *Joplin News-Herald* urged readers, "Don't forget Buckfoot. Vote against Buckfoot. Vote against boss rule. When you go vote, don't forget Buckfoot. Buckfoot will be at Webb City tomorrow working for the Democratic ticket." It sassed, "At last the city jail is full of street walkers. They will probably be kept there until after tomorrow's election. Vote against street walkers."[32]

Election Day was a grim affair as a steady downpour greeted voters. Had carriages not been provided at all polling precincts, turnout would have been light. There was little joking and almost no betting at polling places, with partisans of both tickets working cordially side by side.

BOSS BARBEE TAKES HIS CANDIDATE FOR STATE SENATOR OUT FOR AN AIRING.

Public outcry over prostitution, gambling, and corruption were on the minds of Jasper County citizens thanks to a vibrant local partisan press who connected crime with Democratic boss Gilbert Barbee and his House of Lords. Barbee is shown parading a political candidate on a leash before a saloonkeeper, a gambler, a swindler, and Robert Boatright. *Carthage Evening Press.*

Politicians crowded the county clerk's office as election judges carried in sacks of ballots to be tallied. Phone calls back and forth across the county forecasted a Republican victory. In the early afternoon "Webb City, the Democratic stronghold of the county," reported "a standoff in the result or possibly a small Democratic majority." A few hours later, Webb City conceded a Republican victory. Boatright's stronghold had fallen.[33]

William Phelps and his allies' efforts paid off. The *Globe* howled, "TREASON DEFEATS DEMOCRACY. Phelps and His Lieutenants Betray Their Party and Openly Fight for Republican Success." Republicans now held the offices of the prosecuting attorney, sheriff, recorder, collector, circuit clerk, treasurer, public administrator, county clerk, coroner, probate judge, and two state representatives. The Democratic defeat was due to the "treason which has existed within the party lines in the Eastern district. The republican campaign mangers formed a close combine with the disaffected elements of the democratic party and by this merger a majority was rolled up in the Eastern district that the regular party vote elsewhere in the county was unable to counteract." Unable to cede control of power to Gilbert Barbee's Democrats in western Jasper County, Phelps and his fellow Carthage Democrats boasted "they would knife the ticket from top to bottom" and made good on their threat. No mention was made of the possibility that some disaffected Democrats may have swung Republican because they were tired of county officials ignoring vice and crime. Unfazed, the *Globe* vowed the Jasper County Democratic party would emerge stronger and better equipped to fight future battles having discovered who its enemies were. Boss Barbee would not forget the men who betrayed the Democratic Party.[34]

The *Globe* sourly spat, "The republicans have won. They did it because they were assisted by the corrupt railroad lobby and its king, who succeeded in leading most of the democrats in Carthage over into the republican camp. It is much more a victory for Bill Phelps than it is for the republican party, but even for him it is the traitor's victory." It castigated several local Democratic officials for supporting the Republican ticket after having been elected by Democrats. Cornelius Roach of the *Jasper County Democrat* "supported the republican ticket while he was running what he alleged was a democratic paper."[35]

Elated by the Republican sweep, the *Joplin News-Herald* credited the Republican victory to labor siding with the party and Democrats who resolved to stop voting for the continuation of Buckfootism and political corruption in Jasper County.[36] It was "a newspaper fight. There were no speeches made on the part of the Republicans, the friends of decency depending largely on the press of the county to carry on the campaign against the Globe and its vulnerable methods." The issue was simple. The election was a referendum on the struggle of honest government against boss rule. Now that the shouting was over, newly elected officials were expected to stop protecting Buckfoot and other criminals.[37] In the next campaign, the *Carterville Republican* remarked, citizens would not have to fight prostitutes, gamblers, or fake foot racers because the climate would no longer agree with them.[38]

Phelps partisan Cornelius Roach—a future Missouri secretary of state—offered his analysis of why the Democrats lost the election: the *Joplin Globe*, party boss Gilbert Barbee, and Barbee's much publicized association with gambling, prostitution, and corruption. He also hypothesized voters "refused to be bossed and terrorized by any dictator." Roach reasoned the election results were not a Republican victory. Instead, citizens rebuked the evils of Barbeeism: one-man domination of civil government and the protection of the criminal class.[39]

The *Webb City Sentinel* memorialized Barbee's defeat:

> Here lies the body of Barbee, the boss,
> He's dead as 'Old Heck' and it's not any loss,
> He'll be missed by the gamblers, footracers and thugs,
> The bawdy house keepers, prize fighting pugs.

Departed this life in the prime of his political corruption on Nov. 4th 1902, Gilbert Barbee, age uncertain, character questionable, ability for good nit. His death was due to slow consumption due to exposure to the Republican party, independent and decent democrats.

The deceased was a devoted member of the "Grab it all" gang and the leading spirit in the "Gobble up lodge." He died as he lived, rotten to the core.

He was a kind and affectionate spouse to the lower element, a thoughtful brother to the Buckfoot gang . . .

. . . The pall bearers will be the saloon keepers of Joplin, the House of Lord's bar which he loved so dearly leading by a neck. Chief mourners, the gamblers and ladies of the 'red light district.' The Irish wake will be held at the House of Lord's gambling den; Whirlwind Graham, the wonderful word whizzer, will speak. He will be buried in the grave he digged. *REQUIESCAT IN PACE.*

> Thou art gone but not forgotten,
> All thy deeds so foul and rotten,
> Live to make thy memory cuss'd.

With the election over, it must have disappointed anti-Buckfoot denizens when the US Court of Appeals dismissed charges against James Stewart of using the mails to defraud Jonathan Davis.[40]

In the wake of the election that sought to rid Jasper County of corruption, John W. Cobb arrived in the Ozarks from Texas. He had already lost $10,000 to the gang in Salt Lake City, Utah. Despite realizing he had been swindled, Cobb agreed to a rematch for $17,000. Cobb was accompanied by roper Irven E. Johnson; the two men had known each other for almost two decades.[41] Aurora, a small mining town roughly fifty miles southeast of Webb City, was selected to avoid scrutiny. George Ryan, George Thompson, and Roger H. Williams were already waiting. Before they left for the race a few miles outside of town, they told Cobb he should leave his gun. He refused. When they stopped their hacks to lay out a makeshift racetrack, Cobb picked up as many rocks as he could to avoid a repeat of what happened in Utah.[42]

As the string for the finish line was unspooled, Williams asked for Cobb's gun, saying he was comfortable shooting it since he had used it in Utah. Cobb hesitated. When Williams offered to bet forty dollars against the eighteen-dollar gun, Cobb handed it over. He later remarked, "I thought Johnson was in better shape than I was and if there was any murdering to be done, that he had better do it."[43] Almost immediately after Williams fired Cobb's gun, the Texan knew he had been swindled a second time. After returning home, the next time Cobb saw Johnson was when the latter was in handcuffs after he was indicted for larceny by the Polk County, Texas, grand jury.[44] After Cobb's race, some of the gang departed Jasper County for Hot Springs, Arkansas, where they skinned Nebraska farmer Joel Barto for $4,500 on a fixed wrestling match.[45] After Barto departed Hot Springs so, too, did the men who fleeced him.

As Christmas 1902 approached, the gang faced an increasing number of lawsuits. Boatright's holiday spirits may have dimmed when the Little Rock *Arkansas Gazette* trumpeted, "Officers Probe $12,000 Foot Race. Hot Springs Authorities Still Rounding Up Suspects."[46] The gang had stumbled, but now the question was: Would it fall?

7

"THE CENTER OF GRAVITY"

—*Carthage Evening Press*, MARCH 20, 1903

Howard Bland was a perfect mark. An Ohio native, he had settled in Texas in 1878. He held extensive land holdings, raised sheep and cattle, and cultivated cotton. Bland helped organize one of the first banks in Taylor, Texas, and served as director of two others. He was a partner in a flour mill and actively involved in the town's civic affairs. Bland also loved thoroughbred horseracing.[1] It was no wonder, then, his friend Valentine Hafner, a jeweler in Hillsboro, Texas, told him about a foot race in Hot Springs, Arkansas. Hafner, an alcoholic who favored whiskey, was under the treatment of Dr. Robert E. L. Goddard, who worked as a roper for Boatright. When Hafner told Bland about the race, the banker was all in. The two men journeyed to Hot Springs for what Hafner cackled was a "dead sure thing."[2]

Nestled in the Ouachita Mountains, Hot Springs began in the antebellum era as a collection of ramshackle bathhouses scattered along a series of thermal springs. During Reconstruction the rough settlement transformed into a city of handsome Victorian bathhouses and elegant hotels that attracted clientele from across the country. It had become by the turn of the twentieth century a popular resort city with a reputation for illegal gambling; sports, grifters, and confidence men negotiated with local authorities for influence and access. It was the perfect place for a con.

Bland lost $12,000. Following news of the race, Hot Springs police officers and Garland County deputies spread out through the city to arrest Buckfoot members Roger Williams, Lucius Hindman, Robert E. L. Goddard, George Ryan, and William Nelson, all of whom promptly retained the law firm of Wood & Henderson to represent them. A local woman known as Big Ada gave $5,000 to the firm's attorneys, one of whom subsequently signed a bond for Williams. Before he could be released, however, prosecutor William H. Martin obtained an attachment for the $5,000 and had Big Ada arrested. She refused to tell authorities where she obtained the money and was bailed out of jail. The *Jasper County Democrat* commented, "[Williams] knows the South and Southwest thoroughly and is a smooth individual. He has not been seen in Joplin or vicinity since prosecution was commenced in the courts against the Buckfoot crowd."[3] An additional $35,000 of property belonging to the foot racers was attached by the local court.[4]

Bland slipped out of his hotel room, paid his bill, and left town. Once his absence became known, officers sent telegrams alerting authorities to arrest him. Garland County sheriff Robert L. Williams and Hot Springs police chief Thomas F. Teague were eager to apprehend Bland because without his assistance it would be difficult, if not impossible, to prosecute the gang. Bland's friend Hafner was arrested before he, too, could escape.[5] Hindman was subsequently convicted of grand larceny because he won diamonds and cash from Hafner on a race, but the Arkansas Supreme Court reversed and remanded his conviction.[6]

At the preliminary hearing for the foot racers under arrest in Hot Springs, the judge bound them over to the grand jury on a charge of grand larceny. A ledger in the gang's possession revealed their finances. The top of each page showed the victim's name, how much he lost, and how the funds had been distributed among the gang. One estimate surmised the gang had made $100,000 ($3,467,932) in a month.[7] A St. Louis paper mused, "The sprinters of the eighties, the Collinses, Gibsons, Mouitons, Ecks, etc., pulled off many a sweet job, but they were all fast men, who could break records when they had to. Then the most anyone ever heard of them cleaning up on any one race was some $22,000. The Hot Springs men could not run a lick on earth. Just the same they managed to get men to bet three times as much as the old fast men of the previous decade." Men who knew the crowd said they "were wonderfully persuasive talkers," especially the Honey Grove Kid, who was "credited with spending $1,500 and traveling 15,000 miles with one man" to get $20,000."[8] Yet their smooth talk could only go so far, especially with the courts.

On December 15, 1902, Judge Jacob Trieber issued an order in federal court restraining certain Hot Springs parties from releasing funds in their possession belonging to Roger H. Williams. Having received a judgment in their favor in Jasper County earlier in the year, St. Louis merchants Lang and Becker were after Williams's assets. They asserted in their involuntary bankruptcy filing that Williams had concealed $50,000 from his creditors.[9] Williams was not the only one in financial trouble; Robert Boatright was adjudicated a bankrupt in federal court on December 22, 1902.[10]

As New Year's Eve approached, Williams appeared before Judge Trieber in the US District Court for the Eastern District of Arkansas in

Little Rock. Attorneys Hiram Currey, John Halliburton, and William H. Martin employed multiple lines of questioning in their attempt to make Williams disclose where he had concealed money in Hot Springs. Ably represented by Wilson E. Hemingway of Little Rock, Ralph Davis of Memphis, and James B. Wood of Hot Springs, Williams was no ordinary witness and deftly parried the prosecution's queries. Williams acknowledged he paid a third party $1,200 to ensure he was not accosted while in Hot Springs.[11] In the Missouri Ozarks, business continued.

The year 1903 began with an inauspicious start for gambling houses in Jasper County when new prosecutor Andrew H. Redding ordered them to close after promising to enforce the law. One gambler said he would not even risk a game of pinochle.[12] His fear was unwarranted. A few weeks later Joplin saloons were open on Sunday as some of the more brazen saloonmen sold liquor over improvised bars. The *Jasper County Democrat* warned if Redding did not act within a week, every saloon would reopen; there were rumors gamblers and rowdies had already cut deals with county authorities.[13]

While some worried the rule of law was being undermined, the courts were upholding it. Lightning rod salesman William Barker vowed to spend his last penny to send the gang to the penitentiary. He had seen "Boatright's book showing the receipts and divisions of their foot racing grafts for the last six months" and estimated the gang had won a million dollars. Barker had pursued Leon Lozier and Ed Moore, the sprinters who defrauded him and fellow victim Charles Gregory, to Denver and had caused their arrest. Boatright sent a detective to offer Barker money to get him to ease up, but the Iowan refused as he was "not after money, but blood."[14]

Barker's zeal for justice was rewarded. Despite allegations of attempted jury tampering, Lozier and Moore were found guilty in Council Bluffs, Iowa.[15] Upon hearing the verdict, Lozier looked a decade older. Moore appeared unfazed, but then his face darkened.[16] Each man received the maximum sentence of three years in the state penitentiary.[17] Upon learning of their conviction, the tiny *Chamberlin (SD) Democrat* grumbled, "Chamberlin had a visit from [Lozier] which is well remembered by old timers, while at Sioux Falls the faker only escaped lynching by the convenient passing of a freight train. He has still more coming to him than was awarded him by that Iowa judge."[18] When their conviction was later reversed and remanded by the Iowa Supreme Court, Pottawattamie County prosecutor William Killpack dropped the original charges.[19] Lozier and Moore's chieftain, however, faced desperate odds.

Robert Boatright was a wanted man. Victim Frank Lory had swore out a warrant and promised a substantial reward for the bunco king's arrest. When the law came for him, he was in Monett, an Ozark railroad town forty miles east of Joplin.[20] Within days of being apprehended, Boatright, Ed Ellis, and Bert Bromley were tried in Lawrence County on a change of venue from Jasper County. Many of the region's best lawyers arrayed for battle; the prosecution and defense teams each consisted of six attorneys. Just before the trial began someone broke into Jasper County court stenographer Annie Campbell's hotel room. They stole her handwritten notes of Ed Ellis's testimony from Currey's suit against the Joplin Savings Bank that were to be used as evidence. The thief, however, overlooked Campbell's typed transcript of the notes.[21]

On Wednesday, March 18, 1903, Judge Henry C. Pepper rapped his gavel and the trial began. In the midst of it all, Boatright was "the center of gravity."[22] A reporter favorably described Boatright as a fine-looking man who made friends with ease. Victim testimony about the gang's methods led one paper to marvel, "The plan of campaign of the gang was worthy of a Napoleon." Whenever a state's witness "scored a strong point for the prosecution" the courtroom reverberated with cheers. The defense did not call any witnesses, nor did they put their clients on the stand. Telegrams poured in with the news of Lozier and Moore's conviction in Council Bluffs. "This news," a Mt. Vernon paper confided, "while probably never known to the jury, discouraged the defense and encouraged the prosecution."[23]

On Friday, March 20, 1903, Judge Pepper issued his instructions to the jury: they could find the defendants guilty of obtaining money under false pretenses or grand larceny. The jurors left the courtroom at 7:20 p.m. and returned twenty minutes later. Boatright, Ellis, and Bromley entered the courtroom followed by a flood of anxious onlookers. As the clerk read the verdict, half the crowd rose from their seats as law enforcement officers from other jurisdictions stood ready to arrest the trio in the event of an acquittal. When the guilty verdict was announced, there was an eruption of surprised and satisfied cheers from the audience. For the first time throughout the tedious trial Boatright, Ellis, and Bromley looked crestfallen. Each man received the maximum sentence of three years in the state penitentiary. Pepper discharged the jury and ordered the sheriff to take the prisoners into custody. The defense's motion for a new trial was denied; they vowed to appeal to the Missouri Supreme Court. Judge Pepper assigned Boatright a $7,500 bond and Bromley and Ellis each received $5,000 bonds.[24]

Boatright's change of venue strategy had failed and his hope for a hung jury went unfulfilled. The *Carthage Evening Press* gloated, "There Is No Fake in This." The gang had made the fight of their lives and lost. After years of stymied civil suits, it was the gang's first criminal conviction.[25] Now, the *Webb City Sentinel* opined, "It looks very much like the 'colts' will have a free ride to the Capitol and stripes, molasses and corn bread at the state's expenses."[26] Gilbert Barbee's *Joplin Globe* said little; he likely knew Buckfoot's reign was over.[27]

Civil litigation had depleted Boatright's finances, and he may have been unwilling to cosign his bonds, because Alfred Carter, one of Boatright's loyal bondsmen, withdrew his name from Boatright's bond.[28] Boatright, Bromley, and Ellis were unable to raise the $17,500 to satisfy their bonds and remained in jail at Mt. Vernon. Boatright would not put up the money, he said, because he did not want it to get attached as had happened to Roger Williams in Hot Springs. Charley Parker had been signing bonds on the strength of gang property titled in Parker's name, but he had exhausted all financial resources.[29]

On April Fools' Day, Jasper County sheriff James Owen caught wind Boatright was preparing to leave Mt. Vernon to give bail in nearby Cassville. Suspecting Boatright would try to evade arrest, Owen hurried there. He found Charley Parker and Neosho saloonkeeper Elwin C. "Baldy" Hearrell paying Boatright's bond. Owen then arrested Boatright on two charges of grand larceny. A *Carthage Evening Press* reporter found the foot race chieftain at the Jasper County jail wearing a dark gray suit and hat. Judge Perkins, Sheriff Owen explained, would likely arrange a substantial bond for Boatright, who was already constrained by multiple bonds—$5,000 in Jasper County; $7,500 at Cassville; $5,000 at Fort Scott, Kansas; and $2,500 in Kansas City ($668,195). "What a fall! The mighty prince of confidence in the bull ring with junk thieves and peace disturbers," the reporter hooted.[30]

The following day when the reporter returned, Boatright was sitting on the jail's doorstep playing with the sheriff's four-year-old son; the swindler teasingly called the child a "pretty bad actor." The reporter asked county jailer Frank Hedrick if Boatright was paying for special privileges. Hedrick flinched; "I don't know a thing about it," he replied. The forty prisoners and trusties, the reporter discovered, "are already won over to the silver lined prince of graft. He is hailed as a mighty good fellow prisoner and lives in somewhat of luxury at the jail." A jail trusty divulged, "He's got $70,000 and carries a roll around here with him as big as your leg. He's going to have the best that money will buy and you may gamble on that." Unlike other prisoners, Boatright slept in the jailer's office. For breakfast, Boatright received a platter of fried eggs, breakfast bacon, stewed apples, hot biscuits, butter, and coffee. The other prisoners received gravy, chunks of punk (bread), boiled bull's neck, and black coffee. They were given two meals a day, but Boatright received three, including everything the sheriff had to eat. He was permitted to leave the jail, but never left without permission. US Commissioner David Roper confirmed he had issued two warrants for Boatright on charges made by Hiram Currey.[31] Meanwhile, Boatright's attorneys sought to free him on bond.[32]

A *Jasper County Democrat* reporter was rebuffed one morning after attempting to interview Boatright but found the footrace chieftain in a more talkative mood that afternoon. "Husky in build," Boatright "has keen eyes and in conversation he shows no small amount of intelligence." Lounging in the jailer's office, Boatright told the reporter despite losing his case that he could not complain. His persecutors had used the criminal court to collect a personal debt and that if witnesses had been truthful, he would not have been convicted. He added, "It is nothing less than rank extortion—blackmail. We were all gambling and because I was the heavy winner they wanted me to 'shake down.' "[33] Two weeks later, still stymied by the financial constraints of multiple bonds, Boatright had been unable to make bail.

On April 15, 1903, as Thomas Gilyard, a Black migrant worker, was dragged from the Joplin city jail and lynched, Boatright was safe in the county jail at Carthage. He was in an amiable mood when an *Evening Press* reporter spoke with him. Asked about the lynching, Boatright shrugged, "It's an awful thing, but what are you going to do about it?" Queried about his future, Boatright responded he would soon take care of his bond after some old cases were dropped. He added, "Of course, I suppose as fast as one charge against me is met and disposed, they will get up another one. They will persecute me to the limit I guess, for I have absolutely refused to 'shake down.' That's all it amounts to—persecution— for that's what I call it when a set of lawyers tell a man that he has either got to shake down to them or go to the penitentiary."[34]

He continued, "Why, I have a letter in my pocket now from a Webb City lawyer offering a compromise if I will divide up. But I'll never do it—I wouldn't if I could. The biggest sucker play I ever made was to give up $2,000 in settlement of one of those foot race claims—but my lawyers thought maybe that would settle things for good. But that was a sucker play for the reason that—now for instance, if I am playing you and I find that you will shake down, I naturally keep on playing you as long as I think you have any money." Boatright conceded he was broke and would serve his time. He snorted, "There have been a lot better men than me in the penitentiary, and there'll be better men go there after I come out." He went on: "The point is just this—the state of Missouri has never been once offended by me. It's Currey and Halliburton who are offended—Currey because he got the worst of it in a little $500 suit. My poor old father is just worried to death over this, and is dying now at his home in Webb City. Thanks to the kindness of Sheriff Owen I have been permitted to visit him a time or two since I have been here, going over in company with Jailer Jackson."[35]

Boatright continued as the reporter took notes. "[The lawyers] take these cases against me for one-third of all I'll give up and if I don't give up I must go to the pen. It's persecution because I always gambled fair—of course it was gambling," he admitted. "I frequently lost, but when I saw I was up against a tough gang I didn't play sucker—I played it cautiously so that I needn't lose too much. But there's one thing about these footraces—you'll notice there never was anything wrong about them till the other fellow's man lost the race. Up to that time he thought he was putting me for a sucker. When he found out that he was caught at his own game then he was outraged and his lawyers are offended. It's true that I sent out emissaries to induce bettors to visit Webb City, but they always came with the inward guilty intention of defeating me by some fake scheme in which they believed that they had the advantage of me."[36]

He concluded, "Another peculiar feature of this business is the conduct of many small newspaper men throughout this part of the country. They had a habit of writing to me and enclosing manuscript for a certain article they had prepared against 'Buckfoot.' Of course they didn't want to run it if there was any injustice to me in it, and would I kindly look the article over? Then the writer would go on to say that he represented a half score or more of newspapers, and that the article was worth $20 more or less a column to have it published, etc., etc., etc. Well, you see the point, but pshaw! I never gave any attention to such things—that would be playing sucker again. But I never did holler because I got the worst of it, and I am not crying now. They can send me to the penitentiary but not a cent can they get me to shake down."[37]

To pass the time in jail, Boatright introduced athletics to his fellow inmates, including boxing, shotput, and calisthenics. One evening he boxed "Jack the Ripper," "a bad negro from Joplin." Donning gloves, the

two giants came together in a friendly go and sparred for a time cleverly. Before the third round the fight became spirited and heavy strokes were passed, the encouragement of the on-looking trusties augmenting the heat of the mill as it progressed. A number of stinging blows carried the battle into a desperate phase and the men were soon mixed in hammer and tongs style, Boatright showing the more skill and continually remaining cool and collected. It was in the fourth round, after a fast fight, that 'Jack the Ripper,' made a fierce attempt at a knockout, although showing bad from fatigue and the rain of blows his opponent had given him. Boatright was equal to the onslaught and catching the colored fighter squarely under the jaw with an uppercut felled him.

Fellow trusties revived Jack and he promptly removed his gloves.[38] A few days later Boatright was free after Charley Parker and James Gammon each provided $5,000 on his behalf.[39]

After reading Boatright's interview, victim John Owen—who was swindled with Monroe Griffith in 1900—told the *Carthage Evening Press*, "The [Exchange] bank's attorney came to us last night and acknowledged that there was no getting around this case, and wanted to know if we would compromise with the bank. We told him yes, for the cash, but this morning the attorney went into court, advanced the excuse of President Joe Stewart's broken leg and got the case continued. Of course they're doing this to wear us out." He vowed, "We are going to send Jim Stewart to the penitentiary along with Buckfoot."[40] Stewart had other plans.

James Stewart and the Exchange Bank of Webb City paid Monroe Griffith $4,000 to dismiss his civil suit.[41] The banker denied making a deal with the Kansan. When a *Globe* reporter questioned Griffith's attorney John Halliburton about the deal, he refused to talk. Griffith told a reporter, "There is not much to tell. I was paid $4,000 with the understanding that I would not hold J. P. Stewart or the Exchange bank responsible for any money I had lost to the Boatright gang, and the case will be dismissed at my expense." Doubts emerged if the criminal case against Stewart and others in Lamar would come to trial as several attorneys believed it was the strongest case filed against Stewart and the bank. Perhaps Gilbert Barbee and the *Globe* were trying to dissuade the victims with pending cases to settle.[42]

The *Globe* exulted when Griffith did not appear in court in Lamar for the criminal case against James Stewart. At the insistence of Jasper County assistant prosecutor Harry Green, the trial judge waited to call the case a second time. Victim Jonathan Davis vowed he would get Griffith to appear in court. Davis visited Griffith in person and later sent a telegram to Green saying Griffith would be in court. When Davis and Griffith arrived in Kansas City on their way to Lamar, they met another victim who had declared war against Buckfoot months earlier. The man— Iowan John Black—warned Griffith not to go and, taking him aside, "talked long and earnestly with him." Griffith subsequently announced he was not going to Lamar. Incredulous, Davis pulled Griffith away from

Black. As they started to board the train, Griffith disappeared.[43] The case against Stewart was dismissed and confirmed the theory that the criminal case was brought solely to compel the resolution of Griffith's civil case. Assistant prosecutor Green expressed his belief that Black, despite being "for a short time one of the most active prosecutors of the bunch," was now employed by Buckfoot.[44]

Boatright may have been able to convince Black to switch sides, but he likely never imagined that an attorney would betray him. One of the gang's attorneys, Ralph Davis, was on the run after being indicted for perjury and embezzling $12,500 from Boatright in Hot Springs. Officers soon arrested him in St. Louis.[45] By the time Davis arrived in Hot Springs, the Honey Grove Kid had been convicted of grand larceny and given a five-year sentence in the state penitentiary. The Kid's associates then offered to plead guilty if given the minimum one-year penitentiary sentence, but the judge refused. They requested and received a change of venue.[46] Davis was lucky his father provided his $6,000 bond; his former clients had hoped to "handle him roughly" upon his arrival at the jail.[47]

Although Boatright may not have known it when he hired him, Ralph Davis was crooked as a dog's hind leg. During his trial, Davis explained Boatright—accompanied by Davis's client Michael Haggerty—had visited him at his Memphis office. He accepted Boatright's offer of $10,000 plus $2,500 for expenses to represent the foot racers under arrest in Hot Springs. Davis denied Boatright's attorney George Clay demanded he return the money and also denied telling Clay, "Yes I have got it, and I am going to keep it. Those sons of bitches in Hot Springs are going to the penitentiary, and I am going to keep it."[48] Hot Springs attorney James Wood, who also represented the gang, testified he and Davis agreed Davis would deposit the money with the county treasurer to secure their clients release, but Davis did not comply.[49] The jury found Davis not guilty.[50]

Intrigue surrounding the gang in Arkansas did not end with Davis's case. Garland County sheriff Robert Williams told the Hot Springs press the gang had plotted to assassinate him and prosecutor William Martin. The plan was to have been carried out during the past winter, but the gang changed their minds and decided to enact their scheme when the two men visited the St. Louis World's Fair. The unnamed assassins remained at large, but Roger H. Williams—who had been free on bond—was rearrested.[51]

At seven o'clock on the morning of June 28, 1903, Williams rose to shave in his jail cell. He was stooped over the washbasin, face covered in lather, when fellow prisoner James Dougherty tried to slash Williams's throat with a razor, but the confidence man's hunched position protected his neck. Undeterred, Dougherty opened an eighteen-inch gash across Williams's midsection, almost slicing his liver in half. Williams sank to the floor without making a sound. Dougherty turned to the other prisoners in the cell and waved the bloody razor at them, daring them to avenge Williams. When no one stepped forward, he lunged at Buckfoot roper Irven E. Johnson and yelled, "Beg for your life, you dog; get down upon your knees and do it." Terrified, Johnson complied. Dougherty made Johnson swear he would never testify against a man charged with a crime.

Alarmed by the commotion, Sheriff Williams, accompanied by other officers, burst into the cell. Pointing a pistol in Dougherty's face, he forced him to surrender the razor. Once the homicidal prisoner was subdued, the grievously wounded Williams was removed for medical attention. He was "cool and nervy and made a brave fight, but he died in great agony." Williams's remains were dressed in an evening suit and encased in an expensive casket before being sent to family in Louisville, Kentucky.[52] A paper there acknowledged Williams was "well known" and in his last visit home he was "in the best of spirits and health." Now his luck had run out.[53]

In the wake of Williams's death, news reports indicated no ill will existed between the two men; Williams had conducted himself quietly in jail and had even shared his catered meals with Dougherty. Some believed Dougherty, jailed for the murder of Hot Springs police officer Jack Donahue, had attacked Williams in the hope of creating the impression he was insane and thereby avoid his upcoming execution. As news of Williams's murder spread across Hot Springs, men talked of lynching Dougherty. At midnight a mob converged on the county jail. Sheriff Williams was ordering the men to go home when he was interrupted by the shrill screams of a female inmate. The sheriff ran back inside the jail to a chaotic, bloody scene. Dougherty had hammered the metal ends of his shoestrings flat, fashioned them into a crude blade, and then used one end to cut his throat. Satisfied Dougherty was dead, the mob melted away into the darkness.[54]

"HE WAS NOT DEAD <u>AT</u> ALL, WENT <u>THE</u> STORIES, BUT HAD LONG SINCE TAKEN <u>TO</u> FAR AWAY CLIMES"

—Carthage Evening Press, MAY 31, 1904

On a warm July morning in 1903 George and Neal French, armed with fishing poles, strode across their grandmother's farm west of Carthage. A branch of Pleasant Valley Creek meandered across the land with a small, shallow area that locals called the Flax Pool, and the young brothers were going to try their luck. As they approached the stream, the Frenches saw a dog sitting next to several fishing poles stuck in the bank with their lines set and in the water. The boys then noticed something in the fishing hole. Curious, they used their poles to snag and raise it, then yelled in fright when a mutilated face broke the surface. The boys sprinted to the nearest residence for help. After their father and uncle visited the scene, they called Jasper County deputy sheriff George Eldred. Eldred, in turn, notified the coroner before leaving to investigate.

Upon his arrival Eldred found a man's corpse in the creek; part of his face had been eaten by turtles. He was so disfigured, his identity remained a mystery until Webb City citizens visited the scene and recognized Bert Bromley's body. Searching the area, Eldred found Bromley's coat folded on the creek bank. On top was the dead man's pearl-handled revolver with three empty shells in it. The French brothers told Eldred that Bromley passed their grandmother's farm the previous morning. On further investigation, Eldred confirmed Bromley had taken an electric trolley car from Webb City to Lowery's Crossing and headed off on foot across the country to the Flax Pool. His friends dismissed the theory Bromley had killed himself. They believed he suffered an epileptic fit, rolled into the creek, and drowned.[1]

Bromley avoided fishing alone because he feared he might drown but had not had an episode for two years.[2] Bromley's friends, Oscar "Butch" Gammon and Joseph Fetters, said on fishing trips they had had to pull him from the water after he suffered a seizure. Both agreed "it was when he was in the vicinity of water that he was most subject" to seizure. One claimed that Bromley, during a seizure, had rolled into the water and grasped the root of an underwater plant so tight the rescuer had to uproot the plant to get Bromley to the surface.

Fred Bull, working in a field a short distance from the stream, had heard three shots the evening before Bromley was discovered. Friends surmised Bromley was either shooting at turtles or "felt that a fit was coming on and wished to give an alarm." The body of water Bromley had been fishing was no larger than an ordinary room and roughly four feet deep. The bank was angled in just the right way to make it easy for him to have rolled into the water during a seizure. Deputy Coroner Potter ruled Bromley's death accidental.[3]

Bromley had made his last public appearance in Joplin on June 20, 1903, when he refereed a baseball game between Joplin and Sedalia. Bromley's calls were suspiciously all in favor of Sedalia; the visiting team won 10–3.[4] Like Boatright, Bromley was a member of the Fraternal Order of Eagles, and after a service at the Webb City Methodist Episcopal church, the Joplin aerie carried out his funeral rites. He had been at liberty under roughly $25,000 in bonds; now his bondsmen were free from their obligations.[5]

After Bromley was laid to rest in the Webb City Cemetery, rumors ran rampant the corpse was someone else's.[6] Peck McElhaney, Bromley's brother-in-law, believed the body was that of a different man. Because the remains were in such poor condition when pulled from the creek, Bromley's relatives had not been permitted to look at them; instead, local law enforcement officials identified them.[7] As controversy over Bromley's death lingered, the *Joplin Globe* opined, "Somebody is making a desperate attempt to raise doubts in the public mind as to" the deceased's identity. Those who knew him had no doubt it was Bromley. Bromley's physician J. Albert Chenoweth—who also served as medical examiner for the Joplin Eagles aerie—had examined the body at the coroner's office. He explained, "There was a peculiar square formation of the back of his head, and the curly knot of hair on the top of his head that I suppose gave him his nickname . . . the color of his eyes . . . his stocky trunk, and bow legs, a very deep vaccination scar, and there was also a scar on his right hand" that confirmed Bromley's identity. The most conclusive proof, in Chenoweth's opinion, was the presence of Bromley's dog, who had guarded his master's body overnight.[8]

As soon as Oscar Gammon saw the distinctive scar on the inside of his friend's hand, he had no doubt Bromley was dead. He, along with other friends, had advised the family not to look at Bromley's remains, thus sparking confusion over the deceased's identity. The allegations Bromley murdered and disfigured a man to escape three years in the state penitentiary, the *Globe* huffed, were ridiculous.[9] Another paper thought southwest Missourians were right to be skeptical of anything involving the Buckfoot Gang.[10] Yet as Bromley was laid to rest, so, too, was a case against the gang in Arkansas.

In Little Rock the federal government's case against George Ryan and twenty-nine others charged with five counts of using the mails to defraud fell apart despite several damning letters the men had sent to Roger H. Williams. In one missive, defendant H. W. Kiplinger asked Williams if he was "prepared to handle parties there in the new way, and as Swain Llewellyn and myself have some parties here we think pretty well of, we thought we might be able to drift some of them down there if things are right to do business." Another defendant, Stan (presumably Garrette Stansbury), wrote "Friend Harry" to ask, "Why cant I hear from the *store*, Wrote from Elk City O.T. Got no reply. Write me at once who ever gets this and tell me if the *store is open*. Got some produce want to consign to you." A man named Dan reported in another letter, "I suppose you had about given up hopes of hearing From me But I have Been Bussy [*sic*] as hell Lost one the other Day For 15 But will be their Sunday morning [in Hot Springs] with the Goods he is a brother Elk . . . Feeling Finer than Silk." Judge Jacob Trieber found the letters showed the defendants used the mail to concoct schemes to defraud, but not for the "purpose of carrying them into effect," and that until Congress acted to prohibit the mails from being used for such purposes, the courts were powerless to act.[11]

Perhaps emboldened by the decision, Boatright taunted his enemies. He sent a large safe to his attorney George Clay on a train from Kansas City to Joplin. Its shipment did not go unnoticed by Pinkerton agents, who tipped off federal authorities. The safe, said to hold $53,000 in gold, was intercepted in Joplin after Wells Fargo received an order from Hiram Currey, attorney for the trustee of Boatright's estate, to halt delivery. As George Clay watched, the safe was seized, unloaded, and taken to the Wells Fargo office. With the assistance of Arthur E. Spencer—the referee in federal bankruptcy cases in the Joplin Division of the US District Court—Currey undertook a herculean effort to open the safe with a hammer and chisel. Tucked inside, "grinning at Currey like a skeleton from his closet was a great big buffalo chip." Awkward silence was swiftly followed by a roar of laughter as Currey left in a cold, quiet rage.[12]

Furious, Currey wrote a letter to the *Jasper County Democrat* in which he snarled, "The laugh is on me; I do not object to everybody, that can, enjoying the so-called joke; and yet, when a gang of confessed thieves are . . . are not brought before the court it becomes a serious matter." He claimed once Jasper County sheriff Owen had Boatright in custody at Carthage, he let the bunco chieftain board in hotels, have "daily visits from his concubine," and travel across the state. Boatright even answered the jail's phone and oversaw the office. When Boatright's father died, Owen let him attend the funeral, where he was seen with three confederates who had warrants out for their arrest, but no effort was made to apprehend them. Further, Currey claimed, Owen freed Boatright when he and others were about to locate $29,000 ($968,882) of the gang's illicit funds in St. Louis. US Deputy Marshal Henry Pyatt had asked Owen to tell him when Boatright was released from Owen's custody so he could serve him with warrants, but Owen did not and Boatright slipped away to the lakes of northern Wisconsin.[13]

Currey growled that the gang trying to discredit the attorneys pursuing Boatright's funds "are the same gang that tried to laugh the thefts of the 'Buckfoot gang' into respectability, who cried out its the 'Skinner getting skinned,' 'Let them alone, they are bringing money into the county,' and 'these fellows came here to rob our citizens,' etc." Currey reminded readers the gang hired a fiddler to perform "'I Have Parted with My Money and Cannot Get It Back,' for the amusement of the same class of fellows." The gang had "tried to laugh their thievery into respectability" and now "they are now trying to laugh the criminal concealment of the stolen assets into respectability." It was a felony to receive stolen property "and no number of tricks played by Clay and his associates can make it any less than a felony." Currey hissed, "I have no hesitancy in saying that the conduct of the republican sheriff towards the 'Buckfoot gang' is much more reprehensible than was the conduct of the democratic sheriff."[14] He need not have worried; the gang now had little reason to laugh.

The last of the big Jasper County Buckfoot trials was called in December 1903. The case of *State of Missouri v. James P. Stewart* involving victim Frank Youmans was dismissed, but Jonathan Davis's case against Stewart for obtaining money under false pretenses went forward.[15] If Boatright required financial assistance in the future, he would be without two of his most faithful bondsmen. Daniel Saighman had died of yellow fever in Savannah, Georgia, where he had settled after "war was waged against the gamblers" in Joplin. The *Jasper County Democrat* thought he "was probably better liked by the general public than any other man who followed that vocation."[16] Alfred Carter had succumbed to lung trouble.[17] Boatright now had fewer allies to turn to, something he needed at a time when victims were clamoring for revenge.

More troubling was a judgment against Boatright for $63,338 ($2,116,106) to attorney Frank Lindley (assignee for Frank Lory), $16,588 to John Bacon, and $20,107 to Richard Phipps in the Jackson County Circuit Court at Independence, Missouri.[18] Lory assigned his claim to Lindley because Lory had swindled the attorney and other acquaintances in Illinois on a mining venture.[19] Federal bankruptcy referee Arthur Spencer calculated $260,000 ($8,686,534) worth of claims had been filed. Many of the claimants were allegedly acting with guidance from fellow victim John Black. Whether he was acting on behalf of his own interests or those of Boatright's is unclear. Boatright's ability to influence people, one paper said in wonderment, "appears to be almost beyond the understanding of man."[20] Spencer advanced all the creditors' claims except for Frank Lory's; he received a separate hearing. Despite acknowledging claims in Jackson County Circuit Court, Boatright had not yet been served. Now, the *Globe* noted, it was up to the creditors to prove they were entitled to Boatright's money or get him to disclose his assets in court. Boatright's attorney George Clay swore his client promised to appear before Spencer and give up every cent.[21] Boatright was expected to claim assets of $100,000 and liabilities of more than $200,000.[22] Unsurprisingly he did not appear in bankruptcy court.[23] Although the truth about Boatright's funds remained unresolved, the fate of one of his confederates was sealed.

Buckfoot confederate Irven Johnson went on trial in the US District Court at Beaumont, Texas, for having used the mails to defraud John W. Cobb. The jury could not agree, and a mistrial was declared.[24] Johnson was later tried in Saline County, Arkansas, on a change of venue from Garland County; Lucius Hindman had already been convicted but was free on appeal.[25] Like the Honey Grove Kid, Johnson was convicted and sentenced to five years, but his attorneys appealed the verdict on grounds that improper evidence was admitted. Unsuccessful, Johnson was incarcerated at the Arkansas State Penitentiary.[26]

And then, things quieted down. From March until May 1904, the press was silent as Robert Boatright, Ed Ellis, and the rest of the Buckfoot Gang waited for the Missouri Supreme Court to hear their appeal. A beautiful Ozark spring prepared to give way to a sultry Missouri summer when news unexpectedly came from Kansas City that Robert Boatright was on the verge of death. "One of the most daring men in the Southwest" now weakly requested his mother after he suffered what was initially reported as a severe lung hemorrhage. Webb City physicians acquainted with Boatright cautioned in "a man of his strong physique" it might not be necessarily fatal.[27]

His mother Priscilla immediately left Webb City accompanied by 16 to 1 bartender Sam Jones.[28] Beset by numerous delays, they arrived in Kansas City in the evening. Boatright recognized them upon arrival. Although weak, he lifted his hands toward them to indicate he knew them but could not say more than a few words in a faint voice. Boatright remained semiconscious except when sleeping from the effects of medicine.[29]

Early on the evening of May 25, 1904, the 16 to 1 Saloon's phone rang; Charley Parker answered. The voice on the other end of the line—calling from Kansas City—said Boatright's doctors thought he would recover if he made it through the night. At ten o'clock the next morning, Parker received a telegram informing him Boatright had died at eleven the previous evening.[30] Fittingly a stopwatch, gymnasium set, and revolver were among the items in Boatright's possession at the time of his death.[31]

In early May Boatright had checked into the New Century Hotel under an alias. He posed as a real estate man hoping to sell a refrigerating apparatus patent. The week prior to his death Boatright suffered a serious case of pneumonia. By Sunday night he was confined to his bed and his health quickly deteriorated. Dr. Harry F. Mather was called to care for him. Only after Boatright's death was Mather told Boatright's name so he could accurately fill out the death record; the official cause of death was acute pneumonia. Boatright's bondsmen were forced to reveal his identity so they could be released from their financial obligations. It came as a shock to many that a man described as a former blacksmith of "fine physique" came to such a sudden end. After the death record was submitted to the Kansas City Board of Health, Boatright's body was removed for burial under the watchful eye of Sam Jones, Priscilla Boatright, and an unnamed woman described as his wife.[32]

Boatright's remains were delivered to his mother's home in Webb City, where friends and curious citizens paid their respects. According to Jones, Boatright did not have a hemorrhage. Instead, he strained a heart ligament while exercising and developed a blood clot in his lungs. Boatright then contracted a severe cold that turned into pneumonia. The clot, together with his weakened heart, made medical treatment more difficult than usual.[33]

Not everyone believed Boatright was dead. "Many of the dead man's friends remarked at the change in his appearance," the *Carthage Evening*

Press reported, "probably due to his long sickness and the lack of his mustache; and some of his enemies who saw the body not only remarked at the change but were ready to swear that the remains before them were not those of Robert Boatright." A story spread that the "'Buckfoot gang' had done its greatest fake." Gossip flew that the body of a man who bore some resemblance to Boatright had been procured and was "to be buried while the king of foot racers yet lived. He was not dead at all, went the stories, but had long since taken to far away climes."[34] Even the *Joplin Globe*, Buckfoot's staunch ally, commented that although most of the individuals who viewed the corpse said it was the bunco king, there were one or two close acquaintances who remarked, "Well, I could not swear that was Bob Boatright."[35]

Boatright's mother—not wanting any doubts about her son's death—let Hiram Currey select two physicians, J. Albert Chenoweth and Charles H. Craig, to confirm the corpse's identity. Prior to the funeral, Chenoweth and Craig examined the body as Currey and an unnamed friend of the deceased watched. Currey had no doubt it was Boatright after scars on the right jaw, right side of the neck, and a finger were verified.[36] After the examination concluded, the Reverend James Sullens of the Methodist Episcopal, South Church gave the funeral address. Pallbearers then loaded Boatright's casket into a hearse bound for the Webb City Cemetery. An estimated 250 Eagles from Webb City and Joplin preceded the hearse with numerous individuals in buggies and on horseback bringing up the rear of the procession. At the family mausoleum, attorney Stonewall Pritchett gave the funeral oration surrounded by impressive floral tributes, many sent by Boatright's friends in Kansas City.[37] Currey told a reporter, "No one ever need to have any doubt that it was Bob Boatright who was buried yesterday."[38]

Yet another story circulated. At the funeral Boatright's friends were told "as a strange coincidence, the supreme court, on Thursday afternoon last, just at the time Boatright was near death, had handed down a decision which declared he had been improperly convicted, and reversed the judgment of the lower court." Currey warned the story was without foundation, but it was true.[39] The Missouri Supreme Court reversed and remanded the cases against Robert Boatright, Ed Ellis, and Bert Bromley. The opinion, written by Judge James Britton Gantt, held the men were rightly convicted of grand larceny, but that improper evidence was admitted at trial and Judge Pepper had given erroneous jury instructions. The court expressed its belief Stewart was liable for $4,000 to Monroe Griffith but did not find that Stewart was part of the gang's conspiracy to defraud Griffith.[40] Boatright had pulled off one final victory.

His death did not slow the boys down. Within days George Ryan and Lucius Hindman were accused of participating in a wire scheme. The scheme, which cost Hot Springs pool room operators an estimated $10,000 to $15,000, was believed to be the work of vengeful wire scammers in St. Louis expelled from Hot Springs the previous winter. Ryan, Hindman, Lawrence "Harmony Kid" Varner, and two others were arrested.[41]

The last vestiges of the Buckfoot Gang were auctioned off in the fall at a sheriff's sale in Webb City. Located on North Tom Street, the gang's clubhouse was stripped of its furnishings to satisfy a judgment obtained against Boatright. Boatright's steadfast bondsman Charley Parker oversaw the removal of its contents. Fine bathtub fixtures, an elegant folding bed, a leather couch, a large carpet, two stoves, and a double-sided safe were among the items for sale. The safe was later displayed in the showroom of the Joplin Safe and Scale Company. In 1931 it was unceremoniously sold for scrap.[42]

The safe was not the only specter of the past that resurfaced in the years following the Buckfoot Gang's demise. In the fall of 1907, audible gasps could be heard as pedestrians on Joplin's Main Street stopped to stare in wonder at a man "who was almost the exact counterpart of Robert Boatright." Several Joplin residents questioned him, but he would only say he was from Kansas City and his name was not Boatright.[43] Within weeks, the man was forgotten as word of a new financial crisis spread across the country. The Panic of 1907 threatened to wipe out far more than the wealth of the Middle West's gentry; it threatened the entire existence of the country as the New York Stock Exchange faltered and banks and businesses failed across the United States. Risk was not limited to fixed races and prizefights overseen by men like Boatright; it existed on Wall Street under the watchful eye of the country's financial elite.

Decades later Boatright's fortune was still a topic of underworld gossip. Stories circulated about $200,000 ($6,681,949) he allegedly had in a money belt at the time of his death. Conk Jones, the nom de guerre of gambler Cameron Kunkel, was blamed for the money's disappearance. Few likely dared to broach the subject with Jones; he had forged a tough reputation years earlier in Dodge City. After Jones died his friends refuted the accusations. One crustily declared, "He told me himself he didn't want to take any chances. You don't remember that they jumped on him about any races, do you? No? And don't you supposed he'd have been nipped if they had anything on him?"[44]

When Boatright died in bed at the New Century Hotel, it was an inauspicious ending for the man who began his criminal career with the cold-blooded murder of Charley Woodson. Far from mad, Robert Boatright left the petty grift of St. Louis to become one of the country's most successful confidence men. Operating from an Ozark mining town, he and his confederates swindled stockmen, law enforcement officers, attorneys, businessmen, and even a Yale graduate before the spirit of Progressive reform, an outspoken local press, and a fractious relationship between Democratic party leaders led to their demise.

In life Robert Boatright was known for his appearance; his office was handsomely furnished. This personal preference reportedly extended into the afterlife; Boatright's will, one apocryphal story claimed, had a provision that his $5,000 mausoleum be polished regularly, the grass trimmed, and flowers placed at his grave on holidays and his birthday. For a few years his instructions were followed, but then "something happened to the trust fund; just what no one seemed to know."[45]

"HE USED EVERYBODY FOR ALL HE COULD, AND THAT WAS THE END OF IT"

—MARY E. RICE, *In re Robert Boatright and Ed E. Ellis*

B oatright was dead. The clubhouse was empty and the boys were scattered to the wind as the Ozarks welcomed a new year. On a cold January day in 1905, Mayor George W. Moore, City Attorney Morris Pritchett, and City Marshal Richard T. Mountjoy visited every Webb City saloon and ordered them to close at midnight. They then turned their attention to the city's gambling dens. Officers found Ed Ellis and Al Ballard, both members of the Buckfoot Gang, with five other gamblers in Butch Gammon's joint. They were arrested and taken to Joplin to appear in court. An old rounder groused, "Well, this is the worst closed up town I ever saw, I never saw the time before when I couldn't get a drink in Webb City, but I can't get one today for love or money."[1]

Although Boatright was gone, his cronies remained embroiled in legal disputes born of their association with him. Harry Wasser, alias Harry Price, forfeited his $1,500 bond when he failed to appear in Hot Springs.[2] While he was on the run from the law, Wasser's wife successfully sued for divorce and obtained custody of their son.[3] Arrested in Kankakee, Illinois, Wasser told officers he had typhoid fever. Confined to a hotel room, Wasser escaped but was captured a month later in Springfield, Illinois, where the state fair was in full swing. He sniffed, "If you had let me alone until next week I would have secured plenty of change." Full of bravado, he gloated he had lightened pockets at the Lewis and Clark Centennial Exposition in Portland, Oregon. While returning to Arkansas under guard, Wasser slipped off his handcuffs and jumped out the window of the moving train near Poplar Bluff, Missouri. He stayed ahead of authorities until he was captured at a friend's farm in Illinois and taken to Arkansas. Wasser languished in jail for a month until an anonymous woman furnished him tools to saw his way out of his cell. After that, he appears to have permanently assumed his alias of Harry Price, remarried, and lived in Virginia.[4]

Escape may not have been necessary; the remaining cases against George Ryan, Lucius "Honey Grove Kid" Hindman, and fellow colt Ed Clark in Arkansas were dismissed. The cases, transferred from Garland County to Saline County, had been continued for years, and each man appeared when their cases were called at every term of court. The Saline County prosecutor decided that it was best to dismiss the cases to avoid further expenses.[5] Yet as the tattered remnants of Boatright's affairs continued to fray, one of the late foot race chieftain's confederates remained behind bars.

Irven Johnson, the only member of the gang to serve prison time, was pardoned by Arkansas governor John Isaac Moore after serving eighteen months in the state penitentiary. His freedom was short-lived. Almost a year later, Johnson was convicted in federal court at Beaumont, Texas, and sentenced to the US Penitentiary in Atlanta.[6] He remained, according to a prisoner assessment, "sanguine." Correspondence logs in Johnson's file indicate he only sent and received one letter from a member of the gang, Dr. Robert E. L. Goddard. Although the logs do not indicate he received a letter from Ed Ellis, at some point Johnson communicated with him (perhaps through Goddard), because Johnson's reply to Ellis is included in his prison file.[7]

Ellis's letter has not survived, but Johnson's cheery reply did. "I truly hope you are both in better health and spirits than when I saw you last. . . . You know too the results of my trial was far from our expectations & none of us were prepared for the results as they developed at 'Beaumont.'" He continued, "I sometimes think we were very fortunate all of us to get away from those old 'Springs' alive at all hazards & cost!" Anticipating his release, Johnson said he would have to start over again, but he had a plan. Johnson crowed, "I'll be in clover when many of them are in 'crab grass!'" He guardedly asked Ellis to stay in touch because he might have something that would interest him.[8] Johnson subsequently returned to Texas and became a quack doctor.[9]

As civil proceedings into Boatright's affairs continued, some individuals may have harbored hard feelings toward those litigating the cases. Late one evening in 1905, Hiram Currey stepped into his backyard to enjoy the night air. As he turned to go back into his house someone shot at him from close range. A neighbor, sitting in his yard, heard the gunshot and then saw a man run through the alley adjacent to Currey's property.[10]

"It was surely a deliberately planned attempt to kill me," Currey declared. He explained, "I think the dastardly deed was the direct outcome of my vigorous prosecution of the so-called Buckfoot cases . . . the cases are not through with yet, and a number of them are to come up for trial."[11] The identity of Currey's assailant was never determined, nor was it confirmed that the would-be assassin was connected to the gang. Undeterred, Currey continued to represent the Boatright estate's trustee William H. Waters.

Legal battles over Boatright's assets continued for years as Waters pursued hidden assets on behalf of the estate's claimants.[12] His actions led to two cases that brought new revelations about Boatright, his associates, methods, and efforts to conceal his wealth. In their motion on behalf of Waters, Hiram Currey and John Halliburton alleged George Thompson, Mary "Polly" Thompson, Thomas J. Thompson, and Sarah Thompson took Boatright's money upon his death and concealed it. US district judge Charles F. Amidon issued an order directing "Mrs. Polly Boatright, Boatright's wife" to appear in court and explain why she should not turn over money she received from his estate; he sent a similar order to George Cole, the Thompsons' brother-in-law.[13]

Boatright's purported widow failed to appear. Her attorney explained she was sick due to "nervousness and worry." Her brother George rebuffed Halliburton and Currey's questions.[14] Annoyed, Judge Amidon curtly reminded Thompson he was under oath and then subjected him to an "inquisition." Thompson divulged Boatright, using the alias John Bagwell, deposited $40,000 ($1,336,390) in Windsor, Ontario, Canada, for Priscilla Boatright and "Polly" Thompson and that they had already withdrawn the money. He also disclosed Boatright transferred ownership of a St. Louis County residence valued at $6,000 to keep it from creditors. Thompson allegedly used Boatright's money to purchase the Senate Club at 905 Baltimore in Kansas City. George Cole, Thompson's brother-in-law, admitted Boatright deeded three lots in Clayton, Missouri, to him. These intriguing glimpses—and others—into Boatright's affairs unfolded for years after his death in a series of court cases and depositions.[15]

Although Buckfoot confederate Frank H. Rice was nowhere to be found, his wife Mary E. Rice was deposed.[16] Rice repeatedly asserted her Fifth Amendment right to avoid self-incrimination. When Rice said her husband was a field agent with the Pennsylvania Pneumatic Pump Company of Davenport, Iowa, Hiram Currey retorted he was in Kansas City working as a foot racer. From Currey's line of questioning, it seems the Rices accessed one of Boatright's St. Louis safety deposit boxes. They subsequently purchased a coal mine in Collinsville, Illinois, and put Mary Rice's uncle, Jesse Long, in charge of operations.[17]

Irven E. Johnson. *National Archives and Records Administration.*

Rice and other deponents testified Boatright's mother, Priscilla Boatright, was destitute. Acquaintance G. W. Blake testified Mary Rice told him Boatright's mother was "badly left" because she arrived too late; Boatright's "mistress" got everything. Rice, seemingly enriched by Boatright's fortune, did not volunteer if she had attempted to assist the elderly widow. She disclosed she met with Priscilla Boatright to discuss the Thompson family stealing Boatright's money after his death; the Thompsons, attorney George Clay, and others went so far as to divide Boatright's clothes amongst themselves.[18]

Mary Rice acknowledged some individuals believed there was "more money there than the people knew about." When she stated Boatright lost $60,000 at Hot Springs, Currey snapped, "No, he didn't. There was a book kept there by that crowd that shows how much we captured at Hot Springs, and it shows how much Mr. Rice got." When asked if she knew Boatright took 25 to 75 percent of the gang's winnings, she shot back, "I wasn't supposed to hear these things, they were kept from the women, and what I heard was very little." When Currey asked about Boatright's net worth, Rice spat, "I didn't know that, he didn't tell anybody that, he never made a confidant of anybody, he used everybody for all he could, and that was the end of it." When Currey again asked about Boatright's fortune Rice hissed, "I don't know where it is; if he has any money that woman ["Polly" Thompson] knows it, and she knows the whole thing, when they get her, they will find out as much as they can find of anybody, but she ain't going to trust anybody." No deposition for "Polly" Thompson could be located, leaving many unanswered questions about Boatright's estate.[19]

While Priscilla Boatright may have missed out on much of her son's personal wealth, he tried to provide for her according to testimony in a related case. Boatright wanted to keep his money from the bankruptcy trustee, but he also may have sought to keep it from his associates. Although his actions had been disclosed the previous month, additional information became public when depositions were taken in Joplin before bankruptcy referee Arthur Spencer. George Clay's testimony was saturated with information about Boatright's affairs. Questioned by Hiram Currey and Samuel McReynolds, who represented claimants of the estate, Clay's deposition focused on the $40,000 Boatright deposited in Canada.[20]

Currey scrutinized Clay's finances. As the charges laid out in the bill in equity alleged, Clay and Priscilla Boatright withdrew the money from the Canadian bank for their own use with the "wicked design of defrauding the creditors." Together they purchased lots in Neosho and Webb City as well as land in Newton County, Missouri, in Clay's name and, in some instances, that of Clay's wife, Cora. Clay also used the money to make a series of small, private loans. The trustee estimated Clay and Priscilla Boatright received $29,000 from Boatright's estate.[21] The proceedings were contentious. After Clay stated Currey "tried to scheme with me, and tried to get me to turn up my clients and said we just as well steal that money as let them have it as it was stolen money," he then claimed Currey told him, "There is $20,000 there; that is too much money for that old lady [Priscilla Boatright]; you take $5,000 and I will take $5,000 and we can divide the $10,000 up among the creditors." Furious, Currey called Clay a "damned liar," to which Clay fired back, "You are a damned-son-of-a-bitch." Referee Spencer intervened to prevent a fistfight. Clay insisted the money he delivered to Priscilla Boatright, along with other funds, had been acquired by Boatright after he had been adjudged a bankrupt, and therefore the funds should not be disbursed to the creditors whose judgment liens were attached to the proceedings.[22]

Prior to Boatright's death he had asked Clay to investigate Cuba's extradition laws because he was thinking of moving to Havana. Clay traveled to Cuba with Boatright after his conviction in Lawrence County, but he denied his client deposited $65,000 there. Boatright later traveled to the country alone, but Clay insisted he did not deposit money in a Cuban bank. Currey pressed Clay: "Didn't you say he intended to leave Thompson's and go down into Cuba and take all his funds?" Clay shook his head. "No sir; I told you this, that a short time before his death, that if he came clear of that case he was going to leave this country."

But Boatright may have hidden money somewhere; Clay had told Currey that Boatright's alleged wife possessed Robert Boatright's steamer trunk, which contained evidence of the deposit.[23] Priscilla Boatright received her son's gold watch, a diamond ring, a diamond stud, a three-piece leather parlor set, and $3,000 to $4,000 in cash. She did not get his diamonds valued at $10,000.[24]

George Clay, for his part, deposed Boatright crony Garrette Stansbury; Clay presumably called Stansbury to confirm Boatright's destitution. Stansbury claimed he was no longer in the foot racing business; instead, he was a washing machine mechanic at the Peerless Manufacturing Company in Cherryvale, Kansas. Stansbury said Boatright pulled off tricks in St. Louis County and Kansas City in late 1902 and early 1903; the least amount the gang played for was $300, the most was $41,000 at an event in Clayton, Missouri. In August 1903 he asked Boatright to pay him; Stansbury was owed $6,000 but would settle for $1,000. Together they went over the gang's two account books; Boatright had $55,000. Boatright told Stansbury he was going to deposit money in a Canadian bank for his mother, but that otherwise he was broke; the rest of his money was tied up in Hot Springs.[25] When asked if it was costly to keep the "establishment going," Stansbury replied it was very expensive. Boatright paid everyone's rail fare—victims and ropers alike—as well as $1,000 in protection money to unnamed parties. Clay clarified, "Who squared the officers when they had to be squared?" Stansbury replied, "Bob."[26]

The most intriguing witness, however, was John Black. Hiram Currey believed Black had double-crossed his fellow victims and joined Boatright. In the summer of 1903—with George Clay as an intermediary—Black met Boatright three separate times at the Savoy Hotel in Kansas City. Clay warned him Boatright "was a surly fellow who didn't allow anybody to dictate to him." At their second meeting, Boatright told Black he was ready to stand before the bankruptcy trustee and go broke. He could not hand over "all the money, for a lot of it had got away from him, and that he hadn't made near as much as some people thought he had."[27] Although exactly what happened is unknown, Boatright allegedly convinced Black to help him—presumably in exchange for personal gain. Shortly after his last meeting with Boatright, Black invited victims to meet him in Dallas, Texas, and sign their claims against Boatright over to him; some did. He insisted, "I was going to try and help them get some of their money back."[28]

His actions seemed to prove otherwise. Black denied a litany of accusations: that he acted on Boatright's behalf, that he tried to get a new trustee appointed who would be more favorable to Boatright, and that he agreed to help Boatright avoid prosecution. He also swore, when asked by Currey, that he did not ask Garland County prosecutor William Martin to intercede in exchange for 15 percent of the money recovered from Boatright. He further denied telling Martin he knew where Boatright had hid $75,000.[29] Black conceded he spoke to fellow victim Monroe Griffith on his way to appear in court but denied saying anything to make him return home. Although the extent of his machinations is impossible to discern, it is likely Black was not acting in the best interest of other victims.[30]

US district judge Smith McPherson ruled in favor of trustee Waters. Of Boatright he concluded, "It is doubtful whether, in the history of jurisprudence, there has ever been a greater scoundrel than Robert Boatright. I shall not attempt to enlarge upon this statement. The poverty of the English language does not enable me to do full justice to the subject."[31] McPherson ordered George Clay, Clay's wife, and Boatright's mother to transfer money, jewelry, and land titles to Waters. Claims against the estate now totaled $300,000 ($9,665,307). Gilbert Barbee served as bondsman for the Clays and Priscilla Boatright while the case was on appeal.[32] Waters's pursuit came to an end in 1910 when he informed the court he had concluded his duties as administrator of Boatright's estate and asked to be discharged.[33] Judge McPherson, however, was not finished.

When McPherson consolidated the cases of Stephen Moss and Jonathan Davis against the Exchange Bank, he jovially remarked, "Well, I plainly see I've got to fight these cases to a finish; and here goes. The finish will arrive when I sign the bill of exceptions. I can't get away from them. I found a Webb City footracing case at Des Moines. When I went to Denver I found another one. Then I went to Kansas City and found Buckfoot had left his footprints there. Now I come here and find them in bunches. It seems that Buckfoot was a 'well known citizen.' "[34] Jury selection took most of the morning because Boatright's attorney

George Clay had "too many friends in the jury box." When Hiram Currey made his opening statement, he asserted he would show the Stewarts and the Exchange Bank departed from normal banking procedures to help Boatright. Arthur Spencer, representing the bank and the Stewarts, contended the evidence would show Stephen Moss and Jonathan Davis were the same type of men as Buckfoot and that the bank was a reliable institution.[35]

Late August brought a day of sweltering torture in Joplin's new federal courthouse. Even the "lightest wearing apparel was an agony," a reporter quipped.[36] Perhaps it was the heat. Or maybe they refused to be hoodwinked. After listening to the testimony and closing arguments the jurors returned a guilty verdict against the Exchange Bank for an aggregate of $30,000. This was the second verdict against the bank; Henry Wright won an earlier case for $6,000. The jury found president Joseph Stewart not liable. Cashier James Stewart was not as fortunate—this made Stewart's personal funds fair game for creditors.[37] If Judge McPherson thought he had seen the last of the Buckfoot Gang, he was mistaken. He would meet them again beyond the borders of the Ozarks.

The case's publicity did not hurt Jonathan Davis; he became a perennial candidate in Kansas politics. Despite a failed bid in 1904, he was eventually elected to the state legislature. Derided as "Buckfoot" Davis by his enemies, he did not let his past impede his ambition; Davis ran for governor six times. He succeeded in 1922, but Davis's time as governor was turbulent. Upon leaving office, Davis was prosecuted but found not guilty of selling prison paroles. Further attempts to win elected office failed. He died on June 27, 1943, and was buried in Bronson, where forty-two years earlier he had met a promising young sprinter named Bud Gillett.[38]

The Exchange Bank appealed, but Judge William Hook of the Eighth Circuit Court of Appeals sustained the lower court's ruling in favor of the plaintiffs. A few months later the judgments against Joseph Stewart and the Exchange Bank were paid in full.[39] The Missouri Supreme Court later ruled the bank was liable for the losses of the gang's victims. In 1907, after its shareholders unanimously voted the bank be voluntarily liquidated, James Stewart asked Missouri secretary of state John Swanger to dissolve the bank. Though no reason was given, it is likely the judgments against it in state and federal court may have led to the bank's demise. The Exchange Bank arranged for the newly formed National Bank of Webb City to take over its deposits.[40]

There was one less defendant as other cases proceeded; Joseph Stewart died from a stomach hemorrhage. The *Joplin Globe* lavished praise on "Webb City's Foremost Citizen" in a glowing obituary that

Judge Smith McPherson. *History of Iowa from the Earliest Times to the Beginning of the Twentieth Century* (1903).

Jonathan Davis. *Library of Congress.*

recalled Stewart's role in founding the Center Creek Mining Company, the Stewart & Matthews Lumberyard, the Exchange Bank, and the Webb City Iron Works. When his cousin James Stewart died after a long illness, he, too, received a flattering death notice. Neither obituary mentioned the men's affiliation with the Buckfoot Gang.[41]

The Exchange Bank was not the only Buckfoot-affiliated financial institution to suffer difficulties. On the morning of May 28, 1906, a sign in the window of the Joplin Savings Bank informed customers, "This bank is in the hands of the secretary of state." The bank had failed; it was reportedly the first in Joplin's history. President George Layne, the subject of scrutiny in *Currey v. Joplin Savings Bank*, had carried out his own fraudulent scheme. Layne, who was also president and sole owner of the Ozark Coal and Railway Company, had made several overdrafts and loans to the company. The railway owed the bank $40,000, which violated state law prohibiting corporations from borrowing over 25 percent of a bank's capital stock. "The assets of the bank," the *Joplin News-Herald* noted, "are practically nothing." Layne vowed to pay depositors in full. The state-appointed receiver found $13,000 in assets to be divided between 1,542 depositors with $85,710.48 on deposit.[42] Layne was charged with embezzlement. The case, which lingered in Lawrence County Circuit Court from 1906 until its dismissal in 1911, resulted in two separate hung juries.[43]

Like the short-lived Joplin Savings Bank, many of those connected to Boatright did not outlive him for long. Priscilla Boatright died at her sister's home in De Soto, Missouri, in 1910. The *Webb City Register* described her as "probably one of the best liked women in Webb City." George Clay, accompanied by Boatright's housekeeper Ola McWhirt, escorted her remains to Webb City for interment.[44] A few months later the woman who bested Priscilla Boatright and the authorities in their pursuit of Robert Boatright's assets, Mary "Polly" Thompson, died of heart failure in Los Angeles.[45] She left behind a husband, Robert L. Fargo; the couple had married two years earlier in St. Joseph, Michigan.[46] Although one might suspect Fargo of being Robert Boatright by another name, records indicate he was not. Her estate, valued at $5,000 ($161,142), consisted of an interest in the Olympic Theater, an automobile, cash, jewelry, and extensive wardrobe.[47] Buried together in the family plot at Elmwood Cemetery in Kansas City, the Thompson family—who profited from their tight-knit familial bonds during their lives—remained together even in death.[48]

George Clay, Boatright's pugnacious attorney, was entangled in his client's affairs long after Boatright's death. Like his former client, he met an early demise. In 1913 Clay died of typhoid fever just shy of his forty-second birthday.[49] Clay's counterpart George E. Booth, whose relationship with Boatright never seemed as close as that of Clay, died in 1928 after suffering a suspected heart attack in Kansas City.[50] Their legal nemesis, Hiram Currey, succumbed to heart failure in 1921.[51]

Charley Parker sold the 16 to 1 Saloon in 1908. After years of failing health and substantial financial losses, Parker died in 1911 at the age of fifty-nine.[52] It was just as well; following a revival held by evangelist Billy Sunday in Joplin, prohibition came to Jasper County in 1910. Twenty-nine saloons fell silent—twelve in Webb City alone. Among the saloon-men affected by local option were Buckfoot associates Sam Jones and William "Bill" Fahrman.[53] Fahrman's establishment, the Ben and Bill Saloon, was the first victim of local option in Webb City.[54]

Jasper County saloons were not the only institutions to fall that year. Gilbert Barbee's reign as the Democratic boss of Joplin ended in 1910. In the wake of Buckfoot's demise, he continued to vie with William Phelps for control of the Jasper County Democratic Party. As time passed, Barbee's grip slowly loosened on the Fifteenth District. In 1904 he wrecked the political career of Congressman Maecenas E. Benton, a Neosho attorney and the father of artist Thomas Hart Benton, whose first visit to the House of Lords launched his artistic career. Although it is unclear why Barbee soured on Benton, a local paper hinted the congressman aggravated the political boss in some manner and was a "man of some backbone" who Barbee and his sycophants could not use in their "schemes." Benton attempted a comeback, but Barbee crushed him.[55] In 1906 Barbee's *Globe* lost the services of Bart Howard, who had worked there as city editor, editorial writer, associate editor, and managing editor. Despite reports the two fell out over how to handle publication of a local politician's record, Howard published a statement to the contrary. He was leaving, he said, because of a better business opportunity—though one wonders if working at the *Columbia (OH) Sun* was exciting as working for the mercurial Barbee.[56] That same year, Phelps triumphed over Barbee in the local elections. The *Joplin News-Herald* cheered, "Once again the Carthage boss outgeneraled the Joplin boss . . . It was the finesse of political cunning against the brutal coarseness of bulldog methods, and, as usual, strategy won."[57]

The *News-Herald* kept after Barbee even after the newspaper was sold to Perlee Ellis "P. E." Burton. Burton, like Edward Hosmer, was no fan of Barbee and boss rule. His first job was working for the venerable William Allen White at the *Emporia Gazette*. Undaunted, Barbee retaliated against Burton's attacks.[58] An unusual event in the fall of 1907, however, almost united the two men.

On the evening of September 13, 1907, explosions rocked downtown Joplin. A saboteur dynamited the *Joplin News-Herald*'s printing plant; all four Linotype machines and the press were badly damaged. One stick failed to detonate, saving the press from utter destruction.[59] The *Globe* bellowed it was the result of "vile and vicious anarchy." Barbee offered his rival the use of the *Globe*'s presses, but the goodwill was short-lived.[60] The first issue of the *News-Herald* published in the wake of the explosion proclaimed, "There is this consolation—that the attempt to annihilate the News Herald by an attack on its physical property is simply the death struggle of Buckfootism and Saighmanism."[61] The *Carthage Evening Press* agreed: "Because it stood for decency in politics—municipal, county, state and national, the Joplin News Herald lost its plant last night."[62]

The story eventually faded from the headlines, but Barbee was still sore over the affair six years later when the *News-Herald* provoked his ire over Buckfoot. He fired back by reminding readers Burton was allegedly seen running from the scene of the bombing.[63] This may have led to Barbee's funeral dirge when, in 1908, the "Rebel Democrats of Joplin" declared open war against the Boss. Barbee was denounced for using the party machinery for his own gain and dumping Democratic nominees for Congress because of grudges; further, he had "belittled the professional standing, questioned the private character and scattered the most malicious insinuations concerning the every action of almost everyone who has refused to bow the knee in humble submission." Barbee lashed out at Burton's provocative editorials and cartoons and referred to him as a lady.[64] Although Burton tried to counter Barbee's influence, a new foe, Alfred H. Rogers, would bring the Boss to heel.

Rogers was the opposite of Barbee. A Harvard graduate, he was a lawyer, banker, and founder of the Southwest Electric Railway Company. Barbee's *Globe* fought the railway, with much of its anger directed at Rogers. Rogers established the short-lived *Joplin American*, which employed Thomas Hart Benton as a cartoonist, to compete with Barbee. Years later, local politicians would revisit "why Colonel Barbee did the thing which forever took the scepter out of his hands": in 1910, Barbee sold a large amount of his *Globe* stock to Rogers, perplexing his friends. Barbee told them not to worry; he still controlled the *Globe*. "Men under the spell of his personality" held the majority of the paper's stock and would vote according to Barbee's instructions. When the next stockholder's meeting was held, every director Barbee proposed was elected; Rogers's slate of candidates was defeated. Rogers reportedly said, "Well, Gib, you certainly put one over on me. I'll have to hand it to you for that. It's all right, and you won't hear any squalling out of me. When it comes to controlling a political situation, you know all about it and I know nothing. But when it comes to a fight for the control of a corporation, I believe I know a good deal more than you do. So I'm going to tell you now that, while I haven't figured out just how I'm going to do it, when the next meeting of stockholders occurs it will be me, and not you, who elects the slate of directors." As veteran publisher Arthur Aull observed, "Rogers was as good as his word." He "easily voted a majority of the stock, and the Daily Globe, that had been such a powerful factor in the politics of the Fifteenth district, passed once and forever out of the hands of Gilbert Barbee."[65]

After Rogers wrested ownership of the *Globe* from Barbee, the battle-hardened boss founded the upstart *Joplin Morning Tribune,* which, during its brief existence, published sarcastic parodies of the *Globe* called the Interurban Jr. edited by "A. Snitch" with the motto "Our Polyticks are on the Side of the Fence Where the Most Money Is."[66] Launched in 1911, the paper could not attract enough advertisers and folded in the spring of 1913. Barbee's health declined and he spent much of his time at Texas health resorts. Still, he frequently returned to his native Ozark hills. A year before his death, Barbee was spotted in Neosho. When asked what he was doing there, he replied in characteristic salty fashion: "Damned if I know."[67] In 1924 Barbee passed away in his suite at the Keystone Hotel, located near the old House of Lords and a stone's throw from his former prized possession, the *Joplin Globe.* Former *Globe* editor Bart Howard remarked, "The drama of newspaper life attracted him, just as the power of political life. Drama and power. Those were his things."[68] He at least had the satisfaction of outliving his political rival, William H. Phelps, who had died following an operation at the Mayo Clinic in 1916.[69]

The *Globe* generously called Barbee "the most widely known man in southwest Missouri." He was remembered for helping establish the Joplin Children's Home and advocating for the construction of Joplin's Union Station. After funeral services at St. Philip's Episcopal Church, Barbee was laid to rest on the city's western edge in Fairview Cemetery under an unremarkable headstone. It was a far cry from the ornate mausoleums that many of his peers—among them his rival, Alfred H. Rogers—had in Mount Hope Cemetery. Instead, it had more in common with the resting place of Robert Boatright.[70]

When the House of Lords met its demise in 1922, it barely resembled the fabled restaurant and saloon that had made Main Street famous. "If the old House of Lords were personified," the *Joplin Globe* remarked, "it probably would rise up and laugh with scorn and derision at the temerity of the final bearer of its title in holding forth under a name that is known perhaps in every corner of the globe."[71] After years of hosting

Barbee, Boatright, and the state's political luminaries, it lost its luster before meeting its demise at the hands of Prohibition. Despite a brief resurrection, the final reincarnation of the House of Lords closed its doors on January 31, 1956. The building was demolished in 1964, leaving only memories of the infamous painting behind the bar and a political boss who sheltered one of the early twentieth century's greatest con men.[72]

Boatright was dead. The Webb City Athletic Club gymnasium was empty. The gang was just a memory. But beyond the borders of the Ozarks a paunchy Mississippian who bore an eerie resemblance to the fallen foot race chieftain stood to inherit his kingdom—though perhaps he was not a worthy heir. A new Millionaire's Club, with many familiar faces, was carrying out athletic schemes across the country but much like Buckfoot's colts, it too would stumble.

10

THE MAN WITH THE RED AUTOMOBILE

T here were stories. One of the earliest surfaced in 1905 when William Gordanier, a farmer from Makato, Kansas, was fleeced by five men on a foot race south of Kansas City. "It was all fixed up for the other crowd to get skinned," he said sheepishly, "but I was the sucker, all right."[1] In 1907 Dr. Charles E. Nelson of Phillipsburg, Kansas, asked authorities for help finding the four well-dressed men who swindled him out of $9,000 on a fake fight in Denver. Whether or not they were associated with the Buckfoot Gang was unclear, but the hallmarks were the same.[2] The following year farmer Eddie D. Steinbaugh lost $2,500 on a fake wrestling match in Wichita. When one of the wrestlers began to spurt blood from his mouth, someone yelled an artery had burst in the man's neck. A frenzy ensued as spectators shouted the police would arrest them for murder, and the stakeholder bolted with the purse. Steinbaugh was hurried from the scene, only realizing later he had been cheated.[3] Two of the men implicated in the crime, Duke Bishop and Garrette Stansbury, were members of the Buckfoot Gang. The con had evolved.

Lumberman John E. Cavanaugh of McAlester, Oklahoma, informed New Orleans police he had lost $37,000 ($1,236,571) to a party of men in the city who posed as representatives of well-known local sporting clubs. Cavanaugh was roped on a wrestling match involving wrestler George "Ole" Marsh. He bet on Marsh, who won the first fall but began bleeding profusely from the nose and mouth during the second. A doctor examined Marsh and declared he was dying. Advised to leave, Cavanaugh took a train to Memphis where he read the papers in vain for news of Marsh's death.[4]

When a Colorado banker groused he was conned out of $12,500 in Council Bluffs, Iowa, he drew attention to one "of the biggest and cleverest gangs of confidence men the country has ever seen."[5] The gang had prizefighters, foot racers, jockeys, two race horses, "a big red automobile, two smartly dressed women, and half a dozen business looking men about whom there is nothing flashy—simply well dressed, prosperous looking business men." Nothing less than $5,000 interested them; allegedly a banker from Spokane lost $60,000 on a horse race.[6] While the newspapers reported only vague details, they all led back to Council Bluffs.

Speculation abounded about an office in the city's impressive Merriam Block. It sported a billiard table, pool table, chairs, tables, and other expensive furniture. The occupants installed a typewriter, desks, and a refrigerator stocked with cigars and mineral water. There was little else to indicate what business took place behind closed doors. The man who occupied it, however, drove a flashy red Stevens-Duryea automobile. Dubbed "the man from Omaha," he would suddenly arrive in Council Bluffs accompanied by strangers. A frenzy of activity would then ensue around the office before growing quiet once more. Rumors circulated the office housed a syndicate of high rollers that skinned suckers from across the country through a variety of fraudulent schemes. After the Colorado banker went public, the office was locked and shuttered.[7]

A search of the abandoned office turned up typewritten lists of arrival and departure times of the mail and express trains as well as a long list of telephone numbers. Further investigation revealed the numbers were for telephones in Council Bluffs and Omaha; one was for an Omaha saloon thought to be the gang's headquarters in that city.[8] William Walter, who repaired a sideboard and desk for the office's occupants, recalled one had inquired about a local jockey named Leo Bryson; the man had driven a red automobile.[9] Now both the man and his car had disappeared.

US postal inspector John Swenson was determined to find them. Originally from Sweden, he was a naturalized citizen and University of Nebraska graduate who originally joined the US Postal Service as a mail carrier.[10] His attention was brought to bear on the mysterious men after a postal inspector in San Francisco forwarded him a cryptic letter in the spring of 1908. The letter, mistakenly delivered to and opened by a private detective, seemed to indicate the mail was being used to conduct illegal activities. The letter stated:

New Orleans, La., March 1, 1908

Friend 39:
Owing to a change of administration here, we move to Council Bluffs, Ia., where conditions are perfect. Drop us a line and keep us posted as to your whereabouts. With best wishes, 735.

Merriam Block, Council Bluffs Ia.

Merriam Block, Council Bluffs, Iowa. *Courtesy of the Council Bluffs Public Library.*

Enclosed in the letter were slips of paper that read: "Address all mail, Post office Box 4, Council Bluffs, Ia.; Address all telegrams, A. B. Craft, Council Bluffs, Ia."[11]

Suspecting a counterfeiting scheme, Swenson surveilled the post office box rented by "Barrett and Johnson." He verified letters mailed by the fictitious firm were sent to confidence men, gamblers, and sports. Swenson then confirmed prominent saloonmen and gamblers had signed Barrett and Johnson's post office box application. When he visited the address on file, he found "Southern Land and Timber Company" neatly painted in gold lettering on the firm's door. Although the men had raised red flags, they had not yet violated any postal laws as there was "no law against confidence men using the mails of the country for legitimate purposes." Swenson suspected local authorities protected the men. Proceeding with caution, he determined confidence man John C. Mabray was at the center of his investigation.[12]

Swenson discovered multiple victims, but they were unable to furnish evidence that the gang used the mail to defraud them. US attorney Marcellus L. Temple was not convinced a case could be made, but

US Postal Inspector John S. Swenson. *Mabray and the Mikes* (1910).

Swenson persisted.[13] He learned victim Samuel Sutor of Cass Lake, Minnesota, went to Council Bluffs and drew a check on his bank for $5,000. Because he did not have that amount on deposit, Sutor was forced to write to the bank's cashier in Minnesota. Roper Barney Martin wrote and signed the letter for Sutor, who was unable to write legibly. Temple told postal inspectors he thought Martin could be indicted, but not the others.[14]

Undeterred, Swenson convinced Sutor to file charges and John Hess, county attorney for Pottawattamie County, Iowa, to act. Two days before John Mabray was to be arrested in Council Bluffs on November 17, 1908, he and other members of the gang fled. Postal inspectors blamed the botched arrest on local authorities. Postmasters across the country were asked for their assistance in locating the gang.[15]

John C. Mabray. *National Archives and Records Administration.*

As Swenson searched for Mabray, a parallel investigation emerged. The mystery of the man with the red automobile would not be solved in Council Bluffs. Instead, the answer emerged four months later in Little Rock, Arkansas. In January 1909, two men opened the F. M. Clarke Mining & Land Company in the city's first skyscraper, the ten-story Southern Trust Building. They also rented safety deposit boxes at two trust companies. Shortly after their arrival a red automobile with a Nebraska registration was delivered to the stately home they rented in the fashionable suburb of Pulaski Heights. Neighbors observed well-dressed, bejeweled men and women coming and going at all hours. Neither party made social advances toward one another. "You need something more than mere 'show' to break in, in Little Rock," noted the *Kansas City Star*, but these arrivistes "didn't care a rap if anyone called or not."[16] Their presence, however, had not gone unnoticed by local authorities.

When Pulaski County deputy James J. Hawkins—acquainted with the Honey Grove Kid from the days of the Buckfoot Gang—saw the Texan in the company of Hot Springs sports and strangers in Little Rock, he got suspicious.[17] He noticed the Kid and fellow Buckfoot roper George Ryan made frequent trips between Little Rock and Hot Springs. Hawkins and fellow deputy Louis Reichardt watched the men's rented quarters. After a local transfer company made a large delivery of trunks to the residence, Hawkins visited the firm pretending to look for a stolen trunk. Through his ruse, he learned the individuals renting the mansion planned to stay six months. The deputies then discerned their headquarters were in the Southern Trust Building and arranged surveillance.[18]

Around the same time assistant postmaster Fred Johnson of Hot Springs, Arkansas, noticed Buckfoot stalwart George Ryan had recently returned home after a long absence. Johnson wondered if he might be a member of the gang that fled Council Bluffs. The answer came when a special delivery letter addressed to Ryan was sent to Hot Springs. At that time, such letters arrived unsealed so that the assistant postmaster could officially seal it prior to final delivery. Johnson read the letter, which said in part, "I have him almost ready, and I understand the store is now located at Little Rock." He immediately contacted Inspector Swenson. Johnson's lead was confirmed when deputies Hawkins and Reichardt approached Little Rock assistant postmaster C. J. Cate about their investigation and asked him to request an inspector. Upon being notified the men were in Little Rock and that victim John Cavanaugh had filed a complaint, Swenson moved swiftly to arrest them.[19]

Armed with warrants, Swenson organized a raid for Tuesday, February 23, 1909. That morning US deputy marshal Henry Bickers trailed Mabray confederates Monte McCall and Isador Warner as they walked to the Little Rock Trust Company to retrieve their money. The con men noticed they were being followed and ducked into the Marion Hotel. Entering an elevator, they gave the attendant five dollars to tell anyone who followed them that they had gotten off on the fifth floor. The subterfuge worked. Bickers fruitlessly waited on the fifth floor for the men to emerge from a room while they backtracked and retrieved their money. When Swenson and other officers entered the gang's office in the Southern Trust Building it was empty. A search of their safety deposit boxes revealed only one had a small sum of cash in it.[20] Echoes of Council Bluffs must have crossed Swenson's mind.

Sensing the men may have been tipped off, the officers rushed to the Pulaski Heights mansion.[21] After neighbors confirmed the men were inside, Hawkins and another deputy headed for the back door just in time to see two men sprint from the house. One of the officers fired a shot to alert the others their quarry was on the run.[22] A chase ensued, but the duo was overtaken. One man, John C. Mabray, was armed with a revolver. The other, Isador J. "Kid" Warner, carried a revolver and a pump shotgun. Monte McCall started out of the house but darted back inside. James Johnson pulled up to the house in a car just in time to be taken into custody.

Monte McCall. *Mabray and the Mikes* (1910).   Isador Warner. *Mabray and the Mikes* (1910).

The four men were taken to the US District Court and arraigned before US commissioner William S. Allen. Allen set Mabray's bond at $15,000 and the others' at $10,000. The con men hired the firm of Bradshaw, Rhoton & Helm to represent them.[23] Interestingly Lewis Rhoton, while serving as Sixth District prosecuting attorney from 1904–1908, had fought political corruption in Arkansas. He was likely annoyed when Warner was caught in court ripping up a letter from a private detective in Denver warning him Frank Minter, former sheriff of Mercer County, Missouri, was searching for the gang on behalf of victim Thomas Ballew.[24] Swenson had almost missed his quarry again.

The gang had been on the verge of leaving town. McCall had moved the furniture out of the gang's office for shipment to Denver under an alias. US deputy marshal Guy Caron took possession of the furniture, four horses, two dogs, and a goat. Additional items included wrestling mats, guards, gloves, saddles, and other athletic paraphernalia. Money held in McCall's name, as well as the infamous red automobile, was seized.[25] Swenson, Sheriff Burl Roberts, and Deputy Hawkins found a trunk containing the gang's records at the residence. There were photographs of

Mabray, athletes, and victims taken together prior to contests. A ledger listed every foot race, horse race, wrestling match, and prizefight the gang had pulled off, along with the names of victims, their ropers, the amount of money wagered, and how it was divided among the gang. Mabray also had a small red ledger containing the names of hundreds of his associates, each identified by a unique number. Several dozen envelopes contained a complete record of each transaction in the form of a narrative report as well as meticulous correspondence. Notably, the gang used the term *mike* to refer to their victims instead of the commonly used term *mark*. Victims hailed from such far-flung places as San Antonio; St. Louis; Denver; Toledo; Fergus Falls, Minnesota; Hardin, Montana; and Vancouver, British Columbia. Among the victims was Thomas Cale, a former delegate from the District of Alaska to the US House of Representatives.[26] Mabray's decision to keep the ledgers and other incriminating evidence at his residence was critical in the federal government's ability to build a case against him.[27] A cursory assessment revealed the Mabray Gang used the same con as the Buckfoot Gang to ensnare victims; it was successful and there was little need to alter it. The only difference was that Mabray snared richer suckers.[28]

Officers pored over the papers. Inspector Charles S. Ranger joined Swenson; over the course of the investigation, postal inspectors from across the country and Canada assisted them. John Mabray was aware of the federal Buckfoot case, *US v. George Ryan, et al.*, in which the court ruled "letters passing between conspirators only, for the purpose of keeping each other informed of their movements not to be shown intended victims, was insufficient to base an indictment under the fraud statute." The gang therefore sought to evade—not break—postal laws. They used the mail to communicate with each other, but not to induce a victim. Mabray was confident they were immune from federal prosecution.[29]

Newspaper accounts and court records—save for one federal case—never indicated US postal inspectors investigated the Buckfoot Gang, but following the Civil War this small corps of federal investigators pursued numerous confidence men who used the mail to defraud victims. During Reconstruction there was a notable increase in the number of individuals using the mail for nefarious purposes. Scholar Wayne Fuller noted the expansion of postal routes and rail transportation—as well as cheap postage—meant con men increasingly used the mail for fraudulent schemes. In response, Congress enacted the first mail-fraud statute in 1872, but it failed to deter criminals, who often received light sentences in federal court.[30] The number of cases assigned to inspectors rose from 29,569 in 1880 to 197,996 in 1900. In 1907 there were only 377 postal inspectors tasked with conducting routine inspections and investigating mail fraud, postal robberies, and the use of the mails to send obscene material.[31] The Mabray Gang was one of the largest postal investigations of the early twentieth century; fortunately, the gang's records provided a wealth of damning information.

Some of the most intriguing finds were photographs. The Little Rock *Arkansas Gazette* ran a photo of Mabray, victim W. B. Wood, and members of the gang smiling and shaking hands prior to a fixed wrestling match. Additional photographs appeared. The Council Bluffs *Evening Nonpareil* noted the irony. Mabray used the photographs as a form of self-protection; if a victim threatened to go to authorities, the images were "used as clubs to beat him into submission." It was a method Boatright used; Inspector William F. Allmon obtained a similar photograph of Boatright, two sprinters, and spectators as part of the investigation.

Mabray and his three associates were indicted by the grand jury in Little Rock. Mabray, the only one charged with violating postal laws in Council Bluffs, was held on behalf of federal authorities in Iowa. The others, however, were released on bond; they departed for Hot Springs.[32]

John Mabray, hat in hand, shakes hands with victim O. L. Cramer of San Francisco prior to a fixed contest. Darby Thielman is in the black trunks. *Mabray and the Mikes* (1910).

Joseph G. Kile, who lost $10,000 to the gang in Little Rock, identified Mabray and the others as the men who swindled him. When Pulaski County prosecuting attorney Roy Campbell brought the case to trial, Kile could not be located, nor could the state's other witness, Oklahoman F. E. Ray. Authorities learned Johnson's wife took Kile and his wife on a trip to prevent them from testifying against the gang.[33] She did not need to work her magic on Ray; he told officers he would not help prosecute the gang because he had traveled to Little Rock with the intent to fleece them. Mabray agreed to return Ray's money, but because Mabray and his associates were under bond they could not leave the state. They did not want Ray to come to Arkansas; otherwise, he could be arrested, held as a witness, and forced to give bond. A compromise was struck: Ray met the men at the Arkansas/Oklahoma state line where they returned his money and he signed a statement absolving the gang of any wrongdoing. Without Kile and Ray's cooperation, the case was dismissed.[34]

Inspectors were not only searching for victims like Kile and Ray; they were also looking for $50,000 purportedly taken from the gang's deposit box and shipped out of town. Both Warner and Johnson had sent packages to Monte McCall's brother Wally in Davenport, Iowa. It was not out of the realm of possibility for the gang to have that much in cash; early estimates put the gang's income for the past three years at $500,000. As authorities scoured the gang's records, some believed it could have been upwards of $1 million ($33,420,841).[35] The gang's cook Lulu Bland remarked, "They lived the grandest I ever saw. I'se worked for fine people, but these here sure did live fine. If they wanted something, they got it, and didn't ask about the cost." Another servant said the men ate dinner with "revolvers in front of their places" and "money flowed about the house like water."[36] Asked about the packages, Mabray laughed, "That might have been two quarts of Arkansas booze we shipped up to our friends. Whisky is one of the good things they have in Arkansas."[37]

Whiskey was not in short supply in Davenport. A veritable Sodom and Gomorrah on the Mississippi River, the town was no stranger to confidence men. At its height, Davenport, which had flirted with reform over the years, boasted two hundred saloons, sporting resorts, theaters, and brothels in its Bucktown District. In 1903 Bishop Henry Cosgrove deemed it "the wicked city of its size in America."[38] Reverend William Lloyd Clark fussed, "If I owned Hell and Davenport, I would sell Davenport and keep Hell. Davenport is saturated with rum and catacombed with houses of ill-fame from her vile levee districts to the top of her polluted hills."[39] A sucker could find games along East Third Street and play alongside "seasoned old racetrack workers, bookmakers, railbirds, and touts" in an atmosphere of "con for con—take or get took." Mabray confederates Monte McCall, Kid Warner, and Walter Nolan could be found alongside "a regiment of tinhorns, comeons, dealers, stools, steerers, lookouts, pork-and-beaners, and cheap pikers that did the cappin' to keep the old machine greased."[40]

Mabray reportedly had a branch office in the city, which came as no surprise; Mabray associate John Dobbins was a well-known figure in local sporting circles. For his part in swindling Thomas Ballew out of $30,000 on a horse race, Dobbins was indicted by the Pottawattamie County grand jury. He was much like "our own 'Monte' McCall," a Davenport paper mused, "one of the most gentlemanly and polished of any of the men who have lived for a while in Davenport without any visible means of earning the money which they spent lavishly, living well and treating their friends with a liberality that made them popular everywhere."[41] Wally McCall denied any knowledge of the contents of the packages as authorities and attorneys wrangled over their possession.[42] When opened, they contained office supplies and condoms the gang filled with chicken blood to conceal in their mouths during fixed contests. In shipping the latter they unwittingly violated the Comstock Law, which prohibited individuals from mailing contraceptives. Warner and Johnson, out on bond, were rearrested.[43]

Mabray was in a foul mood when a reporter visited him in jail. "Four-fifths of the things which are attributed to me by the papers are manufactured," Mabray spat. "This is a put-up job."[44] His mood further darkened when Thomas Ballew arrived looking for the men who swindled him. He gave authorities a letter from one of the gang's ropers who wanted to get even with Mabray. The letter, addressed to Ballew, was dated February 17, 1909. The anonymous writer, later identified as retired confidence man George Howard Simpson, advised Ballew he had made a mistake in having John Dobbins arrested. If he wanted his money back, he should pursue John Mabray and Kid Warner in Little Rock. Simpson warned:

> They have a strong protection there, so don't make an attempt to catch them with the assistance of the local officers. You also want Chas. Wilhelm, now of Omaha, who did the jockey work for the gang. You will find Walter Nolan, who helped Dobbins with you, at Hot Springs; he lives in Chicago. Warner lives at Denver, and Ellis, the other big fellow, is also at Little Rock and be careful not to be seen you will get your men, and you can get a quick settlement as they have a barrel of money.
>
> You had better work very carefully or you won't find any one as they are all very keen people, and the officers will slip them away if they know

you are after them; but if you can get either Warner or Mabray you can get a quick settlement, but Dobbins and Nolan are broke and you can only get a conviction against them.[45]

Despite the occasional petulant outburst, Mabray used the charm that made him a successful confidence man to win over his fellow inmates.[46] He organized a minstrel show among the other prisoners, including "rugged mountaineers" serving time for manufacturing moonshine. Mabray taught them humorous songs, many of which he composed, and they taught him to square-dance. Every day the fleeting sounds of voices calling out "ladies dosee," "grand right and left," and "promenade" could be heard throughout the jail.[47]

Jailhouse follies likely provided Mabray little comfort upon learning that additional victims were willing to cooperate with federal officials and several of his associates had been arrested.[48] Even worse, on March 9, 1909, the grand jury in Council Bluffs indicted Mabray and roper Barney Martin. Influence was then brought to bear on US attorney William Whipple in Little Rock and US attorney Marcellus Temple in Iowa to prevent Mabray's removal as the "whole gambling and crooked sporting fraternity of the country" watched. "Powerful influences" sought "to prevent the exposure of conditions at Council Bluffs which had made Mabray's operation there possible." Whipple spoke to US attorney general George W. Wickersham, and Mabray was subsequently removed from Little Rock and transported to Des Moines. There, in a furnished room equipped with a telephone, he awaited the continuance of his case with an aggregate bail of $140,000 ($4,678,918).[49] The *Arkansas Democrat* jeered, "Good bye, Mabray. Hope you like the Iowa climate as well as you do this." Despite the Pottawattamie County grand jury returning ten indictments against Mabray for conspiracy and grand larceny, he cheerfully predicted he would not be convicted.[50] Perhaps overly confident, he granted interviews upon his arrival in Iowa.

With his attorney present, Mabray selectively recounted his life story to reporters. He did not discuss his youth in Mississippi; instead, he skipped to 1886 when he worked with Jim Dahlman on Nebraska governor James Boyd's ranch. After Boyd sold his herd, Mabray went to Chadron, Nebraska, where he worked in the livestock business and then moved on to Crawford, Nebraska. He pulled up stakes in the spring of 1891 and headed to Galveston, Texas, intent on making a fortune in real estate. Four years later Mabray returned to Crawford with less than three cents in his pockets. After learning to make rubber stamps in Kansas City Mabray went on the road, but when the spring breezes of 1896 began to blow, he was running an Omaha boarding house. For reasons left unexplained, he visited New Orleans, San Francisco, and other major cities. After the close of the 1898 Trans-Mississippi and International Exposition he sold the boarding house but remained in Omaha for a few years. He then entered the hotel business in Kansas City; while there he allegedly patronized Buckfoot confederate Thomas J. Thompson's Senate Club saloon. In 1903 Mabray visited Denver, Cheyenne, and his old Nebraska haunts before visiting Tacoma, Washington. He did not elaborate further about his past, but his future was beginning to resemble that of a certain Webb City swindler.[51]

US attorney Temple still had doubts about the case. In a letter to the attorney general, he argued the states of Iowa and Arkansas could "administer a much more severe punishment" than the federal government. Both he and Judge McPherson "now wish that the state courts had taken jurisdiction first and should certainly not have disturbed them. We feel that this is a dangerous, desperate gang of criminals and that they ought to be adequately punished." Temple cautioned the gang's records indicated they used disreputable means to secure immunity from local and state authorities.[52] Inspector Swenson spoke to Sylvester Rush, special assistant to the US Attorney General in Omaha, and persuaded him of the merits of the case. With the US attorney general's blessing, Rush joined the prosecutorial team, and the case took on a different tone. He decided the gang should be indicted for committing an offense against the United States by using the mails in a scheme to defraud. Rush then directed that everyone connected with the Mabray Gang within the statute of limitations should be prosecuted. Swenson swiftly prepared an indictment for over eighty members of the gang.[53] Mabray, however, may have believed that he had a trump card that authorities could not beat: Benjamin Marks.

11

"THE WHOLE STORY WILL NEVER BE TOLD"

—Kansas City Star, MARCH 7, 1909

I n Council Bluffs a man so "plain and unassuming in appearance" he might be mistaken for "a prosperous, benevolent old farmer" followed the Mabray case. An avid reader, he preferred history. His hair was graying, but he still sported a small sandy mustache and goatee. Perhaps the only feature that betrayed his intelligence was his "shrewd, gray blue eyes." Benjamin Marks, "boss gambler of Council Bluffs," had reason to stay informed. The fate of John Mabray was, in many ways, intertwined with his own.[1]

A mythology has grown up around Ben Marks that makes it difficult to discern what is fact and what is folklore. David Maurer stated Marks developed the "Dollar Store" con, the crude forerunner of the big store con Boatright and Mabray perfected. What is indisputable is that Marks was influential in Council Bluffs. His notoriety grew after his death, but even while alive, his story captured the press's imagination. In 1907 a boy working for the *Omaha Evening World-Herald* attempted to photograph Marks's residence but was stopped by Officer Jack O'Neil who threatened to arrest him. Confronted later by a reporter, O'Neil protested he was only kidding.[2] The incident offered a glimmer of Marks's omniscience and influence. The paper asserted, "To Ben Marks, the czar of Council Bluffs, the city pays allegiance and obeisance—and occasionally tribute. In the latter, it is joined by the two Omahas." Marks's enemies dismissed him with insults: "He blew in out of the swamps. He is the tail end of the Mormon procession. He was the confrere of gamblers and race track men."[3]

The son of Irish immigrants, Marks grew up in Waukegan, Illinois. A resident of Council Bluffs by 1870, he was in his early twenties when he fell in with the city's most influential gambler, Canada Bill Jones. It was from Jones and other knights of the green cloth that Marks learned the trade. Jones had one redeeming quality: a charitable heart. "No suffering or destitute person ever applied in vain to the sympathies of Canada Bill," it was said, and Marks may have adopted this trait from his mentor. Or, he may have simply recognized it as good business.[4]

"And still they come" the *Nonpareil* remarked in 1874 after a man lost $500 to Ben Marks in a game of three-card monte.[5] The following year the paper, "no apologist of men who follow in evil paths," reported that Marks, "who plays cards, pays his bills, and molests no one," had been viciously assaulted by a trio of gunmen.[6] The incident did little to persuade Marks to enter a legitimate line of work. Four years later he and another man robbed a bank in Galesburg, Illinois, but the charges were dropped.[7] In 1882 he was a prominent figure in a public spat that broke out among the city's gambling house proprietors.[8] Through it all, Marks pursued a path to power in Council Bluffs.

Founded in 1853, Council Bluffs was eclipsed by Omaha across the Missouri River but remained an important crossroads. It was also small enough for one man to dominate city politics. A word from Marks "gave the possessor immunity from arrest in more than one big city. It opened prison doors, and it put to work strange and sinister, but powerful influences. It made mayors, and unmade them, in Council Bluffs for more than two decades, and Boss Tweed at the height of his power never had the absolute control over his dominions as Marks had over his." City leaders paid no heed to the revenue furnished by saloons, brothels, and gambling houses leading the Bluffs to become "the Monte Carlo of the west." Newcomers had to obtain Marks's approval first; only after he determined the expenses could they open for business. Crime was said to be negligible; on rare occasions when a robbery occurred the perpetrator would be given up to authorities by Marks, who sometimes asked Tom Dennison, his Omaha counterpart, for assistance. Marks frowned upon familial discord; if a wife complained to him that her husband had gambled away his paycheck, he blacklisted the man. This kept Ben in the good graces of many women even though brothels and saloons ran wide open; a local joked "if any of them had a key it was a mighty rusty one." The practice also kept trouble at bay.[9]

A savvy student of men, Marks ensured patrons of his gambling establishment were given two streetcar tickets upon their arrival: one to use if they were too destitute to pay the fare and one for their eventual return visit.[10] The tickets were used frequently by customers of the 1:30 a.m. streetcar to Omaha known as the "gambler's special." To shut down Marks's gaming houses would mean a significant loss of revenue for the city's coffers. Accordingly, influential residents of Council Bluffs refused to speak ill of Marks; one local confessed, "Ben Marks owns Council

Bluffs, lock, stock and barrel. . . . There has not been a move in this city for years, either politically or commercially," the man continued, "that Ben Marks has not approved. If he opposed it, it just naturally ceased to exist." The *World-Herald* lamented Marks and Council Bluffs were profiting at the expense of Omaha, whose citizens flocked across the river after the lid shut on their wide-open town.[11]

Over it all, Marks kept close watch. When a traveling carnival diverted revenue from gambling interests, Marks made a sizeable donation to a local church and informed the preacher of the carnival's sinful attractions. Horrified, the congregation fought to have the carnival closed. In another instance, Marks engineered the dismissal of two preachers who denounced gambling. The grand jury was of no use because Marks had too many friends in town. Politicians who disagreed with the gambling czar, the *World-Herald* claimed, were removed after one term in office.[12]

Marks's method of dealing with political reformers, an acquaintance explained, was simple. He visited them alone in their office, expressed regret at their actions, and then suggested the reformer act differently. If not, trouble would ensue. Should the reformer refuse to listen, Marks would stick a gun in the man's ribs and repeat himself more forcefully. He promised to come back if necessary and, if the reformer was a sinner, tell him about it while prodding the man with his gun.[13] Marks was even less fond of cheats. He employed a man to observe the gaming room floor from a tiny hole in the ceiling. From his bird's eye view he could see if dealers were going to "go south," a euphemism for taking more of their fair share of money from the table. If two watchers confirmed a dealer was trying to cheat the house, Marks dismissed the man, who knew better than to argue.[14]

Marks exuded quiet confidence. He freely gave interviews to reporters who remarked on his "suave, gentlemanly, courteous" demeanor. He was known to say, "A man's word is his main collateral. No matter how much money he has, he don't go far in business, if his word is no good." A Council Bluffs resident observed, "He can size up the caliber of a man better than any man in the world today. And Ben Marks has never yet invested a dollar either in charity or business without a keen eye to the returns."[15] When asked why he did not pursue a legitimate livelihood like banking, Marks explained loaning money at 6 percent was a good—but slow—way to make money. In his gambling house, which Marks insisted ran fair and honest games of chance, the odds were 20 percent in his favor. "I might run a bank like you mean," he shrugged, "but a faro bank's my speed."[16] Marks held court at the Hoffman House where, just a few years earlier, Leon Lozier and the Buckfoot Gang had been frequent patrons.[17]

When not in Council Bluffs, Marks was at his farm south of Lake Manawa seven miles outside of town. The farm was an investment, but it was also a rural retreat far from the prying eyes of the public. He built a substantial two-story log residence on the property after an earlier structure was destroyed by fire; the origin of the blaze was unknown. Generous verandas led into an interior that boasted six bedrooms, two bathrooms, a kitchen, smoking room, parlor, dining room, and drawing room. It straddled the Pottawattamie and Mills county line; one apocryphal story alleged Marks planned it that way in the event the sheriff arrived. If occupants were in the middle of an illegal activity, they could just step into the other county to avoid arrest. Fittingly, Mabray held horse races there.[18]

Marks observed, "Politics is the ruin of many a good man. It is a will-o'-the-wisp that lures him to destruction of body and mind." Political intrigue may have grown tiresome even for Marks. In 1907 it was speculated that "the crash of the overthrow of powerful dynasties has reached Council Bluffs and it may be that the czar, who has fought so long, is getting tired of the intoxication of power."[19] Just how long Marks could wield his power remained to be seen as John Mabray and his little red ledger brought unwanted attention to Council Bluffs.[20]

A steady stream of victims contacted Inspector Swenson; several traveled to Little Rock to assist with the gang's prosecution.[21] James F. Tierney had dropped $10,000 on a wrestling match in New Orleans.[22] Joseph P. Walker had lost $5,000 and a diamond stud on a race in Council Bluffs; he shrugged, "It was the usual game." George S. Bedford had been fleeced for $12,500 in the same fashion.[23] Henry Stogsdill of Cabool, Missouri, had lost $3,000 on a race. Stogsdill's case was especially embarrassing; when his letter of credit was denied in Denver, he returned home to borrow money. He still owed creditors $1,000.[24] Perhaps to influence public opinion, Swenson selectively shared information gathered during the investigation.

Among the tantalizing items he released were telegrams from Ben Marks to Mabray and letters from Monte McCall to Isadore Warner. McCall, writing from Omaha to Warner in Denver, said in part:

> Am going to write Jim tonight to see if he wishes to go to work here. It will be to you in his care, so you may do as you like about whether or not to send him. One of the main reasons I formed a partnership with Mabray is because he is too much of a hustler to allow some other joint to heave. Will you send your draft for your hit Monday. Let me hear from you or come over for a trip. How is the political world in Denver. The impression hereabouts seems to be that Dennison is considerably worried over Shercliffe. With best wishes, I am your friend, Mc.

John Mabray and his confederates took photographs with victims to help ensure they would not go to the authorities; this one was taken prior to a wrestling match. From left to right: Leon Lozier; an unidentified victim from Butte, Montana; John Mabray; Darby Thielman; and Ed Leach. *National Archives and Records Administration.*

In another missive to Warner, McCall discussed opening a big store at Davenport, Iowa. There must have been discontent among their ranks because McCall cryptically told Warner, "With such conditions existing, we, I believe, will be able to make more money, besides gain a lot of revenge."[25] The intriguing correspondence led reporters to closely question local authorities.

Council Bluffs police chief George Richmond scowled when asked about Mabray. "[Swenson] never consulted me or called upon me for any assistance," he snapped.[26] When a reporter queried Richmond "why conditions were any nearer 'perfect' in the Bluffs than elsewhere," he cagily replied, "I have not the slightest idea." When pressed, he responded, "If there were no Ballews and no Cavanaughs there would be no Mabrays and Dobbinses." He disavowed knowledge of the gang's activities but admitted he had spoken to victims. One was Max Lindenbaum. In 1907, accompanied by his attorney, he told Richmond he lost $10,000 on a fight.[27] Richmond scolded Lindenbaum, telling him he "did not come to my office with very clean hands." He asserted, "I did not have a thing tangible to warrant me in making a move."[28]

Chief Richmond was not the only one on the defensive. Pottawattamie County prosecutor John Hess insisted he did not know about the gang until the fall of 1908. He acknowledged receiving two complaints from victims, but only one came to Council Bluffs. The grand jury issued indictments for larceny, but the warrants were not served because, Hess conjectured, the swindlers had used aliases and could not be located by the police. When asked if a conviction could be secured against the gang, Hess was reluctant to give his opinion. He believed witnesses could be at a disadvantage since they were men "who started out to do the biting [and] got bitten themselves."

The case took another unexpected turn when allegations of murder and fake identity enveloped Mabray. Lillian Gates, a British citizen living in St. Louis, accused the swindler of being a dead man. Gates swore Mabray was St. Louis horse racing enthusiast James McCann. After McCann was found dead in 1903, the ensuing investigation led authorities to a friend of McCann's who styled himself Lord Seymour Barrington. Revealed as a fraud, Barrington was convicted of McCann's murder in a sensational trial that captivated St. Louis society. "There is nothing to it," Mabray fumed, "The woman is crazy." St. Louisans who knew McCann said Mabray was not the dead man.[29]

Other ghosts from the past resurfaced. Journalists and others linked Mabray's fraudulent activities to Robert Boatright and the Buckfoot Gang. Following Boatright's demise in 1904, his confederates formed individual groups across the country, but the "Mabray gang was the outcome of it all, the culmination of the most gigantic fraud that ever shocked the world."[30] Denverite Joseph Walker identified George Ryan as one of the men who had swindled him. Unbeknownst to federal authorities, Ryan was under indictment in Hot Springs, Arkansas, on a charge of assault with intent to kill on Robert Cardwell. Cardwell asked for repeated continuances until he could travel to Hot Springs. Ryan's good fortune kept him out of Iowa for over a year.[31] After an absence of several years Ed Ellis returned to Jasper County, Missouri, where Sheriff Arch McDonald promptly arrested him for swindling Thomas Ballew. Before his arrest Ellis told friends he had a deal arranged for $65,000. Pottawattamie County Sheriff Thomas McCaffery asked McDonald to hold Ellis as a fugitive. McDonald released him after twenty hours, only for Ellis to be rearrested by Constable Ed Hansford on a warrant charging him with bringing $30,000 of stolen money into the state. At his arraignment he pled not guilty and was released on $500 bond provided by his brother-in-law George B. Flournoy. Ellis denied any connection with Mabray.[32] When Ballew arrived in Joplin, Ellis could not be located. "This is the first time I ever went on anybody's bond," Flournoy sighed, "and it has taught me something. I ought to have my head taken off for signing the bond in the first place."[33]

Buckfoot stalwart Garrette Stansbury was accused of conspiring with Frank Scott to pull off a fake horse race in Fredonia, Kansas.[34] Newspaper reporter and former Buckfoot sprinter Tom S. Robison was arrested on an Iowa farm on charges of conspiracy and grand larceny.[35] James Mayelin of Correctionville, Iowa, had lost $5,000 seven years earlier on a foot race Robison ran near Joplin; he subsequently lost his farm. Locals noticed Robison took mysterious trips and returned flush with money and diamonds. None of his acquaintances defended him.[36] Buckfoot sprinter and Mabray roper Dick Beatte hid at his father's farm outside Woodward, Oklahoma. On one of Beatte's frequent visits to town, an officer sought to apprehend him. Beatte furiously whipped his horse, but the officer shot it dead and unceremoniously ran him down.[37]

As memories of Robert Boatright and his fleetfooted colts reemerged, a Kansas City paper commented on Mabray's "rather startling resemblance to Boatright." Mabray could have easily "passed for Boatright." The Mississippian, however, "never knew him, although he had heard of his races."[38] Like Boatright, Mabray had influential friends. Omaha mayor James "Cowboy Jim" Dahlman told the press, "I knew Mabray well in 1883 to 1886. Mabray was a cracking good cowpuncher."[39]

This prompted an Omaha paper to reproduce two letters Dahlman sent Mabray. In one, from 1907, Dahlman warned Mabray about the distraught wife of a man named Harriman; likely the spouse of Mabray confederate Russell Harriman. In the other, dated 1908, Dahlman told Mabray he had failed to make "arrangements for the money I owe you."[40] The mayor acknowledged he wrote the letters and admitted Mabray loaned him money, but declined to elaborate. The *Omaha Bee* asked Dahlman about a letter Mabray roper William Scott wrote in 1906, in which Scott told Mabray, "I will answer and let you know that I have everything ready to do business. WE CAN PULL IT OFF IN OMAHA, AS THERE WE CAN GET THE BANK ROLL."[41] Dahlman deflected by saying it was "all Greek to me." The reporter wondered, "Was Omaha 'fixed' for the operations of the Mabray bunco gang in 1906?"[42]

Dick Beatte was a sprinter for the Buckfoot Gang; he later worked with
John C. Mabray. *National Archives and Records Administration.*

Dahlman, a Texan who fled to Nebraska after killing his brother-
in-law in 1878, worked as a cowboy before serving as sheriff of Dawes
County, Nebraska. A Democrat, he became mayor of Omaha in 1906.
During Dahlman's eight terms and two decades in office, he was sympa-
thetic toward Omaha's vice and liquor interests. Dahlman was accused of
being a front man for Omaha political boss Tom Dennison, though one
historian has pointed out the relationship between the two men remains
unclear. Nicknamed the Gray Wolf, Dennison remains a "shadowy and
enigmatic figure, cloaked by legend and hearsay." Born to Irish immigrants, he left his family's Nebraska farm and wandered west to work in
gambling houses. When he returned to Omaha in 1892, Dennison's solid
six-foot frame was attired in expensive clothes and diamonds. He consolidated control of the city's Third Ward, whose brothels, saloons, and
gambling dens led to Omaha's reputation as the "wickedest city in the
United States." He forged an important alliance with the *Omaha Bee*'s
Edward Rosewater while his lieutenant William "Billy" Nesselhous kept
a tight grip on the city. Nesselhous served as a reference for the gang's
Omaha post office box application. Dahlman, Dennison, and Marks

could have been among Mabray's allies who sought to help him behind the scenes as was insinuated in the press.[43] They may have feared what Mabray's records revealed.

A tally from Mabray's ledger showed the gang carried out twenty-nine tricks from April 1 to October 13, 1908, for a profit of $162,593 ($5,433,995). From October 28 to November 15, 1908, they brought in $19,000. Inspector Swenson believed Mabray had pulled in $256,000 from the fall of 1907 into early 1908.[44] This meant there were numerous victims, and each one that could be identified would be subpoenaed and summoned before the federal grand jury.[45] The victims who appeared in Little Rock agreed to travel to Council Bluffs to aid authorities, and more were expected to cooperate.[46] Some, like William McGrath, had even conducted their own investigations.

McGrath pursued the gang after he was swindled out of $10,000. He claimed he had evidence the gang made $5 million over two and a half years with big stores in Duluth, San Francisco, Denver, Salt Lake City, Fargo, South Bend, and New Orleans. There were allegedly also stores in Connecticut and New Jersey. McGrath contended "Mabray is a big man, but there are far bigger than he." McGrath believed Mabray's outfit was just one part of a larger organization. He claimed there were two other branches operating in the east and on the Pacific coast. McGrath explained, "They use many of the same men and interchange when things become too hot. The section in the East is separate from the others, apparently, the only connection being in the heads way up the line."[47]

Inspector Swenson believed Mabray was only connected to the Seattle and Denver stores. He did not believe Mabray was involved with the South Bend, Indiana, outfit headed by Russell B. Harriman, Frank W. Brown, and Edward C. Moore. After the men separated from Mabray in 1908 he replaced them with Monte McCall, Isador Warner, and James Johnson. The South Bend big store paid 13 percent for protection—reportedly the highest protection fee ever paid.[48] Its success was brief; shortly after the store opened a victim contacted authorities. The use of the mails to ensnare victims brought about the store's downfall; the government's chief witness was US postal clerk John Alward. Roper William Flemming received a prison sentence for swindling a man out of $10,000. His conviction brought an end to the South Bend store.[49]

With the collapse of the Council Bluffs outfit a cascade of arrests ensued. Ernest Powers was among the first to be apprehended.[50] While a student at the University of Denver, Powers ran a race against James Ashmore—a name associated with the Buckfoot Gang—at Denver's Overland Park. The *Denver Evening Post* predicted, "[Powers] is gaining experience very fast, and if he keeps on he will be a wiser and sadder man before long."[51] Colorado authorities refused to release him to federal authorities in Iowa; he was subsequently convicted on state charges in Denver.[52] After a vigorous series of appeals, Powers entered the Colorado State Penitentiary.[53] His parole application was denied and he remained in prison.[54] Boone B. Jacobs, who helped Powers rope victim J. C. Bowman, fled Denver after he was released on bond.[55] Pursued by authorities, Jacobs committed suicide as officers were on the verge of taking him back to Colorado from the obscurity of a small Kansas farm.[56]

Other arrests followed. Buckfoot and Mabray roper William Gibson was extradited from San Francisco.[57] Wrestler Thomas Gay was arrested and released on bond. Forced to forfeit his bond after the gang's attorney neglected to notify him of his trial date, a livid Gay agreed to serve as a government witness.[58] William Scott dodged a Kansas sheriff by asking him to wait outside his home while he changed his clothes. After some time had passed, the sheriff entered the residence and asked Scott's wife where her husband was. She smiled, "Will went away quite a while ago." Scott had slipped out, grabbed a horse, and galloped off without even so much as a saddle. When the law caught up to him, he gave bond and disappeared.[59]

When John Mabray appeared before the federal grand jury in Council Bluffs, US district judge Smith McPherson, a veteran of numerous Buckfoot trials, presided. US attorney Marcellus Temple told reporters evidence indicated the gang had fraudulently acquired over $1 million from victims. The estimate might have been too low as some victims refused to cooperate. One of the first to testify, Zachariah Pierpont, bet every cent he had on a fake horse race and was broke.[60] Among the pieces of evidence used to show the character of Mabray's operation were letters written in 1908 by George A. Bradley. He informed Mabray he had fixed a town in New Jersey across the river from New York. Bradley had arranged protection for seventy-five dollars a week; that included the sheriff, chief of police, and district attorney's office. If things got too warm for Mabray, Bradley would welcome him in New Jersey but not Mabray's partners. He ended, "This is a great field & as you know the wealth is here. And with a few good agents business would flourish."[61]

Mabray may have wished he had accepted Bradley's offer. On September 24, 1909, John Mabray, Ben Marks, and over eighty others were indicted on charges of conspiring to use the mails to defraud.[62] To the west, an elusive trio was about to receive a fateful visit.

12

RED LEO

In San Jose, California, Russell B. Harriman answered the door at
246 Park Avenue and found US postal inspectors James O'Connell
and William F. Allmon pointing revolvers at him. He whirled back
inside, but when he burst through the rear door Postal Inspector Charles
Ranger and Santa Clara county sheriff Arthur Langford were waiting for
him. A cordon of deputies had surrounded the house. Harriman looked
at Ranger and Langford, shrugged, and surrendered. Inside Harriman's
rental home the officers found Frank W. Brown, Edward C. Moore,
Canadian athlete Walter Knox, and Harriman's wife. Harriman, Brown,
and Moore had evaded arrest for over a year. Now John Mabray's chief
counterparts had been captured along with a large amount of incriminating correspondence. Leon Lozier, across the bay in Oakland when
the arrests took place, was apprehended in Battle Mountain, Nevada.[1]
Harriman, Moore, and Brown fought their extradition for over a year;
Lozier waived extradition and returned to Iowa.[2]

While Lozier was a member of the Buckfoot Gang, Harriman and
Brown came from different backgrounds. Russell Barrett Harriman was
born in 1865 in Owen Sound, Grey County, Ontario, Canada. He worked
as a telegraph operator before becoming a confidence man. Harriman
worked with Mabray until parting ways in 1908; they had alternated
roles as the millionaire and the millionaire's private secretary.[3]

Washingtonian Frank Wilson Brown came from much different
circumstances. Born in 1867, he began chalking stock quotes on a black-
board as a teenager and found he had an affinity for the business. Brown
opened a brokerage on F Street and represented New York firms of the
first- and second-rate variety, though "his interests were of the bucket-
shop order." He developed a habit of failing; when he did, he often left
town for his health, only to return and open a new office. Brown's last
business venture was reportedly in 1895 when he lost around $100,000

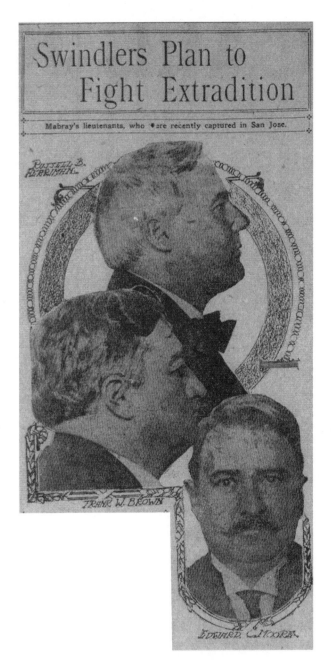

Swindlers Plan to Fight Extradition

Mabray's lieutenants, who *are recently captured in San Jose.

Russell Harriman, Frank Wilson Brown, and Edward Moore.
San Francisco Call.

and took many of his clients with him. Still, Brown was the sort of man everybody liked.[4] While ugly talk followed his last firm's collapse, Brown escaped unscathed. After committing bigamy he and his wife divorced. In 1901 Brown was arrested for his involvement in a stock swindle. Despite his past troubles, acquaintances expressed their surprise he would have been so careless as to get into serious trouble out west.[5] Brown, it seemed, had tempted fate one too many times.

Just three years earlier Harriman, Brown, and Lozier had been implicated in a similar con in Seattle. With the assistance of a local sport, the men secured protection and built a houseboat on Lake Washington, where they staged fake athletic contests. The Seattle Athletic Club and its former director, wrestler Dr. Benjamin F. Roller, were suspected to have been associated with the confidence scheme, but their involvement went unconfirmed by local papers.[6]

Some newspapers incorrectly reported Edward C. Moore was a member of the Buckfoot Gang. In hindsight the mistake is understandable because there were two confidence men who shared that name. It is true that Edward C. Moore of Council Bluffs, Iowa, was part of the Buckfoot Gang, but he and his family moved to San Diego, California, shortly after he and Leon Lozier avoided the Iowa State Penitentiary. Brown and Harriman's partner was, in fact, Edward Cook Moore of Washington, DC. Born to a small-town Pennsylvania clothier turned government employee, Moore grew up in the nation's capital. In 1900 he was a twenty-six-year-old broker living with his parents; though it is unclear how he became a confidence man, his entrée to the criminal world may have been the result of an acquaintance with fellow Washington broker Frank Brown. Now Moore found himself mixing with confidence men and athletes.[7]

Wrestlers George "Ole" Marsh, Jack Carkeek, and others formed the gang's stable of athletes. Their methods would have been uncomfortably familiar to Boatright and Mabray's victims, right down to posing for photographs before an event. An Oregon man reportedly lost $42,500. Others lost anywhere from $2,000 to $15,000. Victims hailed from Anaconda and Butte, Montana; Grand Forks, North Dakota; and Vancouver, British Columbia. The men had reportedly finalized arrangements to open big stores in Tacoma and San Francisco after securing police protection.[8] In all, the gang made $150,000 before the *Seattle Star* exposed them in the summer of 1906.[9] Like a startled covey of quail, the swindlers fled.

Harriman, Lozier, Moore, and Brown were not the only ones apprehended that fall. Officers brought in their quarry from across the country. Joseph E. Wright was caught in San Antonio.[10] Wrestlers Bert R. Shores and George Marsh, and roper Winn S. Harris, were arrested after patronizing

Edward C. Moore of Washington, DC. *National Archives and Records Administration.*

the Alaska–Yukon–Pacific Exposition in Seattle, where Warner caused a sensation when he laid down in the ring before a match with Benjamin Roller. A man in the audience then read a statement from Warner claiming he had agreed to lose twice to Roller. Roller and his entourage erupted in anger; when the match was finally held, he beat Warner in a contest that "savored of pugilism and jiujitsu."[11] Former police judge John C. Smith was apprehended in Streator, Illinois.[12] After brothers Harry and Clarence Forbes were arrested, Clarence told Inspector Swenson "nearly every prize fight is fixed before the principals enter the ring, and in fixing their bouts they had done nothing more than was customary." Wrestling, he claimed, operated the same way.[13] Buckfoot prizefighter Eddie Morris was taken into custody in Amsterdam, New York; boxer Ed McCoy was picked up in Salt Lake City.[14] Dr. Robert E. L. Goddard was apprehended in Fort Worth, Texas, bringing the total of former Buckfoot Gang associates in Mabray's orbit to seven men.[15] By the end of October, over twenty-two members of the gang had been arrested.[16]

As Mabray and an ever-growing number of his confederates awaited their day in federal court, John Dobbins went on trial in Pottawattamie County for swindling Thomas Ballew. Dobbins had been arrested in

New York City where he was a partner in a billiard room.[17] Perhaps signaling Iowa state authorities lacked faith in local officials, Iowa attorney general Howard Webster "Webb" Byers assisted Pottawattamie County prosecutor John Hess. The two men agreed to try Dobbins on larceny.[18] Joining Hess and Byers was Thomas Ballew's attorney John P. Organ. Seated at the defense table were Emmet Tinley and three other attorneys. Former boxer Walter Nolan—who helped swindle Ballew—was absent.[19]

As Dobbins confidently strode into the courtroom a reporter noted his polished appearance. Ballew watched intently as Dobbins walked past him to the defense table; Dobbins gave no indication he noticed his victim. When the trial began on November 15, 1909, the fifty-seven-year-old Ballew took the stand and related his story with "ease and grace." Several times his testimony caused "a murmur of amusement."[20] "The merchant prince of North Missouri" worked as a salesman before he launched fifteen lumberyards, purchased lumber mills, founded a bank, and established a department store in Princeton, Missouri.[21] Far from being a backwoods bumpkin, Ballew's rise from peddler to merchant shows he was a shrewd businessman. His presence in the courtroom, however, demonstrated Ballew was not immune from greed and poor judgment.

Ballew, who had known Dobbins since he was a boy, was aware the younger man liked to gamble. He also knew he had financial issues; Dobbins still owed him $426 for furniture. On October 5, 1908, Walter Nolan—using the alias Walter H. Martin—walked into Ballew's store, handed him a letter of introduction from Dobbins, and told him about an Iowa horse race. Ballew, who repeatedly emphasized during his testimony that he was not a gambler, explained he agreed to participate after Dobbins told him his winnings would help him stop gambling and be able to repay Ballew. He was also, he conceded, motivated by Martin's promise to pay him 10 percent of the winnings. Once in Council Bluffs, Ballew arranged for two banks to send him letters of credit for $30,000.[22]

After the money was secured, Ballew was introduced to the millionaires, bets were taken, and the men were then transported by automobile to a meadow near Lake Manawa. There two jockeys watched from atop their horses as 600 yards were measured off. Once the course was ready, they slowly rode their steeds to the starting line. After a few false starts the horses sprinted down the makeshift racecourse. As they approached the finish line Ballew noticed one of the jockeys was lying on the horse's neck with blood coming from his mouth. A spectator grabbed the reins and helped the jockey from the horse. Ballew heard one of the millionaires exclaim the man had suffered a hemorrhage. Lying prone on the ground, the jockey raised his head and weakly asked, "Did we win?" The stakeholder, a man named Wilson, began to tremble. He told Ballew they had to call a foul race.[23] Arrangements were hastily made for a rematch in Springfield, Illinois. Before Ballew left, Wilson assured him he would return his money within a few days. Instead, he received a telegram from one of the millionaires stating they knew Ballew had participated in a scheme to defraud them. Ballew realized he would never see his money again.

He endured a withering cross-examination by the defense. Attorney Emmet Tinley belittled him as "Buck-'em-all Ballew," but Ballew proved a tough witness.[24] Former Mercer County sheriff Frank Minter testified he ran into Ballew on his way to Council Bluffs. When he asked the businessman if he was worried about trouble, Ballew responded no, as "they were under the protection of the officers at Council Bluffs and under complete protection." Tinley grilled Minter about his alleged attempt to shake down Ballew prior to being hired by Ballew as a private detective.[25]

After Minter finished, several Mabray victims testified. William H. Bedford of Bolckow, Missouri, recounted how he was swindled in 1908. He had just listed his farm for sale when his neighbor, accompanied by a man who introduced himself as William Carson, visited him. After falling for a horse race, he traveled to Council Bluffs. During dinner he felt "queer and unnatural"; Bedford thought he had been drugged. Courtroom spectators laughed when he described Red Leo, the horse he bet on: "I thought I had seen horses that could run faster." Banker John Hermelbracht's exchanges with Emmet Tinley made onlookers laugh several times. Tinley warned, "Hold on, you're not running a vaudeville show." The German shot back, "No circus for me." Farmer Clinton A. Nelson of Alma, Michigan, roped by Herbert "The Brass Kid" Coon in 1908, told the jury after the jockey fell from Red Leo that one of his ropers callously yelled, "I don't care if he does die, I wish he would; he had ought to die."[26]

Dobbins did not take the stand, nor did the defense call any witnesses.[27] On November 23, 1909, after six hours of deliberation, the jury found John Dobbins guilty of larceny. He received five years in the Iowa State Penitentiary.[28] Dobbins's legal battle ended in failure the following year.

Other members of the Mabray Gang faced their own days in court.[29] Roper Frank Scott was tried in Pottawattamie County District Court. Judge Andrew Thornell had presided over the 1903 trial of Buckfoot colts Leon Lozier and Edward C. Moore. Banker John Hermelbracht explained he had met Scott on a train when they were transporting cattle to market.[30] Sheriff Patrick Dorsey recounted how Scott had asked him if had a warrant for his arrest; Dorsey said no. Scott then bragged he had conned Hermelbracht and flashed a large roll of bills. He gloated that he and another man received half of the $5,000; the other half went to men in Council Bluffs.[31] Scott's father-in-law M. S. Campbell appeared for the prosecution; he was angry his daughter had mortgaged her farm for bail money. When the defense asked, "Is it not a fact that you have no use for your son-in-law, the defendant?" Campbell answered, "Well, to tell the truth, I have seen men I have thought more of." Campbell told another witness he did not know if Scott was guilty, but "he should be in the penitentiary anyway."[32] Several key witnesses for the state failed to appear. Because they were Nebraska citizens, the men could not be compelled to appear in Iowa court, leaving Attorney General Byers less than pleased.[33]

In a move that diverged from Dobbins's trial, Frank Scott testified. Scott admitted he approached Hermelbracht and attended the race as a spectator but denied receiving a percentage of the proceeds.[34] The jury deadlocked early and Scott was acquitted.[35] Bowing to jurors as they filed out of the room, Scott shook hands with prosecutor Hess and quipped, "Well, you can't convict an honest man." Hess stiffly replied, "Nothing personal in it with me. I simply want to do my duty as a public officer." Byers was not present; he had already returned to Des Moines. Scott was not entirely off the hook. After the verdict was read, deputy US marshal William Groneweg arrested him on a warrant under the indictment returned by the federal grand jury in Council Bluffs. Hess quickly attempted to raise Scott's bond on the remaining conspiracy charge, but Judge Thornell refused his request and "intimated that acquittal in the larceny case carried the conspiracy case with it."[36]

As John Mabray awaited his day in court, the odds were mixed: Dobbins and Powers had been convicted, but Scott had escaped prison. The gang also had dodged state charges in Little Rock. Just how Mabray viewed his odds of escaping justice is unknown, but he was a gambling man. Whether his luck would hold was yet to be seen.[37]

13

"THE BIG STORE IS CLOSED"

—Omaha Daily Bee, MARCH 27, 1910

A s barren Iowa fields forlornly awaited the spring planting season, federal prosecutors in Council Bluffs prepared for one of the most sensational cases of their careers. Efforts were made to capture the remaining members of the gang who had evaded authorities. Roper Willard "Waco Kid" Powell was arrested in Jacksonville, Florida, where he frequented the races. Over one hundred witnesses were subpoenaed; authorities worried the courtroom they planned to use was not large enough to accommodate both witnesses and the public.[1] Federal prosecutors Marcellus Temple and Sylvester Rush announced that should Mabray and the others be convicted in Council Bluffs it would preclude trial under the Omaha indictment, which may have brought some comfort to the gang.[2]

As victims and cons gathered in hotel lobbies to compare notes about each other's misfortunes, a rumor emerged that Mabray and his codefendants would plead guilty. On March 9, 1910, the Mississippian and fifteen of his associates appeared in court before Judge McPherson and did the opposite. Among those who appeared were Buckfoot stalwarts Leon Lozier, Eddie Morris, and Dr. Robert E. L. Goddard. Several received court-appointed counsel. Ben Marks, too ill to appear, was granted a continuance. Watching with intent interest were several newspapermen and citizens. Noticeably absent from the courtroom were Russell Harriman, Frank Brown, and Edward Moore; they were fighting extradition from California.[3] Also missing were Monte McCall, Isador Warner, and James Johnson; after state charges were dropped against them in Little Rock, they gave authorities the slip in Hot Springs, Arkansas.[4]

Prior to being arraigned, Mabray, sporting a new suit and a tie with a "frolicsome, happy tint," called out to reporters, "You may say for me that I am innocent, neither a liar nor a thief, and in good health." He then flashed a "twinkle of a smile" at his codefendants.[5] Mabray spoke to the press again during a brief recess. "I don't bear anybody any grudges," he explained, "but when I get my liberty, which will not be very far off, I have a thing or two to remember on both sides of the score." He joked he had not missed a meal in the fourteen months he had been in jail before playfully complaining about an Omaha scoundrel who sent him a postcard that said, "Nobody loves a fat man."[6]

Rumors persisted Mabray would enter a last-minute guilty plea, but not to avoid a harsh prison sentence, since the maximum was two years in prison. Instead, it was believed, Mabray wanted to prevent "the most sensational and interesting details" of the gang's activities from being exposed.[7] Prior to the trial Iowa attorney general Byers met with Mabray and offered him a deal: plead guilty in federal court and testify before the Pottawattamie County grand jury against his associates, and all charges against him in state court would be dropped. The Mississippian responded, "You can hang me first before I will turn on those fellows."[8] Like a true gambler, Mabray kept his cards close to his vest.

On Thursday, March 10, 1910, the most highly anticipated trial in the Midwest opened. As Omaha boss Tom Dennison paced outside the courtroom, several farmers, a jeweler, and a retired grocer were selected to serve on the jury. Seated in the courtroom were eighteen defendants represented by a "little army of lawyers." Lead counsels Emmet Tinley and George Wright were assisted by six additional attorneys. The prosecution consisted of Marcellus Temple, George Stewart, and Sylvester Rush.[9]

At the request of US attorney Charles Goss, Rush joined the prosecution with the title of special assistant to the attorney general; his authority was subsequently expanded by US attorney general George Wickersham, who closely followed the case.[10] In a confidential report to Inspector-in-Charge W. W. Dickson, Swenson wrote: "On account of the extraordinary entangling influences brought to bear on behalf of the defense in this case, such a special prosecutor is of the utmost importance." Mabray had boasted, "We have the chief of police, we have the sheriff, we have the prosecuting attorney and we have a bank." Swenson went on, "On account of this implication of officials and prominent men and through the money in possession of the gang, extraordinary efforts are made for the defense, both openly, and secretly." A detective, masquerading as an attorney, had traveled the country on the gang's behalf. Defense attorney George Wright, Swenson claimed, was hired because he was a close friend of Judge McPherson and prosecutor George Stewart. Temple "cannot consult freely or trust his own assistant in this case. On account of these unusual conditions, a special prosecutor from the office of the Attorney General, who will be in a position to stand up fearlessly against the corruption, is particularly needed."[11] Despite Swenson's concerns about undue influence, McPherson was wary of outside interference affecting the trial.

From his bench in the crowded courtroom Judge McPherson warned the jury, "The town is full of detectives and spies on both sides. Make no mistakes. It seems to me that there is a bevy of men about here who are attempting to peddle out what they call facts. You will try this case on what you hear from the witness stand."[12] Notably, several women watched the proceedings; one reporter estimated women made up one-third of the audience. When asked what she thought, a woman replied, "After you have been laughed at for buying things you didn't want from an agent, and pursuing bargain sales it sort of bolsters up your self-respect to see how men are occasionally played upon."[13]

What spectators heard during the trial remains mostly unknown. Because the three volumes of witness testimony are missing from the trial records, newspaper accounts—despite their limitations and challenges—offer the only record of what transpired in the courtroom. After opening statements, victims Alexander Delain, Peter Voorhees, Henry Stogsdill, Zachariah Pierpont, and Clinton Nelson testified. Spectators repeatedly laughed at Delain, who stopped to apologize to the court for his lack of education. McPherson threatened to expel the next man who laughed.[14] Roper William Scott and his wife both took the stand. Scott's reluctance to discuss events in detail led McPherson to sarcastically remark, "The witness is either unwilling or stupid, I don't know which."[15] Government witness Thomas S. Gay, however, had no difficulty in recounting his role in swindling victims. Without flinching, Gay looked at his former associates as he explained how he bit on a bag of blood and pretended to die during wrestling matches. Known as "100" in correspondence, Gay provided critical information about the gang in Los Angles, New Orleans, Seattle, and San Francisco.[16]

While the Mabray trial occupied everyone's attention, legal proceedings of another sort occupied state authorities. Iowa attorney general H. Webb Byers filed a petition in Pottawattamie County District Court to oust Council Bluffs police chief George Richmond from office. Byers charged Richmond with multiple crimes including "willful and habitual neglect and refusal to perform the duties of this office, willful misconduct in office, extortion," and attempted bribery. The charges were signed by William Killpack, president of Council Bluff's Law Enforcement League. The legal proceeding was brought under Iowa's so-called Cosson Laws, passed the previous year. George Cosson, a young Progressive Republican legislator, had successfully fought inadequate enforcement of the state's liquor and vice regulations and secured tougher enforcement statutes. These laws "included a recall mechanism that empowered private citizens to seek a judicial remedy against local officials who failed to uphold the law." Their passage helped Cosson establish a statewide reputation as a reformer and succeed Byers as Iowa attorney general in 1911.[17]

In the wake of Byers's action, the *Nonpareil* believed public sentiment in Council Bluffs and Iowa had changed. Illegal practices previously tolerated by citizens "for the sake of public revenue, or in a spirit of moral indifference" could no longer be justified. One anonymous local was not convinced. He snorted, "The whole affair looks to me like peanut politics" with Richmond as a scapegoat. He pointed out Killpack must have forgotten when he was county attorney "the saloons were notoriously wide open." Judge Eugene Woodruff found Richmond guilty of several charges, save for aiding Mabray, and ordered his removal from office.[18]

Two days into Mabray's trial, Judge McPherson was irritable. He grumbled, "Time is being wasted on trivial matters. There is no use in repetition of details as to how these witnesses lose their money. Their stories are all much the same." Instead, the morning was spent deciding whether to admit the evidence Swenson had seized in Little Rock. The defense argued it would be akin to forcing Mabray to testify against himself, but McPherson overruled their objection and admitted the papers into evidence. Victims Samuel Sutor and Joshua H. Secrest recounted their stories; explosions of laughter erupted throughout the courtroom after Sutor said the gang had him "going like a motion picture show."[19] Mabray, after court ended, mocked Secrest, "You ought to go home and preach that to your grandchildren. The idea of sitting up there and dealing out that stuff. Oh, no, you didn't bet that money; oh no."[20] He remained silent, however, when his associates took the stand.

Michigan wrestlers Ernest Fenby and James Coon testified about their participation in fixed matches. Wrestling enthusiasts readily recognized Fenby when he appeared in court fresh off his loss to Stanislaw Zbysko.[21] Mabray's athletes, the *Omaha Bee* observed, "were not mere imitations, but men who had attained to proficiency in their professions, degraded to the purposes of the gang."[22] Harry Forbes, whose parents hoped he would become an accomplished violinist, was a former world bantamweight champion. His brother Clarence was a capable bantam- and featherweight fighter.[23] Former minor league baseball player Rudolph "Darby" Thielman also figured in Mabray's retinue.[24] Based on the gang's size, it is probable there were far more athletes who were a part of Mabray's outfit; indeed, the names of other prizefighters and wrestlers are

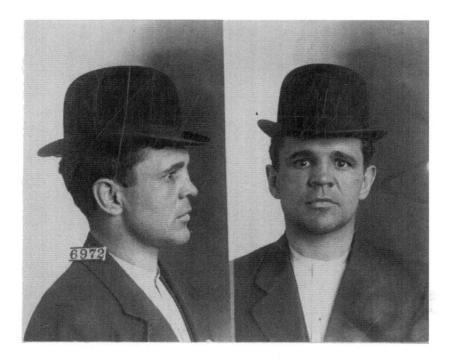

Harry Forbes. *National Archives and Records Administration.*

mentioned in court records and press accounts. For example, former boxing champion Joe Gans and Omaha pugilist Clarence English were rumored to be on the prosecution's witness list. The extent of other disgraced athletes' involvement will likely never be known, but they were just one part of Mabray's complex organization.[25]

Others, however, were not athletes but accomplished confidence men and gamblers. Claudius Willard Powell was, like John Mabray, a son of the South. Born in Mississippi to a Confederate veteran and his schoolteacher wife following the war, he moved with his family to Waco, Texas. Fond of animals, it was perhaps no surprise he became a turfman—that is, a horseman who followed the races.[26] After he left home at sixteen, Powell became a fixture in Fort Worth. Although the Waco Kid was only thirty-two in 1910, he was already well-known to Texas officials.

In 1901 Powell roped a storekeeper into a crooked poker game. Later that year he was arrested for assaulting his wife. Powell was subsequently arrested for swindling; he threatened to file a lawsuit after the police roughed him up. The Kid continued to appear in Fort Worth papers for various crimes until he caught a case he could not beat. In the summer of 1902, as his parents watched, he was convicted of running a con.[27] The case was reversed and remanded on appeal, but the self-described whiskey salesman served two concurrent terms for theft and swindling in the Texas State Penitentiary. Discharged in February 1905, it is unknown when Powell became affiliated with Mabray.[28] Now he found himself contemplating another prison stint.

While the presence of former athletes like Harry Forbes was undoubtedly sensational for some, the star witness was confidence man Howard Simpson. A former member of the gang, he traveled from his home in Spokane, Washington, to testify for the government. Simpson, the newspapers claimed, had made enough money to invest in real estate and retire. He was the individual who mailed the anonymous letter to Samuel Sutor that contributed to the gang's downfall. On the stand Simpson reveled in telling stories; he boasted he taught Robert Boatright the big store con before teaching Mabray. He asserted he gathered remnants of the gang following Boatright's death and created a more effective con. One awestruck reporter quipped, "He appeared to know every gambler and 'sure-thing man' between Sing Sing and San Quentin."[29]

Simpson was reluctant to testify against Mabray, but he did not hold back when discussing Edward Moore, Frank Brown, and Russell Harriman. He was unafraid to settle old scores because the statute of limitations had expired on his past transgressions, though some papers reported he was offered immunity in exchange for his testimony. Simpson confirmed the gang's fourteen stores were connected but independently operated. Ropers worked for one or even multiple stores at one time; he was most familiar with the Council Bluffs, New Orleans, Denver, South Bend, and Galesburg, Illinois, operations. He did not divulge the location of the gang's East Coast store. Simpson claimed the gang had made $5 million ($167,104,203) during its existence and boasted there were several cons the government had failed to uncover.[30] He also swore Mabray "fixed" a bank, which may have made Ernest Hart of the First National Bank of Council Bluffs uneasy. Simpson told reporters, "I have nothing against Mabray. He never did anything against me, but you wait until they get Harriman and Brown; then I'll tell you a story that will set the country afire."[31]

Although he delighted in talking to the press, reporters were unable to discover what it was that so angered Simpson. Letters from Simpson to Mabray seized in Little Rock provided a hint. The first letter, addressed to numbers 12, 36, and 66, accused them "of beating him out of certain of the proceeds of former operations and demanding a settlement, or threatening general and complete exposure of the entire operations." It was this missive that led Swenson to Simpson. The postal inspector prevailed upon Simpson for assistance, but the old con refused. Swenson then gathered information on Simpson, who eventually revealed Harriman, Brown, and Moore were in California, which led to their arrest.[32] Simpson may have been the most colorful witness, but the gang's marks unintentionally entertained the courtroom audience as well.

Over the course of the trial, multiple victims explained how they had been snared by Mabray and his ropers. Joseph G. Kile declared, "That punkin' headed jockey fell off, just pitched off like a frog when our hoss was half way down the course and two lengths in the lead." He growled, "If I'd a knowed how that was going I'd a rode that hoss myself."[33] Some marks remained on good terms with the men that swindled them; after Kile stepped down from the witness stand he addressed Mabray. "No hard feelings, John," the elderly farmer said, "but that was a hell of a race." He extended his hand to Mabray who rose from his chair to shake Kile's hand. "It's alright, uncle," Mabray replied.[34] Witnesses were examined, cross-examined, and recalled repeatedly by both the government and the defense during the proceedings.[35] Iowan Frank Marts sheepishly admitted he mortgaged his farm to participate in a fixed wrestling match.[36] Chicago saloonkeeper Otto Graebe was steered by Clarence Class and notorious Chicago confidence man Joseph "Yellow Kid" Weil to the gang's Galesburg, Illinois, store where he lost $4,000.[37] Others, like Dr. Jesse Benton Titterington of Dallas, experienced memory lapses.

Fortunately, when witnesses failed to be forthright the prosecution had plenty of evidence.[38] Court records indicate federal prosecutors used 210 exhibits to their advantage. Photographs of con men posing with victims, correspondence between ropers and victims, bank drafts, betting lists, athletic contest contracts, tally sheets, and the applications and keys for post office boxes were among the pieces of evidence shown to the jury.

No one from the gang took the stand in their own defense; perhaps they believed in Ben Marks's ability to fix a jury. "They haven't got anything on me in this case," Leon Lozier declared, "I haven't run a race since the Gregory affair, and that was outlawed long ago." He boasted, "I beat dem all. There was Johnson, and Bethune, and Archie McCombs, at one time regarded as the fastest seventy-five man in the world." Lozier crowed, "I won over [John] Grimm fairly when Gregory and Barker lost their money at Webb City, just because I was the faster man." He was not involved with Mabray, Lozier insisted; he was a Denver sign painter.[39]

The closing arguments have not survived, but in his instructions to the jury Judge McPherson reminded them, "This case is of importance to

John Mabray shakes hands with a victim wearing a straw boater hat. Edward C. Moore
is in the derby hat in the center of the photo. Darby Thielman is in front of the victim.
National Archives and Records Administration.

the defendants, because, if convicted they will be deprived of their liberty. On the other hand, if they are acquitted wrongfully then this great postal system of ours will not have the encouragement that it should have from all honestly disposed persons." He concluded, "But whatever you do, do it like men with moral courage to do that which is right and honorable, and, regardless of what may be said by others, regarding only what your judgment and consciences approve."[40]

When the guilty verdict was announced, Mabray sat quietly for a few moments and then said, "Oh well, the mikes that convicted us were as guilty in intent as we." Dr. Robert E. L. Goddard was released as the jury could not agree as to his guilt.[41] John Mabray, Leon Lozier, Eddie Morris, Tom S. Robison, Ed Leach, Clarence Forbes, Harry Forbes, and Ed McCoy each received two years and a $10,000 fine. Ropers Winn Harris and

Frank Scott received six months in jail and a $100 fine. Wrestlers Bert Shores and George Marsh received fifteen months in Leavenworth and a $100 fine.[42]

"The Big Store is closed," the *Omaha Daily Bee* declared. The victims, "bankers, lawyers, newspaper men, merchants, farmers, gamblers, miners, ranchers—young and aged, innocent and worldly wise" were hoodwinked by a congenial horse dealer turned con man who was "a master of the ways of the mind and the ways of men." If only they had heeded Mabray's own advice to a roper, "Let every man look into his own affairs and keep on the square with his fellow men and he will have little trouble. As soon as a man begins trying to do other people he is bound to be done." Mabray told a reporter, "There have been mikes since the world was born and there will be plenty of mikes to the end. Jacob was the first Biblical miker when he turned that little trick for getting the striped cattle. Jacob knew he wasn't exactly on the square. He would have made a good American." He shrugged, "Americans in business and baseball make all they can out of the rules. That was our game, too, but the court says it went too far." In awe of the gang's accomplishments, the *Bee* pronounced "Mabray Most Stupendous Swindle of Modern Times."[43]

After sentencing, Mabray and the others were escorted to a Burlington passenger train. On what must have seemed like a long ride on the short journey to Kansas, Mabray endured verbal abuse from his associates. The *Omaha Daily Bee* warned other inmates "would do well to put padlocks on their pockets."[44] They were received at the US Penitentiary in Leavenworth, Kansas, on March 22, 1910. Some were released on bond pending appeal but subsequently returned to prison to serve out their sentences. Their time at Leavenworth was mostly unremarkable. Each man worked various jobs; some—including Mabray—became trusties. His time at Leavenworth was not entirely smooth as he and Leon Lozier, both assigned to the prison's east gate, frequently quarreled.[45] What led the men to hurl epithets at each other is unclear, but Lozier likely blamed Mabray for his troubles. They were reassigned to separate duties; Mabray to the brick machine, Lozier to the laundry. The other members of the gang, though, seemed content to quietly serve their time, as reflected in the information contained in their inmate files.

Their records provide glimpses into their lives. Lists of letters sent and received reveal tantalizing hints of friendships, relationships, and publishing projects that never came to pass. George Marsh's inmate file reveals his sister Tillie Lurton contacted her husband's relative, US Supreme Court Justice Horace H. Lurton, about George's case. E. C. Hunt of the *Omaha World-Herald* asked for the warden's assistance in helping Tom Robison supply him with information for a proposed book project.[46] Other Mabray confederates were luckier.

The 1910 arrest of jockey Luther "Lute" West revived memories of the Buckfoot Gang in Jasper County, Missouri. Inspector Charles Ranger found West had worked with Mabray from May 6 to November 16, 1908, during which time the gang made $80,690. West received 1 percent of the proceeds—just under $807—as well as six months' salary of $75. In total, he received $1,256.90 ($42,007) for his services. West told Ranger he might be able to find out Ed Ellis's whereabouts from a friend, but had no other information. Webb City postmaster Walter Tholburn informed Ranger that West had never been in trouble and while he could "consume lots of liquor, especially when working saloons where he could get it free, he never got drunk or quarrelsome, or never gambled."[47] George Flournoy, Ed Ellis's brother-in-law, told Ranger that West cared for his horses. He found West "ignorant, but honest and trustworthy." Buckfoot stalwart Charley Parker employed West for fifteen years and let him race his string of horses. After anti-gambling legislation put an end to horse racing, he employed West as a porter in his saloon, which Ranger noted was the Buckfoot Gang's old haunt. West was "perfectly honest, but shiftless; far from smart, but would do anything he was told, but was a fellow who could never seem to get a dollar ahead." Ranger observed he never made flashy purchases because of his family's dire circumstances.[48]

West was the sole support for his mother-in-law and blind brother; he idolized his eight-year-old son, and his wife worked in a boarding house. Ranger remarked, "There is no question but that he is a poor, shiftless excuse for a man, has never amounted to much, has no education, no natural ability, is weak and an easy victim for anybody. He was offered the chance to ride . . . by Ed. Ellis, one of the flashiest and smoothest of the bunch, a fellow townsman of his, and simply took the job because he needed the money." He was, Ranger asserted, "simply a handy tool for Mabray, Ed Ellis and the other sharpers." The inspector recommended clemency.[49]

Instead, West was sentenced to six months in jail and fined $100. Others met a similar fate. Dick Beatte, an old Buckfoot sprinter, received one year and a day at Leavenworth plus a $100 fine. "I'm crooked and I know it," he told a reporter, "and I am doing the best for myself. I could make enough money at legitimate foot racing for the ordinary man, but not enough for what I want to spend. The 'gang' took me up and showed me where the cash was and I fell to it. I am ready to serve my time without a murmur."[50] Boxer W. E. Godfrey received a year in jail and a $100 fine.[51] A week after roper Barney Martin was apprehended, wrestler Jack Carkeek was fined $200.[52]

Surprisingly, one athlete went straight, perhaps to settle old scores. Harry Forbes—convict turned government informant—traveled to New York. He could not find Herbert "The Brass Kid" Coon but learned the Honey Grove Kid frequented a Seventh Avenue gambling resort. Armed with Forbes's information, officers watched the location. Detective Joseph Daly thought he recognized Hindman at Seventh Avenue and Thirty-Seventh Street. A few minutes later he heard someone say, "Well, how is the 'Honey Grove Kid' these days?" Daly rushed the Texan and arrested him. Postal inspectors said Hindman was also wanted for helping swindle a Philadelphia banker out of $55,000.[53] He pled guilty rather than risk a jury trial.[54]

Less kind fates befell the West Coast trio. Russell Harriman did not live long enough for Howard Simpson to get revenge; he died in 1910 after undergoing surgery for stomach cancer in Oakland, California. When told the government would only pay $250 toward his medical costs, Harriman quipped, "The government is cheap."[55] Harriman escaped Leavenworth, but Frank Brown was not as fortunate. The US Supreme Court ruled he and Edward Moore had to appear before the federal court in Omaha. Chastened by the news, Brown either overdosed or died from a preexisting heart condition. On July 22, 1912, he was found dead in bed at his apartment in San Jose, California, while out on bail.[56] Brown returned "feet-first" to Washington, DC "where he was known as the daring broker, the handsome man of pleasure, the festive spender, the fine and genial companion." Even though his Washington brokerage failed, Brown "lost no glamour." "He was an irresistible sort of man," his acquaintances agreed. Now his "meteoric career" had come to an end, far from where it all began.[57] Edward Cook Moore, the sole survivor of the West Coast trio, pled guilty in September 1912 and received a year and a day in Leavenworth.[58] Several cases remained, but for some the cost of justice seemed too high to pursue.

In early 1911 the Pottawattamie County Board of Supervisors ordered county attorney Frank Capell to dismiss all remaining charges against Mabray and his associates. Some suspected the board had been bribed, but their reluctance to prosecute the gang arose from financial concerns; the estimated court costs could exceed $100,000 ($3,222,839) and bankrupt the county. Iowa attorney general George Cosson, who succeeded H. Webb Byers, vehemently disagreed. He ordered the court clerk to enter his appearance in all the cases.[59] A few additional cases were resolved in federal court when Thomas Davies, George Ryan, C. F. Philpot, and William Crider pled guilty. They received $1,000 fines and short jail terms. Ben Marks again asked for a continuance due to ill health, which led Judge

McPherson to bark, "Mr. Marks seems to be afflicted with a strange sort of a malady that only makes him sick in March and September, when this court is in session." He granted the continuance, but Marks soon faced new legal troubles.[60]

Nor was the law finished with John Mabray. While at Leavenworth one of his many visitors was Inspector Swenson. Mabray wrote a signed confession for Swenson stating Ben Marks provided police protection for the gang.[61] He was later taken to Des Moines to meet with Iowa attorney general George Cosson. Mabray reportedly refused to cooperate until Cosson told him each mike meant a separate case against him in state and federal court. Faced with additional prison time, Mabray changed his mind. The jovial con man looked like a "prosperous banker" with a stylish brown crusher hat, polished shoes, silk cravat, and conservatively styled suit. His guard proclaimed Mabray was Leavenworth's best prisoner and swore other inmates thought he was "fine business." Before leaving, Mabray visited county jailer Scott Wise and stopped by the Iowa statehouse where he "shook hands all around." He was later taken to Council Bluffs where he and victims William Bedford and Henry Ruhsert testified before the grand jury in state court.[62]

Mabray's appearance before the grand jury resulted in Ben Marks's arrest.[63] Cosson informed US attorney general George Wickersham that Marks was "the underworld politician of Council Bluffs who has been the cause of more corruption and lawlessness than perhaps any man in Iowa."[64] After his release from Leavenworth, Mabray arrived in Council Bluffs for Marks's trial.[65] There were many familiar faces in the courtroom, although now some were on opposite sides. Marks's defense team included John Organ (who had represented Mabray victim Thomas Ballew) and Mabray's former lawyers George Wright and Emmet Tinley. The young, slender, and bespectacled Cosson was assisted by County Attorney Frank Capell and Assistant County Attorney Harvey O. Ouren.[66]

The trial began with an explosive verbal battle between Organ and Cosson after Organ alleged in his opening statement Inspector John Swenson was acting "as an agent of one of the 'mikes' in an effort to recover his money." When Cosson furiously objected, Organ further alleged, "There was a collusion between Mr. Swenson and the attorney general for the purpose of involving National Committeeman Ernest E. Hart, the First National Bank, J. J. Spindler and others." Cosson leapt to his feet to object; he was not going to have an easy trial ahead.[67]

After tempers cooled the first of many victims testified, but it was the paunchy Mississippian who was the state's most important witness. When word spread Mabray was about to take the stand, spectators jockeyed for seats. He faced a grueling cross-examination by John Organ. As with the federal trial, the testimony for the state case against Marks is missing; all that remains is a small number of court records and press accounts. What survives confirms and fills in some of the missing details from the federal case about the gang's operations and its relationship with Marks.[68] Organ queried Mabray extensively about his early life; when asked what he did after he was a cowpuncher, Mabray airily replied he played cards and sold diamonds obtained from Tom Dennison.[69] In 1906 he entered the big store business in Seattle where he worked as an insideman for Russell Harriman, Frank Brown, and Howard Simpson. Over a period of six to seven months he went from earning 2.5 percent to 6 percent. After he learned the con, Mabray opened a big store in New Orleans with Harriman and Brown and, later, a branch operation in Council Bluffs. In early 1907 Mabray took his share of earnings from the New Orleans store, amounting to around $12,000 to $13,000, and moved to Omaha. He then visited Ben Marks, whom he had known since 1898, and asked Marks to arrange protection from city and county officials. Mabray offered him a flat fee of $800 a month or 8 percent on the assumption the business would generate at least $10,000 a month. After a series of negotiations, Marks received a certain cash percentage in exchange for providing protection. In one instance, Marks helped get Harriman out of jail.[70] Marks took an extra 1 percent of the gang's gross earnings, 1 percent for fixing officials at the First National Bank of Council Bluffs, and 1 percent for fixing the county attorney's office. Letters and telegrams from victims to Council Bluffs police chief George Richmond and Pottawattamie prosecutor John Hess were handed over to Ben Marks. When Organ asked Mabray if he had gotten his money's worth, the swindler responded, "We did our business all right."[71]

Mabray and Marks hunted for a suitable place to hold horse races, finally settling on a strip of land on Marks's farm. Marks directed his tenant to construct a racetrack on a stretch of sandy soil in the middle of an alfalfa field.[72] Mabray carried out a few tricks in Council Bluffs, then suspended operations to return to New Orleans. He reappeared in Iowa in the spring of 1908 after the head of the New Orleans police resigned and the gang lost its protected status. Marks, however, did not want him to resume operations until a certain election had passed. Only once did a Council Bluffs policeman interrupt a fixed athletic contest, but after Mabray reported the incident to Marks there was no further police interference. Business remained steady; the gang made $162,595 from twenty-nine cons they had run up to October 1908. Mabray pointedly noted he and his associates lived in Omaha but did not pull off cons there because they did not have protection outside of Council Bluffs.[73] This prompted Cosson to probe the gang's possible connection with another midwestern boss.

Cosson attempted to uncover what, if any, relationship the men may have had with another regional power broker when he asked Mabray, "When Tom Dennison of Omaha called upon you at the prison what did he say?" Defense attorney Organ's passionate objection was sustained and Mabray was not allowed to answer the question.[74] Organ also asked Mabray if he told his attorney Emmet Tinley in 1909 that Marks was not involved and only turned against Marks after he refused to go on Mabray's bond; Mabray denied it. Organ jabbed at Mabray throughout his cross-examination, but he proved a slippery witness. When he asked the confidence man where he had obtained money to pay for his hotel room, Mabray replied, "I borrowed it from my sister-in-law." Organ glowered as the courtroom audience laughed.[75] When Organ queried Mabray about swindling a victim out of $2,000, he sniped, "What was the matter, was he a poor man?" "No," Mabray chuckled, "My recollection is that he had considerable more than that, but the steerers picked him up in Chicago and got $3,000 of his money playing 'stud' poker on the way out."[76]

One reporter was impressed Mabray was "well informed on a wide range of subjects" and was familiar with the Bible, history, and the classics. He believed Mabray's appearance would lead many to mistake him for "a shrewd, prosperous, intelligent and forceful businessman." Alluding to the corporate titans of the age, he compared Mabray's big store to "a sort of trust development in the gambling world." It robbed men of large sums of money and replaced "old fashioned, slower methods which were counted on the 'tin horn' order by the big operators."[77]

Swenson and Mabray's testimony were supported by additional witnesses. Inspector Charles Ranger testified about telegrams between Mabray and Marks. Multiple police officers, past and present, testified Marks met with Chief Richmond in his office. Mabray roper Thomas Gay appeared on behalf of the state; when Organ asked if he had agreed to appear to avoid prison, Gay shot back, "You bet I would tell the truth to keep out of the penitentiary." Throughout the proceedings, Ben Marks fixed his gaze upon each witness. At times he leaned forward to listen, but showed little emotion.[78]

Marks's attorneys made twin motions to dismiss and for an instructed verdict; both failed.[79] The trial continued with defense witnesses banker Ernest Hart, cashier John Spindler, and former police chief George Richmond refuting Mabray's testimony he had bribed them through Marks. Cosson, however, had secured the bank officials' assistance shortly before the trial and was able to show that in 1907–1908 Marks deposited larger sums of money than he normally did. On cross-examination, Officer Charles Crum admitted Richmond ordered officers not to go into gambling houses or brothels without his permission. Former county attorney John Hess insisted he never accepted bribes and denied giving Marks telegrams from Mabray's victims.[80] Unsurprisingly Ben Marks— among the last witnesses to testify—denied taking money from Mabray, but admitted he owned interests in licensed saloons.[81]

As the trial concluded, onlookers struggled to get into the courtroom; several settled for standing in the crowded doorway. Although only fragments of the closing arguments survive, news accounts indicate the defense and prosecution were in vehement disagreement over the conspiracy charges against Marks.[82] Cosson, in his closing, compared Ben Marks to Omaha's Tom Dennison and New York's Richard Croker. He implored the jury, "If in order to convict a man of crime, we are compelled to have him send out formal printed announcements, or have him call in a bunch of reporters and say 'I'm going to commit a crime' then as I say, I despair for my country."[83] His passionate appeal was not enough. The jury found Marks not guilty precisely at midnight on December 31, 1911. Cosson lamented, "Council Bluffs is not in good civic health."[84] Still, Ben Marks's control of Council Bluffs was weakened. After battling ill health for years, Marks died in 1919. He remained a figure of interest to journalists and local historians in the decades that followed.[85]

If David Maurer's criminal confidants were right that Marks invented the scheme Boatright and Mabray mastered, then the story had come full circle.[86] As a local boss tried in state court, Marks held a better hand than Mabray and Boatright. Inspector Ranger wrote Cosson, "If we didn't win, they at least knew something was happening."[87] The attorney general's response acknowledged Ed Ellis—and other confederates—could be prosecuted, but that it was not worthwhile after Marks's acquittal.[88]

As for Mabray, he surfaced in Kansas City. He wrote Cosson about a job opportunity as assistant manager of the Washington Hotel at the corner of Twelfth and Washington in the city's Quality Hill neighborhood. Cosson advised he should take it.[89] Mabray, anxious about lingering indictments in Iowa, continued to write letters laced with flattery.[90] In February 1912 Mabray told Cosson he had not yet agreed to work at the hotel; instead, an unnamed friend and financial backer from Denver wanted Mabray to go to Los Angeles. Mabray preferred to stay in Kansas City because of friends and unresolved legal issues in Iowa. He confessed, "I could never have believed it so hard for a man to redeem himself after being in prison everyone will tell you yes I am anxious to do anything for you and can but I am afraid it will harm my business now if you can manage to do something else." He acknowledged gamblers had offered him assistance, but had refused their help. Cosson tersely responded he did not care where Mabray went or what he did so long as he remained out of trouble. He told Mabray he would try to resolve the remaining cases during the year.[91]

That same year Mabray was arrested in Kansas City when a pool hall, allegedly operated by his former associate Darby Thielman, led authorities to suspect Mabray had faltered. When Mabray told Police Chief Wentworth Griffin he wanted a chance, Griffin snorted, "Sure, Mabray, I'm willing to give you a chance anywhere—except in Kansas City." He indignantly told a reporter, "Why I couldn't pull off anything in Kansas if I wanted to and I certainly don't want to get in trouble again."[92] Mabray informed Cosson he had been arrested, photographed, and fingerprinted and that three or four hundred people—aldermen, judges, lawyers, businessmen, and fellow Elks—urged him to stay in Kansas City.[93] Cosson counseled Mabray to ignore Griffin's order to leave Kansas City and reaffirmed his confidence in him.[94] When a judge ruled Mabray could stay, Griffin vowed, "The police here will see to it that Kansas City is not made the hangout of criminals whether it can be proved they are operating here or not."[95]

Mabray and Cosson's correspondence dwindled; the last letter was written by Cosson to Mabray's attorney George Mayne. The attorney general wanted Mabray kept "under a sort of suspended sentence for the period of a year and I have not cared to dispose of any cases until I took them all up in their order." Cosson told Mayne he had not heard from Mabray, but understood he was staying out of trouble.[96] In the fall of 1912 Cosson disposed of seventeen remaining Mabray cases.[97] Who can know a man's heart? Yet Mabray's actions in the years that followed show that perhaps he had played yet another long con on Cosson.

Mabray remained in Kansas City and became a fixture in the Quality Hill neighborhood. Founded in the 1850s, it grew exponentially in the 1880s, populated by the city's elite—many of whom were from New England. Quality Hill offered commanding views of the Missouri River, industrial West Bottoms, and the business district. As "one of the most fashionable and prestigious residential neighborhoods" it attracted wealthy residents whose homes were designed by celebrated architects like Stanford White. Shady tree-lined streets, plank sidewalks, and houses with iron grille fences, broad front porches, and side gardens were among its many elegant features. As Kansas City grew southward, the neighborhood lost its luster. The smell of the stockyards was more pungent, and foreign-born and Black laborers now lived a stone's throw away. By 1910 the once stately mansions had been transformed into boarding houses and tenements. This was the shabby world John Mabray inhabited; the man who had posed as a millionaire now lived among the dilapidated remnants of Kansas City's monied elite.[98]

In 1913 an anonymous citizen charged gambling was taking place in a hotel Mabray operated. He responded, "I have had a hard life of it. I have made money and lost it. I am now trying to make an honest living by running the Washington Hotel. It is a clean place and there is no gambling in it."[99] The following year Marcellus Temple and John Swenson agreed the remaining cases should be dismissed. According to their report, fifty-four defendants had been convicted, three were believed innocent, four defendants had had their charges dismissed for other reasons, four Mabray associates had served as government witnesses, seven of the accused had died, two had been duplicated under their aliases, and one had gone free after the jury had disagreed; the identities of six participants could not be ascertained.[100]

Mabray faded from public view until the death of his old associate and business partner "Judge" Henry C. Haley. On the evening of November 25, 1919, Haley, well known in gambling circles, died in convulsions in Kansas City after eating in a hotel restaurant operated by "his opposition."[101] Mabray subsequently sought $9,500 from Haley's estate. Newspapers noted Mabray had been operating a gambling house where he offered private high-stakes poker games with the assistance of a Japanese servant. Mabray argued Haley's money was his; he had merely deposited it in Haley's name for the sake of convenience.[102]

Omaha boss Tom Dennison, administrator of Haley's estate, launched a nationwide search for his friend's heirs. Haley's secretive past made it difficult to locate relatives. Some Webb City locals believed he was a member of the Buckfoot Gang known as Blackie Howard. An attorney who specialized in finding heirs published a notice in Joplin and Webb City newspapers to find Haley's family, but there was little left of the dead man's fortune. Haley had $40,000 to $60,000 in an Omaha bank safety deposit box, but the money disappeared the morning after his death. Only Haley and Mabray had access to the box. "The money," Dennison said sourly, "is gone now. Whether Mr. Mabray took it or not, I do not know."[103]

At trial, Mabray prevailed over the heirs of Haley's deceased wife, but not before he was embarrassed by Dr. C. E. Mathis, who testified Mabray attempted to pry a diamond ring from the dead man's finger.[104] The *Kansas City Star* observed Mabray had managed a gambling house disguised as a hotel and later ran a club. A year later, in what may have been a ploy for a presidential pardon, Mabray talked to the *Star* about his hardships.[105] Still, he was far from repentant. "We never stole a dime," he bragged, "We just relieved monkeys of their money." His testimony against Ben Marks in 1911 angered the underworld, he explained, but he had never squealed on his fellow confidence men. If Mabray received a presidential pardon and had his $10,000 fine remitted, he would no longer "be afraid of the bulls who never forget and the criminals who never forgive."[106]

In the summer of 1922 John Mabray informed Kansas City chief of detectives Isaac Walston he was leaving for good; there was nothing for him in the Paris of the Plains.[107] Kansas City proved difficult to leave. Years after other associates successfully applied for presidential pardons, Mabray followed suit. Perhaps the fifty-seven-year-old Mabray wanted relief from the $10,000 fine levied against him that he had thus far been unable to pay. He gathered several endorsements to bolster his application. Federal prosecutor Marcellus Temple commented Mabray had been a good citizen since his release; clearly Temple did not know Mabray was running a gambling house in 1920. A letter written in 1912 by the late Judge Smith McPherson attesting to Mabray's suitability for a pardon was included. An impressive number of Kansas City's wealthy and influential citizens, including banker William T. Kemper, Judge E. E. Porterfield, Pastor Burris A. Jenkins, and Mayor Frank H. Cromwell wrote letters of support. On August 29, 1922, President Warren Harding pardoned him.[108] In 1923 another significant confidence gang trial was held in Denver when Lou Blonger and his cronies were brought to heel, but Mabray was not among the indicted. His name resurfaced in 1925 when he established a gambling house near the Baltimore Hotel.[109] Over the years the old swindler waxed nostalgic about his crimes.

In 1930 Omaha journalist Tom Porter visited the federal courthouse in Council Bluffs to look at the Mabray trial records. He examined the three volumes of court testimony and photographed them to illustrate their substantial size. US deputy court clerk Gladys M. Gretzer confided Mabray had visited her a few months earlier; he had hoped to look at the little red book, known as Exhibit 101, which contained his victims' names. He boldly introduced himself and, despite proclaiming he had gone straight, seemed to take pride in his criminal achievements. Mabray was disappointed when Gretzer informed him that the exhibits could not be located; they may have been sent to Washington.[110] He returned to Kansas City, where he and his wife lived in a rented home on Holmes Street with entertainers, actors, and office clerks as their neighbors.[111]

On February 2, 1952, John C. Mabray died in Kansas City. His passing went unannounced save for a simple death notice. His wife listed his occupation as retired livestock salesman, recalling his days on the frontier, but gave no indication of his status as an aristocrat of crime. He had outlived the golden age of the confidence man in America. The Kansas City Police Department no longer has a file for him nor does the Federal Bureau of Investigation; Mabray's presence in his adopted hometown is as fleeting as the horse races he pulled off in the alfalfa fields of Iowa.[112]

14

WHO COULD EVER REALLY GO STRAIGHT?

None of us can be certain we will be remembered—or, for that matter, that we
will be forgotten. But if we are not consigned to oblivion, then it will be the institutional identities that remain—the names, the vital records, and the fragments
of expression that will offer glimpses into who we once were.

—BENJAMIN MOORE, *The Names of John Gergen*

For some, the law never caught up to them. Time did. No laudatory
obituary was published in Quincy, Kansas, to mark Bud Gillett's
death. Not yet forty at the time of his death in Hot Springs,
Arkansas, his demise in 1909 was due either to malaria, uremia poisoning,
or "some sort of a disorder super-induced by over-sociability in the line of
women, wine, and song."[1] He escaped the long arm of the law; Mabray's
records showed he had worked as a roper.[2] It was at least a far more pleasant fate than the grisly death of Roger Williams six years earlier in the
same city. Not everyone thought poorly of the fallen champion. Glen S.
Slough, who as a child watched Bud run sprints along the train tracks in
Quincy, recalled:

> From time to time Bud returned to his home town with his stylishly
> dressed wife. She is remembered as the only woman in the community to
> wear earrings. One afternoon I was coming home from school with some
> boys when we met Bud outside the town restaurant. He asked for each of
> our names and then delivered a sermon that was short and to the point.
> He told us that he wanted us to stay in school and make the most of our
> education. And not drop out as he had done.[3]

Gillett's fate might have been different. Local historian Jeff Hokanson
observed, "The Flint Hills are actually escarpments noted for their rocky

soils of flint. The area is not good land for farming, and when the Gillett family saw the property they had purchased, they apparently decided not to stay. Had they chosen to keep that property, however, they would have become wealthy. Oil was discovered there in the 1920s. Interestingly, the Gilletts were always trying to find ways to get rich, many times by committing illegal acts. Too bad they missed their opportunity to gain wealth legally!"[4] In what might be considered an epitaph for the Buckfoot and Mabray gangs, Hokanson remarked, "Bud has become legend as much as fact. In many ways there are two Bud Gilletts: one historical and one literary. Sorting out the two is sometimes difficult."[5]

Gillett's fate was far more kind than the one that befell Edward C. Moore of Council Bluffs. After he and Leon Lozier avoided the Iowa State Penitentiary in 1904, Moore and his family moved to California. In the fall of 1912, a body was pulled from the bottom of San Diego's Glorietta Bay, though it was no easy task; someone had weighed it down with an anchor and one hundred pounds of iron. The corpse was initially identified as a woman, but a subsequent reexamination determined it was a man. Using dental work and a darned sock recovered from the body, authorities and Moore's wife identified the corpse as Moore, who had become a San Diego real estate broker since leaving Iowa. He disappeared on September 14, 1912, after telling his wife he was going to a poker game. Last seen on the Coronado ferry, authorities theorized Moore was murdered and tossed into the bay.[6] It was speculated Moore's death may have been related to a criminal organization in San Diego "startling in its magnitude." Officials hypothesized he may have been double-crossed by a group of gamblers. Another local was suspected of being a victim; police wondered if there were others who had fallen prey to the same organization.[7]

Five years after Robert Boatright's protégé Ed Ellis pled guilty alongside his old Buckfoot crony Walter Nolan in US District Court in Davenport, Iowa, he checked into St. John's Hospital in Joplin. The forty-three-year-old Ellis was destitute and racked with tuberculosis. When a friend paid $500 for his care over the course of several weeks, Ellis vowed to repay him. A Florida man arrived and met with one of Ellis's close friends. Although the stranger did not learn about Ellis's precarious financial state, he handed Ellis's friend seven $1,000 bills and a roll of twenty-dollar bills almost five inches in diameter. "Ellis can have any part of it," the man said, "because if I were broke he'd do the same for me." Ellis had once given him forty dollars when he asked to borrow twenty; the man had taken the money and multiplied it many times over. Now he was returning the favor.[8]

The old days were not far from Ellis's mind. From his hospital bed he confided to a friend, "Boatright died, all right, and the body in his casket was his, not that of someone else." His passing was marked with vivid remembrances of his life. Ellis "had few of the advantages of life, yet he became so polished that he was able to appear to advantage in any society," the *Joplin Globe* recalled. He "became a cosmopolitan, debonair and cultured in a high degree" and yet Ellis was the "shrewdest, oiliest and yet the coldest blooded of the old gang." The *Webb City Register* lamented, "Poor Ed Ellis! He has gone the way of all flesh. His sins were many; the things he could have done, he did not. [T]he things he did do, he could have avoided; but who shall say what impelled him to the course that led only to a ruined life—a remorse to himself and regret to his friends."[9]

Ellis was not the only one who struggled financially after the Mabray Gang's downfall. When Eddie Morris was released from Leavenworth, he told a reporter he made $1 million with Boatright and Mabray, but it was gone. He vowed, "I am thru with the game for good. I violated the law and I am sorry, but I paid the penalty. I never murmured and figured that I was getting what was coming to me."[10] Morris assumed a new name— Dr. William Wardell Castelane—and settled in Columbia, Missouri. In 1915, after he was hired by the University of Missouri to train track and baseball athletes, Morris boasted to a reporter he was born in Africa, learned to box in Britain, and earned a medical degree in Liverpool. He then became a protégé of African American boxer Peter Jackson and fought under the name Eddie K. Morris. It was he, Morris bragged, who taught Jack Johnson how to train.[11] Later that year he was identified as "a negro with a turkish bath establishment in the basement of the Guitar Building" after he fought a man over an unpaid bill.[12] In 1920 he purchased the Wayside Inn and launched the Columbia Catering Company.[13] A second marriage did not work out and he got in trouble for carrying a concealed weapon.[14] Morris reportedly did well enough to build a building in Sharp End, the city's Black business district. When he died in 1927 his obituary recounted—without a hint of skepticism—his claims of being a member of an African royal family, an acquaintance of Queen Victoria, and running a bathhouse in Monte Carlo. In his final years Morris operated a bathhouse in tiny Randolph Springs, Missouri; his death certificate said he was a masseur. From all appearances, Morris attempted to stay out of trouble, though his gift for exaggeration remained constant.[15]

For some, the dream never died. In 1919 sixty-nine-year-old Garrette Stansbury was arrested by postal inspectors in Kansas City on a charge of using the mails to defraud. He and at least three dozen other men were accused of staging fraudulent athletic contests and mythical cutoverlands schemes. Among those convicted were the mayor of Muncie, Indiana, and the prosecuting attorney of Delaware County, Indiana; each received the maximum two-year sentence in the US Penitentiary in

Atlanta. Because of his advanced age, Stansbury received one day in jail.[16] After years of conning suckers across the country he died in 1928 at the age of seventy-six in Kansas City. Like Mabray's, there was nothing in his brief obituary about his colorful past.[17]

That same year veteran sprinter Leon Lozier died. Lozier was plagued by his past sins. Upon his release from prison, he learned his wife Jeanette had abandoned him for a bigamous marriage with a Denver grocer.[18] He was accused of luring two young girls into a hotel room, but denied any criminal intent and was released.[19] In 1914 Lozier was arrested on suspicion of trying to swindle a Denver resident on a fake wrestling match.[20] By 1921 Lozier was working as a scenic painter in Omaha. He made the news when he claimed he and evangelist Billy Sunday competed in fixed foot races in the 1880s. When Sunday brought his revival to Omaha Lozier challenged him, but the preacher allegedly declined. The fifty-eight-year-old proclaimed his record for fifty yards was five seconds and announced he would soon go into vaudeville with a "rapid fire landscape painting act."[21] A year before Lozier died his son-in-law was accused of stealing checks and jailed. Lozier's daughter and grandchildren were subsequently stranded in St. Louis. The old confidence man hissed, "I'll see that he gets the limit and that my little girl gets a divorce from him. He never could have married her, if I had known of it." Lozier groused the forger's predilection for gambling had cost him $6,000 and forced him to sell a cherished violin for $500 at a time of great financial difficulty. He swore, "I may be an old man, but I can still make a living for my daughter and my three grandchildren, if I can only get them back to me." His indirect public appeal for financial assistance may have been one last con on Lozier's part, but he could have been penniless.[22] When he died in 1928, Omaha sports enthusiasts reminisced about his athletic prowess, recalling Lozier allegedly inspired the gambler's motto, "I won't bet on anything that can talk."[23]

After Lucius "Honey Grove Kid" Hindman wrote his father in 1907 to say he was moving to California and going to "renounce sin in all its forms, and that henceforth his path would lie in the straight and narrow way," he wrote again announcing he had married and settled in Denver.[24] Who could, after all, ever really go straight? In 1909 Hindman wrote a friend he was in London, England, and "most too far away from Honey Grove to amount to much."[25] While the Kid was serving a short jail sentence for his involvement with Mabray, his brother visited him. He remarked if authorities did not treat the Kid so well jail "would probably make him a better a man."[26] After he finished his sentence, the Kid returned to his old ways.

In 1913 Hindman sent a postcard home to say he had set up shop in Naples, Italy.[27] The next summer a story circulated the Kid had gone down on the RMS *Empress of Ireland*; there had been a similar report when the *Titanic* sank.[28] Hindman was fine; in November he was arrested in New York for allegedly helping Charles Gondorff swindle a man out of $55,000 in a wire scheme.[29] He headed to Denver where police chief Hamilton Armstrong called Hindman "one of the king-pin bunco steerers of the age."[30] In 1922 Margaret Hill, self-described "Queen of the Underworld," published a series of syndicated stories about her career; one described how Hindman purportedly swindled the Duke of Montebello out of $200,000.[31] The Kid returned home to Texas in the early 1920s driving a Model T with a glass casket poking out the back. He was peddling them, he said, on behalf of the American Glass Casket Company in Ada, Oklahoma. Hindman sold several, collected the money, and was never seen again.[32] The Kid's luck ran out at the age of fifty in 1924 when tubercular meningitis claimed his life; his death certificate listed his occupation as promoter.[33]

The Kid's hometown newspaper called him "the best-known person who ever resided in Honey Grove." "Remarkably bright, and of pleasing personality," the Kid "made friends in all classes and he probably knew more people personally than any man in Texas." His career as a confidence man was not mentioned.[34] In 1936 after an editor in California posthumously called the Kid a "one-man crime wave," the *Honey Grove Signal* defended the Kid, saying he "gained world-wide recognition because of his ability to outwit residents of America, as well as Europe."[35]

One of Hindman's Buckfoot cronies had a much more charmed life. After escaping a federal prison sentence for his involvement with Mabray, George Ryan was arrested in 1913 when Indiana millionaire Frank Fox alleged Ryan, his old partner Ed Spear, and other confidence men swindled him out of $20,000 on a fixed roulette wheel in Hot Springs. His counsel, former Mabray attorney Lewis Rhoton, kept his case from coming to trial for three years; in 1915 Ryan's case was dismissed. Ed Spear and "Handsome Jack" Porter were not so lucky. Spear received seven years in the federal penitentiary in Atlanta while Porter received a five-year sentence.[36]

Ryan became involved in the circus world, likely because of the opportunities to grift. He served as a legal representative for Howe's Great London, John Robinson, and Golmar Brothers circuses, which were owned by the American Circus Corporation. Ed Ballard, one of the corporation's cofounders, befriended Ryan. Ballard was a self-made man who invested heavily in real estate, circus, and gambling operations.

During the Great Depression Ballard suffered steep financial losses. In 1936 he visited Ryan in Hot Springs after Ballard sold him the Kentucky Club. Ballard, Ryan, and Ballard's former business partner Robert "Silver Bob" Alexander met in the businessman's room at the Arlington Hotel to discuss Ballard's recent sale of the Palm Island Club in Miami, Florida. Alexander angrily insisted he was entitled to a portion of the proceeds. When Ballard explained Alexander's share only extended to the club's operations and not the actual building, Alexander shot and killed him. A few seconds later more shots rang out; Alexander fell mortally wounded. It was reported he turned his gun on himself, but Ryan later "intimated to friends he was the killer." He was never charged.[37] Ryan partnered with William S. Jacobs, a local gambling kingpin, during the 1930s until his death in 1940.[38]

Avoiding gambling and bad investments, Ryan was the rare confidence man who remained comfortable in old age. At the time of his death in 1937, he lived in a modest home in Hot Springs and owned a lodge on nearby Lake Katherine.[39] That same year his fellow Buckfoot confederate Dr. Robert E. L. Goddard passed away in Dallas.[40] Sprinter Dick Beatte, who partnered with Boatright and Mabray, died in Amarillo, Texas. The former watchmaker was working as a painter when he passed away in 1926.[41]

After he was convicted for his part in defrauding Henry Stogsdill and Joseph Walker, turfman Willard Powell received the two-year maximum sentence and a $10,000 fine. Upon release on bond from Leavenworth in April 1910, Powell and his attorney George Mayne worked to clear his name. Mayne obtained passenger lists from the Peninsular & Occidental S. S. Company showing Powell had traveled from Florida to Cuba at the time he was alleged to have aided Mabray. He also submitted signed, postmarked postcards Powell sent from Cuba to his mother in Texas. This strengthened Mayne's assertion Powell was wrongfully convicted. At the suggestion of federal prosecutor Marcellus Temple, Mayne secured affidavits from two witnesses whose statements cast doubt on Powell's participation. Although Judge McPherson's report on Powell's suitability for a pardon is not included in the file, he believed Powell had been mistakenly identified by victim Henry Stogsdill.[42]

US attorney general George Wickersham, in a memo to President William Howard Taft, stated McPherson believed it was a case of mistaken identity and if he had still had jurisdiction over the case, he would grant a new trial. Postal Inspector John Swenson disagreed.[43] He argued McPherson had been given misleading information by unnamed parties lobbying for Powell's pardon. While he acknowledged Powell returned

Willard Powell. *National Archives and Records Administration.*

$1,000 to victim Joseph Walker, Swenson asserted Powell only did so after he was charged in federal court in order to avoid a felony conviction. Walker, he claimed, was influenced by Powell's actions. Swenson admitted Powell's alibi in the Stogsdill case was likely genuine, but still believed the Kid was guilty of swindling Joseph Walker and John Sizer. US Postal Service chief inspector Robert Sharp concurred.[44]

Their objections were dismissed. On July 12, 1911, President Taft pardoned Powell. Yale professor Edwin Borchard examined Powell's case in *Convicting the Innocent: Sixty-Five Actual Errors of Criminal Justice.* Almost twenty years after the pardon, Powell's attorney George Mayne told Borchard's research assistant E. Russell Lutz, "It was not wholly a case of mistaken identity but also a question as to whether or not there was evidence which would warrant his conviction." Mayne disclosed that after he obtained evidence that proved Powell was out of the country when Stogsdill was swindled, he showed it to Judge McPherson, who suggested Mayne apply for Powell's pardon.[45]

After his pardon, Powell followed the races to South America and Cuba. In 1914 he and other confidence men in Chicago, including Mabray associate Clarence Class, were accused of being part of a police protection scheme. Cook County state's attorney Thomas Maclay Hoyne II charged two police officials and ten detectives as having taken protection money from what he called the "crime trust." Hoyne also obtained indictments against Powell and other confidence men running a payoff joint. They had reportedly taken in $100,000 that summer.[46] Powell fled Chicago and was later indicted for swindling an Iowan out of $10,000.[47] His attempt to fight extradition failed and he went on trial.[48] Despite Hoyne's efforts, he declared in 1918, "Not since 1913 have there been so many confidence men in Chicago as there are now." The Waco Kid denied any connection to them.[49]

Following his troubles in Chicago, the Waco Kid remained in the Midwest. When he registered for the draft in 1918, Powell lived in Tulsa, where he worked as a leaser for the Hanson Oil and Gas Company.[50] Two years later, when the Kid and his wife applied for passports to travel to Cuba, he gave his residence as Kansas City and his occupation as "Horseman."[51] He may have associated with Kansas City's Twelfth Street Gang; he reportedly fleeced a Texan for $5,000 during his time in the Paris of the Plains.[52] The following year found him in Florida.

Powell was far from alone. Confidence men from across the country flocked to Florida's resort cities during the winter season; one estimate that year claimed they netted $2 million in three months from wealthy visitors who lost their money on cards, fraudulent turf exchanges, badger games, and other schemes. Fred Buckminster and a group of Chicago con men operated the International Turf Exchange, a wire outfit, out of a tony Daytona Beach residence. This practice allowed confidence men to run private clubs out of sight of local authorities who were already—in some cases—on the take. After an Indiana banker was skinned for $100,000 at Buckminster's, the local Ku Klux Klan riddled the residence with gunfire on the evening of March 20, 1921. The sole occupant escaped the mob's fury by jumping out of a second-story window. The Klan stormed the house and destroyed the wire operation. Shortly thereafter Buckminster was arrested in West Palm Beach on an old conspiracy charge out of Chicago. Local papers recalled he had fled the city after he was convicted in March 1917. Now he was on his way back to the Prairie State to serve out his sentence.[53]

On the night of March 21, 1921, the Waco Kid strode into the dining room of a St. Augustine hotel where a well-dressed crowd of confidence men were playing whist. The Kid distributed the proceeds from a recent con by slipping rolls of cash into their pockets, then left to briefly speak with his wife Elizabeth on the veranda.[54] It was getting late when a touring car parked nearby and its occupants entered the hotel. They headed for the dining room where the Waco Kid was now sitting with his back to the door. Seated at his table were fellow confidence men Deacon Wheeler, French Henry, and John Idle. Henry was laughing at a joke Idle had just told when a shot rang out; a bullet intended for the Kid's head missed and grazed his neck. The Kid felt his neck as he stood up from his chair. "Don't shoot!" he yelled as a fusillade of bullets struck him. The Kid fell on his face without seeing who fired the fatal shots. A man sitting near Elizabeth Powell on the veranda jumped to his feet, snapped his fingers, yelled, "——'s got Waco!" and ran into the street. Startled by the man's remark, she ran to the dining room and almost collided with Powell's killer as he fled, gun in hand, to the street.[55] As Elizabeth made her way into the room she was almost trampled by panicked con men. She found her husband alone, face down on the floor. She gathered the Kid in her arms, but he could only gasp. A bellboy brought a pillow, water, and towels as Powell's wife yelled for a doctor. When a physician arrived, he refused her pleas to give her husband a blood transfusion and pronounced Willard Powell dead. He was laid to rest in an expensive copper casket in Texas on Easter.[56]

It developed that although Powell had turned state's evidence in Chicago a few years earlier, he had been welcomed back into the fold. Not all his old cronies were pleased, but together they conned suckers for the next few years. He allegedly quarreled with his associates over money shortly before the Klan attacked their wire operation. Powell fled to St. Augustine and, the story went, "decided to play it both ways against the middle." It was rumored he told Chicago authorities where they could find Buckminster. One local historian surmised "either he was overheard at St. Augustine or someone in the Chicago police department betrayed him."[57] Powell's murderer was never definitively identified, but the "Alabama Kid" and another con man were suspected.[58] Authorities dropped their investigation into Powell's murder after several witnesses refused to cooperate.[59]

Chicago Daily News reporter Charles E. Owen offered an alternate explanation. After speaking to Powell's widow and others, Owen challenged the assertion Powell squealed on Buckminster. Instead, he believed, the Alabama Kid had been barred from operating in Florida and blamed Powell. Owen forwarded the Kid's name to Florida governor Cary Hardee on behalf of citizens who wanted him prosecuted and confidence men driven from the state.[60] Evidence submitted to local and state officials led nowhere and he was never charged with Powell's murder.[61]

Life in Chicago brought grief not only to Powell. Former Chicago welterweight Walter Nolan pled guilty in 1911 and received three months in jail and a $300 fine for helping Mabray swindle Thomas Ballew. While still pursuing Nolan, Ballew died at age fifty-nine of chronic interstitial nephritis in Excelsior Springs, Missouri.[62] After Nolan's release from jail, he returned to the Windy City and began passing fraudulent securities. In 1922 he was arrested in New Orleans on a charge of forging and passing American Express money orders. Nolan wistfully told a reporter he might have had a different life had his ankle not given out during a fight.[63] He was later indicted on seven counts of forgery in Cincinnati.[64] In 1938 he, along with Chicago gangster George "Bugs" Moran, was arrested for counterfeiting American Express money orders. He died in 1943.[65]

Tom Robison, another Buckfoot and Mabray Gang member, lived to endure the hardships of the Great Depression. In 1930 the sixty-five-year-old Robison was convicted of possessing counterfeiting materials and conspiracy to defraud. While serving a three-year-term at the Iowa State Penitentiary his second wife died. Released early in 1932, Robison died ten years later in Los Angeles.[66] He was not the only Mabray associate committing crimes in old age. In 1935 Ed Leach was picked up for counterfeiting in Cleveland. He was eighty-one when he died four years later.[67] Former boxer Ed McCoy was arrested by San Francisco authorities in 1913 and in Los Angeles in 1918.[68]

Prison did seem to have a lasting effect on at least one member of the gang. Harry Forbes appealed his conviction. While he waited, he was sent to Leavenworth but was released on June 30, 1910, after his bond was secured. The following year Forbes applied for a pardon. Postal Inspector John Swenson informed US pardon attorney James Finch that Forbes gave the government very little difficulty. After his release Forbes voluntarily helped federal authorities locate Lucius Hindman and Tom Davies; he also helped postal inspectors secure evidence. For these reasons, Swenson recommended a pardon. Judge Smith McPherson also recommended President William H. Taft pardon Forbes, noting that a position as a Cook County deputy sheriff awaited Forbes in Chicago once his legal troubles were resolved.[69] Despite reluctance on the part of federal prosecutor Marcellus Temple, US attorney general George Wickersham recommended Forbes's sentence be commuted to a fine of $100; President Taft did so on August 21, 1911.[70] Forbes remained in Chicago and worked a variety of jobs before dying in 1946.[71] His thirty-six-year-old brother Clarence died on February 12, 1918, at the Illinois State Hospital in Elgin. Later that year, Clarence Forbes's name came up in court; he, along with four other men including Joseph "Yellow Kid" Weil, had colluded together in 1913 on a fixed fight. Old habits died hard.[72]

Isador "Kid" Warner pled guilty in federal court in 1913 and received a $500 fine. Two years later he was spotted at a Denver racetrack.[73] What he did in the years that followed remains mostly unknown. In 1942, when

Warner was sixty-two, he lived in the handsome Parke Apartments in Buffalo, New York, but gave his mailing address as a post office box in Lexington, Oklahoma, where he owned land. When asked who would always know his address, Warner curiously gave the name of a Lexington banker.[74] Warner died in 1974 and was buried alongside his parents in Buffalo.[75]

Like Warner, Monte McCall was fined $500 when he pled guilty in federal court in 1913.[76] When he applied for a passport in 1916, McCall declared he was a motion picture salesman traveling to Europe to buy and sell films. His old partner Isador Warner vouched for him.[77] The pair opened a fur shop in Davenport in the fall of 1917, but the town had changed—a year earlier Iowa passed a statewide prohibition law that tamed McCall's old haunt. After they realized the police were watching them, McCall and Warner packed up and left late one night. Authorities suspected the two men were going to fence stolen property.[78] McCall later moved to Florida where he lived to be eighty-three; his obituary said he was a retired farmer.[79]

Tainted by their association with Mabray, some struggled in their old profession. After his release, George "Ole" Marsh managed Croatian wrestler Marin Plestina.[80] In 1921 Marsh informed the US Department of Justice he had been battling the "wrestling trust." This clique, he claimed, controlled wrestling and, in some cases, boxing matches. The group had distributed Marsh's Leavenworth mugshot across the country and Marsh wanted the Department of Justice to investigate. A US assistant attorney general replied they could not assist him.[81] Marsh worked in the wrestling industry until the 1930s. He died in Oregon in 1952 at the age of eighty-six.[82]

Smith McPherson, who oversaw Robert Boatright and John Mabray's trials from the federal bench, died in 1915.[83] Iowa attorney general George Cosson served three terms. He ran for governor in 1916 but lost the nomination. He returned to private practice, taught law, and made a final, failed attempt to run for public office in 1936. In his final years Cosson spoke out against isolationism, Charles Lindbergh's America First campaign, and McCarthyism before his death in 1963.[84] John S. Swenson, the postal inspector who doggedly pursued Mabray, received a meritorious service award for bringing Mabray to justice. He worked for the US Postal Service until his retirement in 1941. During World War II Swenson served as a special assistant to the US attorney general and spent his final days in Seattle. He died in 1952.[85] Swenson's colleague Charles S. Ranger died in California in 1961 after serving as mayor of El Monte.[86] Fellow postal inspector William F. Allmon had a long career with the US Postal Service before his death in 1945 in Wichita, Kansas.[87]

That each man passed with little fanfare was no judgment upon their careers; despite being one of the oldest law enforcement agencies in the country, the US Postal Inspection Service has long been overshadowed by the Federal Bureau of Investigation and the US Marshals Service. Known as the "Silent Service" because of its reputation for building solid cases with little fanfare, the US Postal Inspection Service earned the respect of confidence men and other criminals. As criminal Chic Conwell noted, "The post-office inspectors are thought to be the most straight and efficient, and they do not frame cases."[88] Swenson's takedown of the Mabray Gang demonstrated the crucial role postal inspectors played in combating crime across the country—a role the service fulfills to this day. Within a few years, the methods of the Mabray Gang were antiquated and postal inspectors moved on to investigate new schemes.

As David Maurer observed, the foot race store was on "its way out while the wire was in its infancy."[89] Confidence men like brothers Fred and Charley Gondorff, whose story was loosely depicted in *The Sting*, refined and mastered the wire (horse race) con the same way Boatright and Mabray refined the fight store years earlier. Small towns would always have suckers, and there were still small-time grifters who employed the same tired schemes, but the con changed over time. Fixed foot races were a thing of the past; now suckers were taken on the wire and stock market (fake brokerage) rackets.[90] Robert Boatright and John Mabray receded from memory as confidence schemes evolved. Confidence men never left American society, but they were soon overshadowed by the gangsters who rose to prominence during Prohibition and the Great Depression. Yet the con men became engrained in local lore; occasionally newspapers recalled their transgressions in nostalgic articles. Seemingly every decade the Omaha newspapers published a story about the Mabray Gang.[91]

Tom Porter of the *Omaha World-Herald* was perhaps among the last people to examine the three volumes of court testimony from Mabray's trial.[92] What happened after Porter looked at them in 1930 is unknown. Surviving records and newspaper accounts indicate there were two copies of the original three-volume set. Of the three sets, one was in the custody of Judge Smith McPherson, the second was in the possession of defense attorney George Mayne, and the third was last seen in Sylvester Rush's Omaha office. Several defendants appealed their convictions, and one might expect a copy of the testimony to have been included in the appellate case. Court records reveal no duplicate was reproduced at the appellate level because the record was too voluminous.[93] If the appellate court had not balked at the expense of duplicating the testimony, we might have a better understanding of the gang, its operations, and the extent of its influence. Until the volumes surface—if they exist—the complete story of Boatright's successor has yet to be told.

After Robert Boatright passed from the scene in 1904, the greatest con to come out of the Ozarks was Alvin C. Thomas, better known as Titanic Thompson. Born a short distance from Webb City, he grew up across the state line in Rogers, Arkansas. Like Boatright and Mabray, the truth surrounding his legendary career is hard to discern, but his skill as a golfer, pool shark, and card player are indisputable. It seems only fitting that Thompson, the king of the proposition bet, earned his nickname while playing pool in Joplin in 1912.[94]

While journalist Westbrook Pegler contended the Mabray Gang was the biggest scandal in American sports prior to the 1919 Black Sox Scandal, none of the men involved in Mabray's schemes towered so high in the American sports world as Shoeless Joe Jackson. Still, there were several men who competed credibly until they were corrupted. Minor league baseball player Rudolph "Darby" Thielman, boxer Harry Forbes, and sprinter Leon Lozier were men of athletic ability. The fixed matches of the Buckfoot and Mabray gangs confirmed what many spectators may have already known—that some amateurs were suspect—but as the Black Sox Scandal demonstrated, even the actions of professional athletes deserved scrutiny.[95]

Robert Boatright and John Mabray had the cooperation of a local bank and protection from authorities, but they could not control the press—an especially partisan press. Unlike Mabray, Boatright was not brought down by his use of the mails to defraud his victims. Instead, his downfall came as the result of feuding factions in the local Democratic party, progressives outraged by the presence of a brazen criminal organization in their county, and victims who overcame their fear of public humiliation to pursue justice in the courts. Like much of America in the late nineteenth and early twentieth centuries, Jasper County was home to a vocal local press that espoused rival political views and championed competing visions for the country's future. Newspapers in Joplin, Webb City, Carthage, and even tiny Carterville—as well as papers in other states—reported on Boatright and the Buckfoot Gang in dozens of articles over a four-year period. This vibrant, democratic press, however sensational at times, provided Boatright's detractors, as well as his allies, a public forum in which to battle for the soul of Jasper County. Although Boatright's enemies succeeded in driving the Buckfoot Gang from Webb City, other reform efforts were slower to take root.

Mabray was far more successful at keeping his big store out of the spotlight, but he, too, was brought down by his victims. Contemporaries remarked Mabray and Boatright were astute judges of character, but not every mark was a stoic who took their medicine. Any efforts he or his allies may have made to sway federal authorities failed. Where Ben Marks may have been able to exert control over city and county officials, his influence did not extend to the US Postal Inspection Service and the US Attorney General's office. Power and influence sometimes have their limits—especially when public servants aided by twelve jurors uphold the law.

While the federal government unsuccessfully pursued Boatright for defrauding Jonathan Davis, local authorities and his victims brought him to heel. Multiple court cases and heavy bonds strained his finances. An unsympathetic jury from outside Jasper County was immune to any possible entreaties he and his attorneys may have made. Although local and state authorities had long ignored corruption in Council Bluffs, the federal government succeeded despite lackadaisical attitudes toward crime. Inadequate federal laws, however, led to Mabray and his cronies serving two years or less. The most meaningful punishment occurred when the government imposed a $10,000 fine; Mabray was burdened with this debt for years.

For those who almost evaded authorities, their jail terms and fines were far less substantial. It is unsurprising many of them continued to pull off cons. As Inspectors Swenson, Ranger, and Allmon argued in 1910, if the federal government had offered rewards sooner, they likely would have caught more members. Several individuals offered to turn in wanted men on multiple occasions, but only if they received a reward. The inspectors asserted Mabray's con was believed to be the most successful confidence game invented and it would be difficult to suppress; there were already reports men who had evaded arrest were attempting to organize a new con.[96]

The lives of Robert Boatright and John Mabray sit at "the intersection of myth and reality."[97] Their stories raise tantalizing questions sources cannot answer. Was, for example, Boatright's Webb City Athletic Club part of a larger—perhaps even nationwide—syndicate? If David Maurer's criminal informants discussed Boatright's role in such a network, he did not mention it. The federal court case that ensnared George Ryan indicated there were ropers located across the upland South and Midwest. Contemporary press accounts as well as testimony from Mabray's trial hint at a national network of confidence men; Mabray's trial may have provided one of the most detailed views into its inner workings, but little about the broader picture was revealed.

While it would be easy to romanticize their exploits, Boatright and Mabray were criminals who wrecked people's lives. They capitalized on technological innovations—the railroad, the telegraph, the telephone—to further their schemes. Men (and it was always men; no women were swindled) were ruined after losing their money—and sometimes the savings of their family and friends—on fake athletic contests. Although we have little insight into how many families were devastated, at least one victim lost his business, another lost his father in a train wreck while coming to his son's aid, and others were humiliated after their stories were publicized. Their victims were not blameless; as Roger Williams said, a man needed to "have enough Grand Larceny in him to make a good first class horse thief" to participate.

There is a tendency to think of confidence men as an urban phenomenon, a symptom of societal ills concentrated in large cities. Yet as Sinclair Lewis and other early twentieth-century social critics demonstrated, small towns were as full of hypocrisy and sin as any metropolis. Boatright and Mabray's ropers found marks across rural and urban America willing to travel to Webb City and Council Bluffs to bet on a sure thing. Both were among the most successful confidence men in early twentieth-century America. Ephemeral as the lies they spun, Boatright and Mabray's lives provide us with greater understanding of crime and politics in the Ozarks and the Midwest; their stories linger in the landscape of local memory.

Few fragments of Robert Boatright's Jasper County remain. The lead and zinc are gone, the wounds of extraction—sinkholes, open-pit mines, and contamination—the enduring legacies of the region's industrial past. Smoke no longer belches from smelters, pumps no longer endlessly hum, and passenger trains no longer cry out their arrival. Joplin and Webb City's once burgeoning downtown districts—or, what is left of them—are quiet, having fallen victim to changing times. Fourth and Main, once the heart of Joplin and the seat of Gilbert Barbee's power, was decimated by urban renewal. The venues where raucous crowds watched prizefights put on by Boatright's Webb City Athletic Club have been demolished, and the gang's racetrack is long gone. What endures, however, is the knowledge it was once an opportune proving ground for one of the more unique and colorful cons in American history, and that the con—while ever evolving—is eternal: to separate the sucker from his money.

NOTES

INTRODUCTION

1. Raymond A. Smith Jr., "John C. Mabray: A Con Artist in the Corn Belt," *The Palimpsest* 64, no. 4 (July/August 1983): 123–39.
2. Jill Lepore, *These Truths: A History of the United States* (New York: W. W. Norton, 2018), xviii. William R. Draper, *True Stories of Peculiar People and Unusual Events in the Ozarks* (Girard, KS: Haldeman-Julius, 1946), 26.
3. David W. Maurer, *The Big Con: The Story of the Confidence Man* (Indianapolis: Bobbs-Merrill, 1940; repr., New York: Anchor Books, 1999).
4. J. Frank Norfleet, *Norfleet* (Fort Worth: White Pub. Co., 1924); Philip S. Van Cise, *Fighting the Underworld* (Boston: Houghton Mifflin Co., 1936), 7–10.
5. Amy Reading, *The Mark Inside: A Perfect Swindle, A Cunning Revenge, and a Small History of the Big Con* (New York: Knopf, 2012), 8.
6. Chic Conwell, *The Professional Thief by a Professional Thief*, annotated by Edwin H. Sutherland (Chicago: University of Chicago Press, 1937), vii, 26–27. For more on Conwell and Sutherland, see Jon Snodgrass, "The Criminologist and His Criminal: The Case of Edwin H. Sutherland and Broadway Jones," *Issues in Criminology* 8, no. 1 (Spring 1973): 1–17.
7. Conwell, *The Professional Thief*, 21, 23n9, 56n13.
8. Conwell, *The Professional Thief*, vii, 26–27.
9. David R. Johnson, "The Origins and Structure of Intercity Criminal Activity, 1840–1920: An Interpretation," *Journal of Social History* 15, no. 4 (Summer 1982): 593–605.
10. Johnson, "The Origins and Structure of Intercity Criminal Activity," 594.
11. Johnson, "The Origins and Structure of Intercity Criminal Activity," 595.
12. Johnson, "The Origins and Structure of Intercity Criminal Activity," 596–97.
13. Johnson, "The Origins and Structure of Intercity Criminal Activity," 594, 597, 599.
14. Johnson, "The Origins and Structure of Intercity Criminal Activity," 599.
15. Johnson, "The Origins and Structure of Intercity Criminal Activity," 600.
16. Johnson, "The Origins and Structure of Intercity Criminal Activity," 602–3.
17. *Joplin Globe*, December 24, 1994, 5B.

CHAPTER 1

1. "Edward Woodson," 1860 US Census, 1870 US Census, St. Louis City, Missouri; Testimony of the Reverend Edward L. Woodson before the American Freedman's Inquiry Commission, Ira Berlin, et al., eds., *Freedom: A Documentary History of Emancipation, 1861–1867*, Series I, Volume 2,

The Wartime Genesis of Free Labor: The Upper South (Cambridge: Cambridge University Press, 2012), 580–81.

2. Charles Johnson explained, "My brother was counsel for young Woodson. I know old man Woodson, and at his request, because I had known him for years, I consented to assist my brother in the case." *St. Louis Globe-Democrat*, March 8, 1876, 7; Marshall D. Hier, "Charles P. Johnson, The Bar's Window on Its Past," *St. Louis Bar Journal* 38, no. 1 (Summer 1991): 34–35, 51; William Hyde and Howard L. Conard, eds., *Encyclopedia of the History of St. Louis* (New York: Southern Historical Co., 1899), 2:1130–32; Walter B. Stevens, *St. Louis: History of the Fourth City, 1764–1909* (Chicago: S. J. Clarke, 1909), 3:908–10.

3. *St. Louis Daily Globe*, March 16, 1875, 8.

4. *St. Louis Daily Globe*, March 16, 1875, 8; *St. Louis Democrat*, March 16, 1875, 4. The Woodsons lived at 722 North Sixteenth Street.

5. "Oscar J. Boatright," *Missouri Death Records, 1834–1910*, Ancestry.com.

6. *St. Louis Globe-Democrat*, March 10, 1876, 3.

7. *St. Louis Democrat*, March 19, 1875, 4; *St. Louis Daily Globe*, March 16, 1875, 8.

8. *St. Louis Democrat*, March 16, 1875, 4.

9. *St. Louis Democrat*, March 16, 1875, 4. Johnson wrote in his diary, "At 3 o'clk when examining witness a young man named Boatright came in stealthily and walked deliberately up and stabbed young Woodson with a huge butcher knife. Woodson died Wednesday. The most terrible sight I ever witnessed." Charles P. Johnson Papers (C4229), State Historical Society of Missouri.

10. *St. Louis Democrat*, March 16, 1875, 4; *St. Louis Republican*, March 16, 1875, 5.

11. Allen Eugene Wagner, *Good Order and Safety: A History of the St. Louis Metropolitan Police Department, 1861–1906* (St. Louis: Missouri History Museum Press, 2008), 119; *St. Louis Daily Globe*, March 16, 1875, 8; *St. Louis Republican*, March 16, 1875, 5.

12. *St. Louis Democrat*, March 16, 1875, 4.

13. *St. Louis Republican*, March 17, 1875, 8.

14. *St. Louis Democrat*, March 19, 1875, 4; Coroner's Inquest, St. Louis City, Reel 31272, Missouri State Archives, St. Louis.

15. *State of Missouri v. R. P. W. Boatright*, St. Louis Circuit Court, Missouri State Archives.

16. "Robert M. Boatright," 1860 US Census, Franklin County, Missouri; James E. McGhee, *Guide to Missouri Confederate Units, 1861–1865* (Fayetteville: University of Arkansas Press, 2008), 202–5; *St. Louis Globe-Democrat*, March 10, 1876, 3; Robert M. Boatright, Company E, Fifth Infantry,

Compiled Service Records of Soldiers Who Served in Organizations from the State of Missouri, National Archives.

17. Patricia Cleary, *The World, the Flesh, and the Devil: A History of Colonial St. Louis* (Columbia: University of Missouri, 2011), 33, 37, 309; James Neal Primm, *Lion of the Valley: St. Louis, Missouri, 1764–1980*, 3rd ed. (St. Louis: Missouri Historical Society, 1998), 154–67; Louis Gerteis, *Civil War St. Louis* (Lawrence: University Press of Kansas, 2001), 29–31; James T. Lloyd, *Lloyd's Steamboat Directory, and Disasters on the Western Waters* (Cincinnati: James T. Lloyd & Co., 1856), 264–65; Galusha Anderson, *The Story of a Border City during the Civil War* (Boston: Little, Brown, and Co., 1908), 8.

18. Primm, *Lion of the Valley*, 154–57; Linda A. Fisher, "A Summer of Terror: The Cholera Epidemic of 1849," *Missouri Historical Review* 99, no. 3 (April 2005): 189–211.

19. Primm, *Lion of the Valley*, 255–56, 266–67.

20. L. U. Reavis, *St. Louis, The Future Great City of the World* (St. Louis: St. Louis County Court, 1870).

21. Anderson, *The Story of a Border City*, 3.

22. 1867 *Edwards' Annual Directory of St. Louis* (St. Louis: Edwards & Co., 1867), 204; 1868 *Edwards' Annual Directory of St. Louis* (St. Louis: Richard Edwards, 1868), 178; 1869 *Edwards' Annual Directory of St. Louis* (St. Louis: Charles Pub. & Mfg. Co.), 179; 1870 *Edwards' Annual Directory of St. Louis* (St. Louis: Southern Pub. Co., 1870), 157; 1871 *Edwards' Annual Directory of St. Louis* (St. Louis: Southern Pub. Co., 1871), 112; 1872 *Edwards' Annual Directory of St. Louis* (St. Louis: Southern Pub. Co., 1872), 71; *Gould's St. Louis Directory for 1873* (St. Louis: David B. Gould & Co., 1873), 110; *Gould's St. Louis Directory for 1874* (St. Louis: David B. Gould, 1874), 128; *Gould's St. Louis Directory for 1875* (St. Louis: David B. Gould, 1875), 129.

23. Joseph A. Dacus and James W. Buel, *A Tour of St. Louis; Or, The Inside Life of a Great City* (St. Louis: Western Pub. Co., 1878), 417–18, 513; Landmarks Association of St. Louis, *From Kerry Patch to Little Paderhorn: A Visit in the Irish-German Communities of Nineteenth Century St. Louis* (St. Louis: Landmarks Association of St. Louis, 1966), 4–5; *1867 Edwards Directory of St. Louis*, 204. Christy Avenue was later renamed Lucas Avenue. William B. Magnan, *Streets of St. Louis* (Groton, CT: Right Press, 1994), 169. In 1873 Boatright Sr. sued the St. Louis *Globe* after it claimed he was among those on the payroll of the city's street-cleaning department who rendered no services for money received. In a retraction, the *Globe* stated instead of "deserving censure" Boatright "figured very creditably in the investigation" and apologized. *Fort Scott (KS) Daily Monitor*, December 27, 1873, 2.

24. Dacus and Buel, *A Tour of St. Louis*, 417.

25. Dacus and Buel, *A Tour of St. Louis*, 519.

26. Dacus and Buel, *A Tour of St. Louis*, 515; "Preliminary Report of the Board of Managers of the St. Louis House of Refuge," *The Mayor's Message with Accompanying Documents to the City Council of the City of St. Louis, at Its May Session* (St. Louis: St. Louis Times Co., 1872), 5.

27. Bonnie Stepenoff, *The Dead End Kids of St. Louis: Homeless Boys and the People Who Tried to Save Them* (Columbia: University of Missouri Press, 2010), 58–63; "Preliminary Report of the Board of Managers of the St. Louis House of Refuge," *The Mayor's Message with Accompanying Documents to the City Council of the City of St. Louis, at Its May Session* (St. Louis: St. Louis Times Co., 1872), 5.

28. Stepenoff, *The Dead End Kids of St. Louis*, 62; St. Louis House of Refuge, Journal of Commitments, July 25, 1854–January 28, 1899, Missouri Historical Society; Dacus and Buel, *A Tour of St. Louis*, 517; "Lillie Boatright," *Missouri Death Records, 1834–1910*, Ancestry.com.

29. *St. Louis Post-Dispatch*, February 21, 1876, 1.

30. Edward Woodson died from pneumonia on January 29, 1876. *St. Louis Post-Dispatch*, February 21, 1876, 1; "Edward Woodson," *Missouri Death Records, 1834–1910*, Ancestry.com.

31. *St. Louis Post-Dispatch*, March 7, 1876, 4.

32. Marshall D. Hier, "The Rise and Fall of 'Adonis' Judge James C. Normile, Part I," *St. Louis Bar Journal* 42 no. 3 (Spring 1996): 44–47; Marshall D. Hier, "The Rise and Fall of 'Adonis' Judge James C. Normile, Part II," *St. Louis Bar Journal* 42 no. 4 (Spring 1996): 34–36.

33. Hier, "Rise and Fall of 'Adonis' Judge, Part I"; Hier, "Rise and Fall of 'Adonis' Judge, Part II"; *St. Louis Missouri Democrat*, April 8, 1872, 4. The insanity defense was first used successfully in the United States in 1859 by politician Daniel Sickles. Thomas Keneally, *American Scoundrel: The Life of the Notorious Civil War General Dan Sickles* (New York: Anchor Books, 2003).

34. Hier, "Rise and Fall of 'Adonis' Judge, Part I," 44–47; Hier, "Rise and Fall of 'Adonis' Judge, Part II," 34–36. In 1886 Normile was elected to the St. Louis Criminal Court. When the *St. Louis Post-Dispatch* criticized Normile, he sued. The paper hired John D. Johnson to represent them in the case. During a deposition Johnson got to Normile to admit he lied about his education. Normile committed suicide on August 9, 1892.

35. *St. Louis Globe-Democrat*, March 8, 1876, 7; *St. Louis Post-Dispatch*, March 7, 1876, 4; *State v. R. P. W. Boatright*.

36. *St. Louis Globe-Democrat*, March 9, 1876, 3.

37. *The Bench and Bar of St. Louis, Kansas City, and Jefferson City* (St. Louis: American Biographical Pub. Co., 1884), 169–71.

38. *St. Louis Globe-Democrat*, March 9, 1876, 3. Boatright later used the alias John Bagwell.
39. *St. Louis Globe-Democrat*, March 9, 1876, 3.
40. *St. Louis Globe-Democrat*, March 9, 1876, 3.
41. *State v. R. P. W. Boatright.*
42. *State v. R. P. W. Boatright.*
43. *St. Louis Globe-Democrat*, March 9, 1876, 3.
44. *St. Louis Globe-Democrat*, March 9, 1876, 3.
45. *St. Louis Globe-Democrat*, March 9, 1876, 3.
46. *St. Louis Globe-Democrat*, March 9, 1876, 3.
47. *St. Louis Globe-Democrat*, March 9, 1876, 3.
48. *St. Louis Globe-Democrat*, March 10, 1876, 3.
49. *St. Louis Republican*, March 10, 1876, 8.
50. *St. Louis Globe-Democrat*, March 10, 1876, 3; *St. Louis Post-Dispatch*, March 9, 1876, 4; Max A. Goldstein, ed., *One Hundred Years of Medicine and Surgery in Missouri* (St. Louis: St. Louis Star, 1900), 101. Dr. Louis Bauer founded the St. Louis College of Physicians and Surgeons and specialized in orthopedic surgery. Dr. William B. Hazard studied medicine at Bellevue Hospital in New York and served on the faculty of the St. Louis College of Physicians and Surgeons. *St. Louis Medical and Surgical Journal* 54 (December–June 1888): 392.
51. *St. Louis Globe-Democrat*, March 10, 1876, 3.
52. *St. Louis Globe-Democrat*, March 11, 1876, 8.
53. *St. Louis Globe-Democrat*, March 12, 1876, 5.
54. *St. Louis Post-Dispatch*, March 11, 1876, 4.
55. *St. Louis Globe-Democrat*, March 12, 1876, 5; *St. Louis Republican*, March 12, 1876, 10.
56. *St. Louis Republican*, March 14, 1876, 5; *St. Louis Globe-Democrat*, March 12, 1876, 5.
57. *St. Louis Republican*, March 14, 1876, 5; *St. Louis Globe-Democrat*, March 14, 1876, 8.
58. *St. Louis Post-Dispatch*, May 17, 1876, 4; *St. Louis Post-Dispatch*, June 5, 1876, 4.
59. *St. Louis Republican*, June 19, 1876, 8; *St. Louis Republican*, September 12, 1876, 8.
60. *St. Louis Republican*, November 21, 1876, 8.
61. *St. Louis Globe-Democrat*, December 19, 1876, 8; December 20, 1876, 3.
62. *St. Louis Globe-Democrat*, December 22, 1876, 3; *St. Louis Globe-Democrat*, December 23, 1876, 8; *St. Louis Globe-Democrat*, December 24, 1876, 5; *St. Louis Times*, December 24, 1876, 8.
63. *St. Louis Globe-Democrat*, December 25, 1876, 4; *St. Louis Globe-Democrat*, December 28, 1876, 8.

NOTES   205

64. *Gould's St. Louis Directory for 1877* (St. Louis: David B. Gould, 1877), 132; *Gould's St. Louis Directory for 1878* (St. Louis: David B. Gould, 1878), 130; *Gould's St. Louis Directory for 1879* (St. Louis: David B. Gould, 1879), 155; *Gould's St. Louis Directory for 1880* (St. Louis: David B. Gould, 1880), 159; *St. Louis Post-Dispatch*, February 24, 1880, 8; "Elijah Gates Boatright," *Missouri Death Records, 1834–1910*, Ancestry.com.

65. *St. Louis Post-Dispatch*, February 24, 1880, 8.

66. *St. Louis Post-Dispatch*, April 29, 1880, 5.

67. *St. Louis Post-Dispatch*, May 1, 1880, 3; Dacus and Buel, *A Tour of St. Louis*, 401, 474; *The Revised Ordinance of the City of St. Louis* (St. Louis: Times Printing House, 1881), 620–23. See also *The Whole Story Told. The Dark and Mysterious Places of St. Louis* (St. Louis: Globe Pub. Co., 1885).

68. *Gould's St. Louis Directory for 1881* (St. Louis: David B. Gould, 1881), 157; *Gould's St. Louis Directory for 1883* (St. Louis: David B. Gould, 1883), 157; *Gould's St. Louis Directory for 1884* (St. Louis: David B. Gould, 1884), 162; *Gould's St. Louis Directory for 1885* (St. Louis: David B. Gould, 1885), 166. A Robert Boatright of Missouri is listed as a "clerk/steward" on a Mississippi River survey between Ohio and Illinois in *The US Register of Civil, Military, and Naval Service, 1863–1959*, Ancestry.com. The *Post-Dispatch* recalled an earlier episode when "Bob Boatright, a local desperado" and two men conspired to rob and murder a saloonkeeper. A fellow criminal alerted police and the plan was foiled. Boatright was arrested for vagrancy and sentenced to the city workhouse. *St. Louis Post-Dispatch*, May 18, 1887.

69. *State of Missouri v. Robert Boatright*, Jasper County Circuit Court, Jasper County Records Center, Carthage, MO; *State of Missouri v. Robert Boatright*, case no. 6087, Kansas City Court of Appeals (October 1892).

CHAPTER 2

1. Jarod Roll, *Poor Man's Fortune: White Working-Class Conservatism in American Metal Mining, 1850–1950* (Chapel Hill: University of North Carolina Press, 2020); Arrell M. Gibson, *Wilderness Bonanza: The Tri-State District of Missouri, Kansas, and Oklahoma* (Norman: University of Oklahoma Press, 1972), 27–30; *Families and Histories of Webb City, Carterville, and Oronogo, Missouri* (Webb City, MO: Webb City Area Genealogical Society, 2007), 5–7; Thomas L. Thompson and Charles E. Robertson, *Guidebook to the Geology along Interstate Highway 44 (I-44) in Missouri* (Rolla: Missouri Department of Natural Resources, 1993), 158. For mining names, see Evelyn Milligan Jones, *Tales about Joplin . . . Short and Tall* (Joplin, MO: Harragan House, 1962), 100–102.

2. *Carthage Evening Press*, September 21, 1922; for more on the Joplin and Carthage feud, see the editorials, "As to Joplin," *Carthage Evening Press*, January 2, 1901; "Joplin v. Carthage," *Carthage Evening Press*, January 26,

1901; Virginia Jeans Laas, *Bridging Two Eras: The Autobiography of Emily Newell Blair, 1877-1951* (Columbia: University of Missouri Press, 1999), 80.

3. *Families and Histories of Webb City, Carterville, and Oronogo, Missouri*, 5–7.

4. Norval M. Matthews, *The Promise Land* (Point Lookout, MO: School of the Ozarks Press, 1974), 132–33. Matthews mentions the Buckfoot Gang and the Exchange Bank but was too young to be knowledgeable of the gang, as his inaccurate description of their activities shows.

5. Joel T. Livingston, *A History of Jasper County, Missouri* (Chicago: Lewis Pub. Co., 1912), 1:306. The Stewarts became principal owners of the Center Creek Mining Company in 1885; the company "controls and operates the Exchange Bank." *Engineering and Mining Journal* 50, no. 9 (August 30, 1890): 253. The bank was incorporated in 1889 with a capital stock of $20,000. Joseph Stewart controlled the most shares of any shareholder. Exchange Bank of Webb City, Charter No. 572, box 13, folder 23, Bank Charters, Record Group 132, Missouri State Archives. The bank was located at 108 North Allen Street. *Hoye's Joplin, Carthage, Carterville, Webb City, and Jasper County Directory 1905-1906* (n.p., 1906), 189.

6. Henrietta Crotty, *A History and Economic Survey of Webb City, Missouri* (Webb City, MO: Webb City Daily Sentinel, 1937), 4–6; Norval M. Matthews, *An Amazing City: A Mini-Account of Webb City, Missouri* (Webb City, MO: Sentinel Printing Co., 1976), 19; Table 5—Population of States and Territories by Minor Civil Divisions: 1890 and 1900, Missouri, *Population of the United States by States and Territories, Counties, and Minor Civil Divisions as Returned at the Twelfth Census: 1900* (Washington, DC: Census Printing Office, 1901), 241; Livingston, *A History of Jasper County, Missouri, and Its People*, 1:415–21; Brooks Blevins, *A History of the Ozarks, Volume 3: The Ozarkers* (Urbana: University of Illinois Press, 2021), 77.

7. "Southwest Missouri as a Mission Field," *The Christian-Evangelist* 28, no. 35 (August 27, 1891): 556. The gang favored the Newland Hotel at 30 South Allen. *Hoye's Joplin, Carthage, Carterville, Webb City, and Jasper County Directory 1905-1906*, 193.

8. Carthage *Jasper County Democrat*, August 24, 1899. Boatright's associate Charley Parker was charged with selling liquor to minors.

9. For Wenrich, see Rudi Blesh and Harriet Janis, *They All Played Ragtime: The True Story of an American Music* (New York: Alfred Knopf, 1950), 124. For "metropolis," see Laas, *Bridging Two Eras*, 79. For Barde, see *Sedalia Democrat*, October 25, 1899, 2.

10. *Joplin Daily Globe*, December 15, 1899.

11. *Joplin Daily Herald*, December 2, 1899.

12. *Joplin Daily Herald*, December 3, 1899.

13. *Joplin Daily Herald*, December 3, 1899.

14. *Joplin Daily Globe*, December 15, 1899.

15. *Joplin Daily Globe*, December 24, 1899.

16. *Joplin Daily Herald*, December 14, 1899.

17. Glen S. Slough, Undated, unpublished memoir, Greenwood County, Kansas, Historical Society; Zenith Lindamood, "The Fastest Runner in the World," *Kanshistique* (May 1995): 12–13. Bud's full name was Louis B. Gillett; see *Arkansas Deaths and Burials, 1882–1929; 1945–1963*, Familysearch.org.

18. Foot racing is barely mentioned in Robert K. Gilmore's *Ozark Baptizings, Hangings, and Other Diversions: Theatrical Folkways of Rural Missouri, 1885–1910* (Norman: University of Oklahoma Press, 1984). Despite the title, it is hardly mentioned in Murry R. Nelson, ed., *Encyclopedia of Sports in America: A History from Foot Races to Extreme Sports*, 2 vols. (Westport, CT: Greenwood Press, 2009).

19. *Eureka (KS) Democratic Messenger*, July 27, 1894.

20. *Eureka (KS) Democratic Messenger*, September 14, 1894.

21. Greenwood County Historical Society, *History of Greenwood County, Kansas* (Wichita, KS: Josten's Publications, 1986), 1:114.

22. *Eureka (KS) Herald*, October 19, 1894. The most popular version of this story has Bud, his opponent, and two promoters fleeing town in a buggy with locals chasing them. No such version of this story appeared in newspapers that have survived. Two similar versions of this race appear in the *Fort Scott (KS) Daily Tribune*, December 31, 1901, and the *Fort Scott (KS) Daily Monitor*, December 4, 1901; it was thought this was Gillett's first race as a Buckfoot colt. Jim Hoy, *Flint Hill Cowboys: Tales from the Tallgrass Prairie* (Lawrence: University Press of Kansas, 2006).

23. *Yates Center (KS) News*, reprinted in the *Buffalo (KS) Advocate*, October 26, 1894. S. Morgan Friedman, "The Inflation Calculator," www.westegg.com /inflation; hereafter cited as Friedman, "Inflation Calculator." All conversions rounded to the nearest dollar.

24. *Toronto (KS) Republican*, reprinted in the *Eureka (KS) Herald*, November 2, 1894, 4.

25. *Eureka (KS) Democratic Messenger*, October 4, 1895.

26. *Weir City Sun*, reprinted in the *Galena (KS) Evening Times*, July 8, 1897.

27. *Eureka (KS) Democratic Messenger*, July 15, 1897.

28. Not all confidence men went by monikers. For those who did, "it fits the personality of the bearer well and is often the only permanent name a grafter has; once it is applied and accepted, it becomes one of his few permanent possessions. It is tagged to him for life." Maurer, *The Big Con*, 283–84.

29. For "Sodom and Gomorrah" quote, see note 17, US Department of the Interior, National Park Service, National Register of Historic Places

Registration Form, 217 West Main Street Building, Sedalia, Pettis County Missouri, accessed December 6, 2021, https://mostateparks.com/sites /mostateparks/files/Building%20at%20217%20W.%20Main%20St..pdf; *Sedalia Democrat*, February 2, 1899; February 10, 1899; Rhonda Chalfant, *The Midland's Most Notorious: Prostitution in Sedalia, Missouri, 1867– 1900* (PhD diss., University of Missouri, 2005); Michael Cassity, *Defending a Way of Life: An American Community in the Nineteenth Century* (Albany: State University of New York Press, 1989).

30. *Sedalia Democrat*, February 10, 1899. Coon can is a nickname for Conquian, a card game from which rummy originated.

31. *Sedalia Democrat*, February 2; February 3, 1899. Witnesses stated Strand did not threaten Hindman.

32. *Sedalia Democrat*, February 2, 1899; *Sedalia Democrat*, May 1, 1900.

33. *Sedalia Democrat*, February 2, February 3, and February 5, 1899.

34. *Sedalia Evening Sentinel*, February 2, 1899; *Sedalia Democrat*, February 5, 1899.

35. *Sedalia Democrat*, February 3, 1899, February 8, 1899; *Sedalia Sunday Democrat*, February 5, 1899.

36. *Honey Grove (TX) Signal*, February 17, 1899, quoted in the February 15, 1929, issue, 5.

37. *Sedalia Democrat*, February 8, 1899.

38. *Sedalia Democrat*, April 4, 1899; October 29, 1899.

39. *Sedalia Democrat*, April 29, 1900; May 2, 1900; May 4, 1900. For Strand's written statement, see *Sedalia Democrat*, February 2, 1899; February 3, 1899.

40. "Obrzycko," in Shmuel Spector and Geoffrey Wigoder, eds., *The Encyclopedia of Jewish Life before and during the Holocaust* (New York: New York University Press, 2001), 3:923; "Isaac Loser," Staatsarchiv Hamburg, *Hamburg Passenger Lists, 1850–1934*, Ancestry.com. Lozier's surname was Loser and he often appeared in newspaper articles as "Leon Loser." See "Leon Lozier," Records of the Bureau of Prisons, 1870–2009, Record Group 129, National Archives, Kansas City. Conwell, *The Professional Thief*, 24–25.

41. For an example, see the *St. Paul (MN) Globe*, April 13, 1885. Friedman, "Inflation Calculator."

42. *Bismarck (ND) Weekly Tribune*, August 26, 1892; September 2, 1892; for a physical description, see Lozier's file in the Records of the Bureau of Prisons, 1870–2009, Record Group 129, National Archives, Kansas City.

43. *Chicago Tribune*, August 11, 1882; *Lawrence (KS) Daily Herald-Tribune*, October 18, 1884.

44. *Waterloo (IA) Courier*, July 8, 1885; *Sioux Falls Argus-Leader*, May 10, May 12, 1893, February 4, 1930; *Sioux City Journal*, June 26, 1885; May 10, 1893.

45. *Sioux Falls Argus-Leader*, May 10, May 12, 1893; February 4, 1930; *Bismarck (ND) Weekly Tribune*, September 2, 1892; *Waterloo (IA) Courier*, July 8, 1885; *Sioux City Journal*, June 26, 1885; May 10, 1893.

46. *Rapid City Daily (SD) Journal*, July 19, 1888.

47. *St. Louis Post-Dispatch*, October 18, 1888.

48. William H. Copple (1885–1937) of Bancroft, Nebraska, was a professional sprinter. *Omaha World-Herald*, February 28, 1937; *Bancroft (NE) Blade*, February 25, 1937.

49. *Janesville (WI) Gazette*, August 12, 1892.

50. *Sioux City Journal*, May 9, May 16, September 26, 1893; *Iowa City Daily Citizen*, May 11, 1893; *Omaha World-Herald*, January 12, 1895.

51. *Council Bluffs Nonpareil*, January 20, 1894. Lozier appears in Council Bluffs city directories as Leon Loser. He was listed as a painter, sign writer, and sign painter. See, for example, *Council Buffs City and Pottawattamie County Directory for 1894–5* (Omaha: J. M. Wolfe Directory Co., 1895); *McAvoy's Council Bluffs City Directory for 1902–3* (Omaha: Omaha Directory Co., 1903); *Council Bluffs City Directory for the Year Commencing August 1st, 1889* (Council Bluffs, IA: Frank-Orff Pub. Co., 1899). A 1937 story claimed that when the mob called for Lozier to be lynched a gambler hollered, "Sure! Let's get him! Bust the jail down! Get him out and turn him loose!" The mob went quiet and someone yelled, "Turn 'im loose? What for?" "Because," said the gambler, "because I've been wantin' to find out for years just how fast that son of a bitch can run!" The crowd roared. *Omaha World-Herald*, February 28, 1937.

52. *Report of the Adjutant-General to the Governor of the State of Iowa, for Biennial Period Ending November 30, A.D., 1895* (Des Moines: F. R. Conaway, 1895), 7–8; *Council Bluffs Nonpareil*, January 20, 1894.

53. *Council Bluffs Nonpareil*, February 4, 1894.

54. *Omaha Daily Bee*, April 18, 1895.

55. *Decatur (IL) Herald-Dispatch*, March 12, 1898.

56. See Eddie K. Morris, Records of the Bureau of Prisons, 1870–2009, Record Group 129, National Archives, Kansas City; "William Wardell Castelane," (Morris's alias at death), Missouri Death Certificate Database, https://s1.sos.mo.gov/records/archives/archivesmvc/deathcertificates/. The *Topeka (KS) Daily Capital*, September 4, 1900, said Morris had been a boxer since 1893. Bob Long, another African American boxer, may have also been a member of the gang.

57. *Evening-Times Republican* (Marshalltown, IA), November 4, 1911. Roger H. Williams disputed Morris was a member of the Buckfoot Gang. See *In Re R. H. Williams*, US District Court of Colorado, Record Group 21, National

Archives, Kansas City. While their fellow white con artists may not have viewed Morris and Long as equals, their participation in the gang was invaluable.

58. *Joplin Globe*, July 24, 1903; *Galena (KS) Post*, January 3, 1896. Local papers referred to him as Bromley and Brumley; I have opted for the spelling that appears on his marriage certificate and headstone. *Missouri, Marriage Records 1805–2002*, Ancestry.com. For an article about Bromley as a Buckfoot sprinter, see *Fort Scott (KS) Daily Monitor*, December 9, 1901. For Bromley as umpire, see *Joplin News-Herald*, July 10, 1903; *Galena (KS) Evening Times*, May 28, 1900; as a boxer, see *Galena (KS) Evening Times*, June 20, 1901.

59. *Kansas City Journal*, September 29, 1896.

60. *Sedalia Democrat*, September 29, 1896; "Webb City Elite," *Joplin News* reprinted in *Galena (KS) Daily Times*, September 30, 1896.

61. *Baxter Springs (KS) News*, July 16, 1898; *Galena (KS) Evening Times*, January 6, 1899.

62. *Galena (KS) Evening Times*, September 5, 1898; *Galena (KS) Evening Times*, August 29, 1898.

63. George C. Swallow, *Geological Report of the Country along the Line of the South-Western Branch of the Pacific Railroad, State of Missouri* (St. Louis: G. Knapp, 1859), 36–37, 92; *McDonald and Newton County Sections of Goodspeed's Newton, Lawrence, Barry and McDonald Counties History* (Pineville, MO: McDonald County Historical Society, 1972), 301–2.

64. *Springfield Missouri Patriot*, July 13, August 10, 1865; Dixie Haase, *Granby Mo. Scrapbook, Volume II* (Granby, MO: Granby Historical Society, 1991), vii.

65. "James R. Ellis," 1880 US Census, Newton County, Missouri, Ancestry.com.

66. *Joplin Globe*, February 1, 1916; *Webb City Register*, February 1, 1916.

67. *Mt. Vernon Lawrence Chieftain*, July 21, 1921; *Lawrence County Missouri History* (Mt. Vernon, MO: Lawrence County Historical Society, 1974), 100; *Lawrence County Historical Society Bulletin* (April 1998): 13–14; *Mt. Vernon Lawrence Chieftain*, September 12, 1889.

68. Maurer, *The Big Con*, 14–15; *Mt. Vernon Lawrence County Record*, February 4, 1937.

69. Williams's birth date is variously given as 1858, 1862, and 1865. "Roger Williams," 1880 US Census, Carroll County, Kentucky; "Ella B. Brandt," Kentucky Marriages, 1785–1979, Familysearch.org; "Arthur Williams," 1900 US Census, Jasper County, Missouri; *In Re R. H. Williams*. Painter seems to have been a common occupation for confidence men; Leon Lozier, Irven Johnson, and Dick Beatte all worked as painters.

70. *In Re R. H. Williams.*

71. *In Re R. H. Williams; Louisville (KY) Courier-Journal,* June 29, 1903.

72. *Kansas City Star,* September 6, 1903.

73. "Elisha Stansbury," "Louisa Jane Stansbury," Find-A-Grave.com; *Parsons (KS) Daily Eclipse,* February 24, 1883; *Parsons (KS) Weekly Sun,* March 8, 1883.

74. *Chicago Inter Ocean,* April 9, 1887; *Cherryvale (KS) Republican,* December 5, 1899; "G. O. Stansbury," 1900 US Census, Montgomery County, Kansas, Ancestry.com. *Kansas City Star,* February 25, 1929; "Garrette Orville Stansbury," Missouri Death Certificate Database, https://s1.sos.mo.gov /records/archives/archivesmvc/deathcertificates/.

75. Wasser was seventeen when sentenced in Jasper County on September 14, 1893. He was released September 10, 1895. "Harry Wasser," 1880 US Census, Girard, Crawford County, Kansas, 1900 US Census, Webb City, Jasper County, Missouri, Ancestry.com. *Pittsburg (KS) Daily Headlight,* February 6, 1893; *Independence (KS) Daily Reporter,* February 7, 1893. See Record Group 225: Department of Corrections: Missouri Training School for Boys (Boonville), Alphabetical Register (1888–1922, Volume 20) 302, number 307 and Numerical Register (Volume 1), number 307.

76. "Louisville Medical Students," database, Kornhauser Health Sciences Library, University of Louisville, https://webservices.library.louisville .edu/test/doctors/index.php?page=84; *Kentucky School of Medicine and Hospital in the City of Louisville, Register of Students, 1894; Circular of Information, 1895, 39th Annual Session* (n.p., 1895), 17; "Early County Doctors Page," Van Zandt County Genealogical Society, accessed May 5, 2011, www.rootsweb.ancestry.com/txvzcgs/vzgsdoc7.htm. Goddard does not appear in the *Gazetteer of Deceased Texas Physicians. Gazetteer of Deceased Texas Physicians,* accessed November 19, 2018, https://digitalcommons. library.tmc.edu/gazetteer/; "Robert Goddard," 1900 US Census, Dallas, Texas, Ancestry.com.

77. *Fort Scott (KS) Daily Tribune,* April 25, 1902, 4. $100,000 in 1900 would be worth $3,367,552.55 in 2022. Friedman, "Inflation Calculator."

78. *Joplin News-Herald,* November 14, 1911, 7; *Joplin Globe,* November 12, 1911, 7; *Thirteenth Annual Report of the State Mine Inspectors of the State of Missouri* (Jefferson City, MO: Tribune Printing Co., 1900), 286. See *State of Missouri v. Charles Parker,* Jasper County Circuit Court (December 1880); *State of Missouri v. Charles Parker,* Jasper County Circuit Court (March 1881). Parker likely named his saloon the 16 to 1 after the 1896 Democratic platform called for "free and unlimited coinage of both silver and gold at the present legal ratio of 16 to 1." 1896 Democratic Party Platform, accessed April 22, 2019, https://web.archive.org/web/20220901051757/http: //projects.vassar.edu/1896/chicagoplatform.html. The saloon was located

at 117 North Allen. *Hoye's Joplin, Carthage, Carterville, Webb City, and Jasper County Directory 1905–1906* (n.p., 1906), 197.

79. *Carthage Evening Press*, April 24, 1902, 3.

80. *In Re R. H. Williams.* Other members of the gang named in this case were James Raff, Tom Perkins, James Ashmore, Irven E. Johnson, William H. Gibson, Al Ballard, Frank H. Rice, Charles Weaver, Jack Jones, Arthur Dolan, Knight, and [Alexander] McCarren. Only surnames were provided for the last two individuals listed. "Jesse Ansel," 1885 Kansas State Census, McPherson, Union County, Kansas; "Jesse Ansel," 1900 US Census, Tonkawa, Kay County, Oklahoma. John "Jack" Kivlin ran against Leon Lozier in Davenport, Iowa. See *Davenport (IA) Weekly Leader*, May 26, 1896; *Davenport (IA) Quad-City Times*, July 4, 1938, 13. Ed Moore ran against Leon Lozier in Maroa, Illinois. See *Decatur (IL) Morning Herald-Dispatch*, March 9, 1898. Dick Beatte was in the fixed foot race game as early as 1895; see *Larned (KS) Eagle-Optic*, October 11, 1895, 3. There were likely other boxers who were also in on the game, but their names do not appear in court records, leaving their possible involvement open to conjecture. Bob Long and "Cherokee" Tom Cox are among those who were likely in on the scam. In 1902 Walter Nolan assaulted one-armed railroad switchman Robert Warke. Nolan was acquitted of Warke's murder. *Chicago Inter Ocean*, June 1, 1902, 2; July 26, 1903, 5; August 16, 1903, 16; *Daily News* (Chicago), May 30, 1902, 8; "Robert Warke," Cook County Coroner's Inquest Records, volume 56, page 34, May 31, 1902; "Robert Warke," Chicago Police Department Homicide Record Index, volume 1, page 173B, May 29, 1902; both located at Illinois Regional Archives Depository System, Northeastern Illinois University.

CHAPTER 3

1. *Fort Scott (KS) Daily Monitor*, October 16, 1901, 1; *Fort Scott (KS) Daily Tribune*, October 16, 1901, 1.

2. George R. Clay (1870–1913) served two terms as prosecuting attorney of McDonald County, Missouri. He chaired the Newton County Democratic Central Committee and practiced in Neosho for several years before moving to Joplin. *Neosho Daily Democrat*, May 23, 1913, 1; "George R. Clay," Missouri Death Certificate Database, https://s1.sos.mo.gov/records /Archives/ArchivesMvc/DeathCertificates/. George E. Booth (1861–1928) testified in *W. H. Waters (Trustee) v. Davis*, case no. 1495, Transcripts of US District Court Records, 1891–1952, US Circuit Court of Appeals for the Sixth Circuit, Record Group 276, National Archives, Chicago. John Black claimed Boatright never talked favorably about Booth. *In re Robert Boatright and Ed E. Ellis.* For Boatright boasting about owning local officials,

see testimony of Henry Wright and Robert Duncan in *R. E. Hobbs v. Exchange Bank of Webb City and J. P. Stewart*, Missouri Supreme Court, Missouri State Archives. "Men of no reputation" is from a criminal complaint written by Robert Mooneyham that appears in *State of Missouri v. Robert Boatright, Ed E. Ellis, and Bert Bromley*, case no. 11883, Missouri Supreme Court, Missouri State Archives.

3. In June 1889 and June 1890 Boatright was fined for keeping a gaming house. In June 1891 Boatright was convicted of keeping a common gaming house in Carterville. Several witnesses, including the city marshal, testified Boatright ran a gambling joint on Main Street. *State of Missouri v. Robert Boatright*, case no. 6087, Kansas City Court of Appeals (October 1892); *State of Missouri v. Robert Boatright*, Lawrence County Circuit Court (June 1893), Missouri State Archives; *State of Missouri v. Robert Boatright*, case no. 5827, St. Louis Court of Appeals (March 1895). Boatright associates Charley Parker and Sam Jones served as bondsmen.

4. Ed Ellis was charged with keeping a gambling house on December 12, 1894. Bert Bromley was charged twice for the same offense on June 19, 1897. See Tim Fisher, *Vices of Joplin: A Finding Aid and Statistical Overview of Vice Crimes from 1877–1897*, Missouri State Archives, Local Records Preservation Program, Jasper County, Missouri, Records Center, December 2007, 19–21. See also *State of Missouri v. Bert Bromley*, case no. 1248, Jasper County Circuit Court (1897); *State of Missouri v. Ed Ellis*, case no. 1130, Jasper County Circuit Court (December 1895). City officials in Joplin and Webb City informed me municipal court records were discarded, making it difficult to better understand crime and vice at the local level in turn-of-the-century Jasper County and the urban Ozarks. Joplin Municipal Court Administrator Lamonte Ratcliff, email to author, October 18, 2013.

5. During a deposition Garrette Stansbury told attorney John Halliburton he was an original organizer of the gang. Halliburton then asked, "You are the one that initiated Bob Boatright out at Carl Junction or there about?" Stansbury responded, "Initiated him, how do you mean?" Halliburton clarified, "O, took him through the ropes." Stansbury shrugged, "Well they had a foot race out there." Halliburton asked, "Bob was the one you took through wasn't he, it was his money?" Stansbury replied, "Oh no, he was on the inside there. He didn't lose any money on the foot race." *Waters v. Clay*, case no. 59, US District Court, Southwestern (Joplin) Division of the Western District of Missouri, Bankruptcy Act of 1898 Case Files, Record Group 21, National Archives, Kansas City.

6. For 1897, see opening statement of attorney John W. Halliburton in *State of Missouri v. Robert Boatright, Ed E. Ellis, and Bert Bromley*, case no. 11883, Missouri Supreme Court, Missouri State Archives. For 1891 account, see

Atlantic Cass County (IA) Democrat, June 4, 1903, 11. The Buckfoot Gang was not the first; in 1895 a gang of foot race swindlers came through the area. See *Carthage Evening Press*, June 13, 1895, 4; June 14, 1895, 4; June 17, 1895, 4; June 20, 1895, 4, 9, 10; June 21, 1895, 2; June 27, 1895, 1. Leon Lozier ran against fellow member Jack Kivlin; see *Davenport (IA) Daily Leader*, May 22, 1896, 7.

7. *St. Louis Post-Dispatch*, June 2, 1895, 24. Attorney Thomas J. Roney believed the gang began in 1895 or 1896. See *R. E. Hobbs v. Exchange Bank and J. P. Stewart*. An 1899 article announcing an upcoming fight mentioned "Manager Boatright of the Webb City athletic club." *Empire City (KS) Journal*, October 5, 1899, 3.

8. See testimony, *R. E. Hobbs v. Exchange Bank and J. P. Stewart*.

9. Draper, *True Stories of Peculiar People*, 26.

10. Christina Miller, Missouri State Archives, email to author, August 29, 2019. Ms. Miller checked incorporation filings between 1885 and 1909. Victim Henry Wright stated he saw Stewart's name on the club's letterhead. Joseph Stewart admitted his name—as well as that of Alfred A. Hulett (a business partner of Harry Wasser's grandfather)—appeared on the letterhead, but Stewart said Boatright denied using the stationery. Stewart noted a bicycle track was built south of town between Webb City and Center Creek. See testimony, *R. E. Hobbs v. Exchange Bank and J. P. Stewart*.

11. Maurer, *The Big Con*, 285; Johnson, "The Origins and Structure of Intercity Criminal Activity," 599.

12. Maurer, *The Big Con*, 161. This is also explored in Conwell's *The Professional Thief*; see 27–32.

13. Maurer, *The Big Con*, 161, 289. Conwell said the existence of most con mobs was short, but successful ones remained active for years. See *The Professional Thief*, 27.

14. Maurer, *The Big Con*, 19, 109, 299, 304, 138. Traveling salesman Daniel Maloney—a physically imposing man—figures prominently in the Hobbs case. Ed Ellis's and Robert Boatright's fathers acted as eager bettors. David R. Johnson mentions using locals as shills; see "The Origins and Structure of Intercity Criminal Activity," 600. Ed Ellis said shills were given anywhere from five to twenty dollars for their services, sprinters received one-third of the money, and Boatright the remainder. See *Currey v. Joplin Savings Bank*.

15. Maurer, *The Big Con*, 296.

16. Maurer, *The Big Con*, 143, 155.

17. Maurer, *The Big Con*, 19, 298.

18. Maurer, *The Big Con*, 135.

19. See deposition of Garrette Stansbury in *Waters v. Clay*, case no. 59, US District Court, Southwestern (Joplin) Division of the Western District of

Missouri, Bankruptcy Act of 1898 Case Files, Record Group 21, National Archives, Kansas City. Stansbury said he was number one and that the numbers went as high as 114. *Waters v. Clay.*

20. Maurer, *The Big Con*, 13–14.

21. Maurer, *The Big Con*, 22, 131.

22. *Carthage Evening Press*, April 24, 1902, 3; *Fort Scott (KS) Daily Tribune*, April 25, 1902, 4.

23. Maurer, *The Big Con*, 2; Conwell, *The Professional Thief*, 69n27.

24. *Webb City Sentinel*, reprinted in the *Pittsburg (KS) Daily Headlight*, August 18, 1898, 3. For Purcell, see testimony in *R. E. Hobbs v. Exchange Bank and J. P. Stewart*, Statement and Brief of Respondents. His name appears as H. B. and H. P. Purcell; he worked as a buyer for C. M. Keys Livestock Commission Company. Stewart telegraphed Purcell's bank on August 15, 1898, demanding payment of drafts. The Jasper County Records Center staff could not find this case; attorney Thomas Hackney testified it was dismissed after a witness failed to testify and he filed a motion to strike his petition. *Kansas City Journal*, August 27, 1898, 5. For Gillett, Ansel, and Keagy, see *Alma (KS) Enterprise*, May 12, 1899, 10. Leon Lozier was in trouble in Decatur, Illinois. *Decatur (IL) Herald*, March 18, 1899, 2. Friedman, "Inflation Calculator."

25. See boxing matches in *Pittsburg (KS) Daily Headlight*, July 11, 1899, 3; July 28, 1899, 4; *Galena (KS) Daily Republican*, October 20, 1899, 1. Arly Allen notes, "Although prizefighting was a felony, the word 'prize-fight' was not defined in Missouri law. At the time the law passed, prizefights were assumed to be bare-knuckle bouts that took place outdoors on the turf. The London Prize Ring Rules of 1838 as revised in 1853 governed these rules . . . By the 1890s, however, bare-knuckled outdoor prizefights were giving way to indoor fights with gloves called 'sparring or boxing exhibitions' under the influence of the new Marquess of Queensbury Rules (1865). Since Missouri's prizefight law outlawed 'public' sparring or boxing that took place indoors, membership-based athletic clubs were considered to provide 'private,' and thus legal, bouts." Arly Allen, "Seeking 'The Great White Hope': Heavyweight Boxing in Springfield, 1910–1912, Part I," *Missouri Historical Review* 100, no. 3 (April 2006): 172n41.

26. *Topeka State Journal*, April 6, 1900.

27. *Exchange Bank of Webb City v. McIlroy Banking Company*, case no. 188, US Circuit Court, Western District of Arkansas, Fort Smith Division (1900), Record Group 21, NARA—Fort Worth. The McIlroy Banking Company's answer to the Exchange Bank's amended complaint stated Boatright conspired with others "to swindle C. D. McIlroy" on a race. After getting McIlroy drunk they convinced him to bet a $439 bank draft and write a $2,000 check. McIlroy's bank refused payment, so the Exchange Bank

sued. The case was dismissed at the Exchange Bank's expense in 1901. *R. E. Hobbs v. Exchange Bank of Webb City and J. P. Stewart*; see 277. For more on Charles D. McIlroy, see Fay Hempstead, *Historical Review of Arkansas: Its Commerce, Industry and Modern Affairs* (Chicago: Lewis Pub. Co., 1911), 3:1528–29.

28. *Joplin Daily Globe*, September 6, 1900; reprinted from the *Webb City Register*.

29. *R. E. Hobbs v. Exchange Bank of Webb City and J. P. Stewart*. Griffith and Lane Owen were from Franklin County, Kansas. Buckfoot boxer Eddie Morris fought a bout in Webb City that fall. *Joplin Daily Globe*, October 18, 1900. Harry Wasser was charged with gambling, *Joplin Daily Globe*, December 5, 1900.

30. *Joplin Daily Globe*, December 14, 1900.

31. *Joplin Daily Globe*, December 20, 1900.

32. *Joplin News-Herald*, January 6, 1901; *Joplin Daily Globe*, January 24, 1901. Morris had an upcoming bout with Young Walcott; the Galena Athletic Association used referee Ed F. Burke. *Joplin Daily Globe*, February 5, 1901; *Galena (KS) Evening Times*, February 2, 1901.

33. *Joplin News-Herald*, January 11, 1901; *Springfield Leader-Democrat*, October 9, 1901, 5. The victim's surname is sometimes spelled "Burger."

34. *Galena (KS) Evening Times*, February 16, 1901; reprinted from the *Carthage Review*; Carthage *Jasper County Democrat*, February 21, 1901, 9. *History of Adair, Sullivan, Putnam and Schuyler Counties, Missouri* (Chicago: Goodspeed Pub. Co., 1888), 882. Reger likely thought Stewart was president because that is how he was listed on club letterhead.

35. Prosecutor Robert Mooneyham subsequently filed a criminal conspiracy charge against Boatright and the others, but nothing came of it. The gang may have settled with Reger. *Joplin Globe*, April 11, 1901.

36. *Henry Cohn v. Exchange Bank of Webb City, J. C. Stewart, J. P. Stewart*, US Circuit Court, Southwestern (Joplin) Division of the Western District of Missouri, Record Group 21, National Archives, Kansas City. This case describes the bank's bad actions. Cohn's son Phillip testified Frank Rice offered him $500 if he convinced his father to drop the suit. *In re Robert Boatright and Ed E. Ellis*, Joplin Bankruptcy Case Files, US District Court for the Southwestern (Joplin) Division of the Western District of Missouri, Record Group 21, National Archives, Kansas City.

37. Stephen Ellis Moss (1853–1942) began clerking at a young age, but his ambition led him to become a lightning rod salesman. He was so successful he started his own company. "Stephen Ellis Moss," *Encyclopedia of American Biography*, ed. Winfield Scott Downs (New York: American Historical Company, 1943), 16: 170–71.

38. *Stephen E. Moss v. Exchange Bank, J. C. Stewart, and J. P. Stewart*, US Circuit Court, Southwestern (Joplin) Division of the Western District of

Missouri, Record Group 21, National Archives, Kansas City; hereafter cited as *Moss v. Exchange Bank*.

39. *Moss v. Exchange Bank*.

40. *Moss v. Exchange Bank*. William Crider was identified as "William Segrider." C. F. Landers was likely sprinter Frank Landers. See *Morning Democrat* (Davenport, IA), November 17, 1893.

41. *Moss v. Exchange Bank*.

42. *Moss v. Exchange Bank*.

43. *Moss v. Exchange Bank*.

44. *Moss v. Exchange Bank*. For cottage, see *Joplin News-Herald*, December 8, 1901, 1.

45. *Moss v. Exchange Bank*. The gang skinned farmer Bascom O'Hair for $6,247 on June 13, 1901. He, too, said he was "pretty sick" after drinking with the gang. *O'Hair v. Exchange Bank of Webb City*, US Circuit Court, Southwestern (Joplin) Division of the Western District of Missouri, Record Group 21, National Archives, Kansas City. Friedman, "Inflation Calculator."

46. *Galena (KS) Republican*, June 27, 1901, 1. New Yorker Edmund F. Burke (1855–1914) was a prominent Ozark sport. A former Arkansas middle-weight champion, he moved to Springfield, Missouri, where he bred English Setters, raised racehorses, and operated the Antique Saloon. He and business partner Matthew Kerr owned Burke, Kerr, & Laser, Novelties, based in St. Louis; the company sold slot machines. Burke operated slot machines in Springfield and other area cities. In 1914 Burke committed suicide in San Francisco. "Edmond F. Burke," 1900 US Census, Springfield, Greene County, Missouri; *Springfield Democrat*, August 16, 1893, 5; *Memphis (TN) Daily Appeal*, June 23, 1882, 4; *Little Rock Arkansas Democrat*, July 12, 1901, 4; *St. Louis Post-Dispatch*, October 4, 1900, 1; *Fort Scott (KS) Daily Tribune*, April 6, 1900, 4; *Fort Scott (KS) Tribune*, February 28, 1901, 3; *Springfield Republican*, April 15, 1914, 3.

47. *Joplin Daily Globe*, July 9, 1901.

48. *Joplin Daily News-Herald*, July 8, 1901; Carthage *Jasper County Democrat*, July 4, 11, 1901. For Dabbs's statement to the grand jury, see *Joplin Daily Globe*, July 9, 1901. Although not all Jasper County grand jury reports survived, a number still existed when the author first began research on this book. Since that time there have been staff changes and the records cannot be located. Jon Sexton at the Jasper County Records Center stated that "we do not have grand jury reports on their own that I can find." Email to author, December 18, 2018. Boatright was truthful; James and Joseph Stewart later testified they gave him $30,000 in $1,000 bills in June 1901. The identity of the party who sued Boatright is unknown. *R. E. Hobbs v. Exchange Bank of Webb City and J. P. Stewart*.

49. *Joplin Daily News-Herald*, July 9, 1901. Recounting the same event, the *Jasper County Democrat* sarcastically called Boatright the "king of the foot racers of Olympia Park." Olympia Park was a short-lived summer garden and theater in Webb City. When a Native American mark wised up to the scam, he pulled a gun and chased the sprinter who was supposed to throw the race. The gang let him win. Carthage *Jasper County Democrat*, July 18, 1901, 5; *Galena (KS) News*, June 19, 1901; *Galena (KS) Weekly Lever*, May 29, 1900. Adjusted for inflation, $33,000 in 1901 would be worth $1,190,194 in 2022. Friedman, "Inflation Calculator."

50. *Joplin Globe*, July 14, 1901, 8.

51. Phelps eventually angered his employers for exceeding his authority and left his role as a lobbyist in 1910. He was elected to the state legislature that year and again in 1914. From his seat on the floor of the legislature Phelps waged war on the railroads, loudly heckling their representatives at hearings. *St. Louis Post-Dispatch*, July 26, 1916, 4. For descriptions of Phelps, see *The Independent*, September 14, 1901, 8 and Laas, *Bridging Two Eras*, 28.

52. *Joplin Globe*, October 18, 1924, 1; *Sarcoxie Record*, October 23, 1924, 4; William R. Draper and Mabel R. Draper, *Old Grubstake Days in Joplin: The Story of the Pioneers Who Discovered the Largest and Richest Lead and Zinc Mining Field in the World* (Girard, KS: Haldeman-Julius Publications, 1946); Malcolm G. McGregor, *The Biographical Record of Jasper County, Missouri* (Chicago: Lewis Pub. Co., 1901) 479–80; *St. Louis Post-Dispatch*, October 18, 1924, 11.

53. The House of Lords was established in 1892. Jones, *Tales about Joplin*, 121–25; *Joplin Globe*, January 8, 1922, 1.

54. *Joplin Globe*, January 8, 1922, 1. For Wenrich, see Blesh and Janis, *They All Played Ragtime*, 124. For Benton, see Thomas Hart Benton, *An Artist in America* 3rd ed. (Columbia: University of Missouri Press, 1968), 18–22.

55. Jones, *Tales about Joplin*, 121–25; *Joplin Globe*, January 8, 1922, 1. A drawing of the city block that was home to the House of Lords supports this account. See *Carthage Evening Press*, October 25, 1902. Political cartoons lampooning the third-floor brothel appeared in the *Carthage Evening Press*, November 3, 1902, *Joplin Sunday News-Herald*, October 26, 1902. For more on the walkway, see *Joplin Morning Tribune*, December 15, 1911, 1, 3; *Joplin Globe Publishing Company v. Gilbert Barbee*, case no. 9956, Jasper County Circuit Court (1912), Jasper County Records Center.

56. Carthage *Jasper County Democrat*, November 3, 1903, 1; *San Francisco Chronicle*, November 19, 1903, 6; *Kansas City Journal* as quoted in the *Plattsburg (MO) Leader*, November 6, 1903, 4. See also *Joplin Globe*, January 8, 1922, 1.

57. For the Taylor–Moore shooting, see *Joplin News-Herald*, June 28, 1901, 1; *Galena (KS) Evening Times*, June 28, 1901, 1. Another fatality occurred when Charles "Cimarron" Moore killed gambler A. L. Thurell (sometimes spelled "Thurall"), alias Frank Fay, in the "House of Lord's gambling house." See *Galena (KS) Evening Times*, October 31, November 2, 1901. In another incident, a bartender shot and killed a black porter. *Joplin Globe*, January 8, 1922, 1.

58. Jones, *Tales about Joplin*, 121–25. A drawing of the city block that was home to the House of Lords confirms this account. See *Carthage Evening Press*, October 25, 1902. Alfred H. Rogers, who wrested control of the *Globe* from Barbee, sued the political boss in 1911 over the walkway, or, as Barbee called them, "rooms" that connected the *Globe* to the House of Lords. See *Joplin Morning Tribune*, December 15, 1911, 1, 3; *Joplin Globe Publishing Company v. Gilbert Barbee*, case no. 9956, Jasper County Circuit Court (1912), Jasper County Records Center.

59. Laas, *Bridging Two Eras*, 79.

60. Benton, *An Artist in America*, 22.

61. For more on Dugan and Howard as well as the rivalry between Barbee and Phelps, see *Springfield Leader and Press*, July 8, 1929, 14. For Ben H. Reese, see *St. Louis Post-Dispatch*, August 2, 1938, 2. For Bart Howard, see *St. Louis Post-Dispatch*, February 12, 1941, 1–4. For Barbee's personality, see *Sarcoxie Record*, October 23, 1924, 4.

62. *Joplin Globe*, July 23, 1901, 1, 3; *Springfield Leader and Press*, October 21, 1924, 4.

63. *Carthage Jasper County Democrat*, July 11, 1901, 4.

64. *Joplin Globe*, July 21, 1901, 6. Wilkins Taylor was convicted of Moore's murder. See *Joplin News-Herald*, April 16, 1902, 1.

65. *Joplin News-Herald*, July 28, 1901, 1; August 1, 1901, 1.

66. Carthage *Jasper County Democrat*, August 7, 1901, 8.

67. *Joplin News-Herald*, August 1, 1901, 8.

68. *Joplin News-Herald*, July 22, 1901, 4.

69. The case was *State of Missouri v. Robert Long, Eddie Morris, William Gibson, Cherokee Tom, John Briggs, G. O. Stansberry, Tommie Dixon, John McLarn, J. Moore, Ed Burke, Bob Boatright, and Lehman.* Carthage *Jasper County Democrat*, July 11, 1901, 5. The prizefight was held on July 19, 1901, in Webb City. *Pittsburg (KS) Daily Headlight*, June 20, 1901, 5. As boxing historian Arly Allen explained, "Prize-fighting was outlawed in Missouri ... but the gentleman's agreement which permitted 'sparring and boxing exhibitions' in chartered athletic clubs for the benefit of their members was honored by the police." *Jess Willard: Heavyweight Champion of the World* (Jefferson, NC: McFarland, 2017), 55.

70. *Joplin Globe*, July 23, 1901, 1, 3. Later that year Barbee refuted his connection to gambling in the House of Lords when he published the lease he

signed with businessman George H. Redell, who rented the entire building. Barbee insisted he swore out warrants against gamblers in the building and provided a sworn statement by Joplin deputy constable Ed Portley that he delivered a cease-and-desist notice from Barbee to Daniel Saighman and Redell. Saighman closed from June to September 1901. Barbee prosecuted Al Bean for running a card game before giving Redell final notice in October 1901. See *Joplin Globe*, November 1, 1901, 8. *Joplin Globe*, March 5, 1906; *Joplin News-Herald*, March 5, 1906, 1.

71. *Joplin Globe*, July 23, 1901, 1, 3. Burke, a referee for many of the Webb City Athletic Club's boxing matches, was known as the "Springfield slot machine man." A pointed rebuttal of Barbee's claims was delivered by "Country Democrat" in the Carthage *Jasper County Democrat*, August 7, 1901, 4.

CHAPTER 4

1. *Galena (KS) Evening Times*, July 7, 1901; *Joplin News-Herald*, July 21, 1901, 5; July 22, 1901, 8; July 23, 1901, 2. A Kansas City newsmagazine said, "The chief trouble with Siler is that his eyesight is so bad that he can hardly see. It is hard to believe that he is intentionally 'crooked,' or that he can be 'got to' with money. A good referee must be a young, active man with keen eyes, and Siler does not fill the bill at all." *The Independent*, May 24, 1902, 8.

2. *Carthage Evening Press*, July 24, 1901.

3. *Joplin Globe*, July 24, 1901, 2; *Galena (KS) Daily Republican*, October 10, 1899, 1; October 13, 1899, 4.

4. *Joplin News-Herald*, August 6, 1901, 2; August 7, 1901, 8; *Joplin News-Herald*, August 7, 1901, 2; *Webb City Register*, August 7, 1901, 1. One paper remarked, "The management seem to have run the whole affair for their own benefit, regardless of public or patrons." *Carthage Evening Press*, reprinted in the *Webb City Sentinel*, August 9, 1901, 2. Boxer James Bronson wrote an account of the fight for the *News-Herald*. A decade later Bronson managed the Business Men's Athletic Club. One boxing historian believed he "generally ran a clean and honest operation." While overseeing the American Expeditionary Forces' boxing program he trained Gene Tunney. See Allen, *Jess Willard: Heavyweight Champion of the World*, 55. One sports columnist said "this polished, urbane and articulate little guy gave the grubby racket a lot more class than it ever deserved." *New York Times*, February 10, 1966, 45. Whether he was associated with the Buckfoot Gang remains unknown. For more, see *Joplin News-Herald*, September 9, 1901, 2; September 11, 1901, 5; *Joplin Globe*, May 1, 1932, 20.

5. *Merwin B. Bangs v. Exchange Bank of Webb City, J. C. Stewart, J. P. Stewart*, US Circuit Court, Southwestern (Joplin) Division of the Western District of Missouri, Record Group 21, National Archives, Kansas City. New Yorker Merwin Bolton Bangs (1877–1909) was a graduate of St. Paul's School and

Yale University. A Spanish American War veteran, he worked on Wall Street before moving to Kiowa County, Kansas. He died of diabetes at age thirty-two. "1899," *Obituary Record of Graduates of Yale University Deceased from June, 1900, to June, 1910* (New Haven, CT: Tuttle, Morehouse, & Taylor, Co., 1910), 1280; *Hutchinson (KS) News*, June 16, 1903, 5; December 27, 1909, 1.

6. *Joplin News-Herald*, August 27, 1901, 5.

7. *Joplin News-Herald*, August 28, 1901, 3.

8. Carthage *Jasper County Democrat*, August 29, 1901, 6.

9. *Webb City Register*, August 28, 1901, 1. Editor Kuhn's first name is unknown; he is listed simply as "M. Kuhn" in the *American Newspaper Directory* (New York: Geo. P. Rowell & Co., 1901). The *Rocket* was a Republican paper.

10. *Galena (KS) Evening Times*, August 30, 1901, 4.

11. *Joplin Globe*, September 5, 1901, 7.

12. *Joplin Globe*, September 5, 1901, 7. James "Jack" Cherry worked with an Ohio foot-racing gang under the aliases James Martin and Sommers. He once threw a race by pretending to vomit and then escaped with the purse. The victim fired four shots at Cherry but missed. His "lavish expenditure of money, his diamonds and general appearance" made him a conspicuous character on the streets of Marion, Ohio. See *Chillicothe (OH) Daily Gazette*, September 22, 1894, 1, *Marion (OH) Star*, April 29, 1896, 8.

13. *Joplin Globe*, September 5, 1901, 7; *Omaha Daily Bee*, November 30, 1901, 3; Carthage *Jasper County Democrat*, September 12, 1901, 5. The *Bee*'s sensational account said Sheriff Phillips held Lozier at gunpoint as Cherry escaped. Jasper County sheriff Rich was a Democrat. *Official Manual of the State of Missouri, 1901–1902* (Jefferson City: Tribune Printing Co., 1901), 202.

14. *Joplin Globe*, September 5, 1901, 7.

15. *Joplin Globe*, September 5, 1901, 7; *Omaha Daily Bee*, November 30, 1901, 3; *Joplin News-Herald*, September 10, 1901, 2; Carthage *Jasper County Democrat*, September 12, 1901, 5. Phillips thought he was doped. Sonnenschein said when they got a requisition for the gang's arrest an attorney arrived with Phillips's $5,000. *Fort Scott (KS) Daily Monitor*, October 9, 1901, 1.

16. Carthage *Jasper County Democrat*, September 12, 1901, 9. It is unknown how accurate the *Democrat*'s allegation is that Buckfoot employed seventy sprinters. Boatright needed ropers out on the road to find and steer victims to him, so it is not out of the question he would use several. The Carthage *Jasper County Democrat*, November 19, 1901, said there were thirty-three. Harry Wasser estimated there were forty to fifty members. *Johnson v. State of Arkansas*, Arkansas Supreme Court Briefs and Records, University of Arkansas at Little Rock/Pulaski County Law Library (hereafter cited as

Johnson v. State of Arkansas). Garrette Stansbury thought there were 114 members in *Waters v. Clay*.

17. For Henry Wright and Robert Duncan testimony, see *R. E. Hobbs v. Exchange Bank of Webb City and J. P. Stewart*. Wright's loss was listed as $5,100 in a list of creditors in *In Re R. H. Williams*.

18. For Henry Wright and Robert Duncan testimony, see *R. E. Hobbs v. Exchange Bank of Webb City and J. P. Stewart*; see also *H. S. Wright v. Joseph C. Stewart, James P. Stewart, and Exchange Bank of Webb City*, US Circuit Court, Southwestern (Joplin) Division of the Western District of Missouri, Record Group 21, National Archives, Kansas City; *State of Missouri v. Robert Boatright, Ed E. Ellis, and Bert Bromley*, Missouri Supreme Court, Missouri State Archives.

19. *R. E. Hobbs v. Exchange Bank of Webb City and J. P. Stewart*.

20. Wright later received a default judgment against Boatright and the gang because they failed to appear; his attorneys took a nonsuit against the Stewarts and Exchange Bank. See *Joplin Globe*, January 27, 1903, 3; *Carthage Evening Press*, January 28, 1903, 2; *Joplin News-Herald*, January 28, 1903, 8. *H. S. Wright v. Joseph C. Stewart, James P. Stewart, and the Exchange Bank of Webb City*, case no. 16, US Circuit Court, Southwestern (Joplin) Division of the Western District of Missouri, Record Group 21, National Archives, Kansas City.

21. Carthage *Jasper County Democrat*, September 9, 1901, 4; September 5, 1901, 6.

22. *Joplin News-Herald*, September 13, 1901, 5; Carthage *Jasper County Democrat*, September 26, 1901, 6.

23. *Fort Scott (KS) Daily Monitor*, September 27, 1901, 1; *Fort Scott (KS) Daily Tribune*, September 27, 1901, 1. Documentation for *State of Kansas v. L. B. "Bud" Gillett, Robert Boatright, Ed Ellis, Garrett "G. O." Stansbury, and J. P. Stewart* no longer exists. Bourbon County court clerk Rhonda Cole stated her predecessor destroyed all criminal case files older than fifty years. Rhonda Cole, email message to author, September 5, 2019. Some federal court records survive, but do not reveal much. See *US v. Robert Boatright, J. P. Stewart, E. E. Ellis, L. B Gillett, and G. O. Stansbury*, US District Court, Third Division, Fort Scott, Kansas, Record Group 21, National Archives, Kansas City; the government declined to pursue this case. The witness list contains names of victims who never sued. Davis's testimony can be found in *Moss v. Exchange Bank*; *State of Missouri v. Robert Boatright, Ed E. Ellis, and Bert Bromley*, Missouri Supreme Court, Missouri State Archives.

24. Homer E. Socolofsky, *Kansas Governors* (Lawrence: University Press of Kansas, 1990), 156–57.

25. *Bronson (KS) Record*, January 10, 1901, 4; *Fort Scott (KS) Daily Tribune*, September 27, 1901, 1. For Davis's assertion he was doped, see *Fort Scott (KS) Daily Tribune*, September 30, 1901, 1. Davis was not the only victim to

make this claim. Sheriff Henry Phillips, Stephen Moss, Charles McIlroy, and Dr. James H. Guinn remarked they felt ill, even drugged, after drinking with the gang. For Guinn, see *Wichita Daily Eagle*, June 14, 1903, 1; Little Rock *Arkansas Gazette*, June 16, 1903, 1, June 18, 1903, 2. James Henry Guinn (1856–1941) was an 1886 graduate of the Kansas City Medical College and performed postgraduate work at New York's Bellevue Hospital. "James H. Guinn, M.D.," *Kansas: A Cyclopedia of State History*, vol. 3: part 2 (Chicago: Standard Pub. Co., 1912), 1355–56. Guinn was in Hot Springs sometime around November 15–19, 1902. See testimony in *Lockman v. Cobb*, Arkansas Supreme Court Briefs and Records, University of Arkansas at Little Rock/Pulaski County Law Library.

26. *Fort Scott (KS) Daily Tribune*, September 27, 1901, 1; *Fort Scott (KS) Daily Monitor*, September 27, 1901, 4. Both newspapers reported similar stories, but the *Monitor* provides a more detailed account of Davis's financial difficulties. Five years later the local partisan press defended Davis; one paper asserted he had money to feed his cattle but the Bank of Fort Scott seized them because it was concerned about his solvency. *Fort Scott Semi-Weekly Tribune and Monitor*, October 31, 1906, 7.

27. *Fort Scott (KS) Daily Tribune*, September 27, 1901, 1; *Fort Scott (KS) Daily Monitor*, September 27, 1901, 4.

28. It was alleged the county attorney of McPherson County, Kansas, was a victim. *Fort Scott (KS) Daily Tribune*, September 27, 1901, 1; *Fort Scott (KS) Daily Monitor*, September 27, 1901, 4. Charles B. Griffith (1872–1928) served as Kansas attorney general from 1923–1927. *Fort Scott (KS) Sunday Morning Herald*, June 10, 1928, 1, 4.

29. *Fort Scott (KS) Daily Tribune*, September 27, 1901, 1; *Fort Scott (KS) Daily Monitor*, September 27, 1901, 4.

30. *Fort Scott (KS) Daily Tribune*, October 1, 1901, 1; *Fort Scott (KS) Daily Monitor*, October 4, 1901, 1; *Webb City Register*, October 3, 1901, 1.

31. In 2022, $100,000 would be $3,606,649. Friedman, "Inflation Calculator." *Fort Scott (KS) Daily Monitor*, September 30, 1901, 4. Decades later Norval Matthews echoed Brooks's claim that Boatright was involved in Webb City elections. He recounted the story of an election in which the Buckfoot Gang gave lavish sums to each candidate. Bets were taken on the outcome and Boatright volunteered the use of his personal safe. To guarantee no one would tamper with it "armed guards representing all parties concerned" stood watch. When a winner was declared, a crowd gathered to open the safe. It was empty. "Pandemonium broke loose," Matthews claimed, "fights ensued, the place was wrecked, but the money was not found." The safe, unbeknownst to all but the gang, was double-sided. The Webb City newspapers contain sizeable gaps, and I did not find any reference to this event,

but contemporary newspaper accounts confirm the existence of a double-sided safe in Boatright's headquarters. Matthews, *The Promise Land*, 134.

32. *Fort Scott (KS) Daily Monitor*, October 8, 1901, 1.

33. *Fort Scott (KS) Daily Tribune*, November 2, 1901, 1, December 31, 1901, 3; Carthage *Jasper County Democrat*, November 8, 1901, 1.

34. *Fort Scott (KS) Daily Tribune*, November 4, 1901, 1.

35. *Fort Scott (KS) Daily Tribune*, October 9, 1901, 1; *Carthage Evening Press*, October 9, 1901, 8; Carthage *Jasper County Democrat*, October 11, 1901, 6.

36. *Fort Scott (KS) Daily Tribune*, October 9, 1901, 1.

37. *Fort Scott (KS) Daily Monitor*, November 9, 1901, 1; November 11, 1901, 1.

38. *Fort Scott (KS) Daily Tribune*, November 11, 1901, 4.

39. *Fort Scott (KS) Daily Tribune*, October 9, 1901, 1; *Carthage Evening Press*, October 9, 1901, 8; Carthage *Jasper County Democrat*, October 11, 1901, 6.

40. *Carthage Evening Press*, October 9, 1901, 4; *Joplin News-Herald*, October 9, 1901, 5.

41. *Carthage Evening Press*, October 9, 1901, 3.

42. Berger's surname also appears as Burger. *Springfield Leader-Democrat*, October 9, 1901, 5; October 10, 1901, 1; *Joplin News-Herald*, January 11, 1901. Archivist Sarah LeRoy identified the case as *Guy Berger v. Robert Boatright*, case no. 1, US District Court, Joplin, Missouri, Bankruptcy Act of 1898 Case File, Record Group 21, National Archives, Kansas City. The record is missing; it was requested in 1981 by the district court and was never returned. The docket entry shows Berger asked for a dismissal and an order was filed.

43. *St. Louis Republic*, November 29, 1901, 9; *St. Louis Globe-Democrat*, November 30, 1901, 2. For testimony of Frank Youmans, Henry Wright, and Robert Duncan, see *R. E. Hobbs v. Exchange Bank of Webb City and J. P. Stewart*. Johnny Connors won the world flyweight title in 1894; after he retired from boxing, he operated the Empire Saloon in Springfield, Illinois. In 1903 Connors was involved in a fake-foot-race scandal; a Wisconsin judge alleged he was part of a nationwide swindling ring. Connors, he said, was not the head but the "chief of one portion in the middle west." The judge claimed an Arkansas millionaire backed the gang. Connors may have been allied with Boatright and his men. He was accused of partnering with sprinters Alexander McCarren and Cruthers (Carruthers) in fixed races; both names are mentioned as Buckfoot members. Doug Porkorski, *Heartland Magazine*, Springfield (IL) *State Journal-Register*, June 6, 2003, 10A; *Racine (WI) Daily Journal*, May 20, 1903, 8; June 20, 1903, 8; *St. Louis Globe-Democrat* July 29, 1902, 2. For an exposé of the case, see *Chicago Inter Ocean*, October 25, 1903, Magazine Section. See article about indictment in *Chicago Inter Ocean*, October 8, 1902, 10;

for his conviction in Milwaukee see the *Topeka State Journal*, August 6, 1903, 10.

44. *R. E. Hobbs v. Exchange Bank and J. P. Stewart.*

45. *R. E. Hobbs v. Exchange Bank and J. P. Stewart.*

46. *R. E. Hobbs v. Exchange Bank and J. P. Stewart.* Maloncy must have cut an imposing figure because multiple newspapers commented on Boatright's own physique.

47. *R. E. Hobbs v. Exchange Bank and J. P. Stewart.*

48. *R. E. Hobbs v. Exchange Bank and J. P. Stewart.*

49. *Lamar Democrat*, October 24, 1901, 1.

50. *Joplin News-Herald* quoted in Carthage *Jasper County Democrat*, October 18, 1901, 2.

51. *Joplin News-Herald*, October 18, 1901, 2. The column that sparked the *Register*'s ire could not be located.

52. *Joplin News-Herald*, October 28, 1901, 4; Carthage *Jasper County Democrat*, November 1, 1901, 2.

53. Carthage *Jasper County Democrat*, November 1, 1901, 2; *Joplin News-Herald*, October 28, 1901, 4.

54. *Joplin News-Herald*, October 28, 1901, 4. Fay later died.

55. Carthage *Jasper County News*, November 5, 1901, 3; *Joplin News-Herald*, November 3, 1901, 3.

56. *Chicago Inter Ocean*, November 3, 1901, 20.

57. *Chicago Inter Ocean*, November 3, 1901, 20. This item was reprinted in the *Denver Post*, November 4, 1901, 7.

58. *Webb City Sentinel*, November 6, 1901, 2; November 7, 1901, 2. Everts is sometimes spelled "Evarts." Another paper identified him as "Billy Evans." Carthage *Jasper County News*, November 8, 1901, 3.

59. Carthage *Jasper County Democrat*, November 8, 1901, 7. Joplin policemen Bert Brannon and James Sweeney were shot and killed while trying to apprehend transients. Kimberly Harper, *White Man's Heaven: The Lynching and Expulsion of Blacks in the Southern Ozarks, 1894–1909* (Fayetteville: University of Arkansas Press, 2010), 73.

60. *Joplin Globe*, November 7, 1901, 3.

61. *Webb City Sentinel*, November 8, 1901, 7.

62. *Webb City Sentinel*, November 14, 1901, 5; Carthage *Jasper County News*, November 19, 1901, 3. This race pitted Bud Gillett, using the alias J. D. Owens, against George Thompson. See *Carthage Evening Press*, November 23, 1901, 5; *Fort Scott (KS) Daily Monitor*, November 25, 1901, 1.

63. *Webb City Sentinel*, November 19, 1901, 1.

64. *St. Louis Post-Dispatch*, November 1, 1896, 22.

65. Lang and Becker filed suit in Jasper County against Boatright, Ed Ellis, Bert Bromley, Bud Gillett, Roger H. Williams, and Daniel Maloney for

$2,300. The complaint stated their employee A. N. Randall had bet $6,800 of the firm's money. The gang returned $4,500; the firm sued for the difference. *Webb City Sentinel*, November 25, 1901, 4; *Fort Scott (KS) Daily Monitor*, November 25, 1901, 1.

66. Carthage *Jasper County News*, November 19, 1901, 3.

67. *Carthage Evening Press*, November 15, 1901, 3. Adjusted for inflation, $10,500 would be $378,698 in 2022. Friedman, "Inflation Calculator."

68. *R. E. Hobbs v. Exchange Bank of Webb City and J. P. Stewart.*

69. *R. E. Hobbs v. Exchange Bank of Webb City and J. P. Stewart.*

70. *R. E. Hobbs v. Exchange Bank of Webb City and J. P. Stewart.*

71. *R. E. Hobbs v. Exchange Bank of Webb City and J. P. Stewart.*

72. *R. E. Hobbs v. Exchange Bank of Webb City and J. P. Stewart.*

73. *R. E. Hobbs v. Exchange Bank of Webb City and J. P. Stewart.*

74. *R. E. Hobbs v. Exchange Bank of Webb City and J. P. Stewart.*

75. *Cass County Democrat* (Atlantic, IA), June 4, 1903, 11–12.

76. *Joplin News-Herald*, November 24, 1901; *Fort Scott (KS) Daily Monitor*, November 22, 1901; *Cass County Democrat* (Atlantic, IA), June 4, 1903, 11–12. For a different version see the *Jasper County Democrat*, November 22, 1901. Notably the *News-Herald* used a "double column flare headed article." See *Fort Scott (KS) Daily Monitor*, November 22, 1901.

77. William H. Haughawout was Webb City postmaster from 1898 to 1906. US Appointments of US Postmasters, Ancestry.com.

78. *Cass County Democrat* (Atlantic, IA), June 4, 1903, 11–12; *R. E. Hobbs v. Exchange Bank of Webb City and J. P. Stewart.*

79. *R. E. Hobbs v. Exchange Bank of Webb City and J. P. Stewart.*

80. *Cass County Democrat* (Atlantic, IA), June 4, 1903, 11–12. By the time T. Bond Haughawout died in 1903, his wife had sued him for divorce, alleging infidelity with prostitutes. *Carthage Press,* April 17, 1903; May 1, 1903. For more on Loren L. DeLano, see "Iowa Legislature," accessed March 3, 2019, https://www.legis.iowa.gov/legislators/legislator?ga=30 &personID=3529. See *R. E. Hobbs v. Exchange Bank of Webb City and J. P. Stewart.* Stewart was indicted by the federal grand jury in Fort Scott for using the mails to defraud Jonathan Davis. His writ of habeas corpus was denied, but he successfully appealed. *Fort Scott (KS) Daily Tribune,* November 5, 1902, 4.

81. *Fort Scott (KS) Daily Tribune*, November 22, 1901, 3. Adjusted for inflation, $200,000 in 1901 would be worth $7,213,298 in 2022. Friedman, "Inflation Calculator."

82. *Carthage Evening Press*, November 25, 1901, 4. Plummer said Boatright arrived in Jasper County sixteen years earlier, which would be 1885; the Boatright family disappeared from St. Louis city directories beginning in 1886.

83. Carthage *Jasper County Democrat*, December 6, 1901, 7. Jasper County native Alfred G. Carter (1863–1903) graduated with honors from Drury College. Carter was a stakeholder in the P. E. Mine at Oronogo, Missouri, and vice president of the Ball Land and Mining Company. In 1898 he was elected to the Missouri House of Representatives as a Republican. Carter married Harriet Ellis, Ed Ellis's sister. *Webb City Register*, December 12, 1903, 1. The same day J. H. Maclin appeared before Roper and claimed he lost $4,600. *Webb City Sentinel*, December 6, 1901, 1.

84. *Lamar Democrat*, December 12, 1901, 4; *Fort Scott (KS) Daily Monitor*, December 21, 1901, 1; *Fort Scott (KS) Daily Tribune*, December 21, 1901, 3.

85. *Fort Scott (KS) Daily Monitor*, December 7, 1901, 1.

CHAPTER 5

1. *Joplin News-Herald*, January 1, 1902, 1, 2. Jesse Ansel made the same claim to the *Joplin Globe*. He said Ben Ansel was his cousin. *Joplin Globe*, January 2, 1902, 2.

2. *Joplin Globe*, January 3, 1902, 2; *Joplin News-Herald*, January 2, 1902, 1; *Carthage Evening Press*, January 3, 1902, 11.

3. *Joplin Globe*, January 10, 1902, 3; *Carthage Evening Press*, January 10, 1902, 5, September 13, 1902, 5. More details are provided in *Joplin News-Herald*, September 14, 1902, 3; Carthage *Jasper County Democrat*, September 16, 1902, 3. Charles O. Hodges (1858–1938) owned the St. George Hotel in Dallas, Texas. *Dallas Morning News*, August 12, 1905, 9; October 1, 1934, August 18, 1938.

4. *Joplin News-Herald*, January 20, 1902, 1, January 21, 1902, 1; *Carthage Evening Press*, January 20, 1902, 2. A Hodges case could not be located, but the Honey Grove Kid roped him.

5. Herbert S. Hadley (1872–1927) was a Kansan who made his mark in Missouri. As Missouri attorney general (1905–1909) he successfully pursued high-profile cases against corporate trusts. Subsequently elected governor of Missouri, Hadley championed progressive legislation and achieved accomplishments any Progressive reformer would envy. *Dictionary of Missouri Biography*, s.v. "Hadley, Herbert."

6. *Joplin News-Herald*, January 21, 1902, 1; Carthage *Jasper County Democrat*, January 24, 1902, 3.

7. Carthage *Jasper County Democrat*, January 24, 1902, 3; *Joplin News-Herald*, January 30, 1902, 1; *Kansas City Star*, January 30, 1902, 12.

8. *Joplin News-Herald*, February 3, 1902, 1; *Fort Scott (KS) Daily Tribune*, February 3, 1902, 4.

9. *Carthage Evening Press*, June 14, 1902, 6.

10. *Kansas City Star*, June 17, 1902, 4.

11. *Kansas City Star*, June 17, 1902, 4.

12. *Kansas City Star*, June 17, 1902, 4. This court record was likely destroyed.

13. *Fort Scott (KS) Daily Tribune*, February 11, 1902, 4; *Webb City Sentinel*, February 11, 1902, 4.

14. *Webb City Sentinel*, February 19, 1902, 3. Haywood Scott and his law partner, John W. McAntire, represented Day. Scott later represented Roger Williams in *In Re R. H. Williams*.

15. *Carthage Evening Press*, February 20, 1902, 5; *Joplin News-Herald*, February 20, 1902, 1; *Webb City Sentinel*, February 20, 1902, 4. George Day and Harry C. Armstrong gave brief depositions in *Pittman v. Joplin Savings Bank*, case no. 17, US Circuit Court, Western District of Missouri, Southwestern Division, Joplin, Missouri, Record Group 21, National Archives, Kansas City; hereafter cited as *Pittman v. Joplin Savings Bank*. Day said he was roped by George Ryan's nephew Coke Ryan of Xenia, Ohio. Armstrong selected local firm McAntire & Scott to serve as associate counsel. McAntire later represented the bank in *Pittman v. Joplin Savings Bank*. For more on the gang moving their financial operations to the Joplin Savings Bank, see the testimony of James Stewart and Joseph Stewart in *R. E. Hobbs v. Exchange Bank of Webb City and J. P. Stewart*. The testimony of Henry Wright and Robert Duncan is in *R. E. Hobbs v. Exchange Bank of Webb City and J. P. Stewart*.

16. *Joplin News-Herald*, February 23, 1902, 4.

17. *Carthage Evening Press*, March 13, 1902, 5. The US Supreme Court defined a bucket shop as "an establishment, nominally for the transaction of a stock exchange business, or business of similar character, but really for the registration of bets, or wagers, usually for small amounts, on the rise or fall of the prices of stocks, grain, oil, etc., there being no transfer or delivery of the stock or commodities nominally dealt in." *Gatewood v. North Carolina*, 27 S. Ct 167, 168 (1906).

18. *Webb City Sentinel*, March 19, 1902, 3.

19. *Joplin News-Herald*, March 26, 1902, 1.

20. Powell and Blocker's testimony is in *Hindman v. State of Arkansas*, University of Arkansas at Little Rock/Pulaski County Law Library, Arkansas Supreme Court Briefs and Records (hereafter cited as *Hindman v. State of Arkansas*) and *Pittman v. Joplin Savings Bank*.

21. *Joplin Globe*, March 30, 1902, 1. For other published affidavits, see *Joplin Globe*, March 28, 1902, 1; March 29, 1902, 1. Friedman, "Inflation Calculator." Born in Washington, DC, Hosmer was a Harvard and Columbia University Law School graduate. In the years after he sold the *News-Herald* he went insane and died in 1921. *New York Times*, December 30, 1914, 8; *New York Herald*, August 10, 1921, 7; Harvard College, Class of 1888, Secretary's Report No. 8 (January 1920): 68.

22. *Joplin Globe*, March 30, 1902, 2.

23. *Joplin Globe*, March 30, 1902, 2.

24. *Joplin News-Herald*, March 30, 1902, 4.

25. *Joplin News-Herald*, March 30, 1902, 4. Barbee's defense was that gamblers "got into his building through a subtenant." See *Joplin Globe*, November 5, 1901, 6. Hosmer asserted Barbee and the *Globe* failed to speak out against gambling, but that is inaccurate. The *Globe* made occasional lukewarm statements calling for the end of gambling but only if public sentiment was on the side of city and county officials. See, for example, *Joplin Globe*, November 1, 1901, 4.

26. *Joplin News-Herald*, March 31, 1902, 1.

27. *Joplin News-Herald*, March 31, 1902, 1. Only one of these records could be located: *Frank C. Youmans v. Robert Boatright, et al.*, Jasper County Circuit Court (April 1904), Jasper County Records Center.

28. Carthage *Jasper County Democrat*, April 8, 1902, 3.

29. *H. W. Currey v. Joplin Savings Bank*, Kansas City Court of Appeals (March 1903); hereafter cited as *Currey v. Joplin Savings Bank*.

30. *Currey v. Joplin Savings Bank*.

31. *Currey v. Joplin Savings Bank*. Morris said of the contract he signed with Bob Long, "They all look alike to me when the Sheriff isn't around."

32. *Currey v. Joplin Savings Bank*.

33. *Webb City Sentinel*, April 28, 1902, 4; this article discusses the Joplin Savings Bank getting sued. *Currey v. Joplin Savings Bank*. Currey said he did not warn Carlson and Horner because it was nighttime. He stated, "If a man made a remark he would get his head broke before he got away from that club. They had the hack driver and the n[——], and those two fellows as against Mr. Bowman and I alone; we would be very foolish to make any remark." *Currey v. Joplin Savings Bank*.

34. *Johnson v. State of Arkansas;* affidavit of John I. Pittman in *In re Robert Boatright and Ed E. Ellis*, Joplin Bankruptcy Case Files, US District Court for the Southwestern (Joplin) Division of the Western District of Missouri, Record Group 21, National Archives, Kansas City. In *Pittman v. Joplin Savings Bank*, Pittman described the Webb City Athletic Club's club room as having a gymnasium on one side and a club room on the other.

35. *Johnson v. State of Arkansas*. Doucette was a Canadian who worked for the Kirby Lumber Company in Tyler County, Texas; Doucette, Texas, is named for him. At Johnson's trial the defense accused Doucette of having a wire in his saloon for the 1897 Corbett–Fitzsimmons fight. He was the only victim who said the gang would also "fight bull dogs." "Doucette, Texas," Tyler County, Texas, Historical Commission, accessed October 5, 2019, https://web.archive.org/web/20160731140439/https://tylercountyhc.org

/doucette; "Peter Doucette," 1900 US Census, Tyler County, Texas. He died in 1917 at the age of fifty-nine in Grayburg, Texas. "P. A. Doucette," Texas, Death Certificates, 1903–1982, Ancestry.com.

36. *Johnson v. State of Arkansas*. J. J. Broussard's full name may have been John Jay Broussard.

37. *Joplin Globe*, May 8, 1902, 7.

38. *Joplin Globe*, May 8, 1902, 7. Boatright had also just been arrested for grand larceny and obtaining money under false pretenses. The warrants were sworn out by victims Monroe Griffith, William Barker, Charles Gregory, and Frank Youmans. He paid $1,500 bail on each of the three charges. *Carthage Evening Press*, May 6, 1902, 4.

39. *Kansas City Journal*, May 12, 1902, 8. The letter was reprinted in the *Joplin News-Herald*, May 12, 1902, 2.

40. *Kansas City Journal*, May 12, 1902, 8; *Joplin News-Herald*, May 12, 1902, 2.

41. *Kansas City Journal*, May 12, 1902, 8; *Joplin News-Herald*, May 12, 1902, 2.

42. *Webb City Sentinel*, May 26, 1902, 1; Carthage *Jasper County News*, May 27, 1902, 4. Names of individuals who could confirm the story were reportedly listed in the original article, but the names were not published in the *Jasper County News* reprint. The anonymous author alleged Currey was being groomed by Barbee's Democratic rival William Phelps to run for judge.

43. *Webb City Sentinel*, May 26, 1902, 1. There are no extant copies of the *Register* from 1902. Booth's article does not appear to have been reprinted in any other local papers.

44. *Webb City Sentinel*, May 26, 1902, 3; *Springfield Republican*, May 28, 1902, 2. Blagg was likely William A. Blagg of Denton County, Texas; see "William A. Blagg," 1900 US Census, Denton County, Texas.

45. *Pittman v. Joplin Savings Bank*.

46. For Chambers, see *Pittman v. Joplin Savings Bank*. Charles McClellan "Mac" Chambers (1877–1933) served three terms in the Texas legislature and was mayor of San Antonio.

47. *Webb City Sentinel*, May 26, 1902, 4.

48. Carthage *Jasper County Democrat*, May 30, 1902, 8.

49. *Webb City Sentinel*, June 2, 1902, 2.

50. *Webb City Sentinel*, June 7, 1902, 2; Carthage *Jasper County News*, June 10, 1902, 3. Businessman Robert Drewery hired Forlow and filed suit against Boatright, Roger Williams, Ed Ellis, George Thompson, and Mary Rice for the return of a diamond ring and $100 in damages. *Webb City Sentinel*, June 3, 1902, 3; Carthage *Jasper County Democrat*, June 6, 1902, 7; Little Rock *Arkansas Democrat*, June 2, 1904, 7. *Robert A. Drewery v. Robert Boatright, et al.*, Jasper County Circuit Court, Jasper County Records Center. Drewery's name is sometimes spelled "Drewry" or "Drury."

51. Carthage *Jasper County News*, June 3, 1902, 3.

52. Carthage *Jasper County Democrat*, June 6, 1902, 2.

53. Other examples are Harry Wasser (alias Harry Price) in *Johnson v. State of Arkansas* and Ed Ellis in *Currey v. Joplin Savings Bank*. For Colorado City, see Jan MacKell, *Brothels, Bordellos, & Bad Girls: Prostitution in Colorado, 1860–1930* (Albuquerque: University of New Mexico Press, 2004), 71–72.

54. See *In Re R. H. Williams*. It is unclear if this was Russell B. Harriman of Mabray fame.

55. *In Re R. H. Williams*.

56. *In Re R. H. Williams*.

57. *In Re R. H. Williams*.

58. *In Re R. H. Williams*.

59. Carthage *Jasper County Democrat*, June 20, 1902, 7.

60. Carthage *Jasper County Democrat*, June 20, 1902, 7.

61. Carthage *Jasper County Democrat*, June 20, 1902, 7.

CHAPTER 6

1. *Joplin Globe*, June 27, 1902, 7. Stonewall Pritchett (1870–1955) was a graduate of Vanderbilt Law School and a former Democratic state representative. Harper, *White Man's Heaven*, 65.

2. *Joplin Globe*, July 11, 1902, 8. *Currey v. Joplin Savings Bank*.

3. *Joplin Globe*, July 17, 1902, 1; *Carthage Evening Press*, July 17, 1902, 8. *Currey v. Joplin Savings Bank*. At the same time another victim, Walter Harper, filed suit against Robert Boatright and others for $5,850. He and a man named Tipton who lost $700 combined their claims over losses they sustained on a fake race that took place a month earlier in June. Carthage *Jasper County Democrat*, July 4, 1902, 6. The amount was reportedly $6,500; see *Galena (KS) Evening Times*, July 2, 1902, 1. Harper won his suit won by default against Boatright for $5,850 plus $150 on a second count. See *Webb City Sentinel*, March 13, 1903, 4.

4. *Webb City Sentinel*, August 25, 1902, 4; *Joplin Globe*, August 26, 1902, 5. The Joplin Savings Bank case was appealed to the Kansas City Court of Appeals, which ruled in favor of Currey. See *Kansas City Star*, May 25, 1903, 1.

5. *Carthage Evening Press*, July 24, 1902, 7; August 7, 1902, 4. Buckfoot's father, mother, and housekeeper Ola McWhirt were in Manitou Springs, Colorado. Mary Rice called McWhirt Buckfoot's "concubine" in *In re Robert Boatright and Ed E. Ellis*. Friedman, "Inflation Calculator."

6. Carthage *Jasper County Democrat*, August 8, 1902, 2.

7. *Webb City Sentinel*, August 14, 1902; *Joplin Globe*, August 15, 1902, 7.

8. Carthage *Jasper County Democrat*, August 22, 1902, 2.

9. *Webb City Sentinel*, August 13, 1901, 3.

10. *Webb City Sentinel*, August 13, 1902, 2.

11. *Joplin News-Herald*, January 22, 1903, 2; *Joplin Globe*, January 25, 1903, 2.

12. Bourland's loss is mentioned in *In re Robert Boatright and Ed E. Ellis*. Bourland (1862–1952) was colorful; his wife shot his lover on two separate occasions, killing her the second time. The couple remained married and Bourland served four nonconsecutive terms as mayor of Fort Smith. *Mayors of the City of Fort Smith, Arkansas*, accessed January 26, 2020, www.fortsmithar.gov.

13. *Joplin Globe*, September 21, 1902, 1. The case under Shannon was *State of Missouri v. Robert Boatright* for embezzling $500. The prosecuting witness failed to appear and the case was dismissed. The six cases Mooneyham filed against Boatright are listed in the article; two were dropped after the complainant in each case received their money back and refused to appear in court.

14. *Carthage Evening Press*, October 11, 1902, 6.

15. *Cass County Democrat* (Atlantic, IA), June 4, 1903, 11–12; Carthage *Jasper County Democrat*, October 10, 1902, 3. Black's self-serving story must be taken with a healthy dose of skepticism.

16. *Joplin Globe*, October 7, 1902, 2, 5; *Carthage Evening Press*, October 7, 1902, 5, October 8, 1902; *Joplin News-Herald*, October 7, 1902, 1.

17. *Carthage Evening Press*, October 9, 1902, 8; October 10, 1902, 4; Carthage *Jasper County News*, October 14, 1902, 3; *Joplin Globe*, October 9, 1902. *R. E. Hobbs v. Exchange Bank of Webb City and J. P. Stewart*.

18. Carthage *Jasper County Democrat*, October 25, 1902.

19. Frank C. Lory (1873–1934) later owned the Zero Ice and Fuel Company in Indianapolis. *Indianapolis (IN) News*, February 13, 1934, 3; *Men of Indianapolis Affairs 1923* (Indianapolis: American Biographical Society, 1923), 391. *Carthage Evening Press*, October 9, 1902, 4; *Webb City Sentinel*, October 9, 1902, 2. The race was between sprinters Ryan and Dean. *Colorado Springs Gazette*, October 14, 1902; *Colorado Springs Gazette*, January 7, 1903, 2; *Colorado Springs Gazette*, December 24, 1902, 1; Little Rock *Arkansas Democrat*, December 29, 1902, 3. Friedman, "Inflation Calculator."

20. *Colorado Springs Gazette*, December 7, 1902, 12. The gang pulled off fifty-three tricks in the summer of 1902; after local banks refused to handle their money they went to Salt Lake City. See also *Colorado Springs Gazette*, January 11, 1903, 4; testimony of Harry Price in *State v. Johnson*. For police corruption in Colorado Springs see *The Weekly Gazette* (Colorado Springs, CO), July 30, 1903, 1; August 6, 1903, 1, 5.

21. *Carthage Evening Press*, October 10, 1902, 2. The letter first appeared in the Carthage *Jasper County Democrat*. On October 6, 1902, the *Evening Press* reported " 'Kid' Holden, who runs a gambling device in the Barbee

building . . . was robbed on Broadway." The article noted several other robberies in East Joplin and blamed an incompetent police force for the rise in crime. A few days later, citing numerous robberies, pickpockets, and burglaries, the paper declared, "It Is Crime and Carnival" in Joplin. *Carthage Evening Press*, October 21, 1902, 4. A special election was held in early October to elect a successor to murdered Webb City marshal Len Rich. Republican candidate Harrison "Elsie" Marquiss defeated his Democratic challenger. Notably two Republicans were also elected to the city council. "Barbee Rule Condemned," *Carthage Evening Press*, October 8, 1902, 4.

22. *Carthage Evening Press*, October 11, 1902, 2.

23. *Carthage Evening Press*, October 12, 1902, 2; October 13, 1902, 8.

24. Carthage *Jasper County News*, October 14, 1902, 4. James Gammon (1839–1905) did not list an occupation in the 1900 census. James's son Oscar gave his occupation as gambler. The Gammons lived next to Robert Boatright. 1900 US Census, Webb City, Jasper County, Missouri, Ancestry.com. Judge Joseph Dudley Perkins (1851–1935) was the father of Marlin Perkins, host of *Mutual of Omaha's Wild Kingdom*.

25. *Carthage Evening Press*, October 18, 1902, 2.

26. *Carthage Evening Press*, October 25, 1902, 2.

27. *Joplin News-Herald*, October 19, 1902, 12.

28. *Joplin News-Herald*, October 20, 1902, 1; *Webb City Sentinel*, October 31, 1902.

29. *Carthage Evening Press*, November 3, 1902, 1, 2.

30. *Neosho Miner & Mechanic*, November 1, 1902, 4. Barbee sued publisher Charles E. Curtice for malicious defamation. Represented by Boatright's attorney George Clay, Barbee demanded $30,000 in damages. Clay intimated this was just the first in a series of lawsuits Barbee planned against newspapers critical of him. See Carthage *Jasper County Democrat*, December 15, 1902; December 19, 1902, 1; *Joplin Globe*, April 26, 1903, 1, 11. Barbee printed excerpts from depositions taken prior to Curtice's capitulation. Henry Price, a newspaper publisher in Aurora and Carterville, testified that Phelps loyalists tried to pay him to print a similar anti-Barbee squib, but he refused. His testimony reveals much about the behind-the-scenes machinations between the two rivals. Judge W. B. Brown, who rented an office in the House of Lords, testified he did not know of any gambling dens or brothels. In 1911 Barbee and Rogers were in court regarding the passageway Barbee built years earlier connecting the *Globe* building to the House of Lords. Testimony in this case confirmed its existence. See the *Joplin Morning Tribune*, December 15, 1911, 1; *Joplin Globe Publishing Company v. Gilbert Barbee*, case no. 9956, Jasper County Circuit Court (1912), Jasper County Records Center.

31. *Joplin Globe*, November 2, 1902, 2.

32. *Joplin News-Herald*, November 3, 1902, 4.

33. *Carthage Evening Press*, November 4, 1902; November 5, 1902.

34. *Joplin Globe*, November 5, 1902, 1.

35. *Joplin Globe*, November 5, 1902, 4.

36. *Joplin News-Herald*, November 5, 1902, 1.

37. *Joplin News-Herald*, November 5, 1902, 4.

38. *Carthage Evening Press*, November 7, 1902, 2. No issues of the *Carterville Republican* are known to exist.

39. Carthage *Jasper County Democrat*, November 7, 1902, 6.

40. *Webb City Sentinel*, November 4, 1902, 2; *Fort Scott (KS) Daily Tribune*, November 5, 1902, 4.

41. *In Re R. H. Williams*; *Johnson v. State of Arkansas*. Cobb's testimony can be found in both cases; his account varies slightly between the two. I have taken the liberty of interweaving facts from both transcripts so that his experience makes more sense. Friedman's Inflation Calculator says $27,000 in 1902 would be worth $936,342 in 2022.

42. *In Re R. H. Williams*; *Johnson v. State of Arkansas*.

43. *In Re R. H. Williams*; *Johnson v. State of Arkansas*. In *Johnson*, Cobb admitted he lost $27,000 and a six-shooter.

44. *In Re R. H. Williams*; *Johnson v. State of Arkansas*. For Johnson, see "J. E. Johnson," Atlanta Federal Penitentiary Case Files, National Archives, Atlanta. Johnson's first name, Irven, was often mistaken for a J, thus his record appears as "J. E. Johnson." He was indicted in 1903 in Polk County, Texas, but a motion to quash was sustained. *Houston (TX) Daily Post*, April 6, 1908, 9.

45. *In Re R. H. Williams*; it contains a brief deposition from Barto. In *In re Robert Boatright and Ed E. Ellis*, Barto claimed he lost $5,000.

46. Little Rock *Arkansas Gazette*, December 7, 1902.

CHAPTER 7

1. *Taylor (TX) Daily Press*, March 10, 1933, 1; *Colorado Springs Gazette*, December 7, 1902, 12.

2. *Hindman v. State of Arkansas*.

3. Carthage *Jasper County Democrat*, December 12, 1902, 3.

4. Little Rock *Arkansas Gazette*, December 7, 1902, 1; Little Rock *Arkansas Gazette*, December 9, 1902, 1; Carthage *Jasper County Democrat*, December 12, 1902, 3. Upon learning of Bland's loss, the *Honey Grove (TX) Signal* remarked, "Bonham people inform us that the 'Honey Grove Kid' and his pals attempted to work their game there last winter and had

to leave town at night to escape violence at the hands of citizens." *Honey Grove Signal*, December 12, 1902, 1. Nelson's alias was Noland. Little Rock *Arkansas Gazette*, June 9, 1903, 1.

5. Carthage *Jasper County Democrat*, December 12, 1902, 1. On March 16, 1899, Sheriff Williams was involved in a gunfight between members of the Hot Springs Police and the Garland County, Arkansas, Sheriff's Office. The two agencies vied for control of the city's illegal gambling activities. "Hot Springs Shootout," Encyclopedia of Arkansas, accessed September 8, 2019, https://encyclopediaofarkansas.net/entries/hot-springs-shootout-7467/. Ed Spear, who operated a fight store with George Ryan in Hot Springs, was a deputy at the time of the shootout. See Orval E. Allbritton, "A City Drenched in Blood," *The Record* (1996): 23–37.

6. Little Rock *Arkansas Democrat*, June 12, 1904, 7; *Hindman v. State of Arkansas.*

7. Little Rock *Arkansas Gazette*, December 18, 1902, 1; Friedman, "Inflation Calculator."

8. *St. Louis Republic*, February 3, 1903, 4, reprinted from the *Sedalia Democrat*, February 3, 1903, 1–5.

9. Little Rock *Arkansas Gazette*, December 16, 1902, 6. City Marshal Thad Wells of Morrilton, Arkansas, was said to be a victim. See Little Rock *Arkansas Gazette*, December 16, 1902, 6; Little Rock *Arkansas Democrat*, December 15, 1902, 1. See "T. R. Wells," 1900 US Census, Morrilton, Arkansas. L. W. Boyer was allegedly Williams's common-law wife. *In Re R. H. Williams.*

10. *Waters v. Clay.* See also, *In re Wood and Henderson*, 210 US 246 (1908). *Colorado Springs Gazette*, December 24, 1902, 1; *Denver Post*, December 26, 1902, 2; Little Rock *Arkansas Democrat*, December 29, 1902, 3. Boatright used the alias "Scott."

11. Little Rock *Arkansas Gazette*, December 30, 1902, 2; Little Rock *Arkansas Democrat*, December 29, 1902, 3. Ralph Davis (1866–1952) attended Washington University as a teenager and began practicing law before he was twenty. Elected to the Tennessee House of Representatives, he became the youngest speaker in state history. Shortly thereafter Davis was found guilty of misappropriating a client's bail money. When he refused to resign, the House declared the speaker's seat vacant and held a new election. Davis was disbarred but convinced fellow attorneys to petition for his reinstatement. He practiced law until his death. *Memphis Commercial Appeal*, December 7, 1952, 1; *News-Sentinel* (Knoxville), December 8, 1952, 4; Robert M. McBride and Dan M. Robison, eds., *Biographical Directory of the Tennessee General Assembly, Volume II: 1861–1901* (Nashville: Tennessee State Library and Archives; Tennessee Historical Commission, 1979), 225.

12. *Joplin Evening Times* quoted in the *Webb City Sentinel*, January 3, 1903, 3; Carthage *Jasper County Democrat*, January 9, 1903, 6.

13. Carthage *Jasper County Democrat*, January 23, 1903, 4.

14. *Carthage Evening Press*, March 13, 1903, 9; *Webb City Sentinel*, March 14, 1903, 3; Council Bluffs *Daily Nonpareil*, March 14, 1903, 3.

15. For Barker's occupation, see *Omaha Daily Bee*, March 30, 1902, 8. For an account of their legal maneuvering in Denver as well as Moore's sister Anna signing his bond, see *Daily Nonpareil*, November 7, 1902, 3 and April 30, 1903, 3; for trial see *Daily Nonpareil*, March 14–18, 1903. For the court case, see *State of Iowa v. Leon Losier, Ed Moore, John Grimm*, case no. 3244, Pottawattamie County District Court, Council Bluffs, Iowa (March 1902). For requisition papers for Lozier, Moore, and Grimm, see file for "Leon Lozier," Office of the Governor, Governors Criminal Correspondence, 1847–1918, State Historical Society of Iowa. For allegations of jury tampering, see *Daily Nonpareil*, March 16, 1903, 5. Presumably one of the men involved in jury tampering efforts was Ben Marks.

16. *Daily Nonpareil*, March 18, 1903, 5.

17. *Carthage Evening Press*, April 28, 1903, 2. *Daily Nonpareil*, March 24, 1903, 3.

18. Reprinted in the *Black Hills (SD) Weekly Journal*, May 8, 1903, 4.

19. *Omaha Daily Bee*, October 4, 1907, 8. See Lozier's file in Office of the Governor, Criminal Correspondence 1874–1998, Record Group 043, Iowa State Archives for Askwith's account of the case.

20. *Mt. Vernon Lawrence Chieftain*, March 19, 1903, 1; *Mt. Vernon Fountain and Journal*, March 19, 1903, 2; *Webb City Sentinel*, March 17, 1903, 4.

21. *Mt. Vernon Fountain and Journal*, March 19, 1903, 3; *Carthage Evening Press*, March 20, 1903, 2. The shorthand notes and transcript of *Currey v. Joplin Savings Bank* contained several incriminating statements by Ed Ellis. *Carthage Evening Press*, March 23, 1903, 8. *State of Missouri v. Robert Boatright, Ed E. Ellis, and Bert Bromley*, Missouri Supreme Court, Missouri State Archives.

22. *Carthage Evening Press*, March 20, 1903, 2.

23. *State of Missouri v. Robert Boatright, Ed E. Ellis, and Bert Bromley*. The record includes closing statements by John Halliburton and T. Bond Haughawout, but none from the defense. *Carthage Evening Press*, March 20, 1903, 2; *Mt. Vernon Fountain and Journal*, March 26, 1903, 2; *Lawrence Chieftain*, March 26, 1903.

24. *Mt. Vernon Fountain and Journal*, March 26, 1903, 2; *Mt. Vernon Lawrence Chieftain*, March 26, 1903, 1; *Carthage Evening Press*, March 21, 1903, 3; *Daily Nonpareil*, March 22, 1903, 3. The *Fountain and Journal* stated Brumley "is said to have been raised in the south-central part of this

(Lawrence) county, and of an industrious family." *State of Missouri v. Robert Boatright, Ed E. Ellis, and Bert Bromley.*

25. *Carthage Evening Press*, March 21, 1903, 3.

26. *Webb City Sentinel*, March 21, 1903, 4.

27. *Joplin Globe*, March 22, 1903, 1; Carthage *Jasper County News*, March 24, 1903, 1.

28. *Joplin News-Herald*, March 23, 1903, 2.

29. *Carthage Evening Press*, March 23, 1903, 8.

30. *Carthage Evening Press*, April 1, 1903, 6. The jail log stated Boatright was five feet, ten inches tall with gray eyes and black hair. He gave his residence as Memphis, Tennessee, and his occupation as blacksmith. Elwin Clay Hearell (1856–1941) was a longtime Neosho, Missouri, resident. *Neosho Daily Democrat*, August 2, 1941, 1. Friedman, "Inflation Calculator."

31. *Carthage Evening Press*, April 2, 1903, 6.

32. *Carthage Evening Press*, April 3, 1903, 5.

33. Carthage *Jasper County Democrat*, April 3, 1903, 5.

34. *Carthage Evening Press*, April 16, 1903, 3; Harper, *White Man's Heaven.*

35. *Carthage Evening Press*, April 16, 1903, 3. On April 19, 1903, sixty-nine-year-old Robert M. Boatright died at home in Webb City. His obituary called him an "old and respected" citizen who once served as justice of the peace. *Webb City Sentinel*, April 20, 1903, 4. The elder Boatright's *Joplin Globe* obituary stated he arrived there in 1895 and had many friends in the county, "having been known to the Bailey and Whitsett families as connected with their former home on the banks of the Merrimac." *Joplin Globe*, April 21, 1903, 7.

36. *Carthage Evening Press*, April 16, 1903, 3.

37. *Carthage Evening Press*, April 16, 1903, 3.

38. Carthage *Jasper County Democrat*, May 1, 1903, 3.

39. *Carthage Evening Press*, May 7, 1903, 6; Carthage *Jasper County Democrat*, May 8, 1903, 5.

40. Owen said he and others had been told Boatright transferred his property to Charley Parker. *Carthage Evening Press*, April 23, 1903, 6. A few weeks earlier Stewart had been struck by a runaway team and suffered a broken leg, bruised chest, and rib fracture. *Webb City Sentinel*, April 6, 1903, 4.

41. *Joplin Globe*, June 7, 1903, 1. Griffith filed a civil suit in May 1902. *Webb City Sentinel*, May 14, 1902, 4. The Cockrill brothers, who roped him, were arrested in Paola, Kansas, on charges of obtaining $4,000 from Griffith under false pretenses. *Joplin News-Herald*, April 14, 1903, 1.

42. *Joplin Globe*, June 7, 1903, 1. The *Globe* also ran a story about Gilbert Barbee's new Joplin racing park. *State of Missouri v. Robert Boatright, James P. Stewart, et. al*, case no. 3095, Barton County Circuit Court (1903).

43. *Joplin Globe*, September 12, 1903; Carthage *Jasper County Democrat*, September 18, 1903, 5; *Fort Scott (KS) Republican*, September 20, 1903, 1. For more on Black's attempt to act as an intermediary for Boatright, see his testimony in *Waters v. Clay.*

44. *Joplin Globe*, September 16, 1903; *Lamar Democrat*, September 17, 1903, 9; Carthage *Jasper County Democrat*, September 18, 1903, 5; *Lamar Leader*, September 17, 1903, 1, 8; *Waters v. Clay*. Bud Gillett, Ed Ellis, and Bert Bromley had cases pending in Barton County due to a change of venue from Jasper County. Bromley's was dismissed after he died.

45. Little Rock *Arkansas Gazette*, June 4, 1903, 5; June 9, 1903, 8; *St. Louis Republic*, June 9, 1903, 5.

46. Little Rock *Arkansas Gazette*, June 11, 1903, 1; June 12, 1903, 1–2; Carthage *Jasper County Democrat*, June 12, 1903, 5.

47. Little Rock *Arkansas Gazette*, June 12, 1903, 1–2.

48. Little Rock *Arkansas Gazette*, February 11, 1905, 2. Hot Spring County circuit clerk Teresa Pilcher could not find "records that dated back that far." Teresa Pilcher, email message to author, October 21, 2019. Some testimony related to this matter is in *In Re R. H. Williams*. Michael Haggerty was a prominent Irish urban Democratic boss in Memphis. He ran the Old Turf saloon "in the politically important Fourth Ward, which became a base of operations for many gangsters." Haggerty died in near obscurity in 1929. Patrick O'Daniel, *Crusaders, Gangsters, and Whiskey: Prohibition in Memphis* (Jackson: University Press of Mississippi, 2018), 33–36. Haggerty testified Williams sent Boatright to talk to him about hiring a "good criminal lawyer." *In Re R. H. Williams*. Haggerty's saloon is mentioned as a notorious hangout for confidence men in Maurer, *The Big Con*, 163–64. In 1904 Davis and Haggerty were ordered to pay the trustee of Roger H. Williams's estate $12,500. See Arkadelphia *Southern Standard*, June 16, 1904, 1; Little Rock *Arkansas Gazette*, June 2, 1904, 3. See also Little Rock *Arkansas Gazette*, June 2, 1904, 3; June 4, 1903, 3; Little Rock *Arkansas Democrat*, May 26, 1903, 6.

49. Little Rock *Arkansas Gazette*, February 11, 1905, 1, 2. For Woods's own Buckfoot issues, see *Henderson et al. v. Denious*, Eighth Circuit US Court of Appeals, 186 F. 100 (1911).

50. Little Rock *Arkansas Gazette*, February 12, 1905, 1. The following year Davis was in federal court in Memphis after trustee William H. Waters sued him. The first trial ended in a mistrial, the second was decided in favor of Davis, and when Waters appealed, the case was remanded for a new trial. The jury found in favor of Waters and awarded the trustee $5,000 to be divided between the gang's victims. *Nashville American*, December 5, 1906, 6; Little Rock *Arkansas Gazette*, December 5, 1906, 3; June 19, 1907, 1;

June 20, 1907, 7; December 12, 1907, 5. *W. H. Waters (Trustee) v. Davis*, case no. 1495, Transcripts of US District Court Records, 1891–1952, US Circuit Court of Appeals for the Sixth Circuit, Record Group 276, National Archives, Chicago.

51. Little Rock *Arkansas Gazette*, June 20, 1903, 8.
52. Little Rock *Arkansas Gazette*, June 28, 1903, 1.
53. *Louisville Courier-Journal*, June 29, 1903, 7; Little Rock *Arkansas Gazette*, July 25, 1903, 8; *Arkansas Deaths and Burials, 1882–1929; 1945–1963*, Familysearch.org. Williams's obituary stated he was a painter and a member of the Elks, Red Men, and Mystic Circle.
54. Little Rock *Arkansas Gazette*, June 28, 1903, 1; "Roger H. Williams," Kentucky, US, Death Records, 1852–1965, Ancestry.com. Williams was buried in an unmarked grave in pastoral Cave Springs Cemetery in Louisville, Kentucky. *Ardmore (OK) Daily Ardmoreite*, June 30, 1903, 1. The name of Williams's assailant is given as "Doughterty" and "Daughtery." A 1911 report suggested Dougherty killed Williams after the con man reportedly warned officers Dougherty was going to escape. *Hot Springs Sentinel-Record*, March 18, 1911, 4.

CHAPTER 8

1. *Carthage Evening Press*, July 10, 1903, 5; *Joplin News-Herald*, July 10, 1903, 2; *Joplin Globe*, July 11, 1903, 7; Carthage *Jasper County Democrat*, July 14, 1903, 4.
2. *Carthage Evening Press*, July 10, 1903, 5; *Joplin News-Herald*, July 10, 1903, 2; *Joplin Globe*, July 11, 1903, 7; Carthage *Jasper County Democrat*, July 14, 1903, 4. The location was called "Lowery's Crossing" and "Lowrie's" in contemporary news accounts. Flax Pool was also called "Flax Pond" and the stream was also referred to as "Miller's Creek."
3. *Joplin Globe*, July 11, 1903, 7; Carthage *Jasper County News*, July 14, 1903, 4. Oscar Gammon is sometimes referred to as Lee Gammon.
4. *Joplin News-Herald*, July 10, 1903, 2.
5. *Joplin News-Herald*, July 10, 1903, 2, and July 12, 1903, 5; *Webb City Sentinel*, July 11, 1903, 4; Carthage *Jasper County News*, July 14, 1903, 4. Joplin police officer Ed Portley, head of the Joplin Eagles, made the arrangements. Bromley left behind his mother and a widow, but no children. *Joplin Globe*, July 11, 1903, 7.
6. *Joplin News-Herald*, July 22, 1903, 2.
7. *Joplin News-Herald*, July 24, 1903, 6.
8. *Joplin Globe*, July 24, 1903, 7.
9. *Joplin Globe*, July 24, 1903, 7. Chenoweth was presumably asked because Bromley may have had burial insurance through the Eagles.

10. *Kansas City World* quoted in *Mt. Vernon Lawrence Chieftain*, August 6, 1903, 1.

11. Little Rock *Arkansas Democrat*, July 4, 1904, 3. See *US v. George Ryan, et al.*, case no. 2421, US District Court, Eastern District of Arkansas, Western (Little Rock) Division (April 1903), 123 Fed. 634. Twenty-nine men—George Ryan, Robert Boatright, George Thompson, Lucius Hindman, Irven E. Johnson, Robert E. L. Goddard, Roger H. Williams, Harry Wasser, George Burns, Ben Ansel, Eddie Morris, Ed Clark, Newt Nelson, C. F. Landis, W. J. Ryan, Ed Ellis, Allis, Black, Stansbury, Ira Pomeroy, Bert Bromley, William "Jack" Massey, Hovey H. Tislow, William H. Rodgers, Ashmore, Edwards, H. W. Kiplinger, Swain Llewellyn, and Ben Teller—were named in the indictment.

12. *Joplin News-Herald*, August 26, 1903, 2; *Carthage Evening Press*, August 27, 1903, 5. This event did occur; see *In re Robert Boatright and Ed E. Ellis*. John Halliburton, as early as 1901, "was offered employment from this gang that would have brought him a great deal more money than he could ever hope to receive from prosecuting them, and that he refused the employment, solely on the grounds, that he would not represent thieves." Carthage *Jasper County Democrat*, September 4, 1903, 3. For Arthur E. Spencer, see Sidney Corning Eastman, *The Bankruptcy Law Annotated Being the National Bankruptcy Act of 1898 as Amended February 5, 1903* (Chicago: T. H. Flood & Co., 1903).

13. Carthage *Jasper County Democrat*, September 4, 1903, 3; *Joplin News-Herald*, August 26, 1903; Friedman, "Inflation Calculator."

14. Carthage *Jasper County Democrat*, September 4, 1903, 3.

15. *Joplin Globe*, December 8, 1903, 3.

16. Carthage *Jasper County Democrat*, November 3, 1903, 1; *Kansas City Journal* quoted in *Plattsburg (MO) Leader*, November 6, 1903, 4.

17. *Webb City Sentinel*, December 12, 1903, 1.

18. *Joplin Globe*, December 16, 1903, 1.

19. *Waters v. Clay*. Lory was said to be so crooked "he could be utilized if ossified as an Archimedean screw." He allegedly swindled investors—including Lindley—out of $300,000. See *The Yukon Sun (Dawson, Yukon Territory)*, March 28, 1903; *Decatur (IL) Daily Herald*, January 2, 1903, 8.

20. *Joplin Globe*, December 19, 1903, 2; Carthage *Jasper County News*, December 22, 1903, 3. See also *Webb City Sentinel*, December 19, 1903, 1. Friedman, "Inflation Calculator."

21. *Joplin Globe*, December 20, 1903, 1.

22. *Joplin Globe*, December 24, 1903, 2.

23. *Joplin Globe*, December 31, 1903, 5.

24. *Galveston (TX) Daily News*, April 16, 1904, 5; *Houston (TX) Daily Post*, April 6, 1908, 9. *US v. I. E. Johnson*, US District Court for the Eastern

District of Texas, Beaumont, Record Group 21, National Archives, Fort Worth, Texas.

25. Little Rock *Arkansas Democrat*, September 21, 1904, 7; Little Rock *Arkansas Gazette*, September 21, 1904, 2.

26. Little Rock *Arkansas Gazette*, January 12, 1905, 2.

27. *Carthage Evening Press*, May 26, 1904, 2.

28. *Joplin Globe*, May 26, 1904, 2; May 29, 1904, 7; *Webb City Register*, May 25, 1904, 3; *Carthage Evening Press*, May 26, 1904, 2.

29. *Joplin Globe*, May 29, 1904, 7.

30. *Webb City Register*, May 26, 1904, 1.

31. The court-appointed administrator of Boatright's estate in Jackson County stated Boatright's personal property consisted of a bedroom set, steamer trunk, stopwatch, diamond ring, photograph camera ($50), Kodak camera ($7), gymnasium set, Smith Premier typewriter and desk, and revolver. See Robert Boatright, case no. K7168, Jackson County, Missouri, Probate Court Record, Jackson County, Missouri.

32. *St. Louis Post-Dispatch*, May 27, 1904, 4. This article provides a physical description of Boatright. *Joplin Globe*, May 29, 1904, 7. Robert Boatright, Jackson County, Missouri, "Missouri, Death Records, 1850–1931," Ancestry.com. The reference to his wife appears in *Joplin Globe*, May 27, 1904.

33. *Joplin Globe*, May 29, 1904, 7; May 31, 1904, 7. The *Globe* remarked Boatright would be remembered as a man of "splendid physical development."

34. *Carthage Evening Press*, May 31, 1904, 3.

35. *Joplin Globe*, May 31, 1904, 7.

36. *Carthage Evening Press*, May 31, 1904, 3.

37. *Joplin Globe*, May 31, 1904, 7. Boatright's pallbearers were Sam Jones (saloonkeeper), Charles Goatley (saloonkeeper), Dave Springs (mine superintendent), B. Dye, Burrell C. Roberson (livery operator), Silas O. "Butch" Gammon (gambler), William Fahrman (saloonkeeper), and A. C. Crandall. The Webb City Eagle Aerie No. 426 posted a notice stating Robert Boatright was a member of Joplin Eagle Aerie No. 152. See *Webb City Register*, May 27, 1904, 2.

38. *Carthage Evening Press*, May 31, 1904, 3.

39. *Carthage Evening Press*, May 31, 1904, 3.

40. *Kansas City Star*, May 31, 1904, 1. James Britton Gantt (1845–1912) was a graduate of the University of Virginia School of Law and former partner of US Senator George Graham Vest. *Proceedings of the Thirtieth Annual Meeting of the Missouri Bar Association Held at St. Louis, Missouri* (Kansas City: F. P. Burnap Stationery and Printing Co., 1913), 173–74.

41. *Fort Smith (AR) Times*, May 27, 1904, 1; Little Rock *Arkansas Democrat*, May 27, 1904, 1. Varner's name does not appear in records associated with the gang. Mitchell's affiliation is unknown. See Little Rock *Arkansas Democrat*,

June 3, 1904, 1. Varner was acquitted of murder charges in New Harmony, Indiana. *Logansport (IN) Pharos-Tribune*, February 16, 1894, 1. David Maurer defined the wire scheme thusly: "A big-con game in which the insideman (passing as a Western Union official) convinces the mark that he can delay the race results going to the bookmakers long enough for the mark to place a bet after the race is run. The roper makes a mistake, and the mark loses." *Language of the Underworld* (Lexington: University Press of Kentucky, 1981), 369.

42. *Webb City Register*, October 1, 1904, 1; October 11, 1904, 1; Draper, *True Stories of Peculiar People*, 26. Webb City tailor Charley Sutherland installed the safe in his shop. The *Register* may have been recounting the events reported in the *Webb City Sentinel*, June 7, 1902, 2 and the Carthage *Jasper County News*, June 10, 1902, 3. Manufactured by the Mosler Safe Company, the back featured "an extension of about a foot which contained an opening into the safe. The extension fitted into a wall, and the face opened into another room, making the contents of the safe accessible from either room." *Joplin News-Herald*, March 19, 1906.

43. *Webb City Register*, September 23, 1907, 1.

44. Maurer, *The Big Con*, 197. Cameron Kunkel (1861–1908) worked for Bat Masterson in Dodge City. Masterson convinced him to change his name to Jones because Kunkel was "too tame for a cowboy gambler." *Kansas City Star*, April 29, 1908, 2; *Topeka Daily State Journal*, April 28, 1908, 8; *Kansas City Journal*, reprinted in the *New Orleans Times-Picayune*, August 29, 1908, 8. For more on Jones, see Joseph G. Rosa, *The Age of the Gunfighter: Men and Weapons on the Frontier, 1840–1900* (Norman: University of Oklahoma Press, 2007), 156. Kunkel's name is sometimes spelled "Kunkle." Jones is not mentioned in accounts of Boatright's death. He escorted Boatright's purported wife, Mary "Polly" Boatright, to a Kansas City bank to withdraw money. See Minerva Thompson's testimony in *In re Robert Boatright and Ed E. Ellis*. John Mabray testified Conk Jones gave him money to "start in the business" in Council Bluffs, Iowa, and repaid him $6,000 or $7,000. *Des Moines Tribune*, December 20, 1911, 12.

45. Draper, *True Stories of Peculiar People*, 26. No will could be located for Robert Boatright in Jasper County, Missouri. Boatright's probate record, filed in 1911, is at the Jasper County Records Center in Carthage.

CHAPTER 9

1. *Webb City Register*, January 23, 1905; January 24, 1905. See Warrant on Information for a Misdemeanor, *State of Missouri v. Ed Ellis*, Jasper County Circuit Court (January 1905), Jasper County Records Center. Ellis's bondsmen were Ben Ensing and William Fahrman.

2. Little Rock *Arkansas Democrat*, September 20, 1905, reprinted from the *Hot Springs News*.

3. When Wasser's wife filed in 1903, she alleged he frequently came home drunk, abused her, and consorted with prostitutes. See Carthage *Jasper County Democrat*, March 27, 1903, 5; *Webb City Register*, March 8, 1905, 1.

4. Little Rock *Arkansas Democrat*, October 2, 1905, 1; *Chicago Inter Ocean*, September 29, 1905, 12; *Decatur (IL) Herald*, October 1, 1905, 2; *Davenport (IA) Times*, October 3, 1905, 1; *Gibson City (IL) Courier*, November 10, 1905, 2; Springfield *Illinois State Journal*, September 30, 1905, 5; November 4, 1905, 1; *Illinois State Register*, October 2, 1905. There are too many coincidences not to believe Wasser and Price are the same man. Wasser's reformatory record states he was born October 10, 1876, to Phillip and Carrie (Manker) Wasser. Harry Price listed Philip and Carrie as his parents on his 1912 Henrico County, Virginia, marriage certificate. Price's World War I draft card provides the same date of birth. His death certificate lists his father's name as "Phillip Price" and his birthplace as Illinois like Wasser. "Harry L. Price," Virginia, Select Marriages, 1785–1940; "Harry Lewis Price," US World War I Draft Registration Cards, 1917–1918; "Harry Lewis Price," Virginia Death Records, 1912–2014; 1880 US Census, Girard, Crawford County, Kansas, Ancestry.com. Whether Wasser remained out of trouble is unknown, but he may have gone straight because his skills were not as versatile. Buckfoot sprinter Dick Beatte had also headed to Portland, Oregon; see Newton *Evening Kansan-Republican*, April 6, 1905, 1.

5. Little Rock *Arkansas Democrat*, March 23, 1907, 6. Roger Williams was murdered, and the Honey Grove Kid's conviction was reversed on appeal to the Arkansas Supreme Court; only Irven Johnson was convicted.

6. *Galveston (TX) Daily News*, April 16, 1904, 5; *Houston (TX) Daily Post*, April 6, 1908, 9. *US v. I. E. Johnson.*

7. For Johnson's federal prison record, see "J. E. Johnson," Atlanta Federal Penitentiary Case Files, National Archives, Atlanta.

8. "J. E. Johnson," Atlanta Federal Penitentiary Case Files, National Archives, Atlanta.

9. Johnson remained in the Atlanta federal penitentiary until July 7, 1909, thereby missing the opportunity to work with John Mabray. He promoted himself as "The noted Rupture specialist, Inventor of Ideal Surgical Appliances." See *Waxahachie (TX) Daily Light*, September 20, 1927, 8. "Irven E. Johnson," 1910 US Census, Mineral Wells, Palo Pinto County, Texas, "Dr. Irven Edmund Johnson," Texas, Death Certificates, 1903–1982, Ancestry.com.

10. *Carthage Evening Press*, June 23, 1905, 4.

11. *Carthage Evening Press*, June 23, 1905, 4.

12. *Webb City Sentinel*, July 26, 1905, 1; *Joplin Globe*, February 12, 1907, 10; *St. Louis Globe-Democrat*, April 2, 1908, 5. See *W. H. Waters, Trustee, Robert Boatright, Bankrupt v. Mary E. Rice and Priscilla Boatright*, Missouri

Supreme Court (1910), Jasper County Records Center. *Webb City Register*, December 12, 1908, 1. See *W. H. Waters v. W. L. Palmer, Daisy Stansbury, and F. B. Timmons* (interpleaded with Oren W. Ainsworth), Jasper County Circuit Court (1909), Jasper County Records Center.

13. *Waters v. Clay* and *In Re Robert Boatright and Ed E. Ellis. Kansas City Star*, March 29, 1905, 5. New Yorker Charles F. Amidon (1856–1937) was appointed to the US District Court for the District of North Dakota in 1896.

14. *Kansas City Star*, March 31, 1905, 16; *Kansas City Journal*, March 29, 1905, 12; Carthage *Jasper County Democrat*, April 4, 1905, 7; Carthage *Jasper County Democrat*, April 4, 1905, 7; *Joplin Globe*, March 29, 1905. Multiple witnesses, including Mary "Polly" Thompson's mother, stated they did not know if the couple was married; Boatright's mother Priscilla said they were not married. See *Waters v. Clay*. Priscilla Boatright's housekeeper, Ola McWhirt, was allegedly Boatright's Webb City "concubine." See testimony of Mary Rice, *In Re R. H. Williams*.

15. *Kansas City Star*, March 31, 1905, 16; *Kansas City Journal*, March 29, 1905, 12; Carthage *Jasper County Democrat*, April 4, 1905, 7; Carthage *Jasper County Democrat*, April 4, 1905, 7; *Joplin Globe*, March 29, 1905. Windsor is located across from Detroit, Michigan. No marriage record for Robert Boatright and Mary "Polly" Thompson has been located; the couple may have had a common-law marriage. In 1905 the Senate Club was under Thomas J. Thompson's ownership. *1905 Hoye's Kansas City Directory* (Kansas City: Hoye Directory Co., 1905). Friedman, "Inflation Calculator."

16. For depositions taken in September 1904, see *In re Robert Boatright and Ed E. Ellis*, Joplin Bankruptcy Case Files, US District Court for the Southwestern (Joplin) Division of the Western District of Missouri, Record Group 21, National Archives, Kansas City. Rice's uncle stated prior to joining the Buckfoot Gang that Rice "had a petrified man and traveled with it on exhibition." Victim John Black said Boatright told him Rice was his secretary because he was an "expert accountant." See *Waters v. Clay*.

17. *In re Robert Boatright and Ed E. Ellis*. The mine was called the Abbey Coal and Mining Company. Frank Rice's death certificate indicates he was a retired coal operator. "Frank H. Rice," Illinois, US, Death and Stillbirths Index, 1916–1947, Ancestry.com.

18. *In re Robert Boatright and Ed E. Ellis*.

19. For depositions taken in September 1904, see *In re Robert Boatright and Ed E. Ellis*.

20. *Waters v. Clay*, case no. 59, US District Court, Southwestern (Joplin) Division of the Western District of Missouri, Bankruptcy Act of 1898 Case Files, Record Group 21, National Archives, Kansas City.

21. *Waters v. Clay*. Two years later, it was reported Boatright had $100,000 in cash and jewelry on his person when he died and had deposited $40,000 in

Canada. In 1904 Clay and Boatright's mother made several bank withdrawals: $4,000 from a Kansas City bank, $10,000 from the Canadian bank, and $15,550 from the Bank of Neosho. The court found Clay and Priscilla Boatright purchased $1,000 of real estate in Webb City and that Clay separately made $3,225 in real estate purchases. He loaned Newton County residents $2,500, taking mortgages as security. Altogether the pair spent $17,575. McPherson held them jointly liable and ordered them to transfer the amount to the trustee as well as Robert Boatright's diamond ring, diamond stud, and gold watch. *Webb City Register*, August 21, 1907, 2.

22. *Waters v. Clay.* On one occasion Currey and another attorney came to blows. When judge and future Missouri attorney general Edward Crow entered the courtroom, the two men had blood streaming down their faces. Crow asked attorney Al Thomas who started the trouble. Thomas meekly responded, "I couldn't say, your Honor, I was under the table." Flanigan, *The First One Hundred Years of the Jasper County Circuit Court*, 14.

23. *Joplin Globe*, April 12, 1905, 8. Judge Henry Pepper represented Clay; Samuel McReynolds and Currey represented creditors. See *Waters v. Clay*.

24. *Waters v. Clay.* Boatright's Jackson County, Missouri, probate record states he died intestate. Although Priscilla Boatright denied under oath Thompson was married to her son, the two women signed a document—in which Polly was identified as Boatright's wife—waiving their claims to administer his estate. See Robert Boatright, case no. K7168, Jackson County, Missouri, Probate Court Record, Jackson County, Missouri.

25. See *Waters v. Clay.* Clay explained Boatright called the fixed athletic contests "tricks." One thousand dollars in 1903 would be equivalent to $33,410 in 2022. Friedman, "Inflation Calculator."

26. *Waters v. Clay.*

27. *In re Robert Boatright and Ed E. Ellis.* Victims William Kyle, Frank Youmans, and Charles Sievert were present.

28. *In re Robert Boatright and Ed E. Ellis.*

29. *In re Robert Boatright and Ed E. Ellis.*

30. Black moved to Texas where he died in 1936. *Davenport (IA) Quad-City Times*, September 25, 1906, 2, and December 28, 1906, 5. "John Robert Black," Texas, Death Certificates, 1903–1982, Ancestry.com.

31. Opinion of Judge Smith McPherson in *Waters v. Clay.*

32. *Fort Scott (KS) Evening Tribune and Monitor*, April 12, 1907, 5. Friedman, "Inflation Calculator." For Barbee, see *Clay v. Waters*, US Circuit Court of Appeals for the Eighth Circuit, Record Group 21, National Archives, Kansas City. Judge John Finis Philips threatened Clay with ten months in jail for contempt of court if he did not turn over property that belonged to the trustee. See *St. Louis Globe-Democrat*, June 16, 1909, 1.

33. *In the Matter of the Estate of Robert Boatright*, Jasper County, Missouri, Probate Court (1910), Jasper County Records Center.

34. *Fort Scott (KS) Daily Tribune and Monitor*, June 16, 1905, 5.

35. *Joplin News-Herald*, August 22, 1905, 1; August 23, 1905, 1, 5; *Joplin News-Herald*, January 14, 1907, 1; *Joplin Globe*, January 18, 1907, 1. Defendants in *Pittman v. Joplin Savings Bank* petitioned to have the depositions suppressed in their cases; see *Joplin News-Herald*, August 22, 1905. Judge Smith McPherson (1848–1915) was a graduate of the University of Iowa College of Law. He served as Iowa's ninth attorney general from 1881 to 1885, followed by one term in the US House of Representatives. Appointed to the federal bench in 1900, he served until his death in 1915.

36. *Joplin Globe*, August 25, 1905, 5.

37. *Webb City Sentinel*, August 26, 1905, 1; *Fort Scott (KS) Tribune and the Fort Scott Monitor*, August 26, 1905, 1. The case was appealed to the Eighth Circuit Court of Appeals; see *Exchange Bank et al. v. Moss; Exchange Bank v. Davis,* US Circuit Court of Appeals for the Eighth Circuit (1906), National Archives, Kansas City; *Kansas City Star*, November 26, 1906, 1.

38. Socolofsky, *Kansas Governors*, 156–57. For an anti-Davis Buckfoot ad, see the *Fort Scott (KS) Republican*, November 1, 1906, 3.

39. *Joplin Globe*, June 22, 1906, 1; *Fort Scott (KS) Semi-Weekly Tribune and Monitor*, January 30, 1907, 4. The suits were brought by Robert Hobbs, Henry Wright, Jonathan Davis, and Stephen Moss. *Stewart et al. v. Wright* was appealed to the US Supreme Court, but the court did not hear the case. *Stewart et al. v. Wright*, 203 US 590 (1906).

40. *Joplin News-Herald*, April 1, 1906, 1. Exchange Bank of Webb City, Charter No. 572, box 13, folder 23, Bank Charters, Record Group 132, Missouri State Archives. This case is *R. E. Hobbs v. Exchange Bank and J. P. Stewart.*

41. *Joplin Globe*, December 28, 1906; *Joplin Globe*, February 18, 1912, 1; *Joplin News-Herald*, February 18, 1912, 6. The federal court docket for 1907 included four separate Buckfoot cases: *John I. Pittman v. Joplin Savings Bank*; *Bascom O'Hair v. Exchange Bank of Webb City*; *Henry Cohn v. Exchange Bank of Webb City*; and *Merwin B. Bangs v. Joseph C. Stewart, et al. Joplin News-Herald*, January 11, 1907, 1. Merwin Bangs filed suit in federal court against the Stewarts and the Exchange Bank for $5,000; see *Joplin News-Herald*, August 24, 1906, 1.

42. *Joplin News-Herald*, May 28, 1906, 1; *Joplin News-Herald*, January 23, 1907, 1.

43. *Webb City Register*, March 6, 1908, 2; January 25, 1910, 1. One woman "died of grief at losing $350." The bank was founded with capital stock of $10,000 on March 27, 1900. Missouri State Archives, Bank Charters, Record Group 132, box 26, folder 4, #1052½. James Stewart claimed in *R. E. Hobbs v. Exchange Bank of Webb City and J. P. Stewart* the bank did not

handle any drafts from Boatright or the gang after November 1901. This may have been because, as Joseph Stewart testified, the bank was garnished in the Bruce Reger and Guy Berger cases. James Stewart insinuated after that the gang had taken their business to the Joplin Savings Bank. For failure to convict Layne, see *Joplin News-Herald*, January 12, 1911, 7; *Joplin Daily Globe*, January 11, 1911, 9.

44. *Webb City Register*, April 3, 1910, 5.

45. *Los Angeles Herald*, July 8, 1910, 5. A sister, Abigail Gray, lived in Los Angeles; this may be why she moved to California.

46. Both gave their residence as Chicago. Fargo's occupation was theatrical man. Robert L. Fargo and Mary H. Thompson Boatright, Michigan, US, Marriage Records, 1867–1952, Ancestry.com.

47. See Mary H. Fargo's probate file for a list of property; the Olympic was located at 523 South Main in Los Angeles. "Mary H. Thompson Fargo," case number P016944, box 4844, location 102463, Los Angeles County Archives and Records Center, Los Angeles, California. Robert was identified in local papers as part owner of the Olympic—not Mary. After years of decline, the theater enjoyed a resurgence after her death. *Los Angeles Herald*, November 14, 1909, 10. Friedman "Inflation Calculator."

48. "Mary H. Fargo," California Death Certificate, Los Angles, Los Angeles County, California. The informant was Robert L. Fargo. Only one Robert Fargo appears in the 1910 US Census in Los Angeles; he is listed as a married forty-one-year-old New Yorker living in a boarding house; no wife is listed. *Los Angeles Times*, July 12, 1910, 16; August 24, 1910, 18. Elmwood Cemetery Records for Ann Thompson family, Lot 10, Block 10 and individual interment records for George R. Thompson and Mary Thompson Fargo. She was buried in the family plot. George R. Thompson, a member of the Buckfoot Gang, died on October 26, 1941, in Los Angeles, California. *Records of Elmwood Cemetery, Kansas City, MO* (Kansas City: The Heart of America Genealogical Society, 1987), 582–83.

49. *Neosho Daily Democrat*, May 23, 1913, 1, "George R. Clay," Missouri Death Certificate Database, https://s1.sos.mo.gov/records/Archives/ArchivesMvc /DeathCertificates/; *Joplin Globe*, June 16, 1909, 1; April 19, 1910, 2; June 27, 1909, 1. Clay's involvement with the Buckfoot Gang made him a pariah; see *Joplin News-Herald*, November 7, 1910, 12. For Judge McPherson suggesting Clay drop his appeals to purge his contempt record, see *Joplin News-Herald*, July 1, 1910, 2. For the dismissals, see *W. H. Waters v. W. L. Palmer, Daisy Stansbury, and F. B. Timmons* and *W. H. Waters, Trustee, Robert Boatright, Bankrupt v. Mary E. Rice and Priscilla Boatright*, Missouri Supreme Court, April Term 1910, Jasper County Records Center; copy also available from the Missouri State Archives.

50. *Kansas City Star*, April 24, 1928; *Joplin Globe*, April 25, 1928, 4. George Edgar Booth (1861–1928) partnered with his brother-in-law John W. Flanigan before going solo. He later practiced in St. Louis and Kansas City.

51. *Webb City Sentinel*, September 8, 1921, 1; *Joplin News-Herald*, September 9, 1921, 2.

52. *Webb City Register*, May 18, 1908, 1; *Joplin Globe*, November 14, 1911, 7.

53. *Webb City Register*, February 5, 1910, 1. Livingston, *A History of Jasper County, Missouri, and Its People*, 1:438. Sam Jones (1853–1917) had been associated with Charley Parker in mining operations and was the former owner of the Sam Jones Saloon at 103 North Allen Street in Webb City. *Joplin Globe*, June 2, 1917, 7; *Joplin News-Herald*, June 2, 1917, 8; "Sam Jones," Missouri Death Certificate Database, https://s1.sos.mo.gov/records/Archives/ArchivesMvc/DeathCertificates/.

54. *Webb City Register*, March 14, 1910, 4. The establishment was named after proprietors William "Bill" Fahrman and Ben Ensing.

55. On Benton, see *Carthage Evening Press*, August 25, 1904, 2; *Springfield Leader*, October 21, 1924, 4; *Webb City Register*, November 1, 1904; *Sarcoxie Record*, January 12, 1922, 4. For Thomas Hart Benton, see Benton, *An Artist in America*, 18–19.

56. *Joplin Globe*, May 27, 1906, 1. Howard left to serve as managing editor of the *Columbia (OH) Sun*. He later worked at the *St. Louis Republic*, the Oklahoma City *Daily Oklahoman*, and the *St. Louis Post-Dispatch* where he won the 1940 Pulitzer Prize in Editorial Writing. See *St. Louis Post-Dispatch*, February 12, 1941, 1, 4.

57. *Joplin News-Herald*, August 10, 1906, 1. Later that year Barbee punched elderly Judge William B. Halyard for saying Barbee did "Joplin more harm than any other influence in the city." *Joplin News-Herald*, October 31, 1906, 1; November 1, 1906, 1; *Joplin Globe*, November 1, 1906, 1, 2.

58. Edward S. Hosmer and his business partner sold the *Joplin News-Herald* to a stock company headed by M. W. Hutchinson of Texas. *Buffalo (NY) Evening News*, April 1, 1903, 8. Perlee Ellis "P. E." Burton (1875–1953) purchased the *News-Herald* in 1905 and sold it in 1921. The *Globe*'s staff drank at the House of Lords; Burton's staff drank at Jim Madeira's. *Editor & Publisher*, 55, no. 43 (March 24, 1923): 22. *Joplin Globe*, May 1, 1932, 20. *St. Louis Post-Dispatch*, February 28, 1953, 2B. "Perlee Ellis Burton," Missouri Death Certificate Database, https://s1.sos.mo.gov/records/Archives/ArchivesMvc/DeathCertificates/.

59. *Joplin Globe*, September 14, 1907, 1, 2.

60. *Joplin Globe*, September 14, 1907, 1.

61. *Joplin News-Herald*, September 14, 1907, 1. Saighmanism referred to the late gambler Daniel Saighman, who ran a club room in the House of Lords.

62. *Joplin News-Herald*, September 15, 1907, 1.

63. *Joplin Morning Tribune*, January 17, 1913, 1.

64. *Chillicothe (MO) Constitution-Tribune*, January 8, 1910; *Joplin News-Herald*, February 2, 1908, 1; *Joplin Globe*, March 17, 1908, 1. The *Constitution-Tribune* claimed after the *News-Herald* was dynamited, the House of Lords was "reduced to the harmlessness of a country hotel," gambling joints were raided, liquor laws enforced, and a local option election was held. "With death-dealing velocity came one thunderclap after another out of the clear sky of aroused public conscience and Boss Gib bethought himself to seek shelter from the wrath of a determined public sentiment."

65. *Carthage Evening Press*, October 20, 1924, 8; Charles A. King, *Ottaway Newspapers: The First 50 Years* (Campbell Hall, NY: Ottaway Newspapers, 1986), 248–49. The account of Barbee losing the *Globe* was written by Arthur Aull of the *Lamar Democrat*. There are no extant copies of the *Joplin American*. In 1911 Barbee and Rogers were in court regarding the passageway Barbee built years earlier connecting the *Globe* building to the House of Lords. See the *Joplin Morning Tribune*, December 15, 1911, 1; *Joplin Globe Publishing Company v. Gilbert Barbee*, case no. 9956, Jasper County Circuit Court (1912), Jasper County Records Center. For more on the Southwest Missouri Electric Railway Company, see Harry C. Hood Sr., *The Southwest Missouri Railroad* (n.p.: Hood, 1975); *Joplin Globe*, June 17, 1973, D1. It was alleged that after a young boy was killed by a Southwest Missouri Electric Railway Company car, Barbee published a headline accusing Rogers of murder and sparked animosity between the two. The headline did not accuse Rogers of murder; see "Fenderless Car Slaughters Babe; Joplin Boy Mangled at Neosho," *Joplin Globe*, May 25, 1906, 1. The company was found liable for the boy's death. *Joplin Globe*, May 26, 1906, 2.

66. *Joplin Morning Tribune*, March 3, 1912.

67. *Joplin Globe*, February 23, 1918; *Neosho Times*, August 30, 1923.

68. *St. Louis Post-Dispatch*, October 18, 1924. Bart Howard's obituary for Barbee reveals much about the man and his personality by someone who knew him well.

69. *St. Louis Post-Dispatch*, July 26, 1916, 4.

70. *Joplin Globe*, October 18, 1924, 1; *Joplin News-Herald*, October 18, 1924, 1. Howard recalled when the Eight Hour bill was before the state legislature, mine owners expressed their displeasure to Barbee. He responded, "Gentlemen, when a man's done eight hours' work underground he's done a hell of a big day's work." Barbee declared his support for the bill soon after in the *Globe*. *St. Louis Post-Dispatch*, October 18, 1924, 11.

71. *Joplin Globe*, January 8, 1922, 1. The House of Lords remains fixed in local memory. Evelyn Milligan Jones recounted an apocryphal story from World

War I when a sailor, originally from Joplin, was asked by a bartender in Panama, "Is the House of Lords still running?" Engineers from the Tri-State Mining District, while traveling in Bolivia and Peru, were queried about the bar. Suffragist Emily Newell Blair recalled, "Waiters in New York, California, and Florida have greeted me by name and when I have expressed surprise have explained that they had waited on me in the House of Lords." Laas, *Bridging Two Eras*, 80.

72. *Joplin Globe*, August 20, 1964, 29.

CHAPTER 10

1. *Kansas City Star*, May 27, 1905, 2.
2. Nelson's creditors later filed involuntary bankruptcy proceedings in federal court after learning of his loss. *Joplin News-Herald*, October 28, 1907, 2; *Topeka Daily Capital*, January 7, 1908, 2. The same month Nelson was skinned, Walter Nolan, Clarence Class, William Flemming, Joseph "Yellow Kid" Weil, and other confidence men associated with John Mabray were accused of swindling former Chicago alderman Thomas Little on a fixed prizefight. See *Chicago Inter Ocean*, October 19, 1907, 3; October 31, 1907, 3. For a similar match and accusations, see *Rock Island (IL) Argus*, April 16, 1908, 6.
3. Steinbaugh lived near Pratt, Kansas. *Topeka State Journal*, February 15, 1908, 3; February 17, 1908, 2; *Wellington (KS) Daily News*, February 14, 1908, 1.
4. "Like the Buckfoot Gang," *Kansas City Star*, March 15, 1908, 4A. The gang skinned so many marks on wrestling matches in New Orleans that they "made wrestling unpopular." Little Rock *Arkansas Democrat*, February 23, 1909, 3; February 24, 1909, 1–7. Friedman, "Inflation Calculator."
5. *Lincoln (NE) Star*, October 10, 1908, 1; *Cedar Rapids Evening Gazette*, December 1, 1908, 10.
6. *Cedar Rapids Evening Gazette*, December 1, 1908, 10; *Des Moines Register and Leader*, November 30, 1908, 10; *Davenport (IA) Quad-City Times*, December 20, 1911, 12.
7. Council Bluffs *Daily Nonpareil*, October 13, 1908, 5; November 15, 1908, 3. These stories rattled the gang. Monte McCall wrote Isador Warner, "Some of the newspapers of the Bluffs had been bad until yesterday. But it is O.K. now." J. J. Hawkins, *Mabray and the Mikes* (Little Rock, AR: Democrat Print & Litho. Co., 1910), 67; text of the letter is also in *US v. John C. Mabray, et al.*, Indictment, US District Court for the District of Nebraska, Omaha Division, Admiralty and Criminal Case Files, 1867–1911, Docket "P" Cases, box 3, case no. 140, Record Group 21, National Archives, Kansas City. For the office's contents, see interview with janitor Ed Pierce in Council Bluffs *Daily Nonpareil*, February 25, 1909, 1.
8. *Evening Nonpareil*, February 10, 1909, 1.

9. For Walter's description, see *Evening Nonpareil*, March 1, 1909, 5. Their horses were shod by blacksmith Charles Gregory, who Boatright had swindled a few years earlier. He was not asked about the Buckfoot Gang. *Evening Nonpareil*, February 25, 1909, 1; March 2, 1909, 1.

10. *Nonpareil*, July 9, 1952, 3; "Omaha, Nebr.," *The Postal Record* 24, no. 1 (January 1911): 27.

11. Craft was one of John Mabray's aliases. Hawkins, *Mabray and the Mikes*, 1–122. John Makris offers a different account. He claims an Omaha physician who rented Post Office Box 4 mistakenly received a letter intended for the gang's post office box. He turned it over to the Council Bluffs postmaster who then alerted Swenson. The letter, sent from Seattle, concerned a visit to the city by John Cavanaugh, who was trying to locate men who swindled him in New Orleans. Swenson contacted Cavanaugh who agreed to cooperate. See John Makris, *The Silent Investigators: The Great Untold Story of the United States Postal Inspection Service* (New York: E. P. Dutton & Co., 1959), 118–19.

12. J. J. Hawkins, *Mabray and the Mikes* (Little Rock, AR: Democrat Print & Litho. Co., 1910) 1–122; *Evening Tribune* (Des Moines), April 26, 1909, 2. John Makris states Swenson determined the gang had a "regular system of protection payments at every point where operations were started." He asserted it would have been impossible for an "efficient police department" to have overlooked the gang's operations. Makris, *The Silent Investigators*, 120. *US v. George Ryan, et al.*, case no. 2421, April Term 1903, US District Court for the Western (Little Rock) Division of the Eastern District of Arkansas (123 Fed. 634). The men who served as references for Mabray's application for the gang's Omaha post office box were William "Billy" Nesselhous and Charles Lewis; Lewis ran the Orpheum Saloon. Nesselhous was a lieutenant of Omaha political boss Tom Dennison. See *US v. John C. Mabray, et al.*, Indictment (Omaha); John Kyle Davis, "The Gray Wolf: Tom Dennison of Omaha," *Nebraska History* 58 (1977): 25–26, Orville D. Menard, *River City Empire: Tom Dennison's Omaha* (Lincoln, NE: Bison Books, 2013). For Council Bluffs indictment, see *US v. John C. Mabray, et al.*, US District Court for the Southern District of Iowa, Western Division, Council Bluffs, Iowa, Criminal Cases 1874–1915, Record Group 21, National Archives, Kansas City.

13. Hawkins, *Mabray and the Mikes*, 43. Mabray's file has extensive correspondence between Temple and US attorney general Wickersham regarding this case; see Record Group 60, Department of Justice, A1/Entry 112: Straight Numerical File, 1904–1937: File # 145885, National Archives, College Park; hereafter cited as John C. Mabray file, US DOJ.

14. Hawkins, *Mabray and the Mikes*, 43. *List of United States Judges, Attorneys, and Marshals* compiled by the Appointment Clerk (Washington,

DC: GPO, 1908), 19. Canadian Samuel Sutor (1864–1920) ran the Endion Hotel in Cass Lake, Minnesota. See "Samuel Sutor," 1910 US Census, Cass Lake, Cass County, Minnesota; 1920 US Census, Bellingham, Whatcom County, Washington; *Pioneer* (Bemidji, MN), November 4, 1910, 1; *Chilliwack Progress* (Chilliwack, British Columbia), July 1, 1920, 4; Washington, US, Select Death Certificates, 1907–1960, Ancestry.com.

15. Hawkins, *Mabray and the Mikes*, chapter 5. Hawkins's and Makris's accounts are slightly dissimilar; I have sought, in conjunction with contemporary press accounts, to present a clear timeline of events.

16. Little Rock *Arkansas Gazette*, February 24, 1909, 1; Little Rock *Arkansas Democrat*, February 25, 1909, 7; *Kansas City Star*, March 7, 1909, 4A.

17. Hawkins, *Mabray and the Mikes*, chapters 3–4; specifically, 33 and 36–37.

18. Hawkins, *Mabray and the Mikes*, 43–45, 48–49; Makris, *The Silent Investigators*, 122.

19. Hawkins, *Mabray and the Mikes*, chapter 5; Little Rock *Arkansas Democrat*, February 23, 1909, 3; February 24, 1909, 1–7; Little Rock *Arkansas Gazette*, February 24, 1909, 1.

20. Hawkins, *Mabray and the Mikes*, 43–45, 48–49; Makris, *The Silent Investigators*, 122; *List of United States Judges, Attorneys, and Marshals* compiled by the Appointment Clerk (Washington, DC: GPO, 1908), 19. Hawkins believed Mabray knew they were on the verge of being arrested as early as Saturday, February 20, 1909. They may have waited until Tuesday to flee in order to get their money out of their safety deposit boxes because the banks were closed on Sunday and remained closed on Monday because it was a national holiday.

21. Little Rock *Arkansas Democrat*, February 23, 1909, 3; February 24, 1909, 1–7; Little Rock *Arkansas Gazette*, February 24, 1909, 1.

22. Little Rock *Arkansas Democrat*, February 23, 1909, 3; February 24, 1909, 1–7. One account stated that four days prior to his arrest, Mabray attempted to sell the red automobile and a pacing mare. He told a potential buyer he had made $97,000 on a timber deal and was headed for South Africa. Little Rock *Arkansas Gazette*, February 28, 1909, 1.

23. Little Rock *Arkansas Democrat*, February 23, 1909, 3; February 24, 1909, 1–7. Willis Montgomery McCall (1876–1963) was born in Missouri, grew up in Iowa, and became a fixture in Davenport's red-light Bucktown District. Isador J. Warner (1879–1974) was born in Crawfordsville, Indiana, to a German immigrant father and American mother.

24. Lewis N. Rhoton (1868–1936) was a graduate of the University of Arkansas Little Rock Law Department. After he left public office in 1908, he returned to private practice. Rhoton unsuccessfully ran for Arkansas attorney general in 1916. "Lewis Nathan Rhoton," Encyclopedia of Arkansas, accessed May 18, 2020, https://encyclopediaofarkansas.net/entries/

lewis-nathan-rhoton-13215/; James F. Willis, "Lewis Rhoton and the 'Boodlers': Political Corruption and Reform during Arkansas's Progressive Era," *Arkansas Historical Quarterly* 76, no. 2 (Summer 2017): 95–124. Mabray later confirmed he was armed; see *Omaha World-Herald*, December 21, 1911, 14.

25. Little Rock *Arkansas Democrat*, February 23, 1909, 3; February 24, 1909, 1–7; April 1, 1909, 3; Little Rock *Arkansas Gazette*, February 25, 1909, 9. The US Circuit Court granted John Cavanaugh's attorney an attachment on the men's property; he later received a judgment of $37,000. For the attachment, see Hawkins, *Mabray and the Mikes*, 44.

26. Little Rock *Arkansas Democrat*, February 23, 1909, 3; February 24, 1909, 1–7; Little Rock *Arkansas Gazette*, February 24, 1909, 7. Hawkins said there were 300 associates listed in Mabray's red ledger. Hawkins, *Mabray and the Mikes*, 57. "Thomas Cale," Biographical Dictionary of the United States Congress, 1774–Present, accessed March 8, 2020, https://bioguideretro .congress.gov/Home/MemberDetails?memIndex=C000042. For an overview of what happened to Cale, see *Evening Nonpareil*, February 27, 1909, 1.

27. Deputy Hawkins observed that, like the Buckfoot Gang, if Mabray determined a mark had more money available and truly believed the fixed contest was on the square, he would offer the man a second contest. W. H. Martin was an alias used by former Buckfoot Gang member Walter Nolan. Hawkins, *Mabray and the Mikes*, 119.

28. Hawkins, *Mabray and the Mikes*, chapters 3–4; Makris, *The Silent Investigators*, 110–17.

29. Hawkins, *Mabray and the Mikes*, 1–122; *US v. George Ryan, et al.*, case no. 2421, April Term 1903, US District Court for the Western (Little Rock) Division of the Eastern District of Arkansas (123 Fed. 634). References for Mabray's Omaha post office box application were William "Billy" Nesselhous and Charles Lewis. Lewis ran the Orpheum Saloon, and Nesselhous was a lieutenant of Omaha boss Tom Dennison. See *US v. John C. Mabray et al.*, Indictment (Omaha); John Kyle Davis, "The Gray Wolf: Tom Dennison of Omaha," *Nebraska History* 58 (1977): 25–26. For Council Bluffs indictment, see *US v. John C. Mabray, et al.*, US District Court of the Southern District of Iowa, Western Division, Council Bluffs, Iowa, Criminal Cases 1874–1915, Record Group 21, National Archives, Kansas City.

30. Makris, *The Silent Investigators*, 100. The statute was amended in 1889 and 1909. Wayne E. Fuller, *The American Mail: Enlarger of the Common Life* (Chicago: The University of Chicago Press, 1972), 248, 250.

31. Makris, *The Silent Investigators*, 100–101, 105. Makris, who seems to have relied heavily on David Maurer's *The Big Con* and J. J. Hawkins's *Mabray and the Mikes*, gives credit to "Buck Boatright" for developing "the most

far-reaching and successful confidence game ever invented." He does not state Boatright was ever investigated by the US Postal Inspection Service.

32. Hawkins, *Mabray and the Mikes*, 62; Makris, *The Silent Investigators*, 123. For the photographs, see Little Rock *Arkansas Gazette*, February 25, 1909, 1; *Evening Nonpareil*, February 27, 1909, 1. The *Nonpareil* stated some wrestling matches were held at Mynster Springs and horse races on the Manawa Road. For photographs, see *Kansas City Star*, March 3, 1909, 1; *Evening Nonpareil*, March 1, 1909. On June 4, 1911, the *Sioux City Journal* published the photograph. Inspector Allman obtained it "after much difficulty" from Cherryvale, Kansas, where Boatright's associates George Thompson and Garrette Stansbury lived. The grainy photograph purportedly shows Boatright prior to a fixed foot race in Carl Junction, Missouri. See *Sioux City Journal*, June 4, 1911. Warren B. Wood (1858–1906) died after a stroke; he must have been an early victim. He worked as a loan officer, hotelier, and served in the North Dakota legislature. *Grand Forks (ND) Evening Times*, December 5, 1906, 5. Otto Lewis Cramer (1854–1932) owned a manufacturing company in 1900, but ten years later he was an apartment manager. See *Crocker-Langley San Francisco Directory 1899* (San Francisco: H. S. Crocker Co., 1899), 1389; "Otto L. Cramer," 1900 and 1910 US Census, San Francisco, California; "Otto Louis Cramer," California, US, San Francisco Area Funeral Home Records, 1895–1985, Ancestry.com. During divorce proceedings in 1909, Cramer claimed after his wife helped dupe him, the gang gave her 15 percent of the $10,000 he lost on a fake wrestling match. *Santa Cruz (CA) Evening News*, October 21, 1909, 5; *Morning Register* (Eugene, OR), October 22, 1909, 1.

33. Hawkins, *Mabray and the Mikes*, 50–51; 61–63. For Kile, see Little Rock *Arkansas Democrat*, March 1, 1909, 1, 10; Little Rock *Arkansas Gazette*, March 2, 1909, 1, 2; *Kansas City Star*, March 7, 1909, 2A. He identified the gang's racetrack as Sweet Home Pike south of Little Rock. Little Rock *Arkansas Democrat*, March 2, 1909, 9. For the correspondence between Kile and Pulaski County Prosecuting Attorney Roy Campbell, see Little Rock *Arkansas Democrat*, November 2, 1909, 1–7. Missourian Frederick Emery Ray (1874–1910) died from typhoid and left a $13,000 estate for his wife and four young children. *Woodward (OK) Democrat*, August 18, 1910, 1; F. E. Ray, "Oklahoma Wills and Probate Records, 1801–2008," Woodward County, Administrators Records, Volume 5, 1909–1917, 361, Ancestry.com.

34. Hawkins, *Mabray and the Mikes*, 50–52; 61–63. Ray is also referred to as "J. B. Ray" in some news accounts. See Little Rock *Arkansas Democrat*, March 7, 1909, 1; Little Rock *Arkansas Gazette*, March 8, 1909, 1, 5.

35. Little Rock *Arkansas Gazette*, February 25, 1909, 1; Little Rock *Arkansas Democrat*, February 28, 1909, 1. Friedman, "Inflation Calculator."

36. Little Rock *Arkansas Gazette*, February 24, 1909, 1; *Davenport (IA) Quad-City Times*, February 28, 1909, 5.

37. *Evening Nonpareil*, February 28, 1909, 1; Little Rock *Arkansas Gazette*, February 24, 1909, 1; *Davenport (IA) Quad-City Times*, February 28, 1909, 5.

38. *Davenport (IA) Quad-City Times*, January 16, 1916, 13, 21, 24.

39. Jonathan Turner, *A Brief History of Bucktown: Davenport's Infamous District Transformed* (Charleston, SC: The History Press, 2016), 13.

40. *Davenport (IA) Democrat and Leader*, February 26, 1909, 7. For more on Davenport's time as a wide-open town, see *Davenport (IA) Quad-City Times*, August 13, 1922, 17; W. L. Purcell, *Them Was the Good Old Days in Davenport, Scott County, Iowa* (Davenport, IA: Purcell Printing Co., 1922), 167–73.

41. *Evening Nonpareil*, February 10, 1909, 1; *Davenport (IA) Democrat and Leader*, February 26, 1909, 7; *Davenport (IA) Quad-City Times*, August 13, 1922, 17. For a description of Dobbins see *Evening Nonpareil*, February 15, 1909, 1.

42. *Davenport (IA) Democrat and Leader*, February 28, 1909, 5; Little Rock *Arkansas Democrat*, February 28, 1909, 1.

43. *Davenport (IA) Democrat and Leader*, April 2, 1909, 7; Little Rock *Arkansas Democrat*, March 30, 1909, 6; *Evening Nonpareil*, March 2, 1909, 1. They were later acquitted of violating the Comstock Law. See *Jonesboro (AR) Daily News*, May 19, 1909, 2.

44. Little Rock *Arkansas Democrat*, February 25, 1909, 1,7, 9; Little Rock *Arkansas Democrat*, February 26, 1909, 2; *Evening Nonpareil*, February 26, 1909, 7.

45. Hawkins, *Mabray and the Mikes*, 47; Little Rock *Arkansas Gazette*, February 25, 1909, 12. Hawkins states Simpson sent the letter to Ballew. Hawkins, *Mabray and the Mikes*, 97. Blank told the grand jury Mabray gave Russell Harriman use of his box at the bank. He and Harriman used the box between May and November 1908. In November 1908 a stranger gave a letter to Blank stating that he, Mr. Clark, be given use of the box as Clark had purchased someone else's interest in the box. See *Evening Nonpareil*, February 25, 1909, 1.

46. Little Rock *Arkansas Gazette*, February 25, 1909, 1; *Evening-Times Republican* (Marshalltown, IA), February 26, 1909, 2.

47. Little Rock *Arkansas Democrat*, March 29, 1909, 2.

48. Little Rock *Arkansas Democrat*, February 27, 1909, 1, 7; February 28, 1909, 1, 10; *Sioux City Journal*, February 28, 1909, 1.

49. Makris, *The Silent Investigators*, 124. For Whipple in Washington, see *Omaha Evening World-Herald*, April 5, 1909, 1; Little Rock *Arkansas*

Gazette, March 30, 1909, 7, and April 5, 1909, 1. For room, see Little Rock *Arkansas Democrat*, April 22, 1909, 3. For indictment, see *US v. John C. Mabray, et al.* (Council Bluffs). John Organ, victim Thomas Ballew's attorney, complained to US attorney general George Wickersham "because of some influence brought to bear upon the officials either here or at Little Rock this man still remains in the custody of the U.S. Marshal at Little Rock, Ark., although there is no charge pending against him in the U.S. Court for that jurisdiction." He asserted, "Both Judge Trieber and the U.S. District Attorney Whipple of Little Rock have done all possible for the removal of this man, so I am informed by the Post Office Inspector, but without avail." Organ added, "It has been widely stated that there are certain influences in this neighborhood that Mabray has been able to enlist in his behalf, and conditions rather establish the truth of such complaints." See letter from John P. Organ to US Attorney General George Wickersham, April 3, 1909, in John C. Mabray file, US DOJ. Friedman, "Inflation Calculator."

50. Little Rock *Arkansas Democrat*, March 21, 1909, 1, and April 13, 1909, 4, 8. Mabray roper William Scott testified Mabray told him that in Council Bluffs, "We have the officers we need; we have the financial institution we need, and we are well protected against possible arrest there." See Hawkins, *Mabray and the Mikes*, 65–66. See also John C. Mabray's file in Office of the Governor, Criminal Correspondence 1874–1998, Record Group 043, Iowa State Archives.

51. *Evening Tribune* (Des Moines), April 26, 1909, 2; *Omaha Morning World-Herald*, December 20, 1911, 1. Mabray knocked a man's eye out in Crawford. The fair was a magnet for countless confidence men. Mabray was in Omaha in 1901; he was in town when his first wife, Mollie, threw carbolic acid in the face of a rival. *Omaha Evening World-Herald*, September 16, 1901, 1, and October 9, 1901, 7. For saloon, see *Kansas City Times*, March 10, 1910, 1.

52. Letter from Temple to US Attorney General, March 25, 1909, in John C. Mabray file, US DOJ. Inspectors Swenson and Ranger were unable to secure indictments against Mabray in New Orleans. Although the gang operated there with the help of police protection, efforts made to secure indictments against them failed. John Cavanaugh complained District Attorney St. Clair Adams had "called in the former District Attorney, Porter Parker, who apparently did not want the thing heard and prevailed on the present incumbent not to grant it, as he previously had done." See Little Rock *Arkansas Gazette*, March 30, 1909, 7. Deputy Hawkins observed McCall, Johnson, and George Ryan had influential friends like Bat Masterson and Omaha mayor James Dahlman. Hawkins also claimed New Orleans district attorney St. Clair Adams Sr. refused to "let the matter be

presented to the grand jury." Hawkins, *Mabray and the Mikes*, 52, 71–72; letter from John E. Cavanaugh to Judge Smith McPherson, July 28, 1910, *US v. John C. Mabray, et al.* (Council Bluffs).

53. Makris, *The Silent Investigators*, 124–25. Mabray's attorney Lewis Rhoton was confident Mabray would be found not guilty in Iowa. See Little Rock *Arkansas Democrat*, March 14, 1909, 1, 10. *US v. John C. Mabray, et al.* (Omaha) indicates ninety individuals were indicted. The US attorney general at this time was Charles Bonaparte; he left office March 4, 1909, and was succeeded by George Wickersham.

CHAPTER 11

1. *Omaha Sunday World-Herald*, August 25, 1907, 22–23.
2. *Omaha Evening World-Herald*, August 24, 1907, 1; August 27, 1907, 3. For Maurer, see *The Big Con*, 5–6.
3. *Omaha Evening World-Herald*, August 24, 1907, 1; August 27, 1907, 3.
4. 1850 US Census, Waukegan, Lake County, Illinois; 1870 US Census, Council Bluffs, Pottawattamie County, Iowa; *Omaha Sunday World-Herald*, August 25, 1907, 22–23.
5. Council Bluffs *Weekly Nonpareil*, February 4, 1874, 3. David Maurer says Marks mastered three-card monte, then came up with his Dollar Store con, the forerunner of the big store. See Maurer, *The Big Con*, 6–7.
6. *Daily Nonpareil*, March 2, 1875, 4.
7. *Daily Nonpareil*, August 14, 1879, 4; August 17, 1879, 4.
8. *Daily Nonpareil*, December 8, 1882, 8.
9. *Des Moines Register*, May 4, 1919, 16M; Lawrence H. Larsen, Barbara J. Cottrell, Harl A. Dalstrom, and Kay Calamé Dalstrom, *Upstream Metropolis: An Urban Biography of Omaha and Council Bluffs* (Lincoln: University of Nebraska Press, 2007).
10. 1870 US Census, Council Bluffs, Pottawattamie County, Iowa; *Omaha Evening World-Herald*, August 24, 1907, 22; *History of Pottawattamie County, Iowa* (Chicago: O. L. Baskin, 1883), 221. The 1907 account said Mark's venues included the Manhattan Club, Hoffman Club, and Albany Club. A fourth gambling establishment reportedly belonged to Omaha men. Journalist Louis Cook believed Marks only owned Hoffman House, but the others paid tribute to him. Each house paid $250 a week to the city treasury. No saloon, Cook claimed, opened without Ben's approval. *Des Moines Register*, May 4, 1919, 16M.
11. *Omaha Sunday World-Herald*, August 25, 1907, 22–23. Chic Conwell explained, "In a big city you have an efficient political machine, and the fixing is on a strictly business basis, bought and paid for. In the small town, where the political machine is not so well organized and the system of fixing

is not organized at all, the thief must make his approach directly or indirectly to the political leader, whoever he may be, and he secures the release by political influence." Conwell, *The Professional Thief*, 100.

12. *Omaha Sunday World-Herald*, August 25, 1907, 22–23. For Marks's cynical views, see the 1907 profile. For his habits, see *Des Moines Register*, May 4, 1919, 16M. In 1900 the mayor ordered Council Bluffs gambling joints closed. Marks responded he was glad "the Hoffman club, with which he was connected, would have to close up, for it had not been a very profitable investment for some time, and he was getting tired of running the place on a margin hardly large enough to pay expenses." Marks knew it was temporary and bided his time. *Daily Nonpareil*, April 25, 1900, 4.

13. *Omaha World-Herald*, August 31, 1930, Magazine Section, 7.

14. *Omaha World-Herald*, August 31, 1930, Magazine Section, 7.

15. *Omaha Sunday World-Herald*, August 25, 1907, 22–23.

16. *Omaha Sunday World-Herald*, August 25, 1907, 22–23.

17. *Des Moines Register*, May 4, 1919, 16M.

18. *Omaha World-Herald*, August 31, 1930, Magazine Section, 7; *Daily Nonpareil*, October 13, 1905, 5; *Omaha Morning World-Herald*, April 20, 1905, 3. The house was still standing as of 2021 at 17012 Allis Road, Council Bluffs, Iowa. See https://www.realtor.com/realestateandhomes -detail/17012-Allis-Rd_Council-Bluffs_IA_51503_M81207-62312, accessed February 22, 2020.

19. *Omaha Evening World-Herald*, August 25, 1907, 22–23; September 1, 1907, 17.

20. The ledger indicated the gang had at least 306 ropers and from 1906–1908 it made over $400,000. *San Francisco Call*, March 28, 1909, 1.

21. Little Rock *Arkansas Gazette*, March 2, 1909, 1, 14; March 3, 1909, 1.

22. Little Rock *Arkansas Democrat*, March 1, 1909, 1, 10. Tierney was a railroad contractor. See *Kansas City Star*, March 7, 1909, 4A.

23. *Omaha Daily Bee*, March 2, 1909, 8. Swenson found a "flash roll" Mabray used to impress victims. Bedford was conned by Herbert "The Brass Kid" Coon and the Honey Grove Kid. McCain, whose name is also sometimes given as McClain, was roped by Ed McCoy and Leon Lozier. Walker was snared by Willard "Waco Kid" Powell. See *Evening Nonpareil*, February 27, 1909, 2; *Washington Post*, March 21, 1909, Miscellany Section, 1.

24. Little Rock *Arkansas Gazette*, March 3, 1909, 1, 12.

25. *Omaha Evening World-Herald*, March 17, 1909, 1. Frank Shercliffe was convicted of stealing diamonds worth $150,000 from an Iowa train. Upon his release he admitted his guilt, but insisted Omaha boss Tom Dennison was the mastermind. Dennison was then charged and went on trial in 1905 but was acquitted. Davis, "The Gray Wolf: Tom Dennison of Omaha," 35–36.

26. *Omaha Daily Bee*, March 2, 1909, 8.

27. *Omaha Daily Bee*, March 2, 1909, 8; *Omaha Evening World-Herald*, July 29, 1907, 1; *Omaha World-Herald*, December 21, 1911, 14. For more on this, see Council Bluffs *Evening Nonpareil*, July 30, 1907, 1; February 28, 1909, 1; March 2, 1909, 1, 3. Initial reporting incorrectly gave the Kentuckian's name as Henry Hazelbaum; his name was Max Lindenbaum. See *Omaha Evening World-Herald*, July 29, 1907, 1; *Nonpareil*, December 17, 1911, 12.

28. *Omaha Evening World-Herald*, February 28, 1909, 1. For another interview with Richmond, see *Evening Nonpareil*, March 1, 1909, 1. Richmond said he learned Swenson and victim Samuel Sutor approached a Council Bluffs officer for help in locating Mabray. The officer declined and referred them to Richmond. Swenson said he did not want to go to Richmond or the sheriff, nor did he want employees of the First National Bank and the Grand Hotel to know they were looking for Mabray.

29. Little Rock *Arkansas Gazette*, March 4, 1909, 3; April 25, 1909, 1; Little Rock *Arkansas Democrat*, April 25, 1909, 1. *Des Moines Register*, April 26, 1909, 3; *St. Louis Post-Dispatch*, June 29, 1903, 1, 3; *St. Louis Republic*, June 28, 1903, 1; *Evening Tribune* (Des Moines), April 26, 1909, 2. The McCann accusation dogged Mabray, but nothing came of it. For letters and affidavits from Omaha mayor James Dahlman, Tom Dennison, and noted baseball umpire John B. Haskell attesting to his identity, see John C. Mabray file, US DOJ.

30. Hawkins, *Mabray and the Marks*, 35.

31. Ryan was arrested and released on $10,000 bond. His bondsmen argued if he was removed to Iowa he might not return to Hot Springs in time for his trial and they would have to forfeit his bond. They turned Ryan over to Garland County sheriff Jake Houpt, who refused to release him to a US deputy marshal. See Little Rock *Arkansas Gazette*, February 25, 1909, 12, October 30, 1909, 1; Little Rock *Arkansas Democrat*, February 24, 1909, 7. His name appeared in Mabray's ledger. For more on Cardwell, *Joplin Daily Globe*, March 4, 1909; Little Rock *Arkansas Gazette*, March 7, 1909, 1; March 9, 1909, 1. Ryan received five months in the Polk County, Iowa, jail and served his time alongside Buckfoot ropers William Crider and Lucius "Honey Grove Kid" Hindman. See *Evening Nonpareil*, October 6, 1912, 6; Little Rock *Arkansas Gazette*, April 6, 1910, 14. Ryan was the proprietor of the City Hall bar in Hot Springs. *Hot Springs Sentinel-Record*, November 3, 1909. For more on Ryan's legal maneuvering, see Hawkins, *Mabray and the Mikes*, 70–71.

32. *Joplin Daily Globe*, March 27, 1909, 1; *Webb City Register*, March 27, 1909, 1. Ellis's name (as well as Leon Lozier's) first surfaced in a list of the gang's ropers in the *Evening Nonpareil*, February 27, 1909, 1. Ellis's sister Harriet remarried after the death of her first husband Albert "Gib" Carter; her second husband was businessman George B. Flournoy.

33. *Joplin Daily Globe*, March 28, 1909, 1; March 31, 1909, 1; *Webb City Register*, March 30, 1909, 1; *Carthage Evening Press*, March 31, 1909, 6.

34. Little Rock *Arkansas Gazette*, September 24, 1909, 2; *Evening Nonpareil*, September 22, 1909, 1. It was reported Scott and Stansbury went before the grand jury and received immunity. Little Rock *Arkansas Gazette*, October 27, 1909, 10.

35. Hawkins, *Mabray and the Mikes*, 72. He was tried and convicted with Mabray. *Evening Nonpareil*, July 15, 1909, 1.

36. *Omaha Daily Bee*, July 23, 1909, 2. This may have been Irish immigrant James Mayelin of Sac County, Iowa. See 1900 US Census, Sac County, Iowa. "Tom S. Robison," 1900 US Census, Kedron, Woodbury County, Iowa, Ancestry.com; "Tom S. Robison," 1910 US Census, Farmington, Van Buren County, Iowa; Tom S. Robison, US Penitentiary, Leavenworth, Kansas, Records of the Bureau of Prisons, 1870–2009, Record Group 129, National Archives, Kansas City.

37. Little Rock *Arkansas Democrat*, August 12, 1909, 3. The only reference to Stansbury is a brief handwritten note that says "G. O. Stansbury Cherryvail Kans." See *US v. John C. Mabray, et al.*, case no., 2189, folder 5 of 9, box 11, US District Court of the Southern District of Iowa, Western Division, Council Bluffs, Iowa, Criminal Cases 1874–1915, Record Group 21, National Archives, Kansas City.

38. *Kansas City Times*, March 10, 1909, 12.

39. Little Rock *Arkansas Democrat*, February 28, 1909, 1.

40. *Omaha Sunday Bee*, April 25, 1909, 1A, 5A. Photographs of two pieces of correspondence between Mabray and Dahlman survive. See Durham Museum, accessed June 14, 2023, https://durhammuseum.contentdm.oclc.org/digital/search/searchterm/mabray.

41. *Omaha Sunday Bee*, April 25, 1909, 1A, 5A.

42. *Omaha Sunday Bee*, April 25, 1909, 1A, 5A.

43. Hawkins, *Mabray and the Mikes*, 52. Deputy Hawkins believed Dahlman tried to intercede on Mabray's behalf. John Kyle Davis, "The Gray Wolf: Tom Dennison of Omaha," *Nebraska History* 58 (1977): 25–26, 30, 32; Orville D. Menard, *Political Bossism in Mid-America: Tom Dennison's Omaha, 1900–1933* (Lanham, MD: University Press of America, 1989); Larsen, *Upstream Metropolis*, 234. For Nesselhous, see *Omaha Morning World-Herald*, January 3, 1937, 1–2.

44. *Omaha Daily Bee*, March 18, 1909, 8; Friedman, "Inflation Calculator."

45. Little Rock *Arkansas Gazette*, March 16, 1909, 14. This article vaguely states Swenson's investigation revealed "the continually accumulating mass of evidence has brought out another figure—a power exercising more influence than all of the men under arrest." The person's identity is unknown.

46. *Omaha Daily Bee*, March 18, 1909, 8; *San Francisco Call*, March 16, 1909, 3. The cooperating victims were Samuel Sutor, Cornelius C. Vanderbeck, John Hermelbrecht, Joseph P. Walker, and W. H. Bedford. See *Omaha Morning World-Herald*, May 7, 1909, 3.

47. Little Rock *Arkansas Gazette*, March 21, 1909, 17. William H. McGrath (1881–1926) was a graduate of the University of Minnesota. He worked as a reporter before cofounding the Pine City Lumber Company. McGrath later practiced law in Minneapolis. *Minneapolis Star*, February 27, 1926, 1; Augustus B. Easton, ed., *History of the St. Croix Valley*, vol. 2 (Chicago: H. C. Cooper Jr. & Co., 1909), 1267.

48. *Evening Times-Republican* (Marshalltown, IA), June 28, 1909, 3; Hawkins, *Mabray and the Mikes*, 67, 76; *South Bend Tribune*, June 16, 1909, 1; March 9, 1910, 1. Postal clerk J. H. Alward testified about the gang's use of a mailbox that ultimately brought about their downfall. Flemming was sentenced on May 31, 1909. Although riddled with inaccuracies, an entertaining story about William Flemming appears in the *Indianapolis News*, July 4, 1919, 12. He, along with Buckfoot and Mabray stalwart Garrette Stansbury, were caught up in another con in their twilight years. For his penitentiary record, see William Flemming, Prisoner No. 4331, Indiana State Digital Archives, accessed March 14, 2020, https://secure.in.gov/apps/iara/search/Home /Detail?rId=539570.

49. *Evening Nonpareil*, March 8, 1910, 7. See record for William Flemming, Indiana State Prison North, Department of Correction, Indiana State Prison, 1897–1966, Indiana Digital Archives, accessed July 11, 2020, https://secure.in.gov/apps/iara/search/Home/Detail?rId=539570.

50. *Evening Tribune* (Des Moines), April 26, 1909, 2; *Omaha Morning World-Herald*, December 20, 1911, 1.

51. *Denver Evening Post*, December 28, 1900, 7. Ashmore's name is mentioned in news accounts and court records pertaining to the Buckfoot Gang. It is possible that this may have been a Buckfoot-affiliated event.

52. *Denver Evening Post*, March 13, 1909, 4; Hawkins, *Mabray and the Mikes*, 71; Ernest L. Powers, Prisoner no. 8454, Colorado Penitentiary Record, Colorado State Archives. *State of Colorado v. Ernest L. Powers*, Colorado Supreme Court, case no. 7107, History Colorado.

53. *Denver Daily News*, February 18, 1910, 6; *Denver Daily News*, May 21, 1912, 12; *Evening Nonpareil*, January 4, 1910, 8; *Denver Post*, January 3, 1910, 6. Ernest L. Powers, Prisoner no. 8454, Colorado Penitentiary Record, Colorado State Archives.

54. *Denver Daily News*, February 18, 1910, 6; May 21, 1912, 12. November 9, 1912, 4. Ernest L. Powers, Prisoner no. 8454, Colorado Penitentiary Record, Colorado State Archives. Discharged on September 18, 1916, he died in 1968.

55. *Denver Evening Post*, May 1, 1909, 1.

56. *Denver Evening Post*, August 1, 1910, 6. Boone B. Jacobs left a wife and two children. For more on Jacobs, see *Denver Post*, April 27, 1909, 2.

57. *Evening Nonpareil*, May 22, 1909, 2. A member of the Buckfoot Gang, Gibson surfaced in Salt Lake City in 1905. He promoted fights, but local sports realized Gibson's matches were not on the square after Salt Lake City papers called a bout between Billy Stift and George Gardner a fake. Rumors also connected him to a fraudulent wrestling match. *Salt Lake Herald*, November 9, 1906, 8; November 11, 1906, 6; November 20, 1906, 7; September 24, 1907, 10; September 25, 1907, 1; September 27, 1907, 3.

58. Little Rock *Arkansas Gazette*, July 2, 1909, 1; September 24, 1909, 2. Hawkins, *Mabray and the Mikes*, 72. For forfeited bond money, see *Omaha Sunday Bee*, November 14, 1909, 5A; for cooperation with federal authorities, see *Evening Nonpareil*, November 25, 1909, 6. Hawkins said Gay was "one of the best witnesses for the government." Authorities were said to be working to dismiss state charges against him in Illinois in exchange for his cooperation. Thomas Gay (1876–1937) immigrated from England with his parents to Streator, Illinois. After Mabray, he became a hotelier and car dealer. *Streator Daily Times-Press*, October 11, 1937, 3; "Thomas Gay," Illinois Deaths and Stillbirths Index, 1916–1947, Ancestry.com.

59. *Evening Nonpareil*, July 4, 1909, 3; Little Rock *Arkansas Gazette*, July 29, 1909; September 24, 1909, 2. There was confusion in the press about Frank and William.

60. *Omaha Daily Bee*, September 22, 1909, 5; September 23, 1909, 1.

61. The letter was signed, "Yours truly, G.A.B. 32 West 28th NYC, 15." Both letters are quoted in the Philpot case. According to Deputy Hawkins's list, number 15 was George A. Bradley. See Hawkins, *Mabray and the Mikes*, 115. For letter, see transcript of testimony and evidence from *US v. C. F. Philpot*, US District Court, Southern District of California, Southern Division, that appears in *US v. John C. Mabray, et al.* (Council Bluffs). *Omaha Sunday Bee*, April 25, 1909, 5A; *Evening Nonpareil*, September 24, 1909, 1; *Omaha Daily Bee*, September 24, 1909, 1. Additional letters were submitted to the grand jury; see *Omaha Daily Bee*, September 24, 1909, 1, 5.

62. *Evening Nonpareil*, September 23, 1909, 1.

CHAPTER 12

1. *San Francisco Call*, October 1, 1909, 1, 2; October 21, 1909, 5. According to the *Call*, Walter Knox (1878–1951) was exposed after James E. Sullivan, president of the Amateur Athletic Union, called for Knox to be prosecuted for "entering amateur races under false pretenses." Knox then reportedly became a "poker 'shark.'" David F. Town, *Hot Foot: Walter Knox's*

Remarkable Life as a Professional in an Amateur World (Victoria,
British Columbia: FriesenPress, 2014), does not mention Knox's possible
involvement with Harriman and Mabray. Knox was scheduled to compete
at the Alaska–Yukon–Pacific Exposition that Mabray associates George
Marsh, Winn Harris, and Bert Warner attended. The *San Francisco
Chronicle* stated the gang's correspondence indicated there were 321
outside men roping for the gang. *San Francisco Chronicle*, October 2,
1909, 1, 2. See *Frank W. Brown v. C. T. Elliott, US Marshal* in John C.
Mabray file, US DOJ.

2. *Omaha Daily Bee*, October 2, 1909, 12; *San Francisco Chronicle*, October 22,
1909, 20. Brown used the aliases of Hamilton, Potter, Adams, Martin, and
Pomeroy. These names were used by the Buckfoot Gang, but it is unclear if
he was associated with Boatright. James O'Connell (1867–1920) served as
a US postal inspector in San Francisco until 1916 when he was ousted from
the service and his position eliminated. One account blamed his dismissal
on party affiliation. He then joined the US State Department. *San Francisco
Chronicle*, February 26, 1916, 1; *San Francisco Examiner*, March 29, 1916, 9;
San Bernardino County Sun, March 12, 1920, 1.

3. "Russell B. Harriman," 1891 Census of Canada; "Russell B. Harriman,"
Ontario, Canada, Marriages, 1826–1938; "Russell B. Harriman," Ontario,
Canada, Deaths and Deaths Overseas, 1869–1947, Ancestry.com; *San
Francisco Chronicle*, October 2, 1909, 2.

4. *Washington (DC) Herald*, October 15, 1909, 1; July 28, 1912, 1; "Frank
Wilson Brown," US Passport Applications, 1795–1925 (1895–1898),
Ancestry.com.

5. *Washington (DC) Herald*, October 15, 1909, 1; July 28, 1912, 1. For bigamy,
see *Evening Star* (Washington, DC), August 6, 1897, 12; *Evening Star*,
June 2, 1898, 10. For the stock swindle, see *Evening Star*, June 28, 1901, 2.

6. *Seattle Star*, August 23, 1906, 1. Benjamin F. Roller (1876–1933) studied
at DePauw University and graduated from the University of Pennsylvania
School of Medicine. Roller played professional football and taught physiol-
ogy before becoming a professional wrestler. Entry 1571, Benjamin F. Roller,
Alumnal Record DePauw University, ed. Martha J. Ridpath (Greencastle, IN:
DePauw University, 1920), 171.

7. "Caleb B. Moore," *Miltonian* (Milton, PA), December 18, 1919, 5; "Edward
C. Moore," 1900 US Census, Washington, DC; "Edward C. Moore," Records
of the Bureau of Prisons, 1870–2009, Record Group 129, National Archives,
Kansas City.

8. *Seattle Star*, August 23, 1906, 1. George Marsh was from Decorah, Iowa.

9. *Seattle Star*, August 24, 1906, 1. Jack Carkeek (1861–1924) was the son
of Cornish immigrants. He began wrestling in the 1880s and became well
known across the country. Joseph "Yellow Kid" Weil claimed he did two

years in jail. Weil, *Con Man: A Master Swindler's Own Story* (New York: Broadway Books, 2004), 162–63.

10. *Evening Nonpareil*, September 28, 1909, 7.

11. Portland *Oregonian*, October 8, 1909. Bert Shores of Mankato, Minnesota, was rumored to have been part of a crooked wrestling syndicate in 1906. A Minnesota resident wrote to the sporting editor of a Winnipeg, Manitoba, newspaper about a gang of crooked North Dakota wrestlers who were persona non grata throughout Minnesota. See *Grand Forks (ND) Evening Times*, February 23, 1906, 6. For an account of a fixed match he was in, see *Grand Forks (ND) Daily Herald*, March 9, 1909, 10. For more on Roller and Shores, see *Seattle Star*, September 25, 1909, 1–2. Harris roped victim John Cavanaugh. See interview with Cavanaugh in *Evening Times-Republican* (Marshalltown, IA), March 6, 1909, 4. For letters between Harris and Cavanaugh, see *US v. John C. Mabray, et al.* (Council Bluffs).

12. *Omaha Daily Bee*, October 8, 1909, 3.

13. *Omaha Daily Bee*, October 22, 1909, 4; Little Rock *Arkansas Democrat*, October 25, 1909, 3.

14. *Omaha Daily Bee*, November 27, 1909, 12; *Omaha Daily Bee*, December 3, 1909, 4; *Des Moines Tribune*, December 21, 1909, 1; *US v. Eddie K. Morris*, US Commissioner's Court, Northern District of New York (1909) in *US v. John C. Mabray, et al.* (Council Bluffs).

15. *Omaha Daily Bee*, December 29, 1909, 8.

16. Little Rock *Arkansas Gazette*, October 27, 1909, 10.

17. *Daily Gate City* (Keokuk, IA), February 8, 1909, 1; "John R. Dobbins," 1880 US Census, Mercer County, Missouri.

18. *Omaha Daily Bee*, September 1, 1909, 5; *Omaha Daily Bee*, October 28, 1909, 7. Howard Webster Byers (1856–1928) was a former speaker of the Iowa General Assembly. Byers served two terms as Iowa attorney general before returning to private practice. "Notable Deaths," *Annals of Iowa* 16, no. 5 (Summer 1928): 395.

19. *Evening Nonpareil*, November 15, 1909, 1. For Tinley, see *Annals of Iowa* 18, no. 1 (Summer 1931): 73; for Harl, see *Annals of Iowa* 9, no. 5 (1910): 398–99.

20. *Evening Nonpareil*, November 16, 1909, 1; *Omaha Daily Bee*, November 17, 1909, 1.

21. *Evening Nonpareil*, February 28, 1909, 2; November 16, 1909, 1. For Ballew's testimony, see *State of Iowa v. John R. Dobbins*, Supreme Court of Iowa (1910).

22. *Evening Nonpareil*, November 16, 1909, 1; *Omaha Daily Bee*, November 17, 1909, 1; *State of Iowa v. John R. Dobbins*.

23. *State of Iowa v. John R. Dobbins*. The Pottawattamie County Clerk's Office could not locate the original trial records, so I have relied on newspaper accounts and records from Dobbins's appeal to the Iowa Supreme Court.

24. *Evening Nonpareil*, November 17, 1909, 1. Ballew said he earned the moniker when Princeton businessmen "started a lumber yard to fight me, and I started the store to fight them, and they gave it the name 'buck-'em-all.'" *State of Iowa v. John R. Dobbins*.

25. *State of Iowa v. John R. Dobbins*; *Omaha Daily Bee,* November 19, 1909, 1.

26. *State of Iowa v. John R. Dobbins*; *Omaha Daily Bee*, November 19, 1909, 1; November 20, 1909, 1–2; *Des Moines Tribune*, November 19, 1909, 3. A concise account of Bedford's experience can be found in John C. Mabray's file in Office of the Governor, Criminal Correspondence 1874–1998, Record Group 043, Iowa State Archives.

27. *State of Iowa v. John R. Dobbins*; *Omaha Sunday Bee*, November 21, 1909, 1. Swenson received a threatening letter that stated a group of men unknown to Swenson met in Illinois and decided he "had got enough notoriety at the expense of the boys . . . Now these men have got the money and influence to make your road awful rough," the writer warned, "and this town has got men that would put a bum under you for a hundred." It was never clear who threatened him. See Little Rock *Arkansas Gazette*, November 3, 1909, 14; *State of Iowa v. John R. Dobbins*; *Omaha Sunday Bee*, December 12, 1909, 7; December 14, 1909, 5.

28. "J. R. Dobbins," Book Two, Iowa Consecutive Registers of Convicts, 1867–1970, Ancestry.com; *State of Iowa v. John R. Dobbins*. William Henry Bedford (1854–1927) was a native of Andrew County, Missouri. John R. Hermelbracht (1866–1946) immigrated from Germany in 1885. He was president of the First Bank of Bancroft. "About First Bank of Bancroft," accessed April 18, 2020, https://web.archive.org/web/20161016050751/http://www .firstbancroft.com/about_us.htm; *State of Iowa v. John R. Dobbins*; *Omaha Daily Bee*, November 19, 1909, 1; November 20, 1909, 1–2; November 21, 1909, 1–2; November 23, 1909, 1–2.

29. *Evening Nonpareil*, November 20, 1909, 1; November 23, 1909, 1; *State of Iowa v. John R. Dobbins*. "J. R. Dobbins," Book Two, Iowa Consecutive Registers of Convicts, 1867–1970, Ancestry.com; *Nonpareil*, October 19, 1911, 5.

30. *Evening Nonpareil*, February 1, 1910, 5.

31. *Evening Nonpareil*, February 2, 1910, 1.

32. *Evening Nonpareil*, February 3, 1910, 6; *Omaha Daily Bee*, February 3, 1909, 4. In some accounts Campbell's name is H. C. Campbell. See *Omaha Daily Bee*, February 3, 1909.

33. *Evening Nonpareil*, February 3, 1910, 6.

34. *Evening Nonpareil*, February 3, 1910, 6; *Omaha Daily Bee*, February 5, 1910, 12.

35. *Evening Nonpareil*, February 5, 1910, 1; *Evening Times-Republican* (Marshalltown, IA), February 5, 1910, 1.

36. *Omaha Daily Bee*, February 6, 1910, 1–2. Scott was convicted in federal court of using the mails to defraud and sentenced to six months in jail. *Omaha Daily Bee*, March 22, 1910, 1.

37. Mabray likely knew he was going to prison. As Chic Conwell explained, "There is comparatively little fixing of federal agents and federal courts." He believed, "The post-office inspectors are thought to be the most straight and efficient, and they do not frame cases." Conwell, *The Professional Thief*, 114–16.

CHAPTER 13

1. *Evening Nonpareil*, March 2, 1910, 1; February 15, 1910, 5; *Evening Times-Republican* (Marshalltown, IA), March 3, 1910, 3. Federal officials thought some of Judge McPherson's friends tried to prejudice him against the prosecutors prior to trial, leading Rush to reportedly consider dismissing the Council Bluffs case, but either the observers were mistaken or something happened that convinced McPherson to proceed. See Hawkins, *Mabray and the Mikes*, 91–92.

2. Council Bluffs *Evening Nonpareil*, March 1, 1910, 7; March 7, 1910, 1. For Forbes, see *US v. Harry Forbes*, US District Court, Northern District of New York (1910) in *US v. John C. Mabray, et al.* (Council Bluffs).

3. *Evening Nonpareil*, March 7, 1910, 1; March 8, 1910, 7; March 9, 1910, 1, 7. *Omaha Daily Bee*, March 8, 1910, 6; March 9, 1910, 6; March 10, 1910, 3. For who was not present, see *Omaha World-Herald*, March 9, 1910, 11. For the guilty plea, see *Evening Times-Republican* (Marshalltown, IA), March 11, 1910, 3. *US v. Eddie K. Morris*, US Commissioner's Court, Northern District of New York (1909) in *US v. John C. Mabray, et al.* (Council Bluffs).

4. *Evening Nonpareil*, March 7, 1910, 7; Little Rock *Arkansas Gazette* April 9, 1910, 2. US attorney William Whipple informed US attorney general Wickersham, "These men are crafty; having long experience in evading the law; appear to have plenty of money, and are evidently assisted by many friends; as Hot Springs notoriously abounds in men of similar type." He noted Warner, McCall, Johnson, and Ryan disappeared when marshals arrived to arrest them. Federal prosecutor Temple told Wickersham they were hiding on George Ryan's ranch outside Hot Springs having "been sheltered by the local authorities of that part of Arkansas, who have, every time we have sought to arrest these parties, appeared with fictitious and sham charges of violation of the state law, preventing the Federal authorities from taking possession of them. Our officers, both the post-office inspectors and the marshals and deputy marshals, are so well known that it is impossible for them to make the arrest." See Whipple to US Attorney General, February 5, 1910; Temple to US Attorney General, March 22, 1910, in John C. Mabray file, US DOJ.

5. *Evening Times-Republican* (Marshalltown, IA), March 10, 1910, 1.

6. *Omaha Daily Bee*, March 10, 1910, 2.

7. *Evening-Times Republican* (Marshalltown, IA), March 8, 1910, 2.

8. *Omaha Daily Bee*, March 11, 1910, 1. Another account claims Mabray met with Swenson and asked the state charges against him be dropped in exchange for a guilty plea in federal court so long as he did not have to testify against his associates. He agreed to help locate other members. Rush and Temple were agreeable, but Iowa attorney general H. Webb Byers would only agree if Mabray would testify in federal court or "give him such information as would aid him in cleaning out the corruption in Council Bluffs." Hawkins, *Mabray and the Mikes*, 93.

9. *Evening Nonpareil*, March 10, 1910, 1; *Omaha World-Herald*, March 10, 1910, 1, 5; *Omaha Daily Bee*, March 10, 1910, 2.

10. Letter from US attorney general Charles A. Goss to US Attorney General George Wickersham, September 16, 1909; letters from Wickersham to Rush, September 17, 20, 1909.

11. Confidential report from Swenson to W. W. Dickson, Inspector-in-Charge, St. Louis, dated August 7, 1909; Swenson to Inspector-in-Charge Dickson, April 5, 1910; Inspector-in-Charge Dickson to Chief Inspector R. S. Sharp, May 13, 1910, all in John C. Mabray file, US DOJ.

12. *Omaha Daily Bee*, March 11, 1910, 1; *Omaha World-Herald*, March 12, 1910, 1. For more, see *Nonpareil*, March 20, 1910, 10.

13. *Evening Nonpareil*, March 19, 1910, 5.

14. *Evening Nonpareil*, March 11, 1910, 1; *Omaha Daily Bee*, March 11, 1910, 1; *Nebraska State Journal*, March 12, 1910, 2. The witness's surnames are spelled differently in various news accounts. See "Alex Dalin," 1910 US Census, Green Bay, Wisconsin; *Green Bay Press-Gazette*, May 31, 1946, 18. Farmer Clinton Nelson (1850–1925) dabbled in real estate ventures. See *Alma (MI) Record*, September 17, 1925, 1; "Clinton Nelson Sr," Michigan Death Records, 1867–1952, Ancestry.com. Henry Stogsdill (1867–1928) was a farmer and stock dealer from Cabool, Missouri. Peter Voorhees (1856–1942) lived in Alma, Michigan. "Peter Voorhees," 1910 US Census, Alma, Michigan; "Peter Voorhees," Michigan, US Death Records, 1867–1952, Ancestry.com; "Peter Voorhees," *Adrian (MI) Daily Telegram*, December 29, 1942, 6; *Omaha Daily Bee*, March 12, 1910, 6.

15. *Evening Nonpareil*, March 11, 1910, 1.

16. *Evening Nonpareil*, March 11, 1910, 6; *Omaha World-Herald*, March 11, 1910, 11; *Evening Times-Republican* (Marshalltown, IA), March 12, 1910, 3; *Omaha Daily Bee*, March 13, 1910, 1; *Streator (IL) Free Press*, July 8, 1909, 5; *Post Office Department Annual Reports, for the Fiscal Year Ended June 30, 1911, Report of the Postmaster General, Miscellaneous Reports* (Washington, DC: GPO, 1912), 69.

17. "George Cosson," *The Biographical Dictionary of Iowa*, University of Iowa Press Digital Editions, accessed February 22, 2020, http://uipress.lib.uiowa .edu/bdi/DetailsPage.aspx?id=76; *Des Moines Register*, May 4, 1919, 16M. The laws permitted the removal from office any county attorney, mayor, or law enforcement officer for neglect, refusal to perform official duties, misconduct in office, corruption, extortion, felony conviction, or intoxication. *Evening Nonpareil*, March 11, 1910, 1. William Killpack was Pottawattamie County's prosecutor in 1902; he would have known Leon Lozier because he filed requisition papers for him. See file for "Leon Lozier," Office of the Governor, Governors Criminal Correspondence, 1847–1918, State Historical Society of Iowa.

18. This is filed under *State of Iowa v. George H. Richmond*, Pottawattamie County District Court (May 1910); the petition was filed under *State of Iowa, ex. rel., H. W. Byers, Attorney General of the State of Iowa v. George H. Richmond*. Richmond was represented by Mabray attorney Emmet Tinley. From the time he was appointed on April 4, 1904, until his removal in 1910, Richmond charged madams twelve dollars and prostitutes six dollars each month for protection. For Richmond editorial, see *Evening Nonpareil*, March 12, 1910, 4. For anonymous opinion, see *Omaha World-Herald*, March 12, 1910, 11.

19. *Evening Nonpareil*, March 12, 1910, 1, 11; *Omaha Daily Bee*, May 14, 1910, 1. For Joshua H. Secrest (1848–1911), see Charles Cummins Hunt, *A Genealogical History of the Robert and Abigail Pancoast Hunt Family* (Columbus, OH: Champlin Press, 1906), 42–44.

20. *Omaha Daily Bee*, March 12, 1910, 2; March 14, 1910, 1. Deputy Hawkins believed a large amount of the evidence seized in Little Rock under "a search warrant, which, probably if put to the test, would have been found illegal." He believed other letters pertaining to the gang had been illegally opened. Hawkins, *Mabray and the Mikes*, 101.

21. *Evening Times-Republican* (Marshalltown, IA), March 12, 1910, 3. Stanislaus Zbysko was the ring name of Polish wrestler Jan Stanisław Cyganiewicz (1879–1967), a two-time world heavyweight champion whose career peaked in the 1920s. "Stanislaus Zbyszko," accessed May 4, 2020, https://en.wikipedia.org/wiki/Stanislaus_Zbyszko. Ernest Fenby (1874–1946) began wrestling in 1897 and retired in 1921. *Lansing State Journal*, May 9, 1937, Part I, 7; January 24, 1946, 24.

22. *Omaha Daily Bee*, March 27, 1910.

23. *Chicago Tribune*, November 19, 1911, Sports Section, 4B; *Pantagraph* (Bloomington, IL), March 24, 2019, A13.

24. Roper Darby Thielman (1873–1951) was a former minor league baseball player who played with the Seattle Clamdiggers and Spokane Blue Stockings. See Council Bluffs *Evening Nonpareil*, July 30, 1907, 1, February 28, 1909, 1, March 2, 1909, 1, 3; *Omaha Evening World-Herald*, July 29, 1907, 1.

25. *Omaha Daily Bee*, March 14, 1910, 1.

26. Claudius Willard Powell (1878–1921) sometimes appears under the name Claude, but he wrote "Claudius" on his 1920 US Passport application. "Claudius Willard Powell," US Passport Applications, 1795–1925 (1919–1920), Ancestry.com. For parents and childhood, see *Waco News-Tribune*, April 10, 1921, 3. For his father's obituary, see *Waco News-Tribune*, June 29, 1921, 7.

27. *Fort Worth Register*, March 28, 1901, 8; April 14, 1901, 6; April 18, 1901, 5, 6; June 8, 1902, 8. For physical description see, "Willard Powell," Records of the Bureau of Prisons, 1870–2009, Record Group 129, National Archives, Kansas City.

28. *Dallas Morning News*, November 20, 1902, 3. Powell has four entries in the Texas Convict and Conduct Registers, 1875–1945, Ancestry.com. He served two concurrent two-year terms after he was convicted in 1903; one from Hill County, the other from Johnson County.

29. *Omaha World-Herald*, March 16, 1910, 2; *Omaha Sunday Bee*, March 16, 1910, 1A. He allegedly did not like Ed Ellis, but it is unclear if reporters confused Edward Moore with Ellis. For the minister, see Hawkins, *Mabray and the Mikes*, 98–99. The *Omaha Daily News* reported Simpson identified various handwriting in Mabray's red ledger, including those of Ed Ellis and Robert Boatright, making one wonder if it was Boatright's old ledger.

30. *Omaha World-Herald*, March 16, 1910, 2; *Omaha Sunday Bee*, March 16, 1910, 1A. "George Howard Simpson" is a real estate agent in the 1910 US Census, Spokane, Washington. The 1910 and 1911 Spokane city directories list "George H. Simpson"; there are no entries for Howard Simpson. *1910 Spokane City Directory* (Spokane: R. L. Polk & Co., 1910), 1045. In 1912 a man with the same name died in Spokane. A Missourian, he served as mayor of El Dorado Springs before moving to Washington State, where he died at age sixty-three. *Spokane Daily Chronicle*, October 19, 1912, 3; *History of Hickory, Polk, Cedar, Dade and Barton Counties, Missouri* (Chicago: Goodspeed Pub. Co., 1889), 775–76. Howard Simpson briefly testified in *US v. C. F. Philpot*; he curiously said he was a forty-three-year-old Canadian. He said he met Mabray in Kansas City in 1904 or 1905 and that he ran foot races in Hot Springs, Arkansas. A man named Simpson did run for Buckfoot, but his first name remains unknown. The Philpot case appears in *US v. John C. Mabray, et al.* (Council Bluffs). Thomas Gay said the Denver store was operated independently by Harriman, Moore, and Brown. See *Omaha Daily Bee*, March 18, 1910, 2. Friedman, "Inflation Calculator."

31. Little Rock *Arkansas Gazette*, March 16, 1910, 1. For bank claim, see Hawkins, *Mabray and the Mikes*, 66.

32. Hawkins, *Mabray and the Mikes*, 89–90. Mabray was known as number 66 prior to 1908. Harriman was 12; Frank Brown was 36. These letters are not in the court records.

33. *Omaha Daily Bee*, March 17, 1910, 1.

34. *Omaha Daily Bee*, March 17, 1910, 1.

35. The Edwin Montefiore Borchard Papers at Yale contains correspondence between Borchard's research assistant E. Russell Lutz and Willard Powell's attorney George H. Mayne. Lutz borrowed Mayne's 1,834-page, three-volume set of testimony but did not make a facsimile. See Edwin Montefiore Borchard Papers, MS 670, box 116, folder 1102, Yale University Library, and *Convicting the Innocent: Sixty-Five Actual Errors of Criminal Justice* (New Haven, CT: Yale University Press, 1932).

36. *Omaha Daily Bee*, March 15, 1910, 1.

37. *Omaha Daily Bee*, March 16, 1910, 2. This is one of the few instances where a victim implicated Weil, one of the most colorful confidence men of the age, as a member of the Mabray Gang. Weil was convicted on state charges in Illinois in May 1909 for a separate crime and was not released until March 1911. His name does not appear in the Council Bluffs indictment, but he may have been charged under an alias. See Hawkins, *Mabray and the Mikes*, 76; Weil and Brannon, *Con Man*, 113–36, 162–63. See entry for Joseph Weil, inmate no. 1526, Joliet Penitentiary Register, Illinois State Archives. Class and Weil worked together before and after Mabray.

38. *Omaha Daily Bee*, March 16, 1910, 2; March 22, 1910, 2.

39. *Nonpareil*, March 18, 1910, 8.

40. *Omaha Sunday Bee*, March 20, 1920, 2.

41. *Omaha Daily Bee*, March 21, 1910, 1; March 27, 1910. During the trial McPherson instructed the jury to acquit John Beath; the government also dropped charges against ropers Fred Mull and J. R. Morrison after the Canadians they roped refused to testify. Mull contacted Tom Dennison for bail money. *Evening Nonpareil*, March 19, 1910, 7. Beath helped with scams from 1906–1907 but went straight and served as a Deputy US Marshal in Jacksonville, Florida, which led to the dismissal of his charges. Hawkins, *Mabray and the Mikes*, 95.

42. *Nonpareil*, March 19, 1910, 1; March 21, 1910, 1. John Cavanaugh was angered by Harris's light sentence. He wrote Judge McPherson stating Harris played upon McPherson's sympathies with a fake sob story about having an invalid wife and a family. Multiple letters from Harris to Cavanaugh demonstrate how a roper wooed victims. See John E. Cavanaugh to Judge Smith McPherson, July 28, 1910, in *US v. John C. Mabray, et al.* (Council Bluffs).

43. *Omaha Sunday Bee*, March 27, 1910. The paper noted, "Horse trading has long been noted and notorious for its possibilities."

44. *Omaha Sunday Bee*, March 27, 1910, 7F; March 24, 1910, 5.

45. See files for John C. Mabray, Leon Lozier, Willard Powell, Clarence Class, Harry Forbes, Clarence Forbes, Eddie K. Morris, Ed McCoy, Tom S. Robison, George Marsh, Bert Shores, and Frank Myers in the US Penitentiary, Leavenworth, Kansas, Record Group 129, Records of the Bureau of Prisons, 1870–2009, National Archives, Kansas City.

46. John C. Mabray, Leon Lozier, Willard Powell, Clarence Class, Harry Forbes, Clarence Forbes, Eddie K. Morris, Ed McCoy, Tom S. Robison, George Marsh, Bert Shores, and Frank Myers in the US Penitentiary, Leavenworth, Kansas, Record Group 129, Records of the Bureau of Prisons, 1870–2009, National Archives, Kansas City. Tillie Marsh Lurton was the wife of William C. Lurton (1877–1929).

47. US Postal Inspector Charles S. Ranger to Judge Smith McPherson, June 4, 1910, *US v. John C. Mabray, et al.* (Council Bluffs). Friedman, "Inflation Calculator."

48. US Postal Inspector Charles S. Ranger to Judge Smith McPherson, June 4, 1910, *US v. John C. Mabray, et al.* (Council Bluffs).

49. US Postal Inspector Charles S. Ranger to Judge Smith McPherson, June 4, 1910, *US v. John C. Mabray, et al.* (Council Bluffs).

50. *Evening Nonpareil*, July 11, 1910, 1.

51. *Evening Nonpareil*, July 19, 1910, 7; Godfrey's name sometimes appears as "Godefroy." *Post Office Department Annual Reports, for the Fiscal Year Ended June 30, 1911, Report of the Postmaster General, Miscellaneous Reports* (Washington, DC: GPO, 1912), 69.

52. *Evening Nonpareil*, August 27, 1910, 3. Inspector Ranger told McPherson that Martin was a penniless widower who could no longer gamble due to cataracts. Because he swindled only one victim and was willing to plead guilty, Ranger suggested a year in jail. *US v. John C. Mabray, et al.* (Council Bluffs). For Carkeek, see *Evening Nonpareil*, October 6, 1912, 6.

53. Forbes gave authorities information that led to the arrest of Tom Davies; he also found a big store in Boston. Letter from Forbes to Swenson, January 10, 1910; Inspector C. C. James to Swenson, December 20, 1910; Swenson to W. S. Mayer, Inspector in Charge, St. Louis, January 14, 1911; Assistant Attorney General (unsigned) to Postmaster General, February 21, 1911, in John C. Mabray file, US DOJ; *Honey Grove (TX) Signal*, January 13, 1911, 2.

54. *Omaha Sunday Bee*, March 19, 1911, 7A.

55. "Russell B. Harriman," Ontario, Canada, Deaths and Deaths Overseas, 1869–1947, Ancestry.com. Mrs. L. M. Harriman certified his death. For

telegrams about Harriman's surgery, see Letter to AG from Elliott, Marshal, July 11, 1910, in John C. Mabray file, US DOJ.

56. *Washington (DC) Herald*, July 28, 1912, 1; *San Jose Evening News*, July 22, 1912, 1.

57. *Washington (DC) Herald*, July 28, 1912, 1. The initial report in the *San Jose Evening News* stated Brown may have died from a heart condition. The *Washington (DC) Herald* said he committed suicide. Another account said a hypodermic needle and "a few crystals of some drug" were found on Brown's bureau. See *San Diego Union*, July 25, 1912, 19.

58. After his release Moore seemingly went straight; in 1920 he was working in the iron steel industry and a decade later he was vice president of a brake lining firm in Chicago. He died there in 1930 and was buried in his hometown of Washington, DC. *San Diego Union*, September 22, 1912, 34; *Davenport (IA) Quad-City Times*, October 4, 1912, 2; "Edward C. Moore," 1900 US Census, Washington, DC; "Edward C. Moore," Records of the Bureau of Prisons, 1870–2009, Record Group 129, National Archives, Kansas City; "Edward C. Moore," 1920 US Census, Cook County, Illinois; 1930 US Census, Cook County, Illinois ; "Edward C. Moore," District of Columbia, Select Deaths and Burials Index, 1769–1930, Ancestry.com; "Edward C. Moore Death Notice," *Chicago Tribune*, May 25, 1930. Letters from Edward C. Moore to attorneys Birney and Woodward (Washington, DC), July 25, August 9, 1912, in John C. Mabray file, US DOJ.

59. *Omaha Daily Bee*, March 25, 1911, 9; April 8, 1911, 1–10. There were roughly 150 indictments comprising twenty-six bills. Only two men, Frank Scott and John Dobbins, had been tried at this point. Their cases cost almost $2,000 and it was thought that it would cost at least $1,000 to prosecute each case.

60. *Omaha Daily Bee*, March 16, 1911, 1–2; March 17, 1911, 2; *Kansas City Star*, March 16, 1911; *Evening Times-Republican* (Marshalltown, IA), March 22, 1911; *Post Office Department Annual Reports, for the Fiscal Year Ended June 30, 1911*, 69. George Ryan used every legal tactic possible to delay being extradited to Iowa. See Conwell, *The Professional Thief*, 107 for more on how confidence men "fixed" cases. Friedman, "Inflation Calculator."

61. *Omaha Evening World-Herald*, December 21, 1911, 1. For indictment, see *Omaha World-Herald*, October 19, 1911, 3. A handwritten record lists each defendant's status, but does not list every name. *US v. John C. Mabray, et al.* (Council Bluffs).

62. *Nonpareil*, October 17, 1911, 1; October 18, 1911, 1; October 19, 1911, 3. German immigrant Henry Ruhsert (1873–1959) lived with his family on a farm in Chase County, Kansas. See "Henry Ruhsert," 1910 US Census,

Diamond Creek, Chase County, Kansas; "Henry Ruhsert," Kansas, United Spanish War Veterans Reports of Deaths, 1945–1970, Ancestry.com.

63. *Nonpareil*, October 19, 1911, 1, 6.

64. Letter from George Cosson to US Attorney General George Wickersham, October 19, 1911. See John C. Mabray file, US DOJ.

65. *Omaha Evening World-Herald*, December 21, 1911, 1. For indictment, see *Omaha World-Herald*, October 19, 1911, 3.

66. *Omaha Sunday Bee*, December 17, 1911, 12; *Omaha Evening World-Herald*, December 20, 1911, 1, 5. Ouren had previously represented Frank Scott at trial. Cosson was a graduate of Valparaiso University and the State University of Iowa College of Law.

67. *Omaha Sunday Bee*, December 17, 1911, 12; *Omaha Evening World-Herald*, December 20, 1911, 1, 5.

68. *Omaha Sunday Bee*, December 17, 1911, 12; *Omaha Evening World-Herald*, December 20, 1911, 1, 5.

69. For Mabray's testimony in the Marks trial, see *Omaha Evening World-Herald*, December 20, 1911, 1, 5. Mabray said he first moved to South Dakota and later to Nebraska; at the time he was a deputy organizer for the Modern Woodmen of America. He said he acquired many of the diamonds he sold from Tom Dennison. See *Council Bluffs Nonpareil*, December 20, 1911, 1.

70. *State of Iowa v. Benjamin Marks*, Pottawattamie County District County Court, Iowa (1911); *Omaha Evening World-Herald*, December 19, 1911, 1; *Omaha Daily Bee*, December 20, 1911, 5.

71. *Omaha Evening World-Herald*, December 20, 1911, 1, 5, December 22, 1911, 1–2; *Omaha Daily Bee*, December 22, 1911, 2.

72. *Omaha Evening World-Herald*, December 21, 1911, 1; *Council Bluffs Nonpareil*, December 20, 1911, 1. Mabray said he had known Marks since 1898 when he ran a gambling house in Council Bluffs. Marks received 9–10 percent of gross receipts. For the race track, see *Nonpareil*, December 20, 1911, 10.

73. *State of Iowa v. Benjamin Marks*; *Omaha Evening World-Herald*, December 20, 1911, 1, 5; December 22, 1911, 2; *Omaha Daily Bee*, December 22, 1911, 2; *Nonpareil*, December 20, 1911, 10. Mabray said at first it was just him, two partners, and athletes Thielman and Marsh. See *Omaha Evening World-Herald*, December 19, 1911, 2. The gang's $162,595 would be worth $5,434,062 in 2022. Friedman, "Inflation Calculator."

74. *Omaha Evening World-Herald*, December 22, 1911, 1. For testimony of Mabray's wife, see *Omaha Daily Bee*, December 23, 1911, 1, 2.

75. *Omaha Evening World-Herald*, December 22, 1911, 1, 2; *Evening-Times Republican* (Marshalltown, IA), December 21, 1911, 2. Mabray said Jones,

an acquaintance of Boatright, loaned him money for his "bank roll" to become a partner in the big store.

76. *Nonpareil*, December 21, 1911, 1.

77. *Nonpareil*, January 3, 1912, 4.

78. *Omaha Sunday Bee*, December 24, 1911, 1, 2; *Nonpareil*, December 19, 1911, 10. For Gay, see *Nonpareil*, December 23, 1911, 1.

79. *Omaha Daily Bee*, December 28, 1911, 1.

80. *Omaha Daily Bee*, December 29, 1911, 1, 2; *Nonpareil*, December 28, 1911, 1, 6. For Richmond's testimony, see *Omaha Evening World-Herald*, December 28, 1911, 1, 8.

81. *Omaha Daily Bee*, December 30, 1911, 1, 2; *Omaha Evening World-Herald*, December 29, 1911, 1; December 30, 1911, 1, 6. The lawyer was Abner W. Askwith.

82. *Omaha Sunday Bee*, December 31, 1911, 1, 2; *Nonpareil*, December 28, 1911, 6; *Omaha Morning World-Herald*, December 31, 1911, 1. See allegations about Cosson securing Mabray's help in *Omaha Sunday World-Herald*, December 10, 1911, N-7.

83. *Omaha Sunday World-Herald*, December 31, 1911, 2; *Nonpareil*, December 28, 1911, 6.

84. *Omaha Sunday World-Herald*, December 31, 1911, 1; *Omaha Evening World-Herald*, January 2, 1912, 1; Quoted in the *Evening Times-Republican* (Marshalltown, IA), January 9, 1912, 7.

85. *Des Moines Register*, May 4, 1919, 16M; *Evening Nonpareil*, April 26, 1919, 3; *Omaha World-Herald*, August 31, 1930, Magazine Section, 7. Ben Marks died of "pancreas and pylons." His wife gave his occupation as retired farmer and stockman. See "Benjamin Marks," Iowa Death Records, 1904–1951, Familysearch.org.

86. Maurer, *The Big Con*, 19.

87. Charles S. Ranger to Cosson, January 2, 1912, "Benjamin Marks," Office of the Attorney General, Correspondence, Court Cases, Record Group 08, Iowa State Archives.

88. Cosson to Ranger, January 6, 1912, "Benjamin Marks," Iowa State Archives; Cosson to Sutor, January 4, 1912, "Benjamin Marks," Iowa State Archives.

89. Letter from John C. Mabray to George Cosson, January 6, 1912; Cosson to Mabray, January 22, 1912; Mabray to Cosson, January 21, 1912, "John C. Mabray," Office of the Attorney General, Correspondence, Court Cases, Record Group 08, Iowa State Archives. Mabray was living at Flat G on 817 Oak Street in Kansas City. The Washington Hotel was a stone's throw from the New Century Hotel where Robert Boatright died. Chic Conwell

said Kansas City was the easiest city in which to "straighten out a case." See Conwell, *The Professional Thief*, 109.

90. Cosson to Mabray, January 10, 1912; Mabray to Cosson, January 24, 1912, Cosson to Mabray, January 30, 1912, "John C. Mabray," Iowa State Archives.

91. Mabray to Cosson, February 9, 1912; February 20, 1912; Cosson to Mabray, February 22, 1912, "John C. Mabray," Iowa State Archives. *Kansas City Star*, February 7, 1912, 1.

92. *Kansas City Star*, March 21, 1912, 1; March 26, 1912, 1. Republican attorney Wentworth E. Griffin (1873–1928) served as chief of police from 1911 until 1913. *Kansas City Star*, July 6, 1928, 2.

93. Mabray to Cosson, March 23, 1912; Cosson to Mabray, March 28, 1912, "John C. Mabray," Iowa State Archives.

94. Mabray to Cosson, March 23, 1912; Cosson to Mabray, March 28, 1912, "John C. Mabray," Iowa State Archives.

95. *Kansas City Star*, March 25, 1912, 1; March 26, 1912, 1.

96. Cosson to George H. Mayne, September 2, 1912, "John C. Mabray," Iowa State Archives.

97. *Evening Nonpareil*, September 20, 1912, 7.

98. Clifford Naysmith, "Quality Hill: The History of a Neighborhood," Missouri Valley Series No. 1, Kansas City Public Library, 1962; "Quality Hill," Kansas City Register of Historic Places Application and Nomination Form, accessed October 11, 2020, https://clerk.kcmo.gov/Calendar.aspx; see also National Register of Historic Places Registration Form.

99. *Kansas City Star*, November 30, 1913, 2. After Mabray's friend Peter Bond died it was reported Mabray had purchased Bond's remaining interest in the Washington Hotel. *Kansas City Times*, March 26, 1915, 4.

100. *US v. John C. Mabray, et al.* (Council Bluffs). The remaining eight defendants were B. Beamolt, G. W. Debree, A. V. C. McPherson, Charles L. Scott, George Bradley, W. A. Garthie, P. A. Pulley, and J. L. Wright. In 1914 Mabray was listed as the manager of the Washington Hotel; he was a resident of the hotel the following year. 1914 *Kansas City Directory* (Kansas City: Gate City Directory Co., 1914), 1346; 1915 *Kansas City Directory* (Kansas City: Gate City Directory Co., 1915), 1325.

101. *Omaha World-Herald*, February 17, 1921, 2; *Kansas City Times*, November 26, 1919, 6; November 24, 1920, 5; February 12, 1921, 2. An ad placed by the administrator of Henry C. Haley's estate said he "went by the name of H. C. O'Hara in Webb City, Missouri, some twenty years ago; by the name of H. C. Hart in Kansas City shortly thereafter; by the name H. C. Howard in Denver, Colorado until about ten years ago; by the name H. C. Haley in Omaha, Nebraska, for the past ten years." *Diamond Drill* (Crystal Falls, MI), February 14, 1920, 4. He married Maud Smith in Denver, Colorado, on December 24, 1905; they did not have children. She died in 1919 in Los

Angeles. See "Colorado County Marriage Records and State Index, 1862–2006," and "California, US, Death Index, 1905–1939," Ancestry.com. Haley's death certificate indicates he died of "acute dilation of heart" and "acute gastritis." See "H. C. Haley," Missouri Death Certificate Database, https://s1.sos.mo.gov/records/Archives/ArchivesMvc/DeathCertificates. In 1912 Haley was sentenced by Judge Smith McPherson for participating in one of Mabray's swindles. He received a $300 fine and no jail time; he was identified by the name "H. C. Howard." See *Kansas City Star*, March 13, 1912, 12; Hawkins, *Mabray and the Mikes*, 117.

102. *Kansas City Star*, December 12, 1919, 3. The hotel was located at 1106 Baltimore Avenue.

103. *Joplin Globe*, December 31, 1920, 3; January 2, 1921, 1, 4. For Dennison's statement and a photo of Haley, see *Omaha Daily Bee*, February 28, 1920, 5. Dennison said Haley had an additional $9,500 at a bank, $3,600 in cash, Liberty bonds, a house and lot in Omaha near Hascom Park plus a house and apartments in Denver. See Henry C. Haley probate file, Douglas County, Nebraska Probate Court, Omaha, Nebraska.

104. *Kansas City Star*, November 23, 1920, 2; November 27, 1920, 2. The November 23 article notes Mabray had access to Haley's safety deposit box. See *John C. Mabry v. Floyd E. Jacobs*, Administrator of the estate of H. C. Haley, Deceased (1921), Missouri Supreme Court, Missouri State Archives.

105. *Kansas City Star*, March 29, 1921, 1.

106. Reprinted in the *Omaha Morning Bee*, July 26, 1922, 1, 2.

107. *Kansas City Star*, July 1, 1921, 1.

108. Willard Powell and Harry Forbes had already received presidential pardons. John C. Mabray Pardon File, Records of the Office of the Pardon Attorney, Record Group 204, Box 996, National Archives, College Park, Maryland. McPherson, impervious to Robert Boatright's charisma, appears to have been charmed by Mabray when the swindler visited him several times after his release from prison. He found Mabray "thoroughly penitent" and ready to "lead an upright life." Temple claimed that "noted law violators and gamblers have used every effort within their power to hinder him from taking the place he deserves in public life." Mabray was living at 3924 Forest Avenue in Kansas City.

109. For the Blonger Gang of Denver, see Reading, *The Mark Inside; Kansas City Times*, October 31, 1925, 3.

110. *Omaha World-Herald*, June 1, 1930, Magazine Section, 3.

111. "John C. Mabry," 1930 US Census, Kansas City, Jackson County, Missouri; "John C. Maybray," 1940 US Census, Kansas City, Jackson County, Missouri.

112. John C. Mabray married Chloea "Clo" Sarver on November 23, 1903, in Kansas City. She died in 1915. He married Geneva J. Haynes on July 27, 1919, in Kansas City. Whether Geneva died or divorced Mabray is unknown,

but at the time of his death his wife was Ola Collins Mabray. See "Chloea Mabray," *Kansas City Star*, July 1, 1915, 2. "John C. Mabray," Missouri Marriage Records 1805–2000, Ancestry.com; "John C. Mabry," *Kansas City Star*, February 3, 1952, 8; John C. Mabry," Missouri Death Certificate Database, https://s1.sos.mo.gov/records/Archives/ArchivesMvc /DeathCertificates; "Ola Mabray," *Kansas City Star*, January 30, 1992, C3–C4. Email to author from Alan Pierce, Kansas City Police Department Historical Society, May 7, 2019; letter to author, dated November 2, 2020, from Michael G. Seidel, Section Chief, FBI, Information Management Division. His wife spelled his surname "Mabry," although he signed it "Mabray" in surviving documents. Mabray does not have a probate record on file in Jackson County, Missouri. Phone conversation, Jackson County, Missouri, Probate Office, May 9, 2018.

CHAPTER 14

1. *Howard (KS) Courant*, April 22, 1909; *Eureka (KS) Democratic Messenger*, February 15, 1909. See entry for Louis B. Gillett, *Arkansas Deaths and Burials, 1882–1929; 1945–1963*, Familysearch.org. His cause of death was uremia and occupation was carpenter. *Fredonia (KS) Daily Herald*, April 17, 1909, 4. His wife Maude divorced him on grounds of "gross neglect of duty and extreme cruelty." *Neodesha (KS) Register*, July 10, 1908, 8.
2. Deputy Hawkins lists Gillet's number as 6; the swindle occurred in Council Bluffs, Iowa. See Hawkins, *Mabray and the Mikes*, 118. Thomas E. George (1859–1930) was a San Antonio hardware merchant. "Thomas E. George," 1910 US Census, San Antonio, Texas; "Thomas Edgar George," Texas, US Death Certificates, 1903–1982, Ancestry.com. For George, see *Omaha Daily Bee*, March 17, 1910, 2.
3. Undated, unpublished memoir, Glen S. Slough, Greenwood County, Kansas, Historical Society.
4. Letter from Jeff Hokanson, Greenwood County, Kansas, Historical Society, to Gary Purviance, dated November 20, 1996, Gillett Family File, Greenwood County Historical Society, Eureka, Kansas.
5. Letter from Jeff Hokanson, Greenwood County, Kansas, Historical Society, to Gary Purviance, dated October 9, 1996, Gillett Family File, Greenwood County Historical Society, Eureka, Kansas.
6. *San Diego Evening Tribune*, October 19, 1912, 1, 2; October 21, 1912, 1; October 23, 1912, 3; *San Diego Union*, October 20, 1912, 1; October 21, 1912, 10. Edward C. Moore (1858–1912) was the son of Martin and Phoebe Moore. He married Mary Gertrude Schicketanz in 1894 and was living with her and their young daughter in Council Bluffs in 1900. "Ed Moore," 1870 US Census, Pocahontas County, Iowa, Ancestry.com; "Ed Moore," 1900 US Census, Pottawattamie County, Iowa, Ancestry.com; "E. C. Moore," Iowa,

Select Marriages Index, 1758–1996, Ancestry.com. Moore later moved to California. The obituary for Ed's widow stated she moved to San Diego County, California, in 1904. *San Diego Union*, December 12, 1951; "Edward C. Moore," Death Certificate #12–033291, County of San Diego, California.

7. *San Diego Union*, October 24, 1912, 2; October 25, 1912, Section 3, 17, November 5, 1912, 20. The *San Diego Evening Tribune* stated his mother and sister were wealthy residents of Council Bluffs. See October 23, 1912, 3. "Edward C. Moore," Death Certificate #12–033291, County of San Diego, California; *San Diego Evening Tribune*, October 28, 1912, Section 2, 11. No additional stories elaborated on the criminal organization.

8. Each received three months in jail and $300 fines. *Iowa State (Des Moines) Bystander*, October 6, 1911, 4; *Joplin News-Herald*, January 31, 1916, 10; *Joplin Globe*, February 1, 1916, 2; *Webb City Register*, February 1, 1916, 1. Ellis was survived by his sister and brother. His half-brother gave Ed's occupation as merchant. See "Ed E. Ellis," Missouri Death Certificate Database, https://s1.sos.mo.gov/records/archives/archivesmvc/deathcertificates/.

9. *Joplin News-Herald*, January 31, 1916, 10; *Joplin Globe*, February 1, 1916, 2; *Webb City Register*, February 1, 1916, 1.

10. *Evening-Times Republican* (Marshalltown, IA), November 4, 1911, 5.

11. *University Missourian* (Columbia, MO), April 3, 1915, 3. The first reference I could find to Eddie's new identity is in the *Sunday Gate City* (Keokuk, IA), December 6, 1914, 7. "Dr. W. W. Castelane" had a letter at the Keokuk post office. His alias was sometimes spelled "Castellane."

12. *University Missourian*, August 31, 1915, 1. No record of his employment with the university could be found, but the records are incomplete. Email from Gary Cox to author, January 3, 2019.

13. *Columbia Evening Missourian*, July 17, 1920, 1, October 25, 1920, 2.

14. *Columbia Evening Missourian*, November 17, 1921, 1; January 6, 1922, 1.

15. *Columbia Daily Tribune*, July 27, 1927, 4. "Wm. Wardell Castelane," Missouri Death Certificate Database, https://s1.sos.mo.gov/records/Archives/ArchivesMvc/DeathCertificates. His parents were listed as James Steele and Lucinda Garrett of Bedford County, Tennessee.

16. *Fort Scott (KS) Daily Tribune*, July 10, 1919. For details on Stansbury's involvement, see *Indianapolis News*, June 21, 1919, 1, 31. For charges, see *Indianapolis Star*, November 3, 1919. For conviction, see *Indianapolis Star*, November 12, 1919, 1, 13; November 26, 1919, 1, 7.

17. *Kansas City Star*, February 26, 1920, 5B. He is buried in Kansas City's Mount Washington Cemetery.

18. *Denver Post*, November 1, 1911, 1; *Denver Post*, February 20, 1915, 1–2; Jeanette S. Lozier divorced Leon Lozier on September 2, 1914; see "Jeanette S. Loser," Colorado Divorce Index, 1851–1985, Ancestry.com. For the

bigamous relationship, see *Denver Post*, February 20, 1915, 1–2; April 8, 1915, 17.

19. *Denver Post*, January 24, 1912, 2; January 28, 1912, 17; February 27, 1912, 1.

20. *Denver Post*, November 22, 1914, 9.

21. *Omaha Evening World-Herald*, June 3, 1921.

22. *Morning World-Herald* (Omaha), April 26, 1927, 3.

23. Leon Lozier is buried in Omaha's Springwell Cemetery. *Omaha World-Herald*, February 28, 1937, Sports Section, 1B. For 1888 race, see the *Anaconda (MT) Standard*, March 2, 1919, 1.

24. *Honey Grove (TX) Signal*, June 14, 1907, 3; *Bonham (TX) News*, April 23, 1907, 4.

25. *Honey Grove (TX) Signal*, September 10, 1909, 3.

26. *Honey Grove (TX) Signal*, August 18, 1911, 2.

27. *Honey Grove (TX) Signal*, February 21, 1913, 3.

28. *Sentinel-Record* (Hot Springs, AR), June 23, 1914, 6. Hindman supposedly left Hot Springs sometime in 1913. See *Sentinel-Record* (Hot Springs, AR), January 17, 1914, 1.

29. *New York Daily Tribune*, November 19, 1914, 14; *New York Times*, November 19, 1914.

30. *Denver Post*, October 18, 1917, 10.

31. *Washington Times*, June 25, 1922, Magazine Section.

32. *The Roxton (TX) Progress*, September 4, 2008, 7. The Kid allegedly had a weakness for the racetrack; he was also known to play golf "for business reasons." See Maurer, *The Big Con*, 182, 189.

33. "L. E. Hindman," Texas Death Certificates, 1903–1982, Ancestry.com.

34. *Honey Grove (TX) Signal*, August 1, 1924, 1.

35. *Honey Grove (TX) Signal*, September 25, 1936, 1.

36. For an account of Fox's saga to bring the men to justice, see Orval E. Allbritton, "Charlie, the Fixer, and the Brass Kid," *The Record* (1997): 14–83; *St. Louis Republic*, January 18, 1913, 5; Little Rock *Arkansas Gazette*, January 18, 1913, 2; April 7, 1913, 2; April 23, 1918, 1; May 3, 1918, 1. Maurer mentions this case; see *The Big Con*, 241–42. *Mt. Vernon Lawrence County Record*, February 4, 1937. Ryan married Leona (sometimes spelled "Lena") Schaffer in Hot Springs in 1911. Letter to author from Donnie Kilgore, Garland County Historical Society, Hot Springs, Arkansas. Pennsylvanian Frank Fox (1877–1931) was an oil promoter and race car enthusiast. He competed in but did not place in the first Indianapolis 500. *Indianapolis Star*, April 20, 1931, 1, 8.

37. Ryan may have worked in the capacity as a fixer or other criminal capacity for the circuses. See Maurer, *The Big Con*, 173–74; *Mt. Vernon Lawrence County Record*, February 4, 1937; *Hot Springs New Era*, November 11, 1916, 1, October 18, 1922, 2; *Charles Edward "Ed" Ballard: A Story of*

Determination, Self-Education, and Ultimate Success (n.p.: C. E. Ballard
Literary Trust, 1984), 63–65. Robert "Silver Bob" Alexander set up shop
in Detroit in 1915. Ballard's obituaries stated he owned every circus except
Ringling. *Indianapolis Star*, November 7, 1936, 3. One article claimed
Ballard sold the Palm Island Club after Al Capone and his associates
entered the Miami market; Alexander reportedly continued "to oppose the
Capone interests alone." *Lansing State Journal*, November 7, 1936, 3.

38. Letter to author from Donnie Kilgore, Garland County Historical Society,
Hot Springs, Arkansas; *Mt. Vernon Lawrence County Record*, February 4,
1937. Ryan was remembered as a sportsman, poet, raconteur, and a man of
"marked personal magnetism."

39. Maurer, *The Big Con*, 183–84.

40. *Waxahachie (TX) Daily Light*, May 31, 1937, 2.

41. "Richard Beatte," Texas Death Certificates, 1903–1982, Ancestry.com.

42. See file for Willard Powell, Records of the Office of the Pardon Attorney,
Record Group 204, National Archives, College Park, Maryland.

43. Willard Powell, Records of the Office of the Pardon Attorney, Record
Group 204, National Archives, College Park, Maryland.

44. Willard Powell, Records of the Office of the Pardon Attorney, Record
Group 204, National Archives, College Park, Maryland.

45. Willard Powell, Records of the Office of the Pardon Attorney, Record
Group 204, National Archives, College Park, Maryland. The Edward
Montefiore Borchard Papers, MS 670, box 116, folder 1102 contains correspondence between Lutz and Mayne. Lutz noted he believed Powell was
present for one of the cons. Borchard, *Convicting the Innocent*.

46. *Chicago Daily Tribune*, December 2, 1914, 1, 8; December 17, 1914, 13;
December 25, 1914, 17; March 4, 1915, 1, 4.

47. *The Day Book*, March 6, 1915, 8; September 2, 1916, 6. "Queen of the
Underworld" Margaret Hill said Powell and his associates used the badger
game, which was the entrapment of married women for blackmailing pur-
poses. See *Washington Times*, August 6, 1922, 52–53 and Angus McLaren,
Sexual Blackmail: A Modern History (Cambridge, MA: Harvard University
Press, 2002), 90–91.

48. *Chicago Daily Tribune*, October 8, 1917, 17. The final disposition of Powell's
case is unknown because Cook County criminal felony case records from
1900–1927 have been destroyed. Chicago City Government Records, accessed
June 14, 2023, https://neiulibraries.libguides.com/ChicagoCityGovernment
Records/citycourts.

49. *Chicago Daily Tribune*, May 14, 1918, 12. David Maurer repeated a story
about Powell roping a mark for $25,000 when two corrupt Chicago detec-
tives intervened. When the Kid refused to cooperate, they broke his legs.
See Maurer, *The Big Con*, 229.

50. "Claudius Willard Powell," US World War I Draft Registration Cards, Ancestry.com.

51. In his application, Powell stated he had resided in South America and Cuba from March until July 1912. "Claudius Willard Powell," US Passport Applications, 1795–1925 (1919–1920), Ancestry.com.

52. *Kansas City Star*, March 29, 1921, 1.

53. *Fort Lauderdale News*, October 16, 1955, 6; *Miami Herald*, May 22, 1921, 1; *Chicago Daily News*, May 4, 1921, 3. The *Herald* claimed the Klan acted after a widow was swindled out of $12,000. For the mob and Buckminster's arrest, see *Miami Herald*, March 21, 1921, 1. For an editorial lauding the actions of the mob, see "The People Take a Hand," *Miami News*, March 25, 1921, 6. In 1919 confidence men had great success with a wire scheme in Florida; one of the ringleaders was said to be a former member of the Mabray Gang. See *Kansas City Star*, February 11, 1919, 12.

54. *Chicago Daily News*, April 30, 1921, 1.

55. *Chicago Daily News*, April 30, 1921, 1.

56. *Chicago Daily News*, April 30, 1921, 1.

57. *Chicago Daily Tribune*, March 29, 1921, 1; *Chicago Daily News*, April 30, 1921, 1; *Fort Lauderdale News*, October 16, 1955, 6. Powell's testimony was related to a notorious police protection case. His testimony reportedly helped send confidence man Joseph "Yellow Kid" Weil to prison at Joliet. Fred Buckminster and several others eluded authorities. Powell had secured immunity and remained free. Elizabeth Powell recognized the shooter.

58. *Chicago Daily Tribune*, March 29, 1921, 1; *Fort Lauderdale News*, October 16, 1955, 6; *Miami Herald*, May 22, 1921, 1. I could not verify the Alabama Kid's real name.

59. *Tampa Tribune*, May 20, 1921, 3. No grand jury or police records have survived. Email to author from Spencer S. Hathaway, Managing Assistant State Attorney/Public Information Officer, Florida State Attorney's Office of Circuit 7, November 15, 2018; email to author, November 14, 2018, City of St. Augustine Public Records Office; email to author, November 15, 2018, St. Augustine Police Records Office; email to author, November 15, 2018, St. John's County Sheriff's Department. Charles E. Owen of the *Chicago Daily News* reported Powell's widow and friends were not called; he insinuated St. John's County deputy sheriff Raymond Sabate lied when he said they did not wish to testify. See *Chicago Daily News*, May 2, 1921, 4.

60. *Chicago Daily News*, April 30, 1921, 1.

61. *Chicago Daily News*, August 1, 1923, 1, 3; August 3, 1923, 27. This account states Powell caused considerable turmoil in the Chicago Police Department in 1914. The paper claimed he partnered with Buckminster but quarreled in Daytona Beach.

62. *Evening Times-Republican* (Marshalltown, IA), October 4, 1911, 12. Nolan was arrested in a New York City pool room. *Omaha Daily Bee*, May 9, 1911, 3. For Ballew, see *Kansas City Star*, June 13, 1911, 5; *Omaha World-Herald*, September 19, 1911, 9; "Thomas W. Ballew," Missouri Death Certificate Database, https://s1.sos.mo.gov/records/archives/archivesmvc/deathcertificates/.

63. *Chicago Daily News*, December 13, 1922, 25. He reportedly received a six-year sentence for counterfeiting. *Chicago Tribune*, April 23, 1938, 9.

64. *Columbus (OH) Dispatch*, February 7, 1923, 8. One con man remarked, "Stolen money orders are a nasty rap, and very few ex-cons go into it." See Conwell, *The Professional Thief*, 76n33.

65. *Chicago Daily Tribune*, April 23, 1938, 9; September 27, 1938, 13; "Walter Nolan," Illinois Deaths and Stillbirths Index, 1916–1947, Ancestry.com.

66. Tom S. Robison, US Penitentiary, Leavenworth, Kansas, Records of the Bureau of Prisons, 1870–2009, Record Group 129, National Archives, Kansas City. See, specifically, the letter from FBI Director J. Edgar Hoover to the warden of the Iowa State Penitentiary in response to his inquiry about Robison's record. "Tom S. Robison," Book Eight, Iowa Consecutive Registers of Convicts, 1867–1970, Ancestry.com. "Tom S. Robison," 1940 US Census, Atlantic, Cass County, Iowa, Ancestry.com; "Thomas S. Robison," California Death Index, 1940–1997, Ancestry.com.

67. Ed Leach, US Penitentiary, Leavenworth, Kansas, Records of the Bureau of Prisons, 1870–2009, Record Group 129, National Archives, Kansas City.

68. "Edwin McCoy," Utah Death and Military Death Certificates, 1904–1961, Ancestry.com; *Deseret News* (Salt Lake City), August 31, 1925, 7; "Ed McCoy," US Penitentiary, Leavenworth, Kansas, Records of the Bureau of Prisons, 1870–2009, Record Group 129, National Archives, Kansas City.

69. Harry Forbes, Records of the Office of the Pardon Attorney, Record Group 204, National Archives, College Park, Maryland. For payment vouchers and correspondence identifying Forbes as a confidential informant, see John C. Mabray file, US DOJ.

70. Harry Forbes, Records of the Office of the Pardon Attorney, Record Group 204, National Archives, College Park, Maryland.

71. *Pantagraph* (Bloomington, IL), March 24, 2019, A13.

72. *Chicago Tribune*, October 29, 1918, 13; March 4, 1918, 11. For the fixed fight, see *Rockford (IL) Republic*, October 24, 1913, 2.

73. *Oregonian* (Portland, OR), May 3, 1913, 5; Little Rock *Arkansas Gazette*, July 8, 1915, 8. Prosecutor Temple expressed his displeasure at Judge McPherson's decision and groused "the responsibility lies with him." Letter from Temple to the US Attorney General, May 24, 1913, in John C. Mabray file, US DOJ.

74. "Isador Jacob Warner," US World War II Draft Registration Cards, 1942, Ancestry.com; *Daily Oklahoman* (Oklahoma City), May 21, 1954, 14.

75. "Isador J Warner," Forest Lawn Cemetery, Buffalo, New York, Findagrave.com.

76. *Des Moines Register*, June 10, 1913, 1.

77. "Monte McCall," US Passport Applications, 1795–1925, Ancestry.com.

78. *Davenport (IA) Quad-City Times*, November 1, 1917, 13.

79. *Tampa Bay Times*, July 22, 1963, 12. He was a member of the Elks; it was common for confidence men to join fraternal organizations to help gain the trust of their victims.

80. *Omaha World-Herald*, February 8, 1925, Sports Section; *Denver Post*, March 9, 1918, 6; *Decorah (IA) Public Opinion*, February 22, 1922, 1.

81. JC Marsh to US Department of Justice, November 19, 1921, in John C. Mabray file, US DOJ.

82. "George M. Marsh," Oregon Death Index, 1898–2008, Ancestry.com.

83. "Smith McPherson," *Annals of Iowa* 12, no. 1 (1915): 77.

84. "George Cosson," *The Biographical Dictionary of Iowa*, University of Iowa Press Digital Editions, accessed February 22, 2020, http://uipress.lib.uiowa .edu/bdi/DetailsPage.aspx?id=76.

85. *Nonpareil*, July 9, 1952, 3; *Omaha Daily Bee*, November 30, 1910, 5.

86. *Los Angeles Times*, February 5, 1961, F4.

87. "William F. Allmon," 1930 US Census, Wichita, Sedgwick County, Kansas.

88. Conwell, *The Professional Thief*, 115–16.

89. Maurer, *The Big Con*, 27.

90. See Conwell, *The Professional Thief*, 56–62.

91. For example, see Tom Porter's story in the *Omaha World-Herald*, June 1, 1930, Magazine Section, 3.

92. *Omaha World-Herald*, June 1, 1930, Magazine Section, 3. Photographs, correspondence, bank drafts, betting lists, contracts, tally sheets, post office box applications, and post office box keys were among the evidence. After a trial ended, it was common for exhibits to be returned to the US attorney's office. They could then be used in other trials and eventually discarded. Some of the exhibits remain in the surviving records, among them a few photos and letters. What happened to the rest is unclear. I consulted long-time federal archivist Barbara Rust about the common practices of records management at the federal level during the early twentieth-century. Phone conversation with Barbara Rust, National Archives, Fort Worth, Texas, November 2019.

93. *US v. J. C. Mabray, Willard Powell, Ed McCoy, Ed Leach, Tom S. Robison, Harry Forbes, and Clarence Class*, case no. 3474, US Circuit Court of Appeals for the Eighth Circuit (1911), Record Group 276, National Archives,

Kansas City. For Rush, see *Omaha World Herald*, June 1, 1930, Magazine Section, 3.

94. A. C. Thomas with Edwin Shrake, "Soundings from Titanic," *Sports Illustrated*, October 9, 1972; Kevin Cook, *Titanic Thompson: The Man Who Bet on Everything* (New York: W. W. Norton, 2010).

95. *Pittsburgh Press*, November 20, 1937, 9.

96. Letter from Inspectors Ranger, Allmon, Swenson to W. S. Mayer, Inspector in Charge, St. Louis, November 7, 1910, in John C. Mabray file, US DOJ.

97. Interview with Brooks Blevins, *Missouri Times* (State Historical Society of Missouri), Spring 2021.

INDEX

and Moss con, 45–47; move to Colorado Springs, 89–90; move to Jasper County, 20, 227n82; and Phelps con, 58; philanthropy of, 44; and protection, 39, 60, 62–63, 76, 78–80; and Randall con, 67; record-keeping by, 43; in Ryan mail fraud case, 241n11; shakedown complaints, 104–5; and Simpson, 170; skills as inside man, 43; and St. Louis, 19–20; and typhoid, 13; and Watkins con, 74; Woodson killing, 9–11, 14–20; work as young man, 16, 19. *See also* Buckfoot Gang; lawsuits and Buckfoot Gang; prosecutions and Buckfoot Gang; Webb City Athletic Club

Bonaparte, Charles, 258n53

Bond, Peter, 276n99

Booth, George E., 39, 62, 81, 82, 91, 129

bosses, political/criminal: Barbee as, 4, 8, 49–51, 76, 78–80, 129–31; Dennison as, 8, 148, 154; Marks as, 147–50, 179; and vigilante threats, 88–89. *See also* political influence; protection

Bourland, Fagan, 89

Bowman, J. C., 156

Boyd, James, 144

Boyer, L. W., 236n9

Boyle, Louis C., 62, 75

Bradley, George A., 156, 276n100

Bradshaw, Rhoton & Helm, 139

Brannon, Bert, 226n59

bright-lights districts, 7, 8

Bromley, Bert "Curley": arrest, 91; background, 33–34; death of, 109–11; fines, 214n4; Lang and Becker lawsuit, 82, 226n65; and Lory con, 102, 103; and Morris/Long fight, 57; and Moss con, 45;

pending Barton County case, 239n44; reversals of convictions, 115; and Ryan con, 241n11

Bronson, James "Bow Tie," 58, 221n4

Brooks, William, 61–63

brothels and prostitution: and grand jury on crime in Jasper County (1901), 47; and House of Lords, 50; protection fees, 269n18; and vigilante threats, 88; and violence, 85

Broussard, J. J., 81

Brown, Bennett B., 16

Brown, Frank Wilson, *158*; aliases, 264n2; arrest, 157; background, 157–59; death of, 175; and Mabray, 177; and mail fraud trial, 165, 170, 171; Seattle Athletic Club, 159; South Bend operation, 155

Brown, Thomas. *See* Stansbury, Garrette Orville "G. O."

Brown, W. B., 234n30

Bryson, Leo, 134

bucket shop con: defined, 229n17; rise of, 7

Buckfoot Gang: area of operations, 7; formation of, 40–41; members, lists of additional, 37–38, 213n80; members' backgrounds, 26–38; members in Mabray Gang, 5, 137–38, 152–53, 157, 160, 170; name origin, 4; as national, 198; numbers of members, 59; property, loss of, 82–83; property, sheriff's sale of, 116; roles in, 41–43. *See also* Boatright, Robert P. W. "Buckfoot"; fighters and fighting; foot racing; lawsuits and Buckfoot Gang; mail fraud and Buckfoot Gang; prosecutions and Buckfoot Gang; Webb City Athletic Club

Buckminster, Fred, 192, 193

Bulah (prostitute), 85

Bull, Fred, 110

Burke, Edmund F.: background, 218n46; House of Lords affidavit, 54; as referee, 47, 57, 63, 217n32; and slot machines, 218n46, 221n71

Burns, George, 241n11

Burton, Perlee Ellis "P. E.," 129–30

Bush, Carl, 27–28

Business Men's Athletic Club, 221n4

Byers, Howard Webster "Webb," 161, 163, 166, 167–68

c - - - - - -

Cale, Thomas, 140

Campbell, Annie, 102

Campbell, M. S., 163

Campbell, Roy, 142

Capell, Frank, 175, 176

Capone, Al, 281n37

Cardwell, Robert, 152

Carkeek, Jack, 159, 174

Carlson, John, 80, 87–88

Caron, Guy, 139

Carruthers, H. W., 45, 225n43

Carter, Alfred G., 71, 103, 113, 260n32

Carter, William M., 58

Carterville, Missouri, gaming house in, 214n3

Carterville Record, 66

Carterville Republican, 94, 97

Carterville Rocket, 47, 54, 58

Carthage, Missouri: baseball game against Webb City Athletic Club, 39; rivalry with Joplin, 21–22

Carthage Evening Press: on Buckfoot Gang, 4, 102, 103, 106; on Joplin rivalry, 22; on lack of prosecution, 68, 76; and newspaper rivalries, 4, 53, 76, 89, 130; and special election (1902), 91–95

Castelane, William Wardell. *See* Morris, Edward "Eddie" K.

Cate, C. J., 138

Cavanaugh, John E., 133, 138, 252n11, 257n52, 265n11, 271n42

Center Creek Mining Company, 23

Chambers, Charles McClellan "Mac," 82

Chenoweth, J. Albert, 110–11, 115

Cherry, James "Jack," 58–59

circular swindle, 7

circus, 189–90

cities: bright-lights districts, 7, 8; intercity criminal networks, 6–8

Clabby, Andrew, 11

Clark, Ed, 120

Clark, Harry, 73–74

Clark, William Lloyd, 142

Class, Clarence, 171, 191–92, 251n2

Clay, Cora, 123, 125

Clay, George R.: and Barbee's suit against Curtice, 234n30; and Boatright's assets after death, 113, 122, 123–24, 125; as Boatright's attorney, 39; and bribery allegations against Currey, 5; and Davis, 107; death of, 128–29; and death of Priscilla Boatright, 128; shipping of safe to, 111–12

Coakley, Jerry, 19

Cobb, John W., 98, 113

Cockrill, Jerry, 44, 238n41

Cockrill, Stewart, 44, 238n41

codes for correspondence, 43

Cohn, Henry, 45

Cohn, Phillip, 217n36

Cole, George E., 75, 121

Collins, Daniel, 92

Colorado Springs, Colorado: as base for Buckfoot Gang, 4, 7, 88, 89–90; Boatright's shift to, 89–90; as rough town, 83–84; Williams move to, 83–84

con men: intercity criminal networks, 6–8; monikers and, 208n28;

and Mooneyham allegations, 54;
Morris as, 33, 44, 47, 57–58, 63,
66, 80, 84; Morris/Long fights, 47,
57–58, 80, 84; Nolan as, 38, 66;
Purcell fight, 57; rules of, 216n25;
Ryan and fight store, 35; Stift/
Gardner fight, 263n57; Stift/Long
fights, 63, 84
Finch, James, 194
First National Bank of Council Bluffs,
170, 176, 177
Fisher, Bert, 44
Flanigan, John W., 249n50
Flemming, William, 155, 251n2
Flournoy, George B., 153, 174
foot racing: by Ben Ansel, 37, 44; by
Jesse Ansel, 37; by Ashmore, 155–
56; by Beatte, 37, 174, 213n80;
by Bishop, 44; and Black con,
69–70; and Buckfoot Gang, 36, 37,
44–47, 58–59, 64–65, 80–81, 171,
233n19; by Cockrill brothers, 44;
by Connors, 225n43; by Crider, 37,
59; decline of, 196; and Doucette
con, 81; by Fields, 37; by Fisher,
44; by Gillett, 26–28, 44, 45,
226n62; and grand jury on crime
in Jasper County (1901), 47–48;
by Grimm, 37; Hobbs con, 64–65;
by Kivlin, 37, 213n80, 215n6;
and Lory con, 233n19; by Lozier,
30–33, 58–59, 171, 188, 213n80,
215n6; and Mabray Gang, 155–56;
by Moore, 37, 213n80; payments
to sprinters, 215n14; and Pittman
con, 81; popularity of, 26–27;
by Robison, 153; and Simpson,
270n30; by Stansbury, 36; and
Watkins con, 73–74
Forbes, Clarence, 160, 172, 194
Forbes, Harry, *169*; arrest, 160; as

athlete, 168, 197; death of, 194; as
informant, 175, 194; mail fraud
case, 172; pardon, 194, 277n108
Fore, Joseph H., 14
Forlow, Frank, 82
Fox, Frank, 189
Franklin, Elnora, 57
Fraternal Order of Eagles: and
Boatright's funeral, 115; and
Bromley, 110; fight at, 83
French, George, 109
French, Neal, 109

G - - - - - -

Galena, Kansas: as base for Buckfoot
Gang, 7, 44; and Bromley, 34
Galena Athletic Club, 44
gambling: and House of Lords, 50,
53, 57; Jasper County, attempt to
close down by Redding, 101; in
Jasper County, overview of, 21–26;
and Jasper County grand jury on
crime (1901), 47, 53–55, 57, 66; in
Joplin, attempt to control, 25–26;
and Mabray, 181, 182; Marks's
control in Council Bluffs, 147–50;
Webb City as open town, 23–24;
Webb City crackdown on in 1905,
119. *See also* fighters and fighting;
foot racing; wrestling
Gammon, James, 91, 106
Gammon, Silas Oscar "Butch," 110, 111,
242n37
gangs. *See* Buckfoot Gang; Mabray Gang
Gans, Joe, 169
Gantt, James Britton, 115
Gardner, George, 263n57
Garthie, W. A., 276n100
Gates, Lillian, 152
Gay, Thomas S., 156, 167, 178
Geir, "Spooly," 85

Gibson, William H. "Billy," 47, 58, 156, 213n80

Gillett, "Bud" Louis B.: aliases, 226n62; background, 26–28; and Barton County case, 239n44; and Davis con, 60–62, 71, 80; death of, 185; and foot racing, 26–28, 44, 45, 226n62; Lang and Becker lawsuit, 82, 226n65; marriage, 60–61; post-gang career, 185–86

Gillett, Frank, 26, 27

Gilyard, Thomas, 104

Gleason, F. S. W., 13

Globe (St. Louis), 203n23

Goatley, Charles, 242n37

Goddard, Robert Edward Lee: arrests, 160; background, 36; and Bland con, 99; death of, 190; and Johnson correspondence, 120; mail fraud trials, 165, 172, 241n11

Godfrey, W. E., 174

Gondorff, Charles, 189, 196

Gondorff, Fred, 196

Gonter, Charles, 12

Gordanier, William, 133

Graebe, Otto, 171

Granby Stampede, 34

graves: Barbee, 131; Boatright, 3, 8, 115, 117; Lozier, 279n23

Gray, Abigail, 248n45

greed of victims, 4, 41, 44, 84, 105, 199

Green, Harry, 106–7

green goods, 7

Gregory, Charles, 101, 171, 231n38, 252n9

Gretzer, Gladys M., 182

Griffin, Wentworth E., 180

Griffith, Charles B., 61

Griffith, Monroe, 44, 79, 106–7, 115, 125, 231n38

Grimm, John "Cash," 37–38, 171

Groneweg, William, 163

Guinn, James Henry, 224n25

guns, disarming of, 65, 73, 98

H - - - - - -

Hackney, Thomas, 216n24

Hadley, Herbert S., 74–75

Hafner, Valentine, 99–100

Haggerty, Michael, 107

Haley, Henry C. "Judge," 181

Halliburton, John, 101, 105, 106, 121, 214n5, 237n23

Halyard, William B., 249n57

Hamilton, Frank, 68–69

Hansel, Bert. *See* Stansbury, Garrette Orville "G. O."

Hansford, Ed, 153

Hardin, James F., 49

Harding, Warren, 182

Harper, Walter, 232n3

Harrigan, Laurence, 11

Harriman, Mrs., 153

Harriman, Russell Barrett, *158*; background, 157; death of, 175; and Mabray, 155, 177, 256n45; mail fraud prosecution, 157, 165, 170, 171; and Seattle Athletic Club, 159; and South Bend Store, 155

Harris, Joseph R., 18, 19

Harris, Winn S., 159–60, 172–73

Hart, Ernest, 170, 176, 178

Harvey, Austin, 25

Haskell, John B., 260n29

Haughawout, T. Bond, 26, 237n23

Haughawout, William H., 70

Hawkins, James J., 137–38, 139, 257n52, 261n43, 269n20

Hawman, Harvey, 31

Haynes, Geneva J., 277n112

Hazard, William B., 17–18

Hazen, John T., 32–33

Hearrell, Elwin C. "Baldy," 103
Hedrick, Frank, 103
Hemingway, Wilson E., 101
Henry, French, 193
Hermelbrecht, John R., 162, 163, 262n46
Hess, John, 136, 152, 161, 163, 177, 179
Hicks, William, 16
Hill, Margaret, 189
Hindman, Lucius E. "Honey Grove Kid": arrest, 175; background, 29–30; and Bedford con, 259n23; and Bland con, 99–100; and Broussard con, 81; case dismissals, 120; and Chambers con, 82; convictions, 107, 113; death of, 189; Forbes as informant on, 194; and Hodges con, 228n4; incarceration of, 107, 189, 260n31; and Mabray Gang, 137–38; and Moss con, 45–47; move to Little Rock, 137–38; post-gang career, 188–89; as roper, 42, 100; and Ryan mail fraud case, 241n11; and wire con, 116, 189; and Wright/Duncan con, 60; and Youmans assault, 81
Hiner, Maude, 60–61
Hobbs, Robert E., 64–65, 79, 89, 247n39
Hodges, Charles O., 74
Hoffman House (Council Bluffs), 149
Holden, "Kid," 233n21
"Honey Grove Kid." See Hindman, Lucius E. "Honey Grove Kid"
Hook, William, 126
Horner, Samuel, 80
horse racing: and fake death/injuries in con, 161–62; and Mabray Gang, 134, 143, 150, 153, 156, 161–62, 171, 177; Red Leo, 162; and West, 174; and wire con, 196

Hosmer, Edward S., 53, 78–79, 249n58
Hot Springs, Arkansas: as base for Buckfoot Gang, 4, 7, 98; crime in, 99; prosecutions in, 98; raid on Mabray Gang, 138, 139; and wire con, 116
Houpt, Jake, 260n31
Houseman, Lou, 66–67
House of Lords: as Barbee's base, 50–51, 54; decline and demolition of, 131–32; and grand jury on crime in Jasper County (1901), 53, 57, 66; history of, 50; images, 25, 51, 93; ownership and Collins, 92; and special election (1902), 91–97; and violence, 50–51, 66, 85–86, 220n57; walkway, 51, 92, 93, 250n65
House of Refuge (St. Louis), 13–14, 17
Howard, Bart B., 52–53, 129, 131
Howard, Blackie, 181
Hoyne, Thomas Maclay, II, 191–92
Hubbard, Robert L., 84
Hughes, Alex S., 16
Hulett, Alfred A., 215n10
Hunt, E. C., 173–74
Hunter, Bill, 50
Hutchinson, M. W., 249n58

I - - - - - -
Idle, John, 193
insanity defense, 11, 14–20
inside man: Boatright's skills as, 43; role of, 42, 43; and wire con, 243n41
International Turf Exchange, 192

J - - - - - -
Jackson, Peter, 187
"Jack the Ripper" (boxer), 105–6
Jacobs, Boone B., 156
Jacobs, William S., 190

Jasper County, Missouri: as base for Buckfoot Gang, 4; Boatright family's move to, 20, 227n82; gambling houses, attempt to close by Redding, 101; gambling towns in, 21–26; grand jury on crime in (1901), 47–48, 53–55, 57, 66; map of, *22*; mining in, 20; newspaper rivalries in, 4, 48, 53–55, 65–66, 89, 129–30, 197; population growth, 23; Prohibition in, 129; and special election (1902), 90–98

Jasper County Democrat: coverage of Buckfoot Gang, 4, 48, 58, 60, 75, 80, 89, 100, 104; and grand jury on crime in Jasper County (1901), 53–55; on lack of prosecution of crime, 65–66, 67, 83, 88–89, 101, 112; and newspaper rivalries, 4, 53–55, 65–66, 85–86; on Saighman, 113; and special election (1902), 96; on Williams, 100. *See also* Phelps, William H.; Roach, Cornelius

Jasper County jail, 103–6

Jasper County News, 4, 68

Jenkins, Burris A., 182

Johnson, Charles P., 9, 10, 11, 14, 15

Johnson, David, 6, 8

Johnson, Fred, 138

Johnson, Irven E., *122*; as Buckfoot Gang member, 213n80; and Cobb con, 98; incarceration of, 120; larceny by, 98; and mail fraud prosecution, 113, 241n11; as painter, 211n69; pardon, 120; and Pittman con, 80–81; post-gang career, 120; as roper, 42, 80–81; and Williams's death, 108

Johnson, Jack, 187

Johnson, James, 138, 142, 165

Johnson, John D., 9, 203n34

Jones, Canada Bill, 147

Jones, Conk, 116

Jones, Jack, 213n80

Jones, Sam, 114, 129, 242n37

Jones, William Cuthbert, 10, 11, 15

Joplin, Missouri, *25*; attempt to control gambling in, 25–26; growth of, 24–25; reputation of, 50, 51–52; rivalry with Carthage, 21–22

Joplin American, 130

Joplin Globe, 52; on attempts to control gambling in Joplin, 25–26; and Boatright's death, 115; and break in at Boatright's mausoleum, 8; on Bromley's death, 110, 111; connections to Buckfoot Gang, 57, 81, 86, 91–93; coverage of Buckfoot Gang, 4, 48, 58–59, 74, 87, 89, 106, 113; on Ellis, 187; and grand jury on crime (1901), 53–55; and House of Lords, 50–51, 86; and Mooneyham, 67, 76; and newspaper rivalries, 4, 53–55, 76, 78–79, 89, 91–94, 96–97, 129–31; purchase of by Barbee, 52; sale to Rogers, 130–31; and special election (1902), 91–97; staff, 52–53; on Stewart's death, 126–27; and Youmans assault, 81. *See also* Barbee, Gilbert

Joplin Morning Tribune, 131

Joplin News-Herald, 77; coverage of Buckfoot Gang, 4, 48, 53–54, 58, 63, 65–66, 70, 73; dynamiting of, 130; and grand jury on crime (1901), 53–54, 66; on *Joplin Globe*'s endorsement of Mooneyham, 76; on Joplin Savings Bank, 128; on lack of enforcement, 25, 65–66, 89; and newspaper rivalries, 4, 53–54, 76,

Moore, George W., 119
Moore, John Isaac, 120
Moore, Will, 50–51
Moran, George "Bugs," 194
Morgan, William, 14
Morris, Edward "Eddie" K.: aliases,
  187; arrest, 160; background, 33;
  death of, 187; as fighter, 33, 44, 47,
  57–58, 63, 66, 80, 84; and mail
  fraud, 165, 172, 241n11; post-gang
  career, 187
Morrison, J. R., 271n41
Moss, Stephen E., 45–47, 125–26,
  224n25
Mountjoy, Richard T., 119
Mull, Fred, 271n41

background, 37; as bond supplier, 59, 63, 71, 91, 103, 106; death of, 129; and death of Boatright, 114; and grand jury on crime in Jasper County (1901), 53; and selling liquor to minors, 207n8; and sheriff's sale of Club property, 116; and 16 to 1 Saloon, 37, 91, 94, 212n78; and West, 174

Parker, Porter, 257n52

Patton, William "Billy," 50

payments: Boatright's cut, 122, 215n14; Mabray's cut, 177; shills and sprinters, 215n14; and syndicates, 8; and West, 174

Pepper, Henry C., 102, 115

Perkins, Joseph Dudley, 91, 103

Perkins, Marlin, 234n24

Perkins, Tom, 213n80

Phelps, Charles, 49

Phelps, Everett L., 58

Phelps, William H.: and Currey, 231n42; death of, 131; political career, 48–49; rivalry with Barbee, 4, 48, 53–55, 65–66, 76, 131; and special election (1902), 94, 96; speech on lawlessness, 90. *See also Jasper County Democrat*

philanthropy and political influence, 44

Philips, John Finis, 63, 246n32

Phillips, Henry, 59, 224n25

Philpot, C. F., 175

Phipps, Richard, 113

Pickering, E. O., 15–16

Pierpont, Zachariah, 156, 167

Pittman, John I., 80–81

Plestina, Marin, 195

Plummer, Jeff, 71

police: killings of, 88, 226n59; ouster of Council Bluffs chief police, 167–68; violence between police forces, 236n5. *See also* protection

political influence: and Barbee, 4, 8, 49–51, 76, 78–80, 129–31; Conwell on, 258n11; Jasper County special election (1902), 90–98; of Marks, 147–50, 176, 179, 198; need for, 43–44. *See also* protection

Pomeroy, Ira, 241n11

Porter, "Handsome Jack," 189

Porter, Tom, 182, 196

Porterfield, E. E., 182

Portley, Ed, 221n70, 240n5

postal inspectors and services: cons' inability to control, 198; integrity of inspectors, 267n37; numbers of inspectors, 140–41; role of, 196, 198; and stopping delivery, 70. *See also* mail fraud

Potter (Deputy Coroner), 110

Powell, Claudius Willard "Waco Kid," 169–70, 190–93, *191*, 277n108

Powell, Drayton W., 76–78

Powell, Elizabeth, 192–93

Powers, Ernest, 155–56

Price, David, 57

Price, Harry. *See* Wasser, Harry "Bud"

Price, Henry, 234n30

Pritchett, Morris, 119

Pritchett, Stonewall, 87, 115

The Professional Thief by a Professional Thief (Conwell), 6

proposition bet, 197

prosecutions: and lack of enforcement by Mooneyham, 54, 61, 65–66, 67, 79, 83, 85, 89; and ouster of Council Bluffs chief of police, 167–68

prosecutions and Buckfoot Gang: of Boatright for criminal conspiracy, 217n35; of Boatright for embezzlement, 233n13; of Boatright for killing Woodson, 9–11, 14–20;

prosecutions and Buckfoot Gang
(*continued*)

    for Cobb con, 113; for Davis con,
61–63, 71, 79–80, 98, 106–7, 112,
125–26, 227n80; dismissals, 120;
for forged instruments, 74–75;
and petition for grand jury (1902),
76; reversals of convictions, 115;
and Williams's hiding of assets,
100–101; for Youmans con, 112,
231n38

prosecutions and Mabray Gang: and
Ballew con, 160–62, 193–94; dismissals, 175–76, 181; and Kile con,
142; mail fraud, 144, 145, 150–51,
156, 165–73, 176

prostitution. *See* brothels and
prostitution

protection: and Boatright, 39, 60,
62–63, 76, 78–80; for brothels,
269n18; fees, 155, 269n18; and
Howell in Chicago, 191–92; and
Mabray Gang, 135, 143–44, 145,
154–55, 162, 166, 167–68, 177–78,
198; and Marks, 147, 176, 177–79;
in New Jersey, 156; and Seattle
cons, 159

Pulley, P. A., 276n100

Purcell, Frank, 57

Purcell, H., 44

Pyatt, Henry, 112

R------

Raff, James, 213n80

railroads: and access to victims, 8; and
intercity criminal networks, 7–8;
lobbying for by Phelps, 49;
and Webb City transportation
links, 39

Randall, A. N., 67–68

Ranger, Charles: death of, 195;
and mail fraud investigation

and prosecution, 140, 157, 198,
257n52; and Marks trial, 178, 179;
and West arrest, 174

Ray, Frederick Emery, 142

Reading, Amy, 6

Ream, C. L., 16

records and record-keeping: and
Barker testimony, 101; and Bland
con, 100; and Buckfoot Gang, 43;
and codes for correspondence,
43; and Davis con prosecution,
62; and inside man role, 43; and
Mabray Gang, 139–40, 141, 155,
171, 259n20; Mabray trial records,
196; Stansbury on, 124

Redding, Andrew H., 101

Redell, George H., 221n70

Red Leo, 162

Reed, Susan, 15

Reese, Ben H., 52–53

Reger, Bruce, 45, 76

Reger, William, 45

Reichardt, Louis, 137, 138

Republican Party: gains by, 96–97;
Jasper County special election
(1902), 90–98; and newspaper
rivalries in Jasper County, 4, 48,
53–55, 65–66, 89, 197

rewards, 198

Rhoton, Lewis, 139, 189, 258n53

Rice, Frank H., 121, 213n80, 217n36

Rice, Mary, 83, 121–23, 231n50, 232n5

Rich, Albert, 59, 62–63, 67, 83

Rich, Leonard "Len," 54, 88

Richmond, George, 151–52, 167–68,
177, 178–79

Roach, Cornelius: and *Jasper County
Democrat*, 4, 53, 54–55, 60; on lack
of prosecution of crime, 65–66,
67; and special election (1902),
96; on vigilante threats, 88–89

Roberson, Burrell C., 242n37

Roberts, Burl, 139
Robinson, Anselm, 11
Robinson, Belle, 85
Robison, Tom S., 153, 172, 174, 194
Rodgers, William H., 241n11
Rogers, Alfred H., 130–31, 220n58
Rogers, Will, 51
Roller, Benjamin F., 159, 160
Roney, Thomas J., 215n7
Roper, David M., 71, 104
ropers: numbers of in Buckfoot Gang, 222n16; numbers of in Mabray Gang, 259n20, 264n1; role of, 41, 42–43; victims as, 41–42; in Williams deposition, 84–85
Rosewater, Edward, 154
Rossel, Jesse, Jr., 27
Ruhsert, Henry, 176
Rush, Sylvester, 145, 165, 166, 196
Ryan, Coke, 229n15
Ryan, George W.: arrest, 260n31; background, 34–35; and Bland con, 99; and Cardwell assault, 152; and Cobb con, 98; death of, 190; and dismissals, 120; incarceration of, 260n31; mail fraud case, 111, 140, 175, 267n4; post-gang career, 189–90; as roper, 42; shift to Little Rock, 137–38; and Walker con, 152; and wire con, 116
Ryan, Laura Sherman, 34–35
Ryan, William S., 35
Ryan, W. J., 241n11
Ryan (sprinter), 233n19

S - - - - - -
safes, 43, 83, 111–12, 116, 224n31
Saighman, Daniel E., 50, 53, 57, 78–79, 112–13, 221n70
saloons: and closing of gambling houses in Jasper County by

Redding, 101; closing of in Webb City in 1905, 119; and prohibition in Jasper County, 129; and Webb City as open town, 23–24
Salt Lake City, Utah: as base for Buckfoot Gang, 7, 233n20; as base for Mabray Gang, 155
Sarcoxie Farm Record, 66
Sarver, Chloea "Clo," 277n112
Sawyer, Tom, 44
Scanlan, John, 32, 33
Scott, Charles L., 276n100
Scott, Frank, 153, 162–63, 173, 273n59
Scott, Haywood, 84, 229n14
Scott, William, 153, 156, 167, 257n50
Seattle Athletic Club, 159
Seattle cons, 159–60
Secrest, Joshua H., 168
Sedalia, Missouri, crime in, 29
Senate Club (Kansas City), 121, 145
send technique, 42
Sewall, William J., 53, 89, 91, 94
sexual assault: by Bromley and Fetters, 34; by Lozier, 30, 32, 188
Shaley, James, 31
Shannon, Hiram, 25, 26, 89
Sheppard, Jacob, 61, 62, 63
Shercliffe, Frank, 259n25
shills: payment, 215n14; role of, 42, 43
Shores, Bert R., 159–60, 173
Siler, George, 57–58
Simpson, George Howard, 143–44, 170–71, 177
Sinclair, William, 16
16 to 1 Saloon, 37, 91, 94
Sizer, John, 191
Sloane, B. F., 19
slot machines, 218n46, 221n71
Slough, Glenn S., 26
Smith, John C., 160
Sommers, James. *See* Cherry, James "Jack"

Sonnenschein, Fred, 59

South Bend, Indiana, store, 155

Southern Land and Timber Company, 135

Spear, Ed, 35, 189

Spencer, Arthur E., 111, 113, 123, 126

Spindler, John J., 176, 178

Springs, Dave, 242n37

Stansbury, Garrette Orville "G. O.": aliases, 36, 45; arrest, 75; background, 36; on Boatright's assets, 124; and Davis con, 61, 62, 63; death of, 188; and Flemming, 262n48; foot racing by, 36; horse racing con, 153; and mail fraud, 111, 187–88; and Morris/Long fights, 47, 58; on origins of gang, 214n5; post-gang career, 187–88; and Reger con, 45; wrestling con, 133

Steele, Eddie K. *See* Morris, Edward "Eddie" K.

steerers. *See* ropers

Stein, Bernard, 33

Steinbaugh, Eddie D., 133

Stewart, George, 166

Stewart, James: and Black con, 69–70, 71; and Davis con, 62, 71, 98, 112, 126; death of, 128; founding of Exchange Bank, 23; on founding of Webb City Athletic Club, 41; on giving Boatright money, 218n48; and Griffith con, 106, 115; and Hobbs con, 89; and Moss con, 45; and Owen con, 106; and Reger lawsuit, 45; role of in store con, 42

Stewart, Joseph, 23, 70–71, 106, 126–28, 218n48, 227n80

Stift, Billy, 63, 84, 263n57

St. Louis, Missouri, and Boatright, 5, 12–14, 19–20

St. Louis Advertiser, 12

St. Louis–San Francisco Railroad, 49

stock cons: and Brown, 157, 159; rise of, 196. *See also* wire con

Stogsdill, Henry, 150, 167, 190–91

Stone, William Joel, 49, 66, 94

Strahorn-Hutton-Evans Commission Company, 69, 70

Strand, Oscar, 29, 30

Sullens, James, 115

Sullivan, Frank "Kid," 32

Sullivan, James E., 263n1

Sunday, Billy, 188

Sutherland, Charley, 243n42

Sutherland, Edwin H., 6

Sutor, Samuel, 136, 168, 260n28, 262n46

Sweeney, James, 226n59

Swenson, John, *136*; collusion allegations, 176; later career, 195; Mabray Gang mail fraud investigation, 134–36, 138, 139, 140; Mabray Gang mail fraud prosecution, 145, 150, 155, 166–67, 168, 171, 178, 181; and pardons, 194; and Powell conviction, 190–91; on rewards, 198; threats to, 266n27

syndicates, 8, 198

T - - - - - -

Taft, William Howard, 190, 191, 194

Taylor, Wilkins, 50–51

Teague, Thomas F., 100

Teller, Ben, 241n11

Temple, Marcellus L.: and Mabray Gang mail fraud case, 135–36, 144, 156, 165, 166, 181; and pardons, 182, 194; and Powell conviction, 190

Thielman, Rudolph "Darby": as athlete, 168, 197; background,

Waters, William H., 121, 125, 239n50
Watkins, James, 73–74
Watkins, T. J., 73–74
Weaver, Charles, 213n80
Webb, John C., 21
Webb City: closing of saloons in 1905, 119; images of, *24*, *40*; as mining town, 21–22; as open town, 21–24, 26; population growth, 23; and Prohibition, 129; railroad and transportation links, 39
Webb City Athletic Club: baseball game against Carthage, 39; as big store con, 4; in Ellis testimony, 87–88; formation of, 40–41; numbers of members, 59; roles in, 41–43; in Williams deposition, 84–85. *See also* Buckfoot Gang; foot racing
Webb City Register, 65–66, 128, 187
Webb City Sentinel, 60, 67, 82, 97–98, 103
Weil, Joseph "Yellow Kid," 171, 194, 251n2, 282n57
Wells, Thad, 236n9
Wenrich, Percy, 25, 50
West, Luther "Lute," 174
Wheeler, Deacon, 193
Whipple, William, 144, 267n4
Wickersham, George W., 144, 166, 190, 194, 258n53
Wilcox, Hamilton, 70, 89
Wilhelm, Charles, 143
Williams, Leland A., 36
Williams, Robert L., 100, 107
Williams, Roger H.: assets, hiding of, 100–101; background, 35–36; and Bland con, 99–100; and Carlson/Horner con, 80; and Cobb con, 98; and Day con, 76; death of, 107–8, 185; on greed of victims, 4, 84, 199; and Lang/Becker lawsuit,

82, 100–101, 226n65; and mail fraud case, 111; as manager, 43; on Morris, 210n57; and Moss con, 45; move to Colorado, 83–84; and Randall con, 67; representation by McAntire, 229n14; testimony by, 5, 84–85
wire con: described, 243n41; and Hindman, 116, 189; and Johnson, 230n35; rise of, 196; and Ryan, 116
Wise, Scott, 176
Wood, James B., 101, 107
Wood, Warren B., 141
Woodruff, Eugene, 167–68
Woodson, Charles F., 9–11, 14–20
Woodson, Edward, 9, 10, 14
Woodward brothers, 29
wrestling: and Buckfoot Gang, 98; and fake death/injuries in con, 167; and Gibson in Salt Lake City, 263n57; and Lozier post-gang career, 188; and Mabray Gang, 133, 141, 150, *151*, 156, 159–60, 167, 168, 171, 173, 174; and Marsh post-gang career, 195
Wright, George, 166, 176
Wright, Henry S., 59–60, 215n10, 247n39
Wright, J. L., 276n100
Wright, Joseph E., 159

Y - - - - - -
Youmans, Frank C., 63–64, 79, 81, 112, 231n38
Youmans, George W., 64

Z - - - - - -
Zbysko, Stanislaw, 168
zinc mining, 20, 21, 22–23